COMPLETE GARDENER'S DICTIONARY

Barbara W. Ellis

BARRON'S

All inquiries should be addressed to:
Barron's Educational Series, Inc.
250 Wireless Boulevard
Hauppauge, New York 11788
http://www.barronseduc.com

International Standard Book No.: 0-7641-0637-6

Library of Congress Catalog Card No.: 99-62853

Printed in the United States of America
9 8 7 6 5 4 3 2 1

Contents

Introduction

From the outset, *The Complete Gardener's Dictionary* has been a labor of love. What better project for a plant-obsessed gardener who writes and edits garden books? Not only has this dictionary fueled my love of plants, gardening, and botany and all their myriad facets, it also has satisfied a lifelong fascination with words—in this case all the terms we use to describe plants and explain how to grow them in our gardens.

This is a compendium of thousands of commonly used terms from all facets of gardening, horticulture, botany, and landscape design. In it you'll find entries for words that relate to such diverse topics as plant propagation, pruning, garden design principles, tools, and basic gardening techniques, as well as the terms used by specialists such as herb gardeners and soil scientists. You'll also find explanations of the many words botanists and plant taxonomists use to scientifically describe all the plants we love to grow. Each term is accompanied by a definition that is easy-to-understand and informative. Throughout, I've tried to explain terms, not just define them, and have included examples, step-by-step instructions, and illustrations whenever I could to make concepts as clear as possible.

When selecting terms to include, I've tried to delve as deeply into each subject as possible. For example, plant-propagation related terms covered include the specific techniques themselves (cutting, division, layering, and mound layering) as well as definitions of materials and equipment (rooting hormone, nursery bed, and propagation mat) and plant parts and botanical concepts fundamental to propagation (node, internode, asexual propagation, parent plant, and polarity). The discussions of each technique don't just provide a definition and leave it at that. They also include step-by-step instructions, often illustrated, that you can follow to try a technique for the first time or use to review the basics on ones you haven't practiced for a while. You'll also find definitions of all the variations of each propagating technique: In addition to layering, for example, there are definitions for air layering, mound layering, French layering, serpentine layering, tip layering, and trench layering, plus entries on alternative common names for these techniques such as Chinese layering and marcottage. This makes it an easy matter to track down an unfamiliar term. Throughout, references to related entries are indicated in small caps—*See* MOUND LAYERING, for example.

The hundreds of illustrations in the book are especially important because they make the botanical and plant taxonomy terms—flower types, leaf shapes, and so forth—so easy to grasp at a glance. In many cases, I've also provided a specific example of a plant that exhibits that characteristic so you can observe it in your garden or out in the field.

One of the great things about gardeners and gardening is that we have such amazingly diverse interests. With your help, I am hoping we can channel that diversity and make this book into a work-in-progress. I look forward to receiving suggestions from readers on new words to include, meanings to add, and topics to cover that would make future editions more useful. Send them to me in care of Barron's at the address listed on the copyright page.

Acknowledgments

Special thanks to my editor at Barron's, Wendy Sleppin, for her unfailing enthusiasm for this project as well as her dedicated attention to detail. Also, thanks to Rebecca A. Merrilees for her wonderful line drawings, which help the text come to life.

a-, ap-, apo- Prefixes meaning not, lacking, or without. Apetalous means without petals, for example. Astichous means not arranged in rows. Apetiolate means without petioles.

ab- A prefix meaning away from.

abaxial The side of a plant part, such as a leaf, that faces away from the main stem, or axis. The underside of a leaf is abaxial. The same as dorsal.

aberrant Not typical, not normal.

abortive Barely or poorly developed. Rudimentary.

abrupt Terminating suddenly or produced suddenly.

abruptly pinnate *See* EVEN PINNATE

abscission, abscissing Falling away or separating. Used to refer to leaves or other plant parts that drop because a layer of thin-walled cells at their base (the abscission layer) disintegrates.

acanthaceous Prickly or spiny.

acaulescent Stemless or seemingly stemless. Acaulescent plants either completely lack a stem or, more commonly, have a stem that is either extremely short or is underground so that the leaves all seem to be basal, or borne at the base of the plant. Dandelions (*Taraxacum officinale*) are acaulescent.

accent An element in a design that adds contrast in color, shape, or form to lend interest to the overall composition. A clump of bold-textured, variegated hostas can be used to accent a planting of finer-textured ferns and hardy geraniums (*Geranium* spp.), for example. In a flower arrangement, a few darker-colored flowers may add the right touch to an otherwise pastel bouquet.

accent plant A plant that is added to a bed, border, or other planting combination to add contrast in color, form, or texture to a composition and thus add interest to the design.

accessory In addition to.

accessory bud An extra bud or buds borne in the axils of the leaves.

accessory fruit A fruit or cluster of aggregate fruits with a showy, fleshy portion that is formed from the flower's receptacle, rather than its pistil, or female portion. Also called a pseudocarp. A strawberry is an accessory fruit; the true fruits are the tiny seeds (achenes) on its surface.

accessory fruit

acclimatization Gradually introducing a plant to a new and different climate or environment. This term usually is used to refer to the process of gradually bringing tropical houseplants or greenhouse plants outdoors for the summer. If such plants are to make the transition without damage, they need to be exposed slowly to the brighter sunlight and other elements of the outdoors. Acclimatize larger plants just as you would new seedlings. *See* HARDENING OFF

accrete Grafted together naturally.

accumbent Lying against another organ, but not fused or united to it. Used to refer to unlike plant parts such as seed leaves (cotyledons) that lie against the rudimentary root (radicle) in a seed. Cotyledons are accumbent when they are arranged with the radicle lying along one edge. They are incumbent when the radicle lies along the cotyledons' side, rather than the edge.

-aceous/-aceus Suffix meaning belonging to, related to, or "like." Commonly used to refer to plants in related families, for example the terms liliaceous genera or liliaceous plants indicate members of the lily family (Liliaceae). Pomaceous means like a pome or relating to a pome.

acerose Needle-shaped. *See* ACICULAR

achene A dry fruit with a single cavity bearing a single seed that is attached at one point and doesn't open along definite lines when ripe (means it is indehiscent). Many plants bear achenes, including sunflowers (*Helianthus* spp.), dandelions (*Taraxacum officinale*), and windflowers (*Anemone* spp.). Roses (*Rosa* spp.) bear achenes enclosed inside hips, which are often showy.

achene

achlorphyllous Lacking chlorophyll, meaning a plant or plant part that is not green. Indian pipe (*Monotropa uniflora*), a native wildflower, is achlorphyllus. Despite its waxy white appearance, it is a true flowering plant, not a fungus. Instead of depending on chlorophyll to manufacture food, as most plants do, it obtains the nutrients it needs by parasitizing fungi in the soil.

acicular Needle-shaped, and generally round or grooved in cross section rather

than flat. Pines (*Pinus* spp.) have acicular leaves, which are more commonly referred to as needles. Spines, such as those of some cacti, also can be acicular.

acicular

acidophilous Acid-loving or preferring acid soils. Rhododendrons (*Rhododendron* spp.) and mountain laurels (*Kalmia* spp.) are acidophilous.

acid soil Any soil that has a pH below 7.0 is considered to be acid, but soils with pH readings between 6.5 and 7.0 are only slightly acid and considered ideal garden soils. Acid soils are common in areas with high rainfall such the eastern United States and the Pacific Northwest. Below a pH of about 6.0, minerals such as calcium, magnesium, and potassium are less available, while iron, manganese, and aluminum may be too readily available. Acidity also affects soil organisms; they are not as active in acid soils as they are in more neutral ones. To raise the pH of acid soil, you can apply fine-ground limestone (calcium carbonate) or dolomitic limestone (which contains both magnesium carbonate and calcium carbonate). Both are ground-up rock particles: Before you buy, read the label to make sure at least half of the material will pass through a 100-mesh screen. Don't substitute hydrated lime, slaked lime, builder's lime, or quicklime, which are caustic powders that can damage your skin as well as tender plant roots and soil organisms. For best results, have your soil tested and follow the recommendations supplied: The amount of lime needed to change pH depends on the soil's texture and organic matter content. Fine-textured soils like clays, or soils with lots of organic matter, are more resistant to change than sandy soils, for example. In general, to raise the pH of 100 square feet by 1 point (from 5.5 to 6.5) you'll need to spread 7 to 9 pounds of lime on clay soil, about 5 pounds on loam soil, and only 2 to 3 pounds on sandy soil. To change pH more than 1 point, apply lime over the course of 2 or 3 years rather than trying to make a drastic change. Fall is the best time to apply lime (it can be applied at any season, though); that way it has time to do its work before spring planting. Wood ashes also will raise soil pH. Keep in mind that adding organic matter also will help neutralize acid soil. Another option is to grow primarily acid-loving plants such as rhododendrons and azaleas. *See* pH

acorn The type of nut borne by oaks (*Quercus* spp.). An acorn consists of the nut itself and its cap, which is made up of fused, scalelike bracts and is more properly called a cupule.

acroscopic Facing or directed toward the top of a stem or other organ.

actinomorphic A flower that is symmetrical, with its parts radiating from the center, so that a plane or line passed anywhere through the center would yield mirror images. Roses (*Rosa* spp.), tulips (*Tulipa* spp.), and plants with daisy-like flowers such as cosmos (*Cosmos* spp.) and sunflowers (*Helianthus* spp.) have actinomorphic, also called regular, flowers.

actinomorphic flower

actinomycetes Soil microorganisms, active in the composting process as well, that help decompose organic matter and are somewhat like a cross between bacteria and fungi. Most are beneficial, but potato scab is caused by an actinomycete. Since actinomycetes prefer neutral to slightly alkaline pH (6.0 to 7.5), growing potatoes in acid soil prevents this disease.

action hoe *See* HOE

aculeate Prickly or covered with prickles, such as rose (*Rosa* spp.) stems.

aculeolate Covered with very small prickles. Somewhat prickly.

acumen The pointed, tapering tip of a leaf or tepal.

acuminate A base or tip that tapers to a sharp point and has slightly concave sides. At the tip or base of an acuminate leaf, the edges, or margins, come together to form an angle that is less than 45 degrees. A leaf tip or base can be broadly, narrowly, or abruptly acuminate, depending on how suddenly the leaf tapers to a point. An acuminate leaf tip or base is both longer and narrower than an acute one. While most commonly used to describe a leaf base or tip, this term can be applied to other plant parts such as bracts (modified petal-like leaves) or the petals or sepals of a flower.

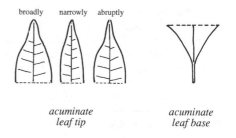

broadly   narrowly   abruptly

acuminate leaf tip   *acuminate leaf base*

acute A base or tip that has straight or only slightly convex sides and tapers to a sharp point. The sides of the point form an angle between 45 and 90 degrees. A leaf tip or base can be broadly, narrowly, or abruptly acute, depending on how suddenly the leaf tapers to a point. An acute tip or base is both shorter and broader than an acuminate one. While most commonly used to describe a leaf base or tip, this term can be applied to other plant parts such as bracts (modified petal-like leaves) or the petals or sepals of a flower.

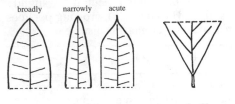

acute leaf tip   *acute leaf base*

acyclic Arranged in a spiral around the stem, rather than in whorls.

ad- A prefix that means to or toward.

adaxial The side of a plant part (such as a leaf) that faces toward the main stem, or axis. The top of a leaf is adaxial. The same as ventral.

adherent, adhering Stuck or clinging together but not actually fused. Used to refer to unlike plant parts that normally are separate.

adhesion The tendency of water to stick to a surface. Water held by adhesion in soil is bonded so tightly that it is unavailable to plants. Water held by cohesion is held by surface tension, mostly in small pores (called micropores). Clay soils, which have many small particles, can retain a large amount of water by adhesion, but the water is held so tightly to the soil particles that roots cannot take up the water they need. As a result, plants can wilt or die even though the soil still holds moisture.

adhesive holdfast *See* HOLDFAST

adnate Fused or united. Used to refer to unlike plant parts that normally are separate, such as stamens and petals. The term connate refers to like parts that are fused together.

adpressed *See* APPRESSED

adventitious Plant parts that develop where they are not normally found, such as buds on leaves or roots on aboveground stems or the branches. Corn (*Zea mays*) produces adventitious roots near the base of the stalk. Sweet potatoes (*Ipomoea batatas*) produce adventitious shoots from their tuberous roots. The roots that form on stem or root cuttings taken for purposes of propagation also are adventitious.

adventive Introduced to an area, and thus not native, but beginning to spread.

aeration The process by which air and other gases enter and move through soil. Aeration depends on the number of soil pores and their relative size. Soils with large pores—rich loams with ample organic matter or sandy soils—tend to be well aerated. Poorly aerated soils are either saturated with water or have very few large pore spaces (and thus poor soil structure). Compost piles also require good aeration if the materials are to decompose. Turning the pile or using a compost aerator are two options for aerating a pile. *See* PORE SPACE, SOIL STRUCTURE, COMPOST

aeration pore *See* PORE SPACE

aerator A tool designed to aerate soil, especially under a lawn, by pulling out soil plugs. Manual as well as power models are available.

aerenchyma Tissue in roots or stems that conducts air and is a feature of some plants that grow in wet, poorly aerated soil. Aerenchymatous tissue has thin cell walls and large spaces between cells. Water hyacinths (*Eichhornia crassipes*) float because they have inflated leaf stalks filled with this type of tissue.

aerial Borne in the air. Commonly used to refer to plant parts that are borne where they are not normally found, such as roots borne above ground or flowers on an aquatic plant that are borne above water.

aerial bulb *See* BULBIL

aerial plant *See* EPIPHYTE

aerial roots Roots that are borne entirely above ground. Ivies (*Hedera* spp.) bear aerial roots, as do many epiphytes.

aerial stems Erect stems borne on a horizontal rhizome.

aerobic Living or active only in the presence of oxygen.

aestival Appearing or flowering during the summer.

aestivation The arrangement of flower parts in an unopened bud.

affixed Attached to.

A-frame An angled wooden support for vining plants such as beans, cucumbers, melons, or annual vines that is covered with strings, wire mesh, wood lath, or plastic netting on which the plants climb.

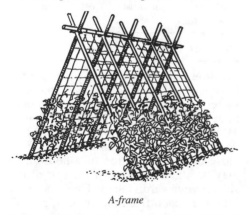

A-frame

after ripening This term refers to changes that occur within dormant seeds or buds that allow them to germinate or grow. Seed that requires a period of cool-moist chilling, or stratification, will after ripen during this process.

agglomerate Crowded together. This term is used to describe individual flowers that are crowded together into a single head, such as those of pincushion flowers (*Scabiosa* spp.).

agglutinate Glued together.

aggregate A cluster of soil particles. Aggregates can be rounded and porous, in which case they are called crumbs, as well as blocky, flattened and layered (called plates), or in shapes that are vertically oriented (called columns or prisms). The sizes and shapes of aggregates influence soil characteristics such as how water and air move through it. *See* SOIL STRUCTURE, PORE SPACE

aggregate flowers A dense, usually rounded, cluster of flowers that resembles but is not a true head, such as those borne by aster-family plants (Asteraceae). Teasels (*Dipsacus* spp.) bear aggregate flowers.

aggregate fruit A dense cluster of separate fruits, commonly referred to as a single fruit, all derived from a single flower (each fruit in the cluster grows from a separate carpel). The "berries" of raspberries and blackberries (*Rubus* spp.) are aggregate fruits. *See also* SYNCARP

aggregate fruit

air drainage This term refers to the fact that cold air sinks to the lowest level that it can reach, pooling at the bottom of a slope or collecting on the uphill side of buildings, hedges, or other structures. Plants sited part way down a slope or on the downhill side of buildings or other structures are somewhat protected from frost, while air drainage causes frost pockets to form in spots where cold air settles. *See* FROST POCKET

air drying *See* DRYING HERBS, DRYING FLOWERS

air layering Inducing roots to form on aboveground stems or branches while they are still attached to the parent plant. Air layering, also called marcottage and

Chinese layering, is often used to propagate houseplants such as dumb cane (*Dieffenbachia* spp.) or figs (*Ficus* spp.), but also is an effective way to propagate many hardy shrubs. To air layer, in spring or early summer remove leaves from a stem or branch and use a sharp knife to wound it by making a shallow, thin 1- to 2-inch-long cut to create a flap or tongue of bark on one side. Take care not to cut too deep. Place a small clump of sphagnum moss that is moist but not wet (like a damp, but not dripping, sponge) in the wound to keep it open. (Otherwise the wound can heal without forming roots.) Wrap a sheet of plastic around the stem below the cut and fasten it with tape or a twist-tie. Then pack moist sphagnum moss all around the branch, covering the cut. Roll the plastic up to cover the sphagnum and pack it tightly against the stem. Then tie at the top; this holds in moisture, which is necessary to encourage rooting. When roots are visible through the plastic, sever the stem just below where they have formed and pot up the new plant. Rooting takes at least a growing season for shrubs outdoors, often more, and can take from 1 to several months or up to 2 years for houseplants. If roots do not form after several months, unwrap the plastic to make sure the sphagnum has remained moist. Wet, if necessary, and rewrap.

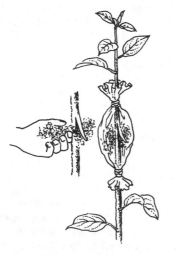

air layering

alate Winged. Commonly used to refer to leaf or flower stems, or fruits, which have a membrane-like wing.

albescent Becoming or turning white or whitish.

albumen The starchy, nutritive material found in a seed. *See* ENDOSPERM

alcohol Rubbing alcohol is an effective insecticide that can be sprayed on plants to control aphids, flea beetles, thrips, and whiteflies. It also is commonly used to control scale or mealy bugs on houseplants, by applying it on the end of a cotton swab to kill each insect individually.

alien Non-native. Used to describe plants, such as garden escapees, that have been introduced from another region or country and are now found growing in the wild. Queen Anne's lace (*Daucus carota*) is an alien species introduced from Europe. *See* INTRODUCED

aliferous Bearing wings.

alkaline soil Soil that has a pH above 7.0 is considered to be alkaline. Also called sweet or chalky soils, these are common in dry parts of the western United States, as well as in areas where the soil is derived from weathered limestone. Soil close to the foundation of a house also may be alkaline—even if the rest of the soil in your yard is acid. That's because lime can leach from the cement, raising the pH. Applying elemental sulfur, also called flowers of sulfur, is the best way to lower the pH of alkaline soil. This yellow powder can lower soil pH in as little as 6 to 8 weeks, but needs to be reapplied every 6 to 12 months. The proper application depends on soil texture and organic matter content. In general, to lower pH add about 1 pound of elemental sulfur per 100 square feet. Organic matter—composted sawdust or bark, composted leaves, and pine needles—releases carbonic acid as it decomposes and will slowly lower pH and have a long-term effect. Replenish organic matter annually by digging in a 1- to 2-inch layer or spreading it over the soil as mulch. While oaks and maples produce slightly acid compost, some trees such as green ash (*Fraxinus pennsylvanica*) can actually contribute to soil alkalinity. *See* pH

allantoid Sausage-shaped. Not surprisingly, the large, woody fruits of the sausage tree (*Kigelia africana*) are allantoid. Botuliform also means sausage-shaped.

allée A walkway or riding path that either is closely lined with trees and shrubs or has been cut through a woodland. The trees and shrubs along either side are commonly clipped like hedges.

allelopathic A plant that produces substances that inhibit the growth of or kill other plants. Walnuts (*Juglans* spp.) are allelopathic and will kill tomatoes as well as azaleas and rhododendrons (*Rhododendron* spp.) planted in their root zone.

allogamy Cross-fertilization.

allotment garden A British term for community garden. *See* COMMUNITY GARDEN

alpine house A greenhouse that is kept cold and well ventilated in order to provide the conditions alpine plants require to grow successfully. An alpine house can reach temperatures as low as 20°F in the winter.

alpine lawn An area, normally found in a rock garden, that has been planted to resemble a flower-filled mountain meadow.

alpine plant A plant that grows naturally in mountainous areas, usually above the treeline.

alternate Leaves that are borne one per node along a stem. The term alternate also can be used to describe pedicels (the stalks of individual flowers in a flower cluster) or branches that are borne singly along a stem or axis. Alternate also can mean petals,

sepals, stamens, or other organs that are borne between (rather than over) one another.

alternate leaves

alternate bearing Producing a heavy crop of fruit or flowers one year followed by a lighter crop the following year. Also called biennial bearing.

alternation of generations Plants that have lifecycles with clearly differentiated sexual and asexual stages exhibit alternation of generations. Ferns are the best known plants that exhibit these phenomena: They have a sporophyte and a gametophyte generation. *See* FERN LIFECYCLE

alulate Having a small or narrow wing.

alveolate Honeycombed or pitted.

ament *See* CATKIN

amentaceous Catkinlike. Bearing catkins.

American garden *See* NEW AMERICAN GARDEN

American pattern hoe *See* HOE

amorphous Shapeless. Lacking a definite form.

amphibious This term is used to describe a plant that can live either on land or in water.

amplexicaul Clasping. A base of a leaf or bract (a modified petal-like leaf) that partially or completely surrounds the stem. A clasping leaf is sessile, meaning it has no stalk. It can have separate basal lobes or a base that widens and wraps around the stem. The leaves of many plants clasp the stems, including New England asters (*Aster novae-angliae*), lady's slipper orchids (*Cypripredium* spp.), and elecampane (*Inula helenium*).

amplexicaul leaf base

ampliate Expanded or enlarged.

ampullaceous Enlarged or swollen in a flasklike or bladderlike manner.

anaerobic Living or active only in the absence of oxygen.

analysis plan *See* SITE INVENTORY

anastomosing Branched and then rejoining to form a netted or networklike pattern. Most often used to describe a pattern of leaf veins. A reticulate (netted) leaf has anastomosing veins.

androecium The male reproductive portion of a flower. A collective term for all the stamens of a flower.

-androus A suffix referring to stamens, usually combined with a prefix that indicates a number. Octandrous means having eight stamens, for example.

anemone-form, anemone A single or semidouble flower with one or more whorls of petals (called guard petals) surrounding a dense cluster of narrow petal-like structures (actually petaloids or staminodes) in the center. Also called Japanese-form blooms, in peonies these differ from bombs in that the petal-like structures clustered in the

center are smaller and narrower than those in a bomb are. 'Bride's Dream', 'Cheddar Supreme', and 'Do Tell' are all peony cultivars with anemone-form flowers. Other flowers, including dahlias and chrysanthemums, come in anemone form. In dahlias, the cluster at the center of the flower consists of tubular disk florets that create a pincushion-like effect.

anemone-form flower

anemophilous Pollinated by the wind. Bearing wind-borne pollen. Most grasses are wind pollinated.

angiosperm A collective term for the flowering plants, which all bear flowers and produce seeds inside an ovary, or fruit. Nearly all common garden plants are angiosperms. The exceptions are gymnosperms, which bear naked seeds and include conifers and cycads, and pteridophytes, which reproduce by spores and include ferns and fern allies.

angular, angulate Angled. Used to describe stems, leaves, or other organs that are angled. Leaves that have broad teeth or lobes with angled edges are angulate. Stems that have clearly defined sides in cross section are angulate. In this case a prefix is added to specify the number of sides. Quadrangular, for example, designates the four-angled stems of mint-family members (Lamiaceae).

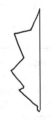

angular leaf margin

animals, soil *See* MACROFAUNA, MICROFAUNA

annual Botanically speaking, an annual is a plant that germinates from seed, grows, flowers, sets seeds, and dies all in one season. For gardeners, the term has a broader meaning: An annual is any plant that can be grown in the garden for a single season, but is killed by frost in fall or early winter. Thus, many so-called "annuals" are actually tender perennials that can be grown outdoors year-round in warmer climates. Zinnias (*Zinnia angustifolia* and *Z. elegans*) and marigolds (*Tagetes* spp.) are true annuals, while wax begonias (*Begonia Semperflorens-cultorum* hybrids) and impatiens (*Impatiens walleriana*) are both tender perennials commonly grown as annuals. Gardeners distinguish several types of annuals, generally because of the plants' cultural preferences, which influence growing schedules. *See* HARDY ANNUAL, HALF-HARDY ANNUAL, COOL-WEATHER ANNUAL, WARM-WEATHER ANNUAL, TENDER ANNUAL Tender perennials also can be grown as annuals. *See also* TENDER PERENNIAL, OVERWINTERING

annual ephemeral *See* EPHEMERAL

annual rings *See* TREE RINGS

annular, annulate Shaped like a ring or arranged in a circle.

annular budding *See* RING BUDDING

annulus The row of specialized cells on the spore-producing bodies of ferns (sporangia) that cause them to open and release the spores contained inside. (*See also* FERN LIFECYCLE) This term is also used to refer to the corona or the edge of the corolla in the flowers of members of the milkweed family (Asclepiadaceae).

antemarginal Within the margin or extending almost to the margin.

anterior The side or portion of a plant part that faces away from or is farthest from the main stem, or axis, and points either out or down toward the base of the plant. Subtending bracts, meaning bracts that are attached under a flower, are anterior. The lower lip on a bilabiate flower such as a snapdragon (*Antirrhinum majus*) or salvia (*Salvia* spp.) is the anterior lip.

anther The pollen-producing portion of a stamen, which is the male reproductive organ of a flower. Generally, but not always, it is attached to the flower by a filament.

antheridium The male reproductive structure of plants that reproduce by spores (called cryptograms) including ferns, mosses, and fungi. The antheridium is equivalent to the anthers of a seed-bearing plant. *See also* GAMETOPHYTE

antheriferous Bearing anthers.

anther sac A saclike portion of an anther, the pollen-producing portion of a stamen that contains the pollen grains.

anthocyanins Pigments in plants that cause reds, purples, and blues in flowers and foliage. Anthocyanins are found in vascular tissue.

anthracnose *See* LEAF SPOTS

anti- A prefix meaning against or opposed to. Plants that are antipathetic, for example, are resistant to forming a graft union. This prefix is also used to form words that mean opposite. Antipetalus means opposite or placed on a petal rather than alternating with petals.

antifeedant A substance that deters feeding by pest insects. The insecticide neem has antifeedant properties.

antitranspirant, antidesiccant Compound that when sprayed on plant foliage reduces water loss through foliage and stems. Applying antitranspirants to broad-leaved evergreens in fall will help prevent winterburn because it reduces the amount of water they lose on warm winter days when the soil is still frozen. Antitranspirants also have been proven helpful in preventing blackspot and other fungal diseases.

antrorse, antrorsely Curved, turned, or pointing up or forward, toward the tip, or apex. Commonly used to describe the position of small plant parts such as thorns or prickles.

anvil pruners A hand-held pruning tool with a straight, sharp blade that cuts when it is pressed down on a narrow anvil. *See* HAND PRUNERS

apetalous Without petals.

apex, *pl.* **apices** The tip of a stem or other organ, such as a leaf.

aphids Tiny green, black, brown, or reddish insects with soft, pear-shaped bodies. Some have wings. Aphids cluster on buds, shoots, and undersides of leaves, sucking plant juices, causing stunted or deformed blooms and leaves. They also exude a shiny, sticky substance called honeydew, which supports the growth of black sooty mold fungus on leaves and stems. Aphids also may transmit plant viruses. To control them, encourage or introduce natural predators, including lacewings and lady beetles. (*See* BENEFICIAL INSECTS) Pinch off and destroy infested plant parts or knock aphids off plants with a strong spray of water. For serious infestations use insecticidal soap or pyrethrins.

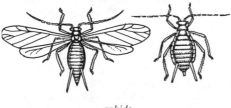

aphids

aphyllous Without leaves.

apical Borne at the tip of a stem or other organ, the apex.

apical dominance The controlling influences that the apical bud (located at the tip,

or apex, of a shoot) has on the growth of the shoot. Auxins produced in the growing tip of a shoot promote growth at the shoot's tip while inhibiting the growth of buds along the sides of the shoot. Cutting off the apical bud when removing a shoot tip cuts off the production of auxins. This allows previously dormant buds (called lateral buds) located along the shoot just below the removed portion to grow into side shoots, called laterals. The topmost bud on the topside shoot nearest the removed tip then becomes dominant and suppresses the growth of buds below it. The topmost bud also often becomes dominant over branches produced by buds below it on the original stem, thereby slowing their growth, too.

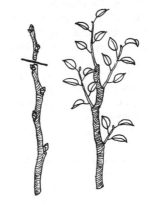

apical dommance

apical meristem *See* MERISTEM

apiculate Abruptly ending in a short, sharp, but flexible point, called an apicule. The point of an apiculate leaf has a length-to-width ratio of 3-to-1 or less. While most commonly used to describe a leaf tip, this term can be applied to other plant parts such as bracts (modified petal-like leaves) or the petals or sepals of a flower.

apiculate leaf tip

apocarpous Bearing separate carpels (rather than syncarpous ones, which are fused together) or separate simple pistils.

apogamy A form of vegetative reproduction that mimics the normal lifecycle of a fern (or fern ally) while bypassing sexual reproduction altogether. Plants that reproduce in this manner bear spores that germinate to produce a prothallus that has male and female organs (antheridia and archegonia), but they are bypassed in the reproduction process. In this case, the prothallus produces a bud that grows into a fern (sporophyte) that is an exact duplicate of the parent plant. Apogamy is actually fairly common: Holly ferns (*Cyrtomium falcatum*), cretan brake fern or ribbon fern (*Pteris cretica*), and some forms of lady fern (*Athryrium filix-femina*) and soft shield fern (*Polystichum setiferum*) reproduce in this manner. It is an especially common adaptation in ferns that grow naturally in dry environments, where lack of water may prevent sexual reproduction. *See* FERN LIFECYCLE

apomictic seed Seeds produced via the process of apomixis. Since this is not a sexual process, they are genetically identical to their parents.

apomixis An asexual reproductive process in which cells in the ovary develop into viable seeds without being fertilized by a male parent. When this happens, the seeds are genetically identical to the female parent. Many citrus trees (*Citrus* spp.) produce seeds this way, as do many lady's mantles (*Alchemilla* spp.), onions (*Allium* spp.), and Kentucky bluegrass (*Poa pratensis*). Kentucky bluegrass produces both apomicts and sexually produced seeds.

apopetalous *See* POLYPETALOUS

appressed, adpressed Pressed against or borne flat on another plant part. Hairs that lie flat against a leaf are appressed. Branches in a fastigiate tree, which are nearly parallel to the trunk, are somewhat appressed.

approach grafting A general term for several different grafting techniques that unite two separate plants that continue growing on their own roots until the graft union has formed. Approach grafting is a valuable technique for uniting plants that are difficult to graft. Approach grafts can be made any time of year, but the unions heal most quickly when the plants are growing actively. To make a spliced approach graft, start with stock and scion plants that are approximately the same size and are close enough together so that the stems will meet. One or both of the plants can be growing in a container. Determine where the stems will meet, and remove a 1- to 2-inch-long sliver of bark and wood from each stem with a sharp knife. Flat, smooth cuts that are exactly the same size are essential to success, so the cambium layers will meet. Tie the two stems securely together with nurserymen's adhesive tape or raffia. Cover the grafted area with grafting wax. Once the graft has formed (this can require several months with difficult-to-graft species), sever the scion below the graft and the stock above it. Remove the tape or raffia. If the stock is relatively small compared to the scion, gradually reduce the top growth on the scion before severing both of them completely. For two other approach grafting techniques, *see* TONGUED APPROACH GRAFT, INLAY APPROACH GRAFT, and INARCHING (a similar technique). *See also* GRAFTING

approach grafting

aquatic Growing naturally in water.

arachnoid Weblike. Covered with white, cobweblike hair. Cobweb houseleek (*Sempervivum arachnoideum*) and cotton or Scotch thistles (*Onopordum* spp.) are arachnoid.

arbor A structure that encloses space to create a shady retreat and has an open roof upon which vines or other plants are grown. Typically, arbors shade a bench and are square. They usually are constructed of wood or timbers. This term has been applied to all types of garden structures. In the 16th century, the term arbor was used for an herb or flower garden as well as a grassy area or an orchard. *See* GALLERY, PERGOLA

arbor

arborescent, arboreous Treelike. Having a treelike habit or stature.

arboretum An area or place dedicated to the collection, culture, study, and exhibition of trees, shrubs, and other woody plants.

arboriculture The science, art, and practice of growing trees for aesthetic purposes, for study, as well as for timber production.

arborist An individual trained in arboriculture and an expert in pruning trees, preventing and curing diseases, and controlling insects. Don't mistake a professional arborist for an unqualified tree trimmer, who may hack up and ruin valuable trees, leaving them open to disease and insect infestation. To find a local arborist certified by the International Society of Arboriculture, write or call ISA, P.O. Box GG, Savoy, IL 61874, (217) 355-9411 for a recommendation.

archegonium The flask-shaped female organ that produces the egg, or female

gamete, in higher ferns and gymnosperms. *See also* GAMETOPHYTE

arching Curving down gently. This term is usually used in reference to branches.

arcuate Curved or arched into a bowlike shape. This term is used to describe leaf veins or other plant parts that are curved rather than straight.

arcuate leaf veins

arenicolous A plant that grows naturally in sand.

areolate Consisting of several small, irregular shapes or spaces.

areole, areola A small space, especially between netted (anastomosing) veins. Also, a small depression or raised area on a cactus stem where the spines are borne.

argenteous Silvery.

argillaceous Clayey. A plant or plants that grow naturally in clay soil.

arhizous Lacking roots.

aril An appendage on a seed that is generally fleshy and can partially or entirely cover the seed. The aril is attached to the seed scar (hilium) or the stalk attaching the immature seed to the placenta in the ovary (funiculus). Some plants depend on ants for seed dispersal, and arils aid in this process because ants are attracted to these fleshy appendages, and thus carry the seeds away. Fringed bleeding hearts (*Dicentra eximia*), twinleaf (*Jeffersonia diphylla*), trilliums (*Trillium* spp.), and some irises (so-called aril irises, which belong to the Oncocyclus, Regelia, and Arilbred groups) all bear seeds with arils. The fleshy red "berries" on yews (*Taxus* spp.) are actually arils surrounding the seeds.

aristate Bearing an awn or bristle at the tip or abruptly tapering to a long, narrow tip. The point, which is an extension of the midrib, has a length-to-width ratio of 3-to-1 or more. While most commonly used to describe a leaf tip, this term can be applied to other plant parts such as bracts (modified petal-like leaves) or the petals or sepals of a flower.

aristate leaf tip

armature Any sharp covering on an organ such as thorns, spines, spikes, or prickles.

armed Bearing prickles, thorns, barbs, or spines.

armyworms These are pale green to greenish brown caterpillars with stripes on their sides and backs, and are the larvae of pale gray-brown moths. Armyworms devour leaves and even whole plants at night and hide under garden debris during the daytime. To control them, attract beneficial predators (*See* BENEFICIAL INSECTS); handpick pests at night, or spray BTK (*Bacillus thuringiensis* var. *kurstaki*) or neem. Use floating row covers as barriers.

arrilate Having an aril.

arrowhead-shaped *See* SAGITTATE

arthropods Cold-blooded animals that have a hard armored skeleton on the outside of their bodies. Insects, spiders, mites,

millipedes, and centipedes all are arthropods.

arthropod

articulate Jointed or seemingly jointed. Having distinct nodes or joints; articulated organs are sometimes swollen at the joints and fall apart easily at them. An articulated fruit can break apart at actual joints or nodes or at sections that are thin or narrow enough to make separation easy.

arundinaceous Reed- or canelike.

ascending Growing upward, usually with a curved stem. Some ferns have rhizomes that ascend to form an upright crown.

asepalous Lacking sepals.

asexual propagation To increase without sex. Also called vegetative propagation, this is a general term used to refer to all forms of propagation that do not involve the fertilization of a flower, and thus the production of seeds. (Apomictic seeds, which are produced without fertilization, are an exception. *See* APOMIXIS for details.) Asexual propagation uses naturally produced plant parts such as bulbils, cormils, offsets, and plantlets, as well as techniques such as taking cuttings, dividing plants, budding, layering, grafting, and tissue culture. Asexual techniques yield plants that are exact genetic duplicates of their parent, whereas seeds, which are the result of a sexual process, do not. *See also* VEGETATIVE PROPAGATION

asexual reproduction Reproducing vegetatively by producing structures such as bulbils, cormils, stolons, or offsets instead of by producing seeds.

ashes, wood *See* WOOD ASHES

asparagus fork Also known as a fishtail weeder, an asparagus knife, an asparagus fork, and a dandelion fork, this is a hand tool with a V-shaped, fishtail-shaped tip at its business end. The blade is inserted into the soil along the length of a root to loosen it and pull it from the soil. Asparagus forks, originally intended for harvesting asparagus, are handy for digging out taprooted perennial weeds in rock gardens and other tight, rocky places.

asparagus fork

asparagus knife *See* ASPARAGUS FORK

assurgent *See* ASCENDING

astemonous Lacking stamens.

asymmetric, asymmetrical Not symmetrical, irregular.

asymmetrical balance A type of balanced design that creates the impression of stability by using different plants or other elements that have similar visual "weight" on either side of a design. Three smaller shrubs can balance a single large shrub, for example. Informal gardens usually feature asymmetrical balance. In a flower arrangement that is asymmetrically balanced, the two sides of the design are composed differently, but have similar visual weights so that the

arrangement does not look like it is about to tip over. *See* SYMMETRICAL BALANCE

asymmetrical balance

asymmetrical triangle A shape used in flower arranging in which the main flowers, leaves, and other plant materials are positioned so that the tips of the materials in the main part of the arrangement outline an imaginary asymmetrical triangle.

asymmetrical triangle

atro- A prefix meaning dark or blackish.

attenuate A base or tip that tapers gradually to a narrow point. While most commonly used to describe a leaf base or tip, this term can be applied to other plant parts such as bracts (modified petal-like leaves) or the petals or sepals of a flower.

attenuate leaf base

-atus A suffix that signifies the presence of a feature or organ. Odoratus means fragrant, for example, and alatus means winged.

auricle An earlike lobe. Some members of the grass family (Poaceae) have auricles on the leaves at the point where the sheath meets the blade.

auriculate Having rounded or ear-shaped lobes at the base. An auriculate leaf has two rounded lobes that stick out at the base, on either side of the stem. The term auriculate-clasping is sometimes used if the lobes encircle the stem.

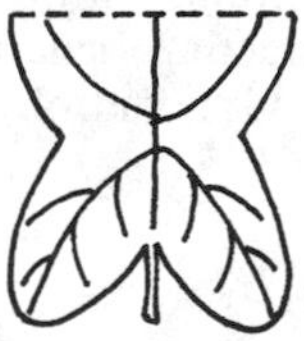

auriculate leaf base

author In plant taxonomy, the author is the first individual to publish a new name for a plant (taxon). In scholarly works, the name of the author, usually abbreviated, follows the botanical name of the plant to precisely identify the type and link it to his or her description. In the name *Hemerocallis fulva L.*, the *L* indicates that Carolus Linnaeus is the author of that particular name. *L. citrina Baroni* refers to Eugenio Baroni, a botanist who lived from 1865 to 1943. *See* BINOMIAL NOMENCLATURE; LINNAEUS, CAROLUS

auxins Plant growth substances that regulate apical dominance and shoot and root elongation. Auxins are produced in meristem tissue, and also are responsible for causing roots to form on cuttings. Synthetic auxins are used as rooting hormones as well as herbicides.

avenue A road or path lined with trees.

awl-shaped *See* SUBULATE

awn A sharp, bristlelike appendage borne at the tip of a leaf or other plant part. Plants in the grass family (Poaceae) have awns on the tips of the bracts at the base of their flower spiklets.

-axial A suffix referring to the axis of a plant or organ. Uniaxial means having one main unbranched stem that ends in a flower.

axil The upper angle that a leaf stalk (petiole), flower stalk (peduncle), shoot, or branch makes with the stem from which it arises. Most often used to designate leaf axils.

axillary Borne or arising from an axil.

axillary flowers

axillary bud A bud borne on the side of a stem, from a leaf axil.

axis The main or central line of a plant around or along which its organs, such as leaves, are attached. A plant's stem, or its central supporting structure, is an axis, as is the central stem of an inflorescence or the main stem of a compound leaf.

ax-shaped *See* DOLABRIFORM

B&B *See* BALLED-AND-BURLAPPED

baccate Berrylike. Soft and fleshy.

bacillus thuringiensis Beneficial bacteria used by organic gardeners that kill various insect larvae by producing crystals that paralyze the larvae's digestive systems. Several varieties are available: BTK (*Bacillus thuringiensis* var. *kurstaki*) kills caterpillars such as cabbage looper, cabbage worm, and tomato hornworm, but keep in mind that it also kills butterfly larvae. It won't harm other insects or animals, however. BTI (*B. thuringiensis* var. *israelensis*) kills larvae of fungus gnats, blackflies, and mosquitoes. BTSD (*B. thuringiensis* var. *san diego*) kills leaf-eating beetles such as black vine weevils, boll weevils, and Colorado potato beetles. *See* MICROBIAL INSECTICIDE

backbulb *See* PSEUDOBULB

backcross, backcrossing Cross-pollinating a plant with one of its parents. Plant breeders use backcrossing to preserve certain genetic traits such as flower color or disease resistance.

backyard wildlife garden *See* WILDLIFE GARDEN

bacterial spot *See* LEAF SPOTS

bactericide A substance that kills bacteria. *See* BORDEAUX MIX

bacterium, *pl.* **bacteria** One-celled organisms that can cause plant diseases. There also are beneficial species of bacteria that help break down organic matter in soil as well as in compost.

bagworms Dark brown caterpillars, the larvae of moths, that hide inside a cocoonlike bag they carry along as they feed. The bags are up to several inches long and are covered with bits of leaves or needles from the host tree. Bagworms eat the foliage of many evergreen and deciduous trees and can defoliate portions of plants. To control them, spray with BTK (*Bacillus thuringiensis* var. *kurstaki*) in early spring to kill young larvae, and handpick and destroy bags during the winter—or any time of the year. Use a knife to cut the cocoons from the twigs; attracting beneficial predators also can help with control. *See* BENEFICIAL INSECTS

bagworms

baking soda Sodium bicarbonate. *See* FUNGICIDES

balance A feature of a design that creates the impression that the individual elements in it are stable and not lopsided-looking. Balance is a consideration in both garden design and flower arranging—a flower arrangement that looks like it is about to tip over because all the flowers are positioned too high or all on one side is not balanced. There are two types of balance: *See* SYMMETRICAL BALANCE, ASYMMETRICAL BALANCE

balanced fertilizer A fertilizer that contains equal amounts of nitrogen, phosphate, and potassium.

balled-and-burlapped A plant that has been dug with a ball of soil around the roots, which are wrapped in burlap. The burlap is either tied or stapled in place. When planting a balled-and-burlapped plant, set the plant in the hole then remove any staples or ties holding the burlap in place. Cut off as much of the fabric as you can easily manage without disturbing the root ball and push the rest down into the bottom of the hole before filling over it with soil. While real burlap is biodegradable, synthetic substitutes are commonly used, and these are not biodegradable. Also called B&B. *See* PLANTING

banded A variegation pattern in which stripes of color (usually referred to as bands) run across a leaf or other surface. Zebra grass (*Miscanthus sinensis 'Zebrinus'*) is banded. *See also* STRIPED

banding Spreading fertilizer along a row of seedlings or plants. *See* SIDE-DRESSING

banner The large, uppermost petal in papilionaceous flowers—sweet peas (*Lathyrus odoratus*), for example. Also called a standard or a vexillum.

barbate Having a tuft or beard composed of long, stiff hairs.

barbed Armed with sharp, short, fishhook-like points.

barbellate Armed with short, stiff hairs, or barbs, called barbellae. Most often used to describe bristles or awns (sharp, stiff hairs) that have barbs down the sides.

bare root A plant that is sold with roots that are bare of soil. A few shrubs, roses, and fruit trees are commonly sold this way, as are many perennials. Bare-root plants are dormant (or should be) and should be planted in spring while they are still dormant. When bare root plants arrive in the mail, keep them packed in the material in which they were shipped, moistening it if necessary. If they were shipped without anything covering their roots, soak them in lukewarm water for an hour or so and then pot them up or heel them in a protected spot with their roots covered with damp soil or compost. Ideally, plant as soon as

you can after they arrive. Before planting, soak perennials in a bucket of water for several hours and shrubs and roses overnight. Carry the plants to the garden in water to make sure the roots don't dry out during planting. Dig a hole that will accommodate the roots, build a cone of soil in the bottom of the hole, set the plant on top of the cone, and spread the roots out in all directions. Be sure to set plants with the crown—where the roots meet the buds or top growth—at the soil surface unless otherwise noted in the instructions that came with the plant. Refill the hole, stopping several times to gently firm the soil around the roots. When the hole is half-full, flood it with water and let the water drain away. Then continue filling and tamping down. (The filling, flooding, and tamping process is important because it eliminates air pockets in the soil.) When the hole is full, form a wide saucer of soil around the plant and water it thoroughly. If bare-root plants have sprouted, cut back new topgrowth by about one-third to give the plants a better chance to recover from the shock of transplanting. Water bare-root plants deeply and thoroughly every week for the entire first season to encourage a vigorous root system. The term bare rooted is sometimes used instead of bare root.

bark A collective term for the protective layers that cover the trunks, branches, and roots of woody plants. Although the term bark is sometimes used to refer to the dead outer covering of the plant, the bark actually includes all of the tissue formed outside the vascular cambium, including the cork and the secondary phloem, which is sometimes called the inner bark.

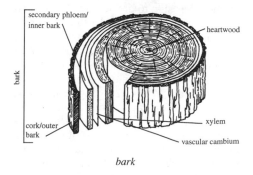

bark

bark grafting A general term for several slightly different grafting techniques that involve slicing through the bark on the stock and fitting a scion against it. Bark grafting is fairly easy and reliable, even for beginning grafters, and doesn't require any special equipment. It can be used to graft onto stock that is 1 inch in diameter or larger. (Since large wounds are slow to heal, very large stock branches—to 1 foot in diameter—don't make good candidates for grafting.) For all bark grafting techniques, the stock needs to be actively growing so that the bark separates from the wood readily. Scions of deciduous species need to be dormant, so collect and store them in winter. (*See* SCION) Scions of evergreen species can be collected and used immediately. Several scions are inserted into each stock branch. To prepare the stock (branch) for the method shown here, saw it off cleanly at a right angle to the branch. For each scion you intend to graft, make a vertical, 2-inch-long cut into the bark to the wood with a sharp knife. Lift the edge of the bark up with the blade of the knife along both sides of the cut. Use 4- to 5-inch-long scions that are ¹/₄ to ¹/₂ inch in diameter; each should have two to three buds. Make a tapered, 2-inch-long cut along one side of the base of the scion, so that it has a flat surface and ends in a point at the bottom. This makes it easy to slip under the bark. If the scion is thick, try to make a gentle L-shaped curve at the top before tapering to the base. Small scions don't need a curved cut, which is used to make thick scions thinner, so the bark flaps don't end up too far away from the wood. (Extremely thin scions will be weak however, and may break off.) Make a second, short cut near the base of the scion on the other side to create a wedge-shaped point. Insert the scions under the bark flaps, with the long cut pressed against the wood. If you made an L-shaped cut at the top, fit the top of the "L" against the flat, top cut on the scion. To fix the scions in place, use ⁵/₈- to 1-inch-long, 19- or 20-gauge wire nails; use two nails on each side to securely nail down the bark. (It tends to curl back otherwise.) Wax the entire cut end of the stock, along the length of the cuts and scions, and dab a bit of wax on the cut end of the scions

as well. (*See* GRAFTING WAX) Scions that have been bark grafted require extra support the first year of growth, so stake them to keep them from being accidentally broken off.

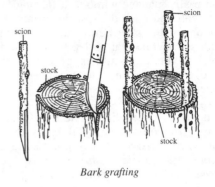

Bark grafting

bark ringing A technique used to slow down vigorous growth on some fruit trees. A ¹/₄-inch-wide strip of bark is removed part way around the trunk with a sharp knife. (Don't cut all the way around, as this will kill the plant.) Cover the wound with electrical tape until it begins to heal, or form callus tissue. Do not push the tape down into the wound; it should not adhere to the cut surface.

basal Growing from or attached at the base. Basal leaves are leaves borne close to the ground, either from the base of the stem or the crown of the plant.

basal cuttage A propagation technique used on certain bulbs, especially hyacinths (*Hyacinthus orientalis*) and other species that form few offsets, to cause large quantities of bulblets to form. It also can be used with other bulbs, including squills (*Scilla* spp.), snowdrops (*Galanthus* spp.), snowflakes (*Leucojum* spp.), daffodils (*Narcissus* spp.), and amaryllis (*Hippeastrum* spp.). There are two types of basal cuttage: scoring and scooping. Collect bulbs for basal cuttage in midsummer, after the leaves have died back and dried. Discard any that show signs of disease. To score a bulb, make three cuts across the base of the bulb that extend through the basal plate and into the growing point of the bulb. To scoop a bulb, use a curve-bladed scalpel, a spoon with a sharpened edge, or a small-bladed knife to scoop out the entire basal plate and destroy the bulb's central shoot. (Depth is important: Scooping out too much tissue can remove the meristem cells responsible for bulblet formation; removing too little also results in few bulblets.) Dust scored or scooped bulbs with a fungicide such as sulfur and store them upside-down in dry sand or on open trays for a week in warm (70 to 78°F), dry conditions to encourage the formation of callus tissue. Then increase the humidity to 90 percent. Bulblets should be visible at the bases of the exposed bulb scales in 3 to 4 months, at which time the mother bulbs should be planted, still upside down, in a cool, protected spot with the bulblets just below the soil surface. Scooped bulbs usually produce more bulblets than scored ones, but they take longer to bloom: Bulblets from scooping bloom in 3 to 4 years, from scoring in 2 to 3 years.

basal cutting, basal stem cutting A cutting taken from a shoot that arises from the base of the plant, usually in spring, and usually from a herbaceous plant. Many hardy perennials can be propagated by rooting basal cuttings; nonflowering shoots are best. Dahlias (*Dahlia* spp.), tuberous begonias (*Begonia* × Tuberhybrida hybrids), and other plants that grow from tuberous roots or stem tubers can be propagated by removing new shoots as well. Collect and root basal cuttings as you would a softwood cutting; some stems have adventitious roots at the base, making them even easier to root. *See* SOFTWOOD CUTTING

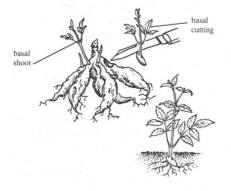

basal cutting

basal shoot

basal cutting

basal plate The compressed stem at the base of a bulb, to which the individual scales are attached.

base map *See* BASE PLAN, BASE MAP

base plan, base map A map that is drawn to scale and indicates the boundary lines of a particular lot or site, along with the location of the house and other buildings. A base map should indicate which way is north, and also record the location of important, semi-permanent or permanent features such as driveways, utility lines, wells, septic fields, easements, and existing trees. (*See* TRIANGULATION for a simple method for accurately locating elements away from the house.) It also can record changes in elevation. A base map is a useful tool for designing a garden: Either make photocopies of your finished base map or use sheets of tracing paper over it to experiment with ideas for plantings and other features. *See also* SITE INVENTORY

basifixed Attached at the base.

basipetalous Opening or developing from the base to the tip. An inflorescence with flowers that open beginning at the bottom is basipetalous.

basiscopic Facing or directed toward the base of a stem or other organ.

bastard trenching *See* DOUBLE DIGGING

bats Beneficial, night-flying mammals that eat a variety of insects. A single bat can consume 1,000 insects a night, including moths, midges, beetles, and mosquitoes.

beak A pointed hornlike protrusion.

beard A line or tuft of hairs. This term is commonly used to refer to the velvety hairs that run along the falls of a bearded iris, but also refers to the bristlelike hairs called awns found in the inflorescence of some grasses. *See also* FALL

bearded Having tufts or patches of hairs, such as those found on the petals of a bearded iris. It also can mean ending in a bristlelike hair, called an awn.

bed An area of cultivated ground in which plants are grown that is usually designed to be seen from more than one side and meant to be appreciated up close. Beds can be of any shape and typically are set alongside paths, patios, or foundations. They can contain all manner of plants, including herbaceous perennials, bulbs, shrubs, trees, woody vines, annuals, and other plants. Because they are meant to be viewed up close and normally are in high-traffic areas, for best results fill beds with perennials and other plants that offer a long season of interest and have attractive foliage. *See also* ISLAND BED, RAISED BED

bedding out Planting bedding plants in the garden, generally in mass plantings.

bedding plants Plants grown temporarily for their flowers or foliage. Typically, bedding plants are annuals, biennials, or tender perennials that are grown to nearly flowering size and then planted in blocks or patterns.

bed system *See* INTENSIVE GARDENING

beetles Hard-shelled, oval to oblong insects that can be pests or beneficials. *See* BENEFICIAL INSECTS for information on beneficial beetles. Common pest beetles include Japanese beetles, asparagus beetles, rose chafers, Colorado potato beetles, cucumber beetles, flea beetles, and Mexican bean beetles. Adult beetles chew holes in leaves, stems, and flowers during the growing season. The grubs, or larvae, of some kinds feed on roots. To control beetles, handpick adult beetles early in the morning and drop them into a container of soapy water. Treat seriously infested plants with neem, pyrethrins, or rotenone. *See* GRUBS for information on beetle larvae and their control.

beetle

bell glass A glass cloche. *See* CLOCHE

belt *See* SHELTERBELT

bench grafting *See* ROOT GRAFTING

bending *See* FESTOON

beneficial animals Animals that eat insects, rodents, and other garden pests or have other beneficial effects in the garden. *See* TOADS, BATS, BIRDS, EARTHWORMS, SNAKES, and SPIDERS, all of which fall into this category.

beneficial insects A general term for insects that have a beneficial effect in the garden. Also called beneficials, these either pollinate flowers or help control pest insects either by parasitizing them or as predators. Bees and wasps are perhaps the best known beneficials: Honeybees are important pollinators in the garden, but parasitic wasps are important beneficials, too. Parasitic wasps inject eggs inside host insects, and the eggs hatch into larvae that feed on them. Brachonid wasps are native beneficials that parasitize aphids, codling moths, cabbageworms, armyworms, and also tomato hornworms; a hornworm covered with tiny ricelike cocoons has been parasitized. Ichneumon wasps also are native wasps that parasitize caterpillars and beetle larvae, as are yellow jackets, which consume flies, caterpillars, and other larvae. Several types of beetles also are beneficial: Lady beetles and their larvae both feed on aphids, mealybugs, and spider mites, while blue-black ground beetles hunt for cabbage root maggots, cutworms, and other pests. Other beneficials include tachinid flies, which parasitize cutworms and various other caterpillars, and syrphid flies, which lay eggs in aphid colonies so their tiny, sluglike larvae can feed on these pests. Native dragonflies eat gnats and mosquitoes, while delicate-looking lacewings, another native beneficial, prey on aphids, scale insects, and caterpillars. Their ferocious larvae, which look something like tiny alligators, also prey on these pests. Other beneficials include minute pirate bugs, spined soldier bugs, soldier beetles, rove beetles, and various predatory mites. To attract beneficials that will help in the fight against garden pests, avoid using toxic sprays in the garden (*See* ORGANIC PEST MANAGEMENT). Leave some areas permanently mulched or covered with ground covers so that beneficials can hide there when the garden is being cultivated or sprayed. The adults of many beneficial species eat pollen and nectar, so a border of plants rich in these foods will help attract them. Consider the following: carrot-family plants, such as caraway, dill, fennel, and parsley; aster-family plants, such as purple or orange coneflowers (*Echinacea* spp. or *Rudbeckia* spp.), daisies (*Leucanthemum* spp.), and yarrow (*Achillea* spp.); and mint-family plants, including catnip, mints, oregano, rosemary, sage, and thyme. A source for water also helps: Fill a shallow basin with rocks, then nearly cover them with water so beneficials can drink without drowning.

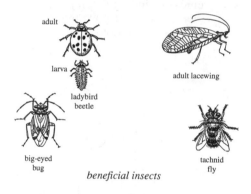

beneficial insects

adult

larva

ladybird beetle

big-eyed bug

adult lacewing

tachnid fly

beneficial microorganisms *See* MICROBIAL INSECTICIDE

beneficials *See* BENEFICIAL INSECTS, BENEFICIAL ANIMALS

berm An elongated mound of soil used to direct runoff. When planted with trees, shrubs, and other plants, a berm also can be used to create privacy. A berm should be about twice as wide at its base as it is high—a 2-foot-tall berm should be 4 feet wide at the base, for example. A berm also is the gradual slope around a paved area such as a terrace or patio and the shoulder of a road.

berry A fruit that contains many seeds, is fleshy or pulpy throughout, and does not open at maturity (is indehiscent). A true berry develops from a single, compound pistil, which bears two or more united carpels. Grapes, tomatoes, and peppers all bear berries.

berry

bi- Two. A prefix that indicates two of a particular organ or characteristic.

bicolor, bicolorous Having two distinct colors.

bicrenate Doubly scalloped, or edged with shallow, rounded teeth that are further divided by a second set of shallow, rounded teeth. This term is commonly used to describe the edge, or margin, of a leaf or leaflet.

bidentate Doubly toothed. Edged with sharp teeth that point out rather than toward the tip of the leaf, with each tooth being further divided into one or more smaller teeth. This term is commonly used to describe the edge, or margin, of a leaf or leaflet.

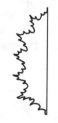

bidentate leaf margin

biennial A plant that takes two years to germinate, flower, set seed, and die. Plant parts also can be biennial: Brambles (*Rubus* spp.) such as raspberries and blackberries produce canes that only have foliage the first year. The second year they produce flowers and fruit, and then they die. Most biennial plants produce a rosette of low-growing leaves the first year and then flower the second. Parsley (*Petroselinum crispum*) and Canterbury bells (*Campanula medium*) are two popular biennials. Plants described as biennials or short-lived perennials generally produce their biggest display of flowers in their second year and bloom poorly, if at all, in subsequent seasons. Foxgloves (*Digitalis purpurea*) and hollyhocks (*Alcea rosea*) are popular biennials or short-lived perennials. For gardeners, the term biennial is as much a growing schedule as a botanical distinction. A variety of plants can be grown as biennials, including true biennials, plants that are biennials or short-lived perennials, and plants that are true perennials. All can be sown indoors or out. Outdoors, sow seeds in spring or summer up to 2 months before the first fall frost where the plants are to grow. Some gardeners sow biennials in a nursery bed, so they can give the plants optimum care, then move them to the spots where they are to bloom in early fall or the following spring. Indoors, sow seeds in individual pots 6 to 8 weeks before seedlings are to be transplanted to the garden, which means in midsummer for biennials that are to be moved to the garden in early fall, or in late winter to have transplants for spring planting. Pull up biennials, including plants being grown as biennials, after they have flowered, or leave them in the garden long enough for their seeds to ripen and self-sow.

biennial bearing *See* ALTERNATE BEARING

bifid Deeply cut to form two lobes or points. The tips of leaves or petals can be forked or cleft to form two points. Some plants have leaves that are covered with hairs that are divided in two, or bifid.

bifoliate Having two leaves.

bifoliolate Having two leaflets.

bifurcate Y-shaped. Forked, with two branches.

bilabiate Two-lipped. Having a calyx (sepals) and/or corolla (petals) divided into upper and lower lip-shaped segments. Members of the mint family (Lamiaceae, formerly Labiatae) such as mint (*Mentha* spp.) or salvia (*Salvia* spp.) have bilabiate flowers.

bilabiate flower

bilateral symmetry The type of symmetry exhibited by a flower that can only be divided into two mirror-image halves along one plane, or line. Zygomorphic flowers such as snapdragons (*Antirrhinum majus*) and orchids (including *Cattleya* spp. and *Phalaenopsis* spp.) display this type of symmetry. *See also* ZYGOMORPHIC

bilateral symmetry

binomial A two-part name. In botany and horticulture, the standard botanical name for a plant is a binomial consisting of a genus name and a specific epithet or the name of a cultivar or hybrid group that belongs to the genus and distinguishes a particular plant or group of plants. Sedum acre and Sedum 'Vera Jameson' are both binomials.

binomial nomenclature Sometimes called the Linnaean system, this is the system of naming plants, animals, and other organisms with two-part names called binomials. Binomial nomenclature, introduced by Swedish botanist Carolus Linnaeus, recognizes the genus as central to the naming and classification of plants and other organisms.

To designate individual species, Linnaeus used a single word, or specific epithet. Previous systems lacked short, definite, technical names and allowed taxonomists to attach any number of epithets to a name. Thus scientific names took on the character of long descriptions. For example, before Linnaeus' system was adopted, one widely recognized "name" for catnip was *Nepeta floribus interrupte spicatis pedunculatis*. Linnaeus classified this plant in the genus *Nepeta*, and attached a single epithet to identify the species, and thus catnip became *Nepeta cataria*. The word *cataria* is Latin and means pertaining to cats.

biocontrol *See* BIOLOGICAL PEST CONTROL

bio-dynamic gardening This is both a philosophy and an organic system for growing plants developed by Rudolph Steiner in the 1920s. Bio-dynamic gardeners use raised beds, succession planting, companion planting, soil building, and other intensive gardening techniques to maximize harvests. They also stress recycling and efficient use of natural resources: A bio-dynamic farm ideally is a self-supporting system, with livestock providing manure to feed plants and plants in turn feeding people and livestock. Bio-dynamics also use moon phases and planetary events to guide activities such as planting or harvest. *See* INTENSIVE GARDENING

biological controls *See* ORGANIC PEST MANAGEMENT

bipinnate Twice cut or twice pinnate. Divided into pairs of segments (leaflets) arranged in a featherlike (pinnate) fashion. The individual segments are further divided into pairs of leaflets.

bipinnate

bipinnate-pinnatifid Twice-cut pinnatifid. Divided into pairs of segments (leaflets) arranged in a featherlike (pinnate) fashion. The individual segments are further divided into pairs of leaflets, which are in turn pinnatifid, meaning they also are divided and have deep indentations (sinuses) that reach from halfway to nearly all the way to the midrib. The individual segments are not separated into individual leaflets.

bipinnate-pinnatifid

bipinnatifid Twice pinnatifid. Divided or cut into pairs of segments arranged in a featherlike (pinnate) fashion, with the indentations, called sinuses, cut from halfway to the middle of the midrib of the leaf but not all the way to the midrib. The segments also are pinnatifid, with deep indentations (sinuses) that reach from halfway to nearly all the way to the midrib. The individual segments (both main and secondary) are not separated into individual leaflets.

bipinnatifid

bipinnatisect Twice pinnatisect. *See* PINNATISECT

birds While some birds are considered garden pests, most are highly efficient beneficial animals that consume a wide variety of insects and other animals. A single house wren can catch 500 insect eggs, beetles, and grubs to consume or feed to young, and a

Baltimore oriole can eat as many as 17 tent caterpillars a minute. Chickadees spend the winter scouring for and eating aphid eggs, which make up more than 60 percent of their winter diet. There's little wonder that gardeners take steps to attract birds to their yards. To make your yard more bird-friendly, plant a variety of shrubs and trees that provide nesting sites, shelter, and food: Berry-bearing shrubs such as viburnums (*Viburnum* spp.) are ideal, as are ever-greens. Also plan for water—a birdbath or water garden with a shallow end that has a bottom that slopes very gradually and is covered with pebbles is ideal. Clean bird-baths every 2 or 3 days and install an electric deicer to be sure water is available in winter as well. Installing a variety of birdhouses also can attract species such as house wrens and bluebirds.

bis- Two. A prefix that indicates two of a particular organ or characteristic.

biserrate Doubly serrate, or doubly saw-toothed. Edged with sharp teeth that point toward the tip of the leaf, with each tooth being further divided into one or more smaller teeth. This term is commonly used to describe the edge, or margin, of a leaf or leaflet.

biserrate leaf margin

bisexual A flower bearing both male and female reproductive organs.

bisexual flower *See* PERFECT FLOWER

bitten *See* PRAEMORSE

black spot A disease that causes black leaf spots with feathery margins on rose foli-age. Infected leaves turn yellow between spots and eventually drop off. To control

black spot, plant rose cultivars that are resistant to this disease. Pick off and de-stroy infected leaves, and prune out affected canes. At the first sign of the dis-ease, spray thoroughly every 7 to 10 days with fungicidal soap or sulfur or use a bak-ing soda spray. *See* FUNGICIDE

bladder An inflated, thin-walled struc-ture.

blade The broad, flattened part of a leaf or a petal.

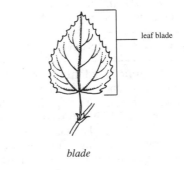

leaf blade

blade

blade-and-hook pruners *See* PRUNING SHEARS

blanching Depriving a plant of light to cause it to form white stems and/or leaves. Asparagus, leeks, and celery commonly are blanched. This can be accomplished by hilling soil up around and even over the tops of the plants, planting in trenches and gradually filling them in with soil (leeks are treated this way), or excluding light by various barriers. Celery can be blanched by fitting each plant with a paper collar or even a paper milk carton with both top and bottom removed. Blanched stems generally are more tender and have a milder flavor.

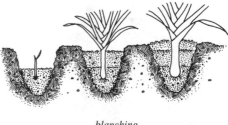

blanching

bleed, bleeding Producing excessive sap flow after a pruning cut or wound. Some species of trees bleed excessively if they are pruned when the sap is rising in late winter or early spring. These include maples (*Acer* spp.), elms (*Ulmus* spp.), walnuts (*Juglans* spp.), and birches (*Betula* spp.). Although the oozing sap doesn't pose any danger to the tree, it can be unsightly, as it attracts sooty molds. Consider pruning bleeders in midsummer, when new growth is hardened off, or in early winter after the leaves have fallen and the tree is dormant.

blight *See* FIRE BLIGHT, LEAF SPOTS

blind This term is used to describe a flower stalk that does not terminate in a bloom because the bud was damaged or aborted. Bulbs that do not produce flowers also are called blind.

blistered *See* BULLATE

blocking This is actually a root-pruning operation used to get seedlings or transplants that have been grown together in a flat or small tray ready for transplanting, either to individual pots or to the garden. Blocking is used for plants that have been spaced out in rows in such containers. It encourages dense, well-branched root systems. Annuals are sometimes sold in 4- by 6-inch trays at garden centers in spring; blocking helps separate the individual plants for transplanting. To block seedlings, a few days before transplanting or before beginning the hardening off process simply cut between the individual plants with a sharp knife. Water thoroughly and set the containers back where they were before. Then transplant as scheduled.

blocking mix A mix of ingredients for making soil blocks. To make it, use a 10-quart bucket and combine 2 buckets of compost, 1 bucket of sphagnum peat, $1/2$ bucket of colloidal phosphate, $1/3$ cup of kelp meal, $1/3$ cup blood meal, and $1/4$ cup ground limestone. Add 1 part water to every 2 to 3 parts of the dry mix and mix thoroughly. *See* SOIL BLOCKS

blocks, soil *See* SOIL BLOCKS

blood, dried *See* BLOOD MEAL

blood meal An organic fertilizer made from dried blood that is an excellent source of nitrogen. It is fast-acting and contains about 11 percent nitrogen. Blood meal also is sometimes spread to repel animal pests such as rabbits.

bloom A whitish covering that is waxy or powdery and found on the surface of fruit, stems, leaves, or other plant parts. Also, a flower. A rapid proliferation of algae in a water garden or pond also is called a bloom.

blossom Flower.

blossom end rot A cultural problem, caused by a calcium deficiency, that begins with a water-soaked spot or bruise on the end of the fruit. The spot gradually turns a tan color, then becomes dark, flattened, and leathery. Blossom end rot affects tomatoes and peppers, and often is related to temperature extremes, uneven watering, or root damage. To prevent it, mulch to keep soil evenly moist and eliminate the need to cultivate around roots. Spray with seaweed extract to give plants a quick calcium boost. Test the soil in fall and add lime, if needed, to correct the deficiency.

blotched A variegation pattern in which color is distributed in large, irregular areas, or blotches.

blunt *See* TRUNCATE

boat-shaped *See* CARINATE, CYMBIFORM, NAVICULAR

bog garden An area designed to grow moisture-loving plants. To build a simple bog garden, dig out a depression, line it with a flexible water garden liner (*See* WATER GARDEN LINER), and fill it with soil. Bog gardens also can be built as part of a water garden—with a shallow area filled with soil partially separated from the deeper water. *See* MARGINAL PLANTS for species that will grow in a bog garden.

bog plants *See* MARGINAL PLANTS

bole The trunk of a tree or treelike plant.

bolt, bolting To form flowers and seeds prematurely, usually because of exposure to excess heat. This term is most often used to refer to biennial crops such as cabbage that begin to set seeds too soon. Lettuce and spinach also commonly bolt in response to warm temperatures.

bomb This rather warlike term actually refers to a flower that has an outer rim of large petals (called guard petals) surrounding a round, pom-pom-like tuft of showy, petal-like structures (actually petaloids or staminodes) in the center. It is most often used to refer to peonies. Peony cultivars 'Angel Cheeks', 'Pink Lemonade', and 'Raspberry Sundae' all produce bombs.

bone meal A fast-acting organic fertilizer that is an excellent source of both phosphate (from 20 to 25 percent) and calcium (about 25 percent). It also contains some nitrogen (from 1 to 5 percent).

bones The visible structure or framework that unifies the elements of a garden. The bones of a garden consist of walls, paved paths or other areas, fences, hedges, trellises, and any other structures that mark its framework. Repeated shapes such as freeform beds that interlock or a pattern of rectangular beds also can be part of a garden's bones. Repeated materials such as brick or stone also play a role in giving a garden a strong framework—called "good bones" by gardeners and designers alike. The bones of a garden are easiest to see in wintertime, when foliage and flowers don't distract from them.

bonsai The ancient Japanese art of creating living, miniaturized trees that are maintained in small containers and trained to echo the shapes and forms of mature, full-size specimens and mirror nature. Roughly translated from the Japanese, bonsai means "shallow pot and tree." The art of cultivating miniature trees first appeared in China (*See* PENJING), and was brought to Japan sometime before 1195, when a bonsai was first depicted in a Japanese picture scroll. Experts develop bonsai from collected specimens and also raise them from seeds and cuttings. The plants are trained and miniaturized by various techniques, including regular pinching and root pruning as well as wiring. Most bonsai are hardy plants that should be maintained outdoors year-round, although tropical species sometimes are trained for use as houseplant bonsai.

bonsai shears *See* SHEARS, GARDEN

bordeaux mix An organically acceptable fungicide and bactericide that contains a mix of copper sulfate and hydrated lime in a wettable powder. Bordeaux mix can be used as a spray or dust to control various fungal diseases such as anthracnose, powdery mildew, and rust, as well as bacterial leaf spots and wilts, and fireblight, also a bacterial disease.

border A long, relatively narrow strip of cultivated ground in which plants are grown. Borders usually are designed to be seen from one side, and commonly are sited in front of a fence, building, or wall, which serves as a backdrop. They also can be sited along either side of a walkway or driveway. Borders can contain all manner of plants, including herbaceous perennials, hardy bulbs, shrubs, trees, woody vines, annuals, and other plants such as herbs, vegetables, and fruit. The plants are arranged with the tallest ones in back and tiers of lower plants in front. For best results, don't be too strict about this rule, however, because varying heights will create a more pleasing, less regimented look.

bordered A variegation pattern in which one color is edged or ringed by a rather broad border of another color. Used to describe the color markings of leaves, petals, or other plant parts. *See also* EDGED

border fork *See* FORK

border shovel *See* SHOVEL

border spade *See* SPADE

boreal From the north. Northern.

borers Tunneling, wormlike larvae of moths or beetles that bore into leaves, stalks, branches, or trunks to feed. Borers are seldom visible, but their symptoms are. The larvae produce small holes in plant parts that have gummy, sawdust-like material around or just below them. The holes often are close to the ground, and affected plants are weakened or killed. Wilting even when the soil is moist is a common symptom of borer infestation on herbaceous plants, including vegetables. If possible, dig out and destroy borers. On trees and shrubs, try inserting a flexible wire into the entrance hole to impale and kill the borer. Injecting parasitic nematodes into borer holes also may help. Dig up iris rhizomes and destroy infested leaves and stems. Avoid damaging tree and shrub stems with lawn-care equipment; wounds provide easy access for borers. Keep borers away from squash, cucumbers, melons, and related plants by covering them with floating row covers from planting to flowering.

borrowed view In landscape design terms, this is an interesting feature or view that is outside the boundary of the garden but is highlighted in the design itself. For example, a view of a nearby church steeple could be framed with plants, thus calling attention to it and making it a feature that adds to the garden's appeal.

boscage, boskage A grove, thicket, or mass of trees and shrubs.

bosket, bosquet A plantation or thicket of trees in a park or garden. This term is primarily used to describe a thicket of trees in a very large garden when the trees are used as a backdrop to a parterre or and allée.

boss A round knob or projection on an otherwise flat surface, such as a leaf. Also used to refer to a showy, dense cluster of stamens or petaloids (petal-like stamens and carpels) in the center of a flower. Fall-blooming anemones (*Anemone hupehensis*,

A. × *hybrida*, and *A. tomentosa*) have a showy boss of stamens in the center. The term boss also is used to refer to the dense cluster of stamens or petaloids in the center of Japanese-style peonies.

bostryx *See* HELICOID CYME

botanical Pertaining to plants or botany. Derived from plants.

botanical garden A garden dedicated to the collection, culture, study, and exhibition of plants.

botanical pesticides Insecticides derived from plants. *See* SABADILLA, SULFUR, NICO-TINE, ROTENONE, RYANIA, PYRETHRIN, NEEM

botanist An individual who specializes in the study of botany or a branch of botany.

botanize To collect and/or study plants in the field for scientific purposes.

botany The branch of biological science devoted to the study of plants. This term is also used to refer to a book or scholarly work on plants as well as the characteristics and lifecycle of a particular plant or group of plants.

botany, economic *See* ECONOMIC BOTANY

botrytis blight *See* GRAY MOLD

bottle garden A terrarium grown in a bottle. *See* TERRARIUM

bottom heat *See* PROPAGATION MAT

botuliform Sausage-shaped. *See* ALLANTOID

bouquets garnis Bundles of aromatic herbs used to flavor soups, stews, and other dishes. To make *bouquets garnis*, tie sprigs of fresh or dried herbs in small bundles or place them in cheesecloth bags. Add them to simmering dishes and remove before serving. These bundles of herbs make it easy to add rich flavor to food without adding flecks of herbs. While classic *bouquets garnis* includes parsley, thyme, and sweet bay leaves, experiment with other ingredients such as tarragon, marjoram, cloves, or peppercorns, and even lemon peels and cinnamon sticks, depending on the dish.

bower A shady nook or recess. This term also is used to refer to an arbor, and it also once referred to a gallery, which is a series of vine-covered arches. *See* GALLERY

bracing A general term for several techniques an arborist can use to provide artificial support to trees that are in danger of being damaged or breaking apart during storms or high winds. Arborists can use flexible cables or rigid rods to strengthen weak crotches and even out the stress load on a tree.

brackish Somewhat salty.

braconid wasp *See* BENEFICIAL INSECTS

bract Actually modified leaves, bracts usually are leaflike or scalelike structures borne at the base of individual flowers, flower clusters, or where a new shoot emerges on a stem. In most cases they are very small (reduced) and scalelike, but the "petals" of many dogwoods, including flowering dogwood (*Cornus florida*) are actually showy, petal-like bracts, as are the red, white, or pink "petals" that make up the blooms of a poinsettia (*Euphorbia pulcherrima*). Sea hollies such as Miss Willmott's Ghost (*Eryngium giganteum*) are grown for their showy, silver-gray, spiny bracts borne beneath cylindrical flower clusters.

bract

bracteate Bearing or borne above bracts.

bracteole, bractlet A very small bract.

brambles, bramble fruit The prickly-stemmed raspberry relatives (*Rubus* spp.), brambles include raspberries, blackberries, loganberries, tayberries, boysenberries, wineberries, and dewberries. Most produce fruit on biennial canes: First-year canes bear foliage only and are called primocanes. The second year the canes, now called floricanes, produce flowers and fruit. Canes that have finished fruiting die: Cut them to the ground after harvest to make room for more new primocanes. (Fall-bearing raspberries are an exception. They bear their fruit on first-year canes at the end of the season; cut the plants to the ground each year in fall.) Brambles are sometimes called cane fruits.

branch A woody stem or division growing from the trunk of a tree, from another branch, or from a primary stem of a shrub.

branch angle *See* CROTCH, CROTCH ANGLE

branch collar The bulging or ridged area at the base of a branch. When pruning off a limb, cut just outside the branch collar. Try to cut parallel to the bark ridges on the main trunk or stem of the plant. Cuts made in this manner heal quickly and cleanly, and keep the plant's natural barriers against pests and diseases intact. *See* NATURAL BARRIER, THREE-STEP CUT

branch leader The main, terminal shoot of a branch.

branchlet A very small, thin branch or twig.

branch nippers A pruning tool used primarily in bonsai that has two curved, concave blades at the front of the tool (perpendicular to the handles). Branch nippers leave a slight depression when they cut, which will heal over without forming a lump. They are also useful for removing hard-to-reach branches.

break A shoot emerging from a bud, especially when the shoot begins to grow after the terminal bud is pinched out. A bud that opens and begins to grow. This also is a general term for a sport or mutation.

breastwood Shoots that grow out from an espaliered tree or shrub that is trained against a wall. These are normally removed.

breed true *See* COME TRUE

bridge grafting Like inarching, bridge grafting is a repair technique in which scions are grafted over a damaged area on the trunk of a tree to make sure nutrient flow isn't interrupted. In this case, scions are grafted over the damaged area to repair trees that have been girdled or have damaged areas caused by lawnmowers, mice or other rodents, or even by cars running or backing into them. Bridge grafting is best done in early spring, just as the established tree begins growing, so that the bark "slips" easily. Scions should be dormant, so collect and store $1/4$- to $1/2$-inch-diameter scionwood the winter before (*See* SCION) either from the plant to be grafted or from the same or a compatible species. Be sure to keep track of which end is up, because they need to be grafted right side up. *See* POLARITY for further information. In an emergency, try bridge grafting any time during the growing season—up to late spring is best—using actively growing stock and scions; in this case, remove any shoots or buds growing on the scions. To prepare the tree for grafting, first trim away the dead and damaged bark around the wound. The cuts used for bridge grafting are similar to those used in bark grafting. (*See* BARK GRAFTING) After cutting back to healthy, living tissue on both sides of the wound, cut slots at the top and bottom of the area to be bridge grafted. Space the slots from 2 to 3 inches apart and leave a 1/2-inch-long flap of bark attached to the tree at the top and bottom of each slot for the scion to slip under. You may decide to cut slots and graft scions one at a time since the slots need to be exactly the width of the scions and they should be long enough to bow out slightly when inserted.

To prepare each scion, make a tapered, 2-inch-long cut along one side of the base of the scion, so that it has a flat surface and ends in a point at the bottom. Then make a second, short cut near the base of the scion on the other side to create a wedge-shaped point. Repeat the procedure at the other end of the scion, making both long cuts on the same side. Check to make sure they will fit into each slot tightly and are long enough to bow out slightly. This allows the trunk to sway slightly without moving them and also ensures good cambium to cambium contact. Insert the tips of the scions under the flaps of bark at the top and bottom of the slot. Then use wire nails to nail each end in place as you would for bark grafting; be sure to nail through the flap of bark and to nail down any loose bark. Then coat the entire area with grafting wax.

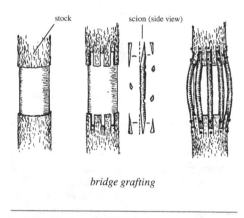

stock   scion (side view)

bridge grafting

bristle A short, stiff hair.

bristly Bearing bristles. *See* ECHINATE, HISPID, SETOSE

broadcasting Sowing seeds outdoors by scattering them over an area. To attain even coverage when broadcasting seeds (such as those of lawngrasses) over a large area, scatter half the seeds while walking a pattern of rows in one direction, then scatter the other half of the seeds while walking in rows perpendicular to the first. To broadcast a drift of annuals in a flowerbed or border, it is sometimes a good idea to "draw" a shape on the soil surface with a stick to outline the final shape of the planting. *See* DIRECT SOWING

broadfork Also known as a cultivating fork, this is a tool designed for loosening up the top layer of soil. It has two handles that are connected to a broad head with about five widely spaced tines. To operate it, step on the head to insert the tines into the soil, then pull back on the handles to loosen the top layer of soil.

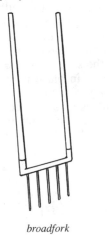

broadfork

bromeliad potting mix *See* EPIPHYTE MIX

brushy twigs *See* PEA STAKES

bryophyte A general, collective term for mosses and liverworts based on the division Bryophyta, recognized by 19th-century botanists. Bryophytes are distinguished from ferns because they have stems and leaves but lack true roots and vascular tissue. *See* DIVISION, PTERIDOPHYTE

BT *See* BACILLUS THURINGIENSIS

bubble diagram A plan for a bed or border in which the plants are indicated by loosely drawn, round, oval, or free-form blobs. These diagrams usually are drawn in pencil and the names of the plants to be used are written inside each bubble. If a bubble diagram is to be useful in determining how many plants you will need for a particular design, draw it to scale, and take the overall spread of each plant into account when drawing the bubblelike shapes.

bud An undeveloped organ such as a flower or leaf or an undeveloped shoot or branch.

bud, axillary *See* AXILLARY BUD

budding A grafting technique used to unite a stock with a scion that consists of a single bud, a small section of bark, and depending on the technique, sometimes some wood. Budding is faster than grafting, makes extremely efficient use of scionwood, and is commonly used with roses and fruit trees. Plants can be budded anytime the bark is slipping (*See* SLIPPING), but midsummer to fall and spring are the best times to bud. To bud in midsummer or fall, collect scions, called budsticks, when you are ready to bud. Budsticks should be from the current season of growth and have leaf rather than flower buds. (The latter tend to be rounder and fatter than the former.) Remove the leaves, leaving on the leaf stalks, which make convenient handles for the buds. Keep budsticks cool and moist until you are ready to use them: Wrap them in moist cloth and set them in a shady spot. *See* T-BUDDING, CHIP BUDDING, and PATCH BUDDING for three techniques to consider. Bud unions should form within 2 to 3 weeks. If the leaf stalk drops off and the bud remains plump, a union has formed. If the leaf stalk does not drop off and the bud or the attached bark turns black, the union has not formed. (You can rebud these if the bark is still slipping.) Let plants with successful buds grow until the following spring. In most cases, the buds will not sprout until then. Just as the buds begin to swell in spring, cut off the top of the stock. Remove any shoots that emerge from the stock. To bud in spring, collect budsticks as you would for fall budding, but after plants have become dormant—from fall to winter—and store them as you would scions (*See* scion). Bud plants as soon as the bark starts slipping in spring (the budsticks should still be dormant). Unions will form on spring-budded plants within 2 to 3 weeks; after that, cut off the top of the scion. *See* GRAFTING, SCION

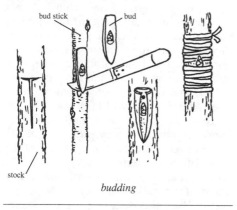

budding

budding knife A knife with a very sharp, rounded blade that has a narrow, blunt, flared section either on the wrong (blunt) side of the blade or on the other end of the knife. This flared section is inserted under the bark after cuts are made to pull out the flaps of bark under which buds are inserted. It can be either a flat or a folding knife.

budding rubbers *See* RUBBER BUDDING STRIPS

bud grafting *See* BUDDING

bud primordia *See* MERISTEM

bud scale A small, bractlike modified leaf that covers a bud. Bud scales protect the dormant bud, and leave a ring of tiny scars on stems that can be used to determine where the current year's growth began. *See* NEW WOOD

bud sport A branch that exhibits a marked change from the parent stock that can be perpetuated vegetatively by techniques such as stem cuttings. Many popular fruit cultivars originate as bud sports. For example, pink-fleshed grapefruits originated on a single branch of a tree. 'Golden Delicious' is a sport of 'Delicious' apple.

budstick A shoot of a scion collected especially for budding.

bud, terminal *See* TERMINAL BUD

budwood A shoot of a scion collected especially for budding.

bugs A general term used to refer to all insects. The term bug is more precisely used to refer to any number of insects that are true bugs. *See* PLANT BUGS

bulb While gardeners commonly use the term bulb to refer to various underground structures, strictly speaking a true bulb is a fleshy storage organ that resembles a bud and is usually underground (bulbs sometimes protrude above the soil surface). A bulb consists of fleshy scales attached to a basal plate, which gives rise to the roots and a compressed stem that contains an embryonic shoot or flower. The scales, which make up the majority of the bulb, are actually modified fleshy leaves that store food for the plant. Daffodils (*Narissus* spp.), tulips (*Tulipa* spp.), onions (*Allium* spp.), amaryllis (*Hippeastrum* spp.), lilies (*Lilium* spp.), and fritillarias (*Fritillaria* spp.) all bear true bulbs. Of these, the first four bear bulbs that consist of a solid mass of tightly packed scales. These sometimes are called tunicate bulbs, because a papery tunic, which protects the bulb from being damaged or drying out, covers the outside. Lilies and fritillarias have bulbs that consist of loose scales, and they are not covered by a protective tunic. Sometimes called scaly or non-tunicate bulbs, these dry out more quickly and are damaged more easily than tunicate bulbs. For best results with loose-scaled bulbs, handle them carefully to avoid bruising or breaking them, and plant them promptly when you bring them home or they arrive in the mail. Most bulbous plants eventually produce clumps that can be dug and divided for propagation. To get the most plants from a single clump, separate the individual offsets and replant them separately. For information on other bulb propagation techniques, *see* BASAL CUTTAGE, CHIPPING, TWIN-SCALING, OFFSETS, BULBILS, BULBLETS. For information on bulblike structures, *see* TUNICATE, CORM, TUBER, RHIZOME. For different types of bulbs, *see* HARDY BULBS, LITTLE BULBS, SUMMER BULBS.

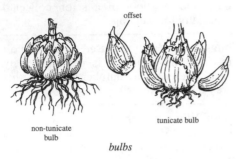

bulbs

non-tunicate bulb

tunicate bulb

offset

---

bulb cutting *See* CHIPPING

---

bulbiferous Bearing bulbils or bulblets. Many lilies (*Lilium* spp.) bear bulblets in the leaf axils, for example, and thus are bulbiferous.

---

bulbiform Bulb-shaped or bulblike.

---

bulbil A small bulb that forms on the aboveground portion of a plant, such as in the leaf axils or in the inflorescence. Some lilies (*Lilium* spp., including many Asiatic hybrid lilies) commonly form bulbils in the leaf axils; some onions (*Allium* spp.) produce them in their flowerheads. To grow bulbils into full-size plants, simply pick them off the parent plant in late summer and handle them as you would bulblets. *See* BULBLETS

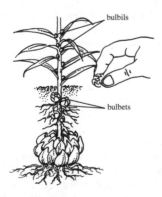

bulbils

bulbets

bulbils and bulbets

---

bulblet A small bulb that forms on the underground portion of a plant, such as

along the stem beneath the soil surface or around the scales of the mother bulb. Lilies (*Lilium* spp.) commonly bear bulblets. To propagate lilies from bulblets, dig the bulbs in fall, pick off the bulblets, and pot them in flats or pots of growing medium. Or plant them outdoors in a nursery bed. Set the bulblets at a depth of about twice their diameter. Keep them in a cold frame or a protected spot outdoors over winter. They will take several years to reach blooming size, and may need annual repotting as they grow. To encourage bulblet formation on a lily, carefully twist off a flowering stalk, leaving the bulb beneath the soil. Clip off the flower, and dust the stalk with a fungicide such as sulfur. Bury the stalk in a shallow trench at a 45-degree angle. Fill the trench with a 50-50 mix of peat and very coarse sand or grit. Pot up the bulblets that form the following summer.

---

bulbous Bulblike.

---

bulb planter A somewhat unusual-looking tool with a round blade designed to dig out holes for bulbs. Both hand-held and long-handled models are available. To use one, plunge the blade into the soil (long-handled models have a foot tread), pull it out with the core of soil it removes, plant, and replace the soil.

bulb planter

bulbs, little *See* LITTLE BULBS

bulbs, summer *See* SUMMER BULBS

bullate Covered with rounded blister-like lumps or puckers. Most often used to describe leaf surfaces.

bun A small, rounded plant, usually an alpine or rock garden plant. *See* CUSHION

bundle scar *See* LEAF SCAR

burlap A rough, strong cloth used to wrap the root balls of plants that have been dug (*See* BALLED-AND-BURLAPPED). Burlap also can be stretched over a frame to shade new transplants or to provide wind protection to broad-leaved evergreens over winter. It also can be spread over a slope and staked in place to prevent erosion while grass seeds germinate or groundcovers (which can be planted in holes cut through the burlap) become established. Burlap is biodegradable, but synthetic forms of it are now common, and these aren't appropriate for erosion prevention (they would have to be removed). The British term for burlap is hessian.

burr, bur A prickly fruit that is covered with hooked spines.

burr

bush This term is commonly used to refer to a small, heavily branched shrub that does not have a distinct trunk. *See* SHRUB

butterfly garden A garden designed to attract adult butterflies and butterfly larvae, or caterpillars. A successful butterfly garden must provide nectar plants for adults as well as food plants for caterpillars. Water and shelter from wind also are important for creating suitable habitat for butterflies. Plants in the daisy family (Compositae) are excellent nectar plants, including asters (*Aster* spp.), sunflowers (*Helianthus* spp.), sneezeweed (*Helenium autumnale*), goldenrods (*Solidago* spp.), tickseed (*Coreopsis* spp.), and yarrow (*Achillea* spp.). Peas, clovers, and other legumes also make good butterfly plants, as do members of the mint family (Lamiaceae) such as hyssops (*Agastache* spp.), lavenders (*Lavandula* spp.), and catmints (*Nepeta* spp.). Milkweeds (*Asclepias* spp.) attract monarch butterflies and a wide variety of other species, and members of the parsley or carrot family (Umbelliferae) attract swallowtails. Larvae feed on various trees, shrubs, and vines, including willows (*Salix* spp.), aspens and poplars (*Populus* spp.), hackberries (*Celtis* spp.), and honeysuckles (*Lonicera* spp.).

buttress, buttress root A wedge-shaped outgrowth from a tree trunk or above-ground roots that extends up the trunk and out from it to provide added support for the tree. Butress roots are found on several species of trees, including figs (*Ficus* spp.), especially when they are growing in shallow, wet soils. *See also* STILT ROOT

butyl, butyl rubber A rubber used to make flexible water garden or pond liners. *See* WATER GARDEN LINERS

bypass pruners *See* HAND PRUNERS

cabling *See* BRACING

cacti, potting mix for *See* POTTING MIX

caducous Falling off early or prematurely compared to similar plant parts on other species. Stipules, the leaflike appendages at the base of a leaf stalk, commonly fall off early, making them caducous.

caepitose, cespitose Growing in dense tufts, clumps, or mats.

caging Supporting plants—especially tomatoes—in round or square wire cages. Commercial models are available, but most of those available are far too small to support the average indeterminate tomato plant at maturity, which can reach 5 or 6 feet. Cages should be made of wire mesh that has at least 5- or 6-inch openings, and they should be at least 2 feet around. Install wooden stakes at the base of each cage and tie the cage to them for added stability. Or "cage" tomatoes by installing four 6-foot-tall stakes around them and then surrounding the stakes with string.

calcarate Spurred. Bearing a spur or spur-like appendage called a calcar. *See also* SPUR

calcareous Containing lime. This term is used to describe soil or rock that has a high lime content. Soil that is calcareous is alkaline, or basic, in pH. *See* pH

calceolate Slipper- or shoe-shaped. The pouched lips of the flowers of lady's slipper orchids (*Cypripedium* spp.) are calceolate.

calcicole A plant that grows naturally in, and therefore thrives on, calcareous soils, which are high in lime and alkaline.

calcifuge A plant that cannot survive and is actually damaged by calcareous soils, which are high in lime and alkaline.

calciphilic Requiring or preferring limestone (calcareous) soils or limestone. Lime-loving.

callose, callous Having a callus.

callus The thick tissue that develops on a cutting that is being rooted, or the protective tissue that forms along a wound on a stem or other plant part, especially in woody plants. Also, a thick, leathery or hard bulge or knob. Also called a callosity.

callused Having a callus. This term is commonly used to refer to plant parts, such as cuttings, that have developed a callus because they were wounded to encourage rooting, or because a plant part has dropped off.

calyx The collective term for all the sepals of a flower, which are located just outside the petals (corolla) and make up the outer whorl of the perianth, which consists of the corolla plus the calyx. A calyx can bear separate sepals or the sepals can be fused together to form a tube (called a calyx tube) at the base of a flower.

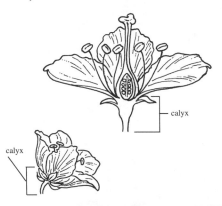

calyx lobe In a flower with fused sepals, the lobe is the remaining free portion at the top of each sepal.

calyx tube Sepals that are fused together to form a tube at the base of a flower. A calyx that is fused may have lobes (called calyx lobes) at the top. This term is sometimes used for hypanthium, which botanically is a slightly different structure. *See* HYPANTHIUM

calyx tube

cambium Cambium is a lateral meristem, meaning an area of undifferentiated cells that actively divide and differentiate, located along the length of a stem or root. Dicots have cambium; monocots such as palms do not. There are two types of cambium: vascular cambium and cork cambium. The vascular cambium is a narrow layer of cells that lies between the xylem (water-conducting tissue) and the phloem (food-conducting tissue). During the growing season, the vascular cambium cells give rise to secondary phloem on the outside of the trunk or stem and secondary xylem on the inside; it is responsible for the thickening of stems as they grow. The cork cambium develops after a stem begins to thicken. It is a thin layer of meristematic cells that gives rise to the elastic, spongy, waterproof, protective tissue called cork, which is the thickest and outermost of the several layers that make up the bark that covers trunks, branches, and roots of woody plants. The cork cambium and the cork it produces protect the phloem in woody stems. *See also* MERISTEM, PHLOEM, XYLEM, BARK

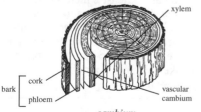

xylem

bark

cork

phloem

vascular cambium

cambium

campanulate Bell-shaped. Lily-of-the-valley (*Convallaria majalis*) and many, but not all, bellflowers (*Campanula* spp.) have campanulate blooms: Canterbury bells (*C. medium*) have classic campanulate flowers, while peach-leaved bellflower *(C. persicfolia*) bears broadly bell-shaped ones, sometimes described as cup-shaped.

campanulate flower

canaliculate Having grooves or channels that run lengthwise.

candelabriform Tiered in whorls or ranks that radiate out from a common point. This term is used to describe branching habits as well as stellate hairs.

candle The tender new shoots of conifers, before the needles have elongated.

candling Pinching back candles of evergreens, breaking them in half, or heading them back with pruning shears to induce more branching or control the size of the plant. Candling only works when the new growth is still quite succulent—the candles usually are lighter green in color than the rest of the needles and they should break easily if bent over. Breaking candles off at about half their length in late spring or very early summer (late May or early June) forces buds to form along the length of the remaining candle or at its base. Candling works on spruces (*Picea* spp.), firs (*Abies* spp.), and most pines (*Pinus* spp.). New growth of junipers (*Juniperus* spp.), arborvitae (*Thuja* spp.), hemlocks (*Tsuga* spp.), and certain other evergreens can be pinched, sheared, or headed back, but they don't produce the recognizable "candles" that spruces, firs, and pines do.

cane A primary stem that arises from the base of a plant, at a height not more than one-quarter the height of the entire plant. Rose stems are commonly called canes, as are the biennial stems of brambles such as raspberries and blackberries (*Rubus* spp.). Hardened, first-year shoots of grapes also are called canes (*See* CANE PRUNING). In addition, the woody, jointed, hollow stems of bamboos, sugarcane, some palms, and some grasses are called canes. Stakes, such as those made of cut lengths of bamboo, also are referred to as canes.

cane fruits More often called brambles or bramble fruits, these are fruit produced by raspberry (*Rubus* spp.) relatives, which produce canes. *See* BRAMBLES

cane pruning A pruning and training system for grapes designed to keep the plants in check so that they produce large clusters of fruit. First train the vine to establish a trunk against a stake and create a basic framework for the plant. (Grapes are generally grown on a 1- or 2-wire trellis.) The first year, let newly planted vines grow unrestrained, free of the support stake. Then in late winter, select the thickest shoot, or cane, to become the trunk, and nip it back just above the third bud from the cane's connection to the original trunk. Cut off any other shoots. This leaves a small plant, but one with an extensive root system that will grow vigorously. The second year, let the vine grow about 6 to 8 inches, then select the strongest, most upright shoot to become the trunk. Tie it loosely to the stake for support. Continue tying it to the stake throughout the summer. When the main shoot grows to within 6 inches of the support wire, pinch off the growing tip to encourage branching. This establishes the "head" or top of the vine. Shoots that grow from this point will be trained along the wires. (To train to 2 wires, pinch out the tip below the first wire and again the following season below the second.) Choose two side shoots that emerge from the head and are the thickness of a pencil, and train them horizontally along the wires so the vine forms a "T" shape. These shoots become the cordons. Remove any other shoots on the trunk. As the cordons grow, loosely tie

them to the wires, occasionally wrapping them around the wires for added support. The second winter, remove any shoots that have grown either from the trunk or the two cordons, leaving a T-shaped vine. Cut the cordons back to 10 or 12 buds if they grew vigorously during the previous summer. The third year, pinch off any flower buds that emerge. Beginning in the third winter, and annually thereafter, select two thick canes that emerge from the base of each cordon. Remove the older cordon, and tie the one that is farthest from the trunk to the wire; it is the fruit-bearing cordon for the coming season. Head back this cordon to between 10 and 12 nodes, which will produce the fruit. Cut the second cordon back to about two or three buds to make a renewal spur that will produce the following year's cordons.

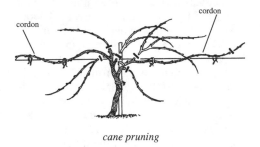

cane pruning

canescent Hoary or frosted looking. Covered with short gray or white hairs that make the surface appear gray or white. Most often used to describe leaf surfaces.

canker Fungal and bacterial diseases that produce discolored spots and dead areas on stems. Affected areas may be covered with small black spores or ooze a slimy or gummy material. Infected shoot tips may turn yellow, wilt, and die. Pruning is the best control for canker: During dry weather, cut off infected parts at least 2 inches below the affected area. Disinfect pruners after each cut by dipping them in a bleach solution (1 part bleach to 9 parts water). Remove and destroy severely diseased plants. To prevent future cankers, avoid wounding bark with pruning or lawn-care tools.

capillary Slender, fine, and hairlike.

capillary pore *See* PORE SPACE

capillary moisture, capillary water Water held in soil by both by adhesion and by forces of surface tension (including cohesion). Water held in this manner doesn't necessarily drain down in response to gravity; it moves in the direction of greatest surface tension through a process called capillary action. Capillary watering systems use this force to water plants, which are set on a wet mat or in sand in a watertight bench. The moisture moves from the wet mat or sand into the drier soil in the pots. Capillary mats usually are made of synthetic fiber: Commercial seed-starting systems and indoor gardening systems are available that incorporate them.

capitate Headlike. A flower cluster, or inflorescence, that resembles a head (capitulum), but may or may not be a true head.

capitulum, *pl.* **capitula** A short, dense cluster of flowers, or inflorescence, that has individual flowers, or florets, that are attached to a common point on the flower stem called a receptacle. *See also* HEAD

capsular Attached to or resembling a capsule.

capsule A dry fruit that opens at maturity (is dehiscent) and is the result of two or more fused carpels. A wide range of plants bear capsules in many shapes and sizes, including poppies (*Papaver* spp.), onions (*Allium* spp.), violets (*Viola* spp.), and okra (*Abelmoschus esculentus*). Surprisingly, buckeyes (*Aesculus* spp.) bear their seeds, which are commonly called nuts, in capsules. Capsules open to release their seeds in different ways. *See* DEHISCENT for information on the major methods.

capsules

carbon-nitrogen ratio The proportion of high-carbon versus high-nitrogen materials in a compost pile. Materials that are high in carbon tend to be brown or yellow and dry: These include dry fallen leaves, straw, sawdust, paper, and pine needles. High-nitrogen materials usually are moist and often green (manure, a high nitrogen material, is an exception). Other high-nitrogen materials include grass clippings, vegetable peelings, and fresh garden trimmings. Ideally, mix about 2 or 3 parts high-carbon materials with 1 part high-nitrogen materials. This proportion allows for optimum decomposition. A pile with too much high-carbon materials will not decompose, while one with an excess of high-nitrogen materials will smell.

carinate Having ridges, or keel-like structures that run lengthwise.

carnivorous Meat eating. A plant that catches or traps, and then digests, insects and other prey. Venus's-flytraps (*Dionaea muscipula*) and pitcher plants (*Sarracinea* spp., *Darlingtonia* spp., and *Nepenthes* spp.) are examples.

carotenoids Pigments in plants that cause yellows, oranges, and reds.

carpel The basic unit of the female reproductive portion of a flower, consisting of a simple pistil (a stigma, style, and ovary), and bearing the ovules that develop into seeds when the flower is fertilized. Carpels can be borne singly or they can be fused together to form a compound pistil. The number and structure of the carpels in a flower is one element that taxonomists use to help them describe and classify plants.

carpellate Bearing or consisting of carpels. This term is often used with a number to indicate the number of carpels a pistil or gynoecium (the female portion of a flower) contains, for example 2-carpellate (or bicarpellate), or 3-carpellate.

carpet bedding A form of bedding out in which an area is filled with very low-growing bedding plants that are arranged in a pattern to create a colorful design of flowers or foliage.

-carpous A suffix referring to fruit, usually combined with a prefix that indicates a particular characteristic. *Pterocarpous* means winged fruits, for example.

caryopsis A dry fruit bearing a single seed that doesn't open along definite lines when ripe (meaning it is indehiscent) and has a seed coat that is fused to the wall of the fruit inside. Members of the grass family, including wheat and corn, bear this type of fruit.

caryopsis

caterpillar A larva, or immature stage, of a butterfly or moth. Caterpillars are soft-bodied, wormlike creatures that can be smooth, hairy, or spiny and can have several pairs of legs. Many different kinds of caterpillars attack garden plants, including armyworms, cabbage loopers, cankerworms, corn earworms, imported cabbageworms, cutworms, and tomato hornworms. These pests chew holes in leaves, flowers, fruits, and shoots. To control them, handpick and destroy caterpillars. Spray plants with BTK (*Bacillus thuringiensis* var. *kurstaki*). Use pyrethrins or neem for serious infestations. *See also* BUTTERFLY GARDEN

caterpillar

cation exchange capacity The measure of a soil's ability to retain fertility as measured by its ability to absorb cationic plant nutrients such as potassium, calcium, and magnesium.

catkin A spike or spikelike flower cluster, or inflorescence, that consists of scalelike bracts and densely packed flowers that usually lack petals (apetalous). A catkin, also called an ament or a nucamentum, commonly is cylindrical and hangs down. It usually bears flowers of one sex only. Willows (*Salix* spp.), birches (*Betula* spp.), filberts (*Corylus* spp.), and oaks (*Quercus* spp.) all bear catkins.

catkin

caudate Ending with a tail-like appendage at the tip. A caudate leaf has concave margins. While most commonly used to describe a leaf tip, this term can be applied to other plant parts such as bracts (modified petal-like leaves) or the petals or sepals of a flower.

caudate leaf tip

caudex Thickened or swollen underground stems and/or roots that give rise to the aboveground stems of the plants. Houseplant enthusiasts grow a variety of succulents (fleshy-stemmed plants) for their unusually shaped caudex bases, including desert rose (*Adenium obesum*). The term caudex is also used to refer to the trunk of a palm tree.

caulescent Producing a well-developed aboveground stem, or stems, called a caulis.

cauliflorus, cauliflory Producing flowers directly from the old wood of branches or trunks. Redbuds (*Cercis* spp.) are cauliflorus.

cauline Attached, pertaining to, or arising from the stems. Foxgloves (*Digitalis purpurea* spp.) have cauline leaves.

-caulous A suffix referring to stems, usually combined with a prefix indicating a particular characteristic. *Pterocaulous* means winged stems, for example.

cavex hoe *See* HOE

cavex rake *See* THATCH

cell The basic unit of living matter or tissue, consisting of a nucleus (or nuclei) and protoplasm contained within a cell wall. The term cell also is used to designate a chamber or compartment within an ovary, anther, or fruit.

cell culture *See* TISSUE CULTURE

cellulose The substance that is the major component of cell walls in plants.

central leader A pruning and training technique that creates a pyramid-shaped tree with a few strong, evenly spaced tiers of branches radiating from the trunk like spokes of a wheel. Dwarf and semidwarf apple trees, pears, as well as sour and sweet cherries can be trained as central leaders. To train a central-leader tree, start with an unbranched whip (the tip of which will become the central leader) and the first growing season select three or four main branches, which will become the scaffold branches. These should emerge from different sides of the trunk, with no two branches on top of one another, and should be separated vertically by 4 to 8 inches. Cut off all the other branches that emerge from the trunk, but leave any secondary branches that arise from the scaffolds. (Some nurseries sell small trees that already have undergone some training and have scaffold branches; in this case, start with second-year pruning.) Spread scaffold branches to widen crotch angles as needed. (*See* CROTCH, CROTCH ANGLE for details.) The second winter or early spring, use thinning cuts to remove any branches that are growing at narrow angles or are competing with the central leader. Cut back the central leader to a bud about 3 to 3 $^1/_2$ feet above the lowest scaffold branch; for dwarf trees cut at about 2 to 2 $^1/_2$ feet to encourage a new tier of scaffold branches to form. Also head back the tips of the scaffold branches by one-third to one-half. In early summer, select a new central leader and remove competing shoots within about 8 inches of its base. At the same time, select another two or three new scaffold branches above the original branches, using the same selection criteria. Again remove all the other branches that emerge from the trunk as well as watersprouts (*See* WATERSPROUTS) and spread branches to widen crotch angles as needed. Repeat the process in the third year, but this time also thin out some of the secondary branches so the center is open to light and air.

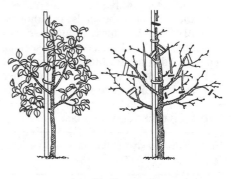

central leader pruning

centrifugal Developing or opening from the center toward the outside or margin. A cyme is a centrifugal inflorescence, for example.

centripetal Developing or opening from the outside or margin toward the center. A corymb is a centripetal inflorescence.

-cephalous A suffix referring to the type or number of heads. Polycephalous means bearing many heads, for example.

ceraceous Waxy looking or waxy textured.

ceriferous Producing wax.

cernuous Drooping or nodding. This term is most often used to describe flowers that have curved or drooping individual flower stalks (pedicels) attached to an erect inflorescence stalk (peduncle). *See also* NUTANT

certified seed, certified plants, certified stock Seed or plants grown under specific standards designed to maintain propagating material that is true to type (exhibits the correct flower color or fruit shape and flavor, for example), and also is free of contaminants as well as insects and diseases.

cespitose *See* CAEPITOSE

chaff A membranelike scale or bract that is dry and thin. This term refers to the small bracts that are attached to the receptacle and encircle the base of the individual disk florets that make up the "eye" of the daisy-like flowers of aster-family plants (Asteraceae). On sunflowers, once the seeds are removed, the chaffy heads are sturdy enough to use as scouring pads. The husks of grains such as wheat are also referred to as chaff. These are separated from the seeds they enclose by winnowing. *See* WINNOW

chaffy Chafflike or having chaff.

chalky, chalky soil Alkaline. *See* ALKALINE SOIL

channeled Marked by one or more long, deep grooves in the surface. *See also* CANALICULATE, SULCATE

chartaceous Thin and papery in texture and generally brown or tan. Used to describe bracts or scales.

chasmogamous flower A flower that opens before it is fertilized and is usually cross-pollinated. *See also* CLEISTOGAMOUS FLOWER

chemical controls *See* ORGANIC PEST MANAGEMENT

chemical fertilizer A fertilizer processed or produced in a chemical plant. Also called a synthetic fertilizer, these products are usually made from nonrenewable resources such as petroleum products or by treating rock powders with acids to increase their solubility. While chemical fertilizers contain mineral salts that are readily available to plants, these salts do not feed beneficial soil organisms and actually repel earthworms by making the soil more acid. They also readily leach out of the soil. Repeated use of chemical fertilizers will reduce biological activity in the soil over time, and this has a negative impact on soil structure. *See* soil, SOIL STRUCTURE

chimera, chimaera A plant that has sections or layers of two or more genetically distinct tissues growing next to one another, because of either a mutation or grafting. Many plants with variegated leaves originated from this type of mutation; variegated geraniums (*Pelargonium* spp.), coleus (*Solenostemon* spp.), and variegated sansevierias (*Sansevieria* spp.) are all chimeras. While most chimeras must be propagated vegetatively, depending on their origin some can be reproduced by seed. In general, chimeras are relatively unstable, and plants can revert to their previous appearance—all green foliage, for example. A chimera can affect part of a shoot tip (sectorial chimera), in which case, buds arising on either side of the shoot may have different characteristics, while a bud that originates on the line that joins the two tissues will exhibit both characteristics. Chimeras that affect a thin layer of tissue covering the entire shoot (periclinal chimera) are relatively stable and can be propagated by stem cuttings or tip layering. Thornless blackberries are an example of this type of chimera: The epidermis (outer layer) of the shoots lacks the gene to produce thorns.

Chinese layering *See* AIR LAYERING

chip budding A budding technique that is not as popular or simple as T-budding, but is valuable nonetheless because it can be used even if the bark is not slipping, either in fall or if growth slows and the bark "tightens up" in summer. It is best used with stock and scions that range from ¹/₂ to 1 inch in diameter. To prepare the stock, make a cut at a 45-degree angle about one-fourth of the way into it. Then, starting about 1 inch above the first cut, make a smooth, second cut that meets the first one and removes a chip of wood. To prepare the bud, make the same two cuts in the bud-stick. The chip removed from the budstick needs to fit exactly into the cut in the stock. After fitting in the bud, fasten the bud in place with a rubber budding strip as you would for a T-bud. *See* BUDDING, T-BUDDING

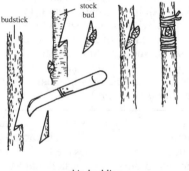

chip budding

chipping A propagation technique, some-times referred to as bulb cutting, used to propagate some bulbs, especially those that are slow to produce offsets, such as snow-drops (*Galanthus* spp.). Collect bulbs for chipping from midsummer to fall and dry them. Discard any that show signs of dis-ease. Use a sharp knife or razor blade to cut from the top through the center of the bulb and down through the basal plate, to make two halves. Cut each piece in half again. It is possible to obtain as many as 16 chips from a single bulb. Make sure that each has a piece of the basal plant. Treat the chips with a liquid fungicide (liquid penetrates the areas between the scales better than

powders do) and let them drain for 10 min-utes or so. Then place the chips in a plastic bag containing moist vermiculite or perlite (about 1 part chips to 2 parts vermiculite or perlite is fine). You can also spread them in layers in a box, deep flat, or pot, to a depth of no more than 6 inches, again using ver-miculite or perlite. Cover flats tightly with plastic wrap, but leave a couple of inches between the top of the medium and the plastic to allow for air to circulate. Store the chips in a dark, warm (68°F) place for 3 months, after which bulblets should have formed. Check regularly and remove any chips that show signs of rot. Harden off bulblets slowly and grow them in a nursery bed or other protected location; they will take 3 to 4 years to reach blooming size.

chlorophyll The green pigment in plants that is primarily responsible for absorbing light during the process of photosynthesis.

chloroplast The body within a cell that contains the chlorphyll.

chlorosis A condition in plants evidenced by very pale green to yellow or almost white leaves that have veins that remain green. Chlorosis is caused when chloro-phyll doesn't develop in the leaves, usually because a nutrient the plant needs to make it is unavailable.

chopped leaves Leaves that have been shredded or chopped by a power shredder. Another option for making them is simply mowing them up off the lawn in a bagging lawn mower.

choripetalous Bearing separate petals. Polypetalous.

chromosome The threadlike body in the nucleus of a cell that contains the DNA and is responsible for the transmission of hereditary characteristics. Chromosomes are divided into units called genes.

chrysalis A butterfly pupa.

ciliate Edged with very small hairs, called cilia. This term is commonly used to describe the edge, or margin, of a leaf or leaflet, but also can be other structures. Water hyacinths (*Eichhornia crassipes* spp.) have ciliate roots, for example, and stocks (*Malcolmia* spp.) have ciliate leaves.

ciliate leaf margin

cion *See* SCION

circinate Coiled or rolled down from the top. A fiddlehead, or unfurled fern frond, is circinate.

circumposition *See* AIR LAYERING

circumscissile dehiscence *See* DEHISCENT

cirrhose Ending with a tendril or a tendril-like tip called a cirrus. While most commonly used to describe a leaf tip, this term can be applied to other plant parts such as bracts (modified petal-like leaves) or the petals or sepals of a flower. Several species of everlasting peas (*Lathyrus* spp., including *L. grandiflorus* and *L. sylvestris*) have leaves ending in tendrils.

cirrhose leaf tip

cirrus, *pl.* **cirri** Tendril.

cladophyll, cladode A flattened stem that looks and functions like a leaf, meaning it has chlorophyll and thus can perform photosynthesis, but it rises from a node bearing a bractlike true leaf. *Ruscus* species, including butcher's broom (*R. aculeatus*) bear showy red fruit on top of cladophylls. Asparagus (*Asparagus* spp.) "fronds" actually consist of leaflike stems, or cladophylls; their true leaves are scalelike.

clairvoyée, clair-voyée An opening in a wall or hedge, usually located at the end of a walkway, designed to provide a view of the surrounding countryside. A clairvoyée can be open or covered with a decorative grill.

clambering Climbing weakly. This term is used to describe vines that grow over other plants or objects without benefit of tendrils or supporting stems. *See also* CLIMBER

clasping Amplexicaul. A base of a leaf or bract (a modified petal-like leaf) that partially or completely surrounds the stem. A clasping leaf is sessile, meaning it has no stalk. It can have separate basal lobes or a base that widens and wraps around the stem. The leaves of many plants clasp the stems, including New England asters (*Aster novae-angliae*), lady's slipper orchids (*Cypripredium* spp.), and elecampane (*Inula helenium*).

class Botanically, a class is a major group of plants that share similar characteristics within a division. Classes are further subdivided into orders. *See* DIVISION, ORDER

classification The systematic arrangement of plants, animals, and other organisms into groups or categories according to a specific overall plan or system. Currently, the primary categories in use are DIVISION, CLASS, ORDER, FAMILY, GENUS, and SPECIES. Species are further divided into VARIETIES, CULTIVARS, forms, and subspecies.

clathrate Pierced by holes or windows. Resembling lattice.

clavate Club- or bat-shaped, with a tapered base and a wide tip.

claw The narrow, stemlike base of some petals and sepals.

claw cultivator *See* CULTIVATOR

claw hoe *See* CULTIVATOR

clay, clay soil One of the three major mineral particles in soil (the other two are silt and sand), clay particles—those less than 0.002 mm across—are so fine they can only be seen with the aid of an electron microscope. Soils high in clay tend to shrink and crack apart when they are dry, hardening into concretelike, dense clods. While clay soils absorb moisture slowly, once they are moist they hold water and the nutrients dissolved in it very tightly. For this reason, clay soils get waterlogged easily after a rainy spell, and can remain sticky and hard to dig for a considerable time. *See also* SOIL TEXTURE, SOIL STRUCTURE

cleaning containers Containers used to germinate seeds or root cuttings need to be scrubbed thoroughly before they are reused so they are relatively free of soil and organisms such as fungi that can cause diseases. Some gardeners take the extra step of "sterilizing" containers before recycling by dipping them in a 10-percent bleach solution, made by mixing 9 parts water with 1 part household bleach.

cleaning seed Separating seeds from pods, stems, flesh, and other plant matter collected with them. Collected seeds need to be cleaned and dried before they are stored. Separating the seeds from other plant matter collected with them reduces bulk in storage and having clean seeds that are free of chaff makes sowing easier. Drying increases storage life and prevents seeds from becoming moldy in storage. Spread dry seeds out on newspaper in a warm, windless but well-ventilated spot for a day or two. During this time seed pods often will open and spill their contents. Place the contents into a paper bag and shake them to release all the seeds. If the seed pods are hard, you may need to gently crush them to release their contents. Open pods to release seeds and/or pick up large seeds and place them in envelopes for storage. To separate small seeds, which are mixed with a quantity of chaff and litter, use seed-cleaning

sieves (available at horticultural suppliers). Sift the seeds from one sieve to another to eliminate as much extraneous material as possible. To remove particles that are smaller than the seeds, sift them out with a smaller sieve. To remove material that is the same size as the seeds, try spreading them on a piece of folded paper and gently blowing away the lighter chaff. *See* WINNOW and THRESH for other options for cleaning dry seeds. Seeds borne in berries, such as those of tomatoes and jack-in-the-pulpits (*Arisaema* spp.), will rot if not separated from the flesh and dried. Soak berries in water for 24 hours; open large ones, like tomatoes, before soaking to release the seeds. Then place them in a sieve or other open-bottomed container (with openings smaller than the seeds) and wash away the pulp. Gently mash the fruits to separate them from the seeds. Spread the separated seeds on newspaper for 2 to 3 days to dry before sowing. *See* STORING SEEDS

cleft Divided into segments that are cut about halfway to the middle of the leaf, petal, or other organ. On a cleft leaf, for example, the indentations, called sinuses, extend about one-half the distance to the midrib. Leaves can be cleft either palmately (into fingerlike segments) or pinnately (in a featherlike fashion). *See also* LOBED, PARTED

cleft leaf

cleft graft A grafting technique commonly used to unite scions with the trunk of a small tree or the main scaffold branches of a larger tree. It is a popular graft for top-working (*See* TOP-WORKING) and is best used for branches (the stock) that are from 1 to 4 inches in diameter. Plants with straight-grained wood that splits cleanly are best. To prepare the stock (branch), saw it off cleanly at a right angle to the branch. The stock should be smooth and free of knots for at least 6 inches below the cut. Use a cleft-grafting tool or a heavy knife (a butcher's knife works for this) to split the cut branch vertically down through the center by pounding the tool or knife with a mallet. The split should be about 2 to 3 inches long. Insert the wedge of the cleft-grafting tool, a chisel, or a sturdy screwdriver into the split to hold it open. Prepare two 3- to 4-inch-long scions, each with two to three buds, for each stock branch you split. To prepare them, make smooth, gently tapering, 2-inch-long cuts on the bottom to create a wedge. For best results, make a slightly lopsided wedge, leaving one edge along the length of the cut slightly wider than the other. When inserting the scions, place the widest edge next to the cambium so that when the split branch springs back together it will put the most pressure on the edge where the cambium is lined up. Spread the split in the stock and insert the scions, lining up the cambium layers. (The outside edge of the scions may be slightly inside the outer edge of the stock when they are lined up.) If the sides of the scion don't line up smoothly with the stock along the length of the cut, try shaving the sides of the stock to create a smoother surface and ensure better contact. Remove the tool used to spread the stub on the stock, which should spring closed and hold the scions firmly in place. Wax the entire cut end of the stock, along the length of the split, and down into the split itself. Dab a bit of wax on the cut end of the scions as well. *See* GRAFTING, GRAFTING WAX

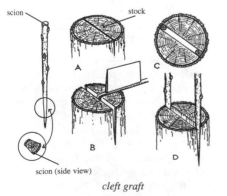

scion
stock

A

C

B

D

scion (side view)

cleft graft

cleistogamous A flower that is fertilized before it opens, and is usually self-pollinated. *See also* CHASMOGAMOUS

climber A plant that climbs or grows upward by one or more of the following adaptations: twining stems (wisteria, *Wisteria* spp.), twining leafstalks (clematis, *Clematis* spp.), adhesive holdfasts (woodbine, *Parthenocissus* spp.), or aerial roots (ivy, *Hedera* spp.). Some climbing plants, such as rambling or climbing roses, do not have any method for holding onto a trellis or other structure: They must be tied up or can hold themselves up by weaving through supports.

cloche A cover, much like a tiny greenhouse, designed to protect a plant or group of plants from cold weather. Historically, cloches were glass bell jars, which were placed over plants at transplant time in spring. These had to be vented manually by tipping them or removing them completely during the daytime because heat builds up under unventilated cloches quite quickly. They also were quite easily broken. Modern-day gardeners can buy paper or plastic cloches, including waxed-paper hotcaps, Wall O'Waters (these plastic devices consist of a circle of cylinders that can be filled with water and that store heat during the day and release it at night), and tunnels covered with plastic or clear fiberglass to cover rows. A simple, homemade cloche consists of a plastic, 1-gallon milk jug with the bottom cut off. Place it over a transplant in spring. Remove the cap to vent the milk-jug cloche on sunny days. Because of the frost protection they provide, cloches allow you to transplant about 2 weeks earlier than you normally would.

clod A mass of soil particles caused by digging or cultivating heavy, or clay, soils when they are wet.

clonal rootstock A rootstock maintained by vegetative propagation for the purpose of grafting. As genetically identical clones, they are used because they offer uniformity and also to preserve certain characteristics such as dwarfing influence on the scion.

clone A group of individual plants that originated from a single parent plant and have been propagated by asexual (vegetative) techniques such as division or cuttings. Because they are propagated asexually, clones are genetically identical; however, site, soil, and other environmental conditions of a particular site or region can affect the appearance and/or performance (phenotype) of members of a clone. In plants that require cross-pollination to set fruit, two individuals of the same clone cannot pollinate one another since they are genetically identical and are technically the same plant.

clouded A variegation pattern in which two colors are blended together.

clove One of the small, new bulbs formed at the side of a parent bulb when the larger parent divides. Mature garlic bulbs are actually tight clusters of smaller bulbs referred to as cloves.

coalescent Growing together to form a single unit.

coat The outer covering of a seed or of another plant part or structure.

cobble A rounded, water-worn stone usually referred to as river rock.

coccineus Scarlet.

cocoon The protective cover for a pupa; the hardened shell formed by insect larvae undergoing complete metamorphosis.

coherent Stuck together. This term is used to indicate similar structures, such as leaves or filaments, that form a unit but are less firmly attached than connate parts.

cohesion *See* ADHESION

cold composting *See* COMPOSTING

cold frame A covered, unheated structure with a sloping, hinged roof that is made of glass or plastic in a wood frame. Cold frames are used for germinating seeds over winter, hardening off seedlings or cuttings, propagation, and overwintering. Cold frames also can be used to grow crops of cold-tolerant vegetables and salad plants.

cole crop A general term for vegetables that belong to the cabbage family (Brassicaceae, formerly Cruciferae), including cabbage, broccoli, cauliflower, and Brussels sprouts.

collar *See* BRANCH COLLAR

collarette A daisylike flower, usually a dahlia, that has two rows of petals, or ray florets: An outer, single row of petals and an inner ruff or collar of smaller petals (actually shorter florets) just inside it. These surround a buttonlike center of disk florets.

collarette flower form

collateral Located or standing side-by-side.

collecting seed *See* SAVING SEED

collenchyma Tissue composed of long, thin cells with stiff walls composed of cellulose that help support stems of young plants. The "strings" on the outer edge of a celery stalk are collenchyma.

colloidal phosphate An organic fertilizer that actually is a clay found between layers of rock phosphate; it washes out when rock phosphate is mined. Colloidal phosphate contains between 16 and 20 percent phosphorus and about 19 percent calcium. About 2 percent of the phosphorus is readily available.

colonnade A row of columns that are regularly spaced.

color break A sport or mutation in which the flower or foliage color varies from the parent plant.

color echo Repeating a color to create harmony and unity in a garden as well as to highlight the features of the plants themselves. Color echoes can be created in many different ways. A streak or blotch of color on the petals of one plant can be picked up and echoed by a clump of flowers or foliage featuring the same hue growing nearby. Combining two different flowers that have the same colors but feature distinct forms, shapes, or sizes will create a color echo. Combining foliage plants that have similar colors but different patterns or textures also creates an echo. The term color echo was coined by horticulturist, photographer, and gardener Pamela Harper (*Color Echoes: Harmonizing Color in the Garden*, Macmillan, 1994).

color temperature Whether colors appear in a garden or in a painting, they convey a feeling of temperature. Blues, purples, and greens tend to look cool, while reds, oranges, and yellows look hot and fiery. *See* COOL COLORS, WARM COLORS

column The structure in the flowers of orchid-family plants (Orchidaceae) that is formed by stamens, which bear the pollen, and the style, the stalk that joins the stigma and the ovary. Flowers of some mallow-family members (Malvaceae) have a column that consists of fused filaments of the stamens.

columnar Column-shaped. This term is commonly used to describe the shape of a fastigiate tree, which is strongly erect with densely clustered, rigidly upright branches and a narrow crown. *See* FASTIGIATE

coma A tuft of hairs on a seed, such as those borne by milkweeds (*Asclepias* spp.). A tuft of leaves or bracts at the top of an inflorescence or a syncarpous fruit (a fruit that actually consists of several individual fruits massed together); the leaves on top of a pineapple (a syncarpous fruit) are an example.

comate, comose Bearing a tuft of hairs on the tip of a seed. The flat seeds of milkweeds (*Asclepia*s spp.), also called silkweeds, are comose, because each is attached to a silky tuft of hair.

comblike *See* PECTINATE

come true Cultivated forms of plants that can be grown from seeds and yield uniform seedlings with predictable characteristics—flower color, foliage form, or fruit character for example—are said to come true from seed. (Both seeds and plants can come true.) Open-pollinated vegetables such as tomato 'Beefsteak', 'Brandywine', and 'Yellow Pear' come true, while seeds collected from hybrids do not. While many popular cultivars of perennials can only be propagated vegetatively, by techniques such as cuttings or division, some do come true from seeds. These include *Campanula carpatica* 'Blue Clips' and 'White Clips', *Coreopsis grandiflora* 'Early Sunrise', *Digitalis purpurea* 'Foxy' and 'Excelsior Hybrids', *Rudbeckia* 'Goldsturum', and *Platycodon grandiflorus* 'Fugi Series' and 'Shell Pink'. *See* OPEN POLLINATED, HYBRID, HOMOZYGOUS

commercial synonym An alternative, but legitimate, name for a cultivar or a shortened form of a cultivar name that is more acceptable commercially. The most common commercial synonyms are names translated from foreign languages in order to create names that are more marketable. For example, German sneezeweed (*Helenium* spp.) cultivars 'Dunkelpracht' and 'Kugelsonne' are commonly sold as 'Dark Beauty' and 'Sunball', respectively. *See* CULTIVAR

common name A name applied to a particular species in the local language of a particular area. Common names vary from region to region and a single species can have many different ones. The same common name also can be used to refer to entirely different plants; thus gardeners are best served by learning and using the accepted botanical name for a particular species. The name lemon lily has been used to refer to both *Hemerocallis lilioasphodelus* and *Lilium parryi*, for example. Dusty miller is used to refer to at least eight different species, including *Artemisia stelleriana*, *Centaurea cineraria*, *Lychnis coronaria*, and *Senecio cineraria*.

community garden An area set aside by a municipality or other public office or institution devoted to provide garden space for individuals and families.

compaction The reduction in soil volume caused by compression of pore spaces due to repeatedly walking or driving on soil or other activities that damage soil structure. Compacted soil lacks pore spaces and thus has reduced amounts of water and air. To correct compaction, loosen the soil by digging or tilling it and adding plenty of organic matter in the process. *See* PORE SPACE, SOIL STRUCTURE

companion planting Interplanting vegetables with herbs, flowers, and other plants to confuse or repel pest insects. Companion planting has a rich tradition in garden lore, often combining folklore with fact, although scientific studies have substantiated the effectiveness of many garden companions. Companion plants can be used to mask or hide a crop from pests: Interplanting marigolds (*Tagetes* spp.) and mints (*Mentha* spp.) with other crops is thought to confuse or repel pests. Trap crops—plants that attract (or seem to attract) pests away from other crops—are another companion planting option. Once the trap crop is completely infested, pull it up and discard or destroy it. Planting crops that attract beneficial insects or feed their young also is a type of companion planting. *See* BENEFICIAL INSECTS

compatibility A grafting term that refers to the ability of two individual plants to form a successful, long-lasting graft union and grow into a complete composite plant.

complanate Flattened or compressed.

complementary colors Technically, complementary colors are pairs of color that

appear white or gray when mixed together in the proper proportions. In terms of the color wheel, complementary colors are pairs of colors consisting of a primary color and the secondary color directly across from it—red and green; blue and orange, yellow and violet. Complementary colors also are contrasting colors.

complete Bearing all of the typical parts. A complete flower has sepals, petals, stamens, and a pistil or pistils.

complete fertilizer A fertilizer that contains nitrogen, phosphorus, and potassium.

complete flower A flower that has pistils (the female reproductive organs), stamens (the male reproductive organs), a calyx (sepals), and a corolla (petals). *See also* INCOMPLETE

complete metamorphosis *See* METAMORPHOSIS

complex A group of closely related or very similar plants that could be placed in a single species but are too well-known separately or too distinct individually to make this treatment acceptable.

complicate Folded together.

composite A member of the aster family, Asteraceae (formerly Compositae). A compound plant part that appears to be a single unit but is actually made up of several distinct parts.

compost Often called "gardener's gold," compost is the end product of the decomposition of various organic materials, produced via the composting process, usually in a pile or specially designed structure. (The word compost also is used in British books to refer to potting soil.) Compost is a valuable soil amendment that can be worked into the soil or used as mulch to improve soil structure while adding organic matter and nutrients. To start a compost pile, select a level, out-of-the-way spot that is convenient to your garden—a spot that is out of sight from your garden and from neighbors' yards is best. Compost in an open pile or contain composting ingredients in a cage, bin, or other structure, which makes your composting area look neater, helps keep the materials evenly moist, promotes faster decomposition by microorganisms, and discourages animals from rooting around in the pile. For fast, efficient composting, plan on a pile or enclosure that is 3 to 4 feet square. Two enclosures are best so you can fill up the second one while materials in the first are breaking down. Compost ingredients include trimmings and clippings from the garden, grass clippings, kitchen scraps, leaves, sod (place it upside down), wood shavings, and manure. Avoid using cat or dog droppings, plant materials that show signs of disease, and weeds that have gone to seed. Also avoid meat, bones, or fat from the kitchen. There are two general composting systems: cold composting and hot composting. Cold composting simply involves tossing ingredients in a pile or other enclosure and then waiting a year or two for them to break down. Turning the pile is optional, although tackling this task once or twice a year will help the materials decompose more evenly. Hot composting takes more time and energy, but produces finished compost in about 3 months. It also is more space efficient and lets you produce more compost per year in the same amount of space. Hot composting gets its name because all the microorganisms busily breaking down materials generate heat within the pile. (*See* MICROORGANISMS) To build a hot compost pile, a proper mix of high-carbon, high-nitrogen materials is especially important. *See* CARBON-NITROGEN RATIO for more on these materials and how they can be combined to speed the composting process. Build the pile in layers or just mix all the materials together. Chopping up or shredding leaves or other large materials speeds up the composting process, but isn't essential. For best results with hot composting, stockpile materials and build the pile all at once: In order to heat up properly, the pile should be 3 to 4 feet square and at least 3 feet tall. As you build the pile, spray it with water periodically unless the materials you are using are very wet. The finished pile should feel lightly moist to the touch—like a damp sponge. The pile will heat up in a day or two. Once it begins to cool off or it feels dry (usually after a few weeks), turn it by dumping the materials into a new pile next to the old one. This aerates the materials; add water if the pile seems dry. Let it heat up again (the heat is produced by microorganisms decomposing materials in the pile) and in another few weeks once temperatures cool off, use the compost aerator or turn the pile again. Finished compost is dark and crumbly, and the original ingredients are mostly unrecognizable. It's fine if there are still some lumps, especially if you plan to work the compost into the soil. *See* SOIL MICROORGANISMS

compost aerator A tool used to dig channels of air within a compost pile and mix materials that consists of a pole with two hinged flaps at the end. To use it, poke the end with the flaps into the pile and pull it out. The flaps open as you pull to mix materials and open up a channel that lets air into the middle.

compost, potting A British term for potting mix. *See* POTTING MIX

compost tea A dilute liquid fertilizer that is easy to make at home. To make compost tea, place a shovelful of finished compost in a burlap sack or old pillowcase, tie the top closed, and let the sack soak in a tub or large bucket of water for several days. When the water looks dark, remove the "tea bag" and toss the contents on the compost pile. Add enough water to dilute the remaining liquid to the color of weak tea. Apply compost tea to the soil around plants with a watering can or sprinkle it onto the leaves. Strain it through a piece of nylon stocking if you want to spray it on the foliage.

compound Divided into or bearing two or more similar parts.

compound corymb *See* CORYMB

compound fruit *See* SYNCARP

compound layering *See* SERPENTINE LAYERING

compound leaf A leaf that is divided into two or more separate leaflets. To distinguish a compound leaf from ordinary simple leaves that are borne on or along a stem, look at the base of the leaves or leaflets. Leaflets on a compound leaf will not have buds at the base of their stems, which are called petiolules. True leaves, both simple and compound, have a bud at the base of the stem, or petiole, although it can be quite small and hard to see. There are two major types of compound leaves, pinnate leaves, which are featherlike in construction, and palmate, which are palm- or hand-shaped, with leaflets radiating out from a common point like fingers. *See also* PINNATELY COMPOUND, PALMATELY COMPOUND

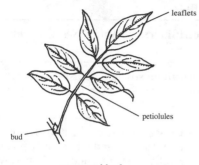

compound leaf

compound umbel This type of flower cluster, or inflorescence, is flat or rounded on top, and bears stalks (pedicels) that arise from the same point on the stem and are more or less equal in length. The individual pedicels are topped by separate, secondary umbels of flowers. Members of the carrot family (Apiaceae, formerly Umbelliferae) commonly bear their flowers in compound umbels, including Queen Anne's lace (*Daucus carota*), dill (*Anethum graveolens*), and fennel (*Foeniculum vulgare*). *See also* UMBEL

compound umbel

compress An herbal remedy that consists of soaking a towel or other cloth in a hot herb tea (below 180°F). After soaking, wring out the towel and place it directly on the skin.

compressed Flattened.

con-, co-, com- Prefixes meaning with or together with.

concolored, concolorous Uniformly colored with a single color.

conditioning flowers A treatment that lengthens the vase life of cut flowers simply by standing them in water for a period of time before arranging them. Most flowers benefit from standing in water for 8 hours or overnight in a deep bucket or other container of cool water that is deep enough to reach the base of the flowerheads. Set flowers that are being conditioned in a cool, dark room. (Darkness encourages stomata in leaves to close, which decreases moisture loss.) High humidity is ideal; try misting flowers and the surrounding area with a spray bottle. When arranging, remove leaves that will be under water. Recut stems as necessary, also under water. *See* VASE LIFE for information on prolonging the life of flower arrangements.

conducting tissue *See* VASCULAR BUNDLE

conduplicate Folded lengthwise, with the upper surfaces together. Cotyledons, or seed leaves, can be folded together in this manner inside the seed. Many grasses have leaves folded in this manner, as do some irises (*Iris* spp.).

cone The common name for the fruit of conifers, including pines (*Pinus* spp.), spruces (*Picea* spp.), ginkgo (*Ginkgo biloba*), and cycads (including *Cycas* spp. and *Zamia* spp.). Botanically speaking, a cone is a dense cluster of cone-scales (sporophylls or spore-bearing leaves) and bracts. Cones can be woody and long lasting, or fleshy and lasting only a short time.

congeneric Belonging to the same genus.

congested Crowded.

congested growth *See* RUBBING BRANCHES, CROSSING BRANCHES

conic Cone-shaped. Evenly tapering from base to tip.

conifer Cone-bearing. Conifers are trees or shrubs, and the most common of them are evergreens such as pines (*Pinus* spp.), cypresses (*Cupressus* spp.), spruces (*Picea* spp.), junipers (*Juniperus* spp.), and yews (*Taxus* spp.). Deciduous conifers include larches (*Larix* spp.), bald cypress (*Taxodium distichum*), and ginkgo (*Ginkgo biloba*).

conifer cuttings Most conifers are propagated by semi-ripe cuttings. *See* SEMI-RIPE CUTTINGS

connate Fused or united. This term is used to indicate similar structures, such as leaves or filaments that are fused to form a unit.

connate-perfoliate Bases of two opposite leaves or bracts (modified petal-like leaves) that are joined and completely surround the stem, making it appear as if the stem is inserted through the middle of the paired leaves. Connate-perfoliate leaves are sessile, meaning they have no stalks, or petioles. Cup plant (*Silphium perfliatum*) and common teasel (*Dipsacus fullonum*) have connate-perfoliate leaves.

connivent Coming together or converging, but not fused.

connivent

conservatory A greenhouse or glass-enclosed room in which plants are grown and displayed.

conspecific Belonging to the same species.

conspicuous Easily visible. This term is commonly used to mean showy or enlarged.

constricted Abruptly narrowed.

container grown A plant that has been grown in a container for at least several months and then sold. Container-grown plants can be transplanted easily with minimal root disturbance.

containerized A plant that has been potted up in a container but has not necessarily been grown there for any length of time.

containers, cleaning *See* CLEANING CONTAINERS

container sowing *See* SEED SOWING, SEED SOWING INDOORS, CONTAINER SOWING OUTDOORS

container sowing outdoors Seed for many perennials and other hardy plants are especially easy to handle when sown in containers and then set outdoors for germinating. Sow as you would for containers to be kept indoors (*See* SEED SOWING INDOORS), then mulch the pots with very small, washed pea gravel (the kind sold in pet stores for aquariums). The gravel prevents moss from forming, which can outcompete seedlings. Set the containers in a protected spot, such as next to a shrub on the north side of the house, for germinating, either in a flat or sunk to within an inch of the rim in the soil. Water as necessary (rainfall often is sufficient). Schedule sowing times depending on the requirements of the seeds. This is an especially easy way to handle plants that need a cold treatment to germinate—sow in winter and set the pots outdoors. For plants that germinate best from fresh seeds, sow in midsummer as soon as seeds are ripe for germination the following spring. Seeds with complex dormancy requirements are easy to handle in containers, too, because they can be left out for several seasons.

contiguous Touching but not fused together.

continuous layering See FRENCH LAYERING

contorted Twisted or bent.

contractile roots Many species of plants with bulbs, corms, or rhizomes produce these thickened roots, which shorten and pull the bulb or other plant part deeper down into the soil.

contrasting colors Technically, contrasting colors do not have any pigments in common: Blue and red, red and yellow, yellow and blue. Gardeners use this term in a broader sense to include any two colors that simply look different—orange and magenta, for example.

convolute Twisted or rolled together lengthwise with margins overlapping. Leaves or petals in a bud can be arranged in this manner.

cool colors Blue, purple, violet, and green—the colors of water—along with pastels such as lilac, lavender, pale pink, pale yellow, and gray are cool colors. As their name suggests, a garden filled with cool-colored flowers and foliage has a cool, restful look. To the eye, cool-colored flowers, along with deep green (especially blue-green) foliage, appear farther away than hot colors such as yellow and orange. This illusion can be used to advantage in a small yard, since a garden filled with cool colors will appear farther away than one filled with hot colors, thus making the yard look larger. See also COLOR TEMPERATURE, HOT COLORS

cool-moist stratification See STRATIFICATION

cool-season grass Grasses that grow best during the spring and fall, and grow slowly or go dormant during the summertime. Cool-season grasses remain green in winter. They grow best at temperatures between 60 and 75°F. Cool-season grasses include red fescue, turf-type tall fescues, bentgrasses, Kentucky bluegrass, and perennial ryegrass.

cool-weather annual Sometimes called hardy or half-hardy annuals depending on how much frost they will tolerate, these are annuals that thrive in cool conditions. In the South, typically they are grown for winter or early spring bloom, but die out or stop blooming when the weather gets warm. In areas with cool summers—the Pacific Northwest, New England, mountainous areas, or more northerly areas, such as Zone 4 and north—they can last the entire summer. Pansies, sweet peas (*Lathyrus odoratus*), larkspur (*Consolida ajacis*), and pot marigolds (*Calendula officinalis*) are popular cool-weather annual flowers. To grow cool-weather annuals in warmer zones, plant or sow in the fall for bloom in winter or the following spring. Or, sow seeds or move transplants in late winter or early spring for bloom from late spring until the plants begin to languish in summer's heat. After that, pull them up and replace them with heat-tolerant plants. In the North, sow cool-weather annuals in late winter or early spring for spring to summer bloom. Some can be sown as soon as the soil can be worked (meaning it is no longer frozen and dry enough to dig without compacting or otherwise damaging it). Others are best sown just before or on the last frost date. Or start them indoors and move plants to the garden as hardened-off transplants on or around the last frost date. Cool-weather annuals also can be planted or sown in midsummer for fall bloom or harvest.

cool-weather crops, cool-season crops Vegetable crops that thrive in cool temperatures, including cabbage, broccoli, cauliflower, lettuce, spinach, kale, collards, beets, carrots, peas, leeks, parsnips, garlic, and shallots. All are grown as cool-weather annuals. See COOL-WEATHER ANNUAL

coping A protective cap on the top of a wall. The coping usually is slightly wider than the wall to keep water from running down the wall's face.

copper An organically acceptable fungicide that still is quite toxic to mammals, including humans, as well as fish. It can be used as a dust or spray to control diseases such as anthracnose, leaf spot, black spot, and downy mildew.

copper naphthenate A wood preservative that is not toxic to plants.

coppice, coppicing A dense thicket of shrubs or small trees. Shoots arising from a stump. For gardeners, this term also refers to a type of pruning, called coppicing. To coppice a shrub or tree, use loppers or a small saw to cut all the stems to the ground in late winter or early spring. Cut back hard—to a height of only 1 to 3 inches above ground—but do not damage the swollen wood at the base of the plant, because this is what gives rise to new stems. Historically, coppicing was used to produce small twigs for firewood and pliable new shoots for basket weaving. Today, it is used to enhance the stem color in shrubs grown for their colorful bark, which is most prevalent on younger stems, as well as to encourage larger or more colorful leaves. Purple-leaved cultivars of smoketree (*Cotinus coggygria*) are coppiced for this latter purpose. Shrubby willows (*Salix* spp.) and dogwoods (*Cornus* spp., including tatarian dogwood, *C. alba*) are coppiced to enhance stem color. Shrubs and trees also are coppiced to produce a steady supply of pea stakes. *See* PEA STAKES

copse A dense thicket of shrubs or small trees. A small, dense woodland.

cordate Heart-shaped. The outline of a cordate leaf is rounded in an egg-shaped fashion, like an ovate leaf, but has a deep indentation, called a sinus, at the base of the leaf where the stem is attached. The widest point of the blade is near the base, where the leaf is attached to the stem. Redbuds (*Cercis* spp.) and katsura tree (*Cercidiphyllum japonicum*) have cordate leaves. The term cordate also is used to describe a leaf base that has an indentation where the stem is attached and two rounded lobes on the sides. The indenta-tion, or sinus, reaches from one-eighth to one-quarter of the distance to the midpoint of the leaf.

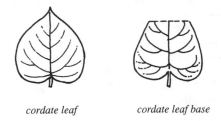

cordate leaf   *cordate leaf base*

cordon A tree, usually a fruit tree, that has a single main trunk with short lateral branches along its length. The trunks are trained at an angle (usually 40 to 45 degrees) to increase fruiting; the sharper the angle the more evenly they bear along their length. Training fruit trees in cordons is extremely space efficient and an excellent option for small gardens because trees can be spaced as close as 2 ½ feet apart yet still are extremely productive. Erect strong support wires on a wall or along a fence to support them. This system is best for spur-bearing cultivars of fruit, especially apples. Cordon is also the term used to refer to the canes of vines. *See* CANE PRUNING

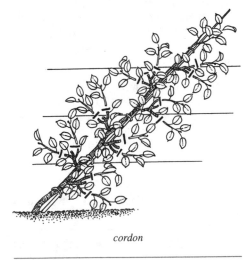

cordon

coriaceous Leathery and tough but with a smooth, pliable texture.

cork An elastic, spongy, waterproof, protective tissue that is the thickest and outermost of the several layers that make up the bark that covers trunks, branches, and roots of woody plants. Cork replaces epidermis on stems of woody plants as they age.

cork cambium *See* CAMBIUM

corky Made up of cork or having corklike characteristics such as texture or porosity.

corm A solid, swollen, underground stem that stores food. Superficially, it resembles a bulb (and is sometimes referred to as such), but a corm is solid inside, not made up of layers of scales. Corms usually are covered with papery, scalelike leaves (a tunic) that protect them from damage and drying out. Many members of the iris family (Iridaceae) grow from corms, the best known of which are gladiolus (*Gladiolus* spp.) Most corms are annual, especially those of plants in the iris family: After the parent plant blooms, the old corm dies and a new one forms at the base of the stem, on top of the old corm, which withers. Even so, cormous plants that are hardy, such as crocuses (*Crocus* spp.), hardy gladiolus (*G. communis*), (*Crocosmia* spp.), and some species of gayfeathers (*Liatris* spp.) can be left in the ground over winter. To overwinter corms of tender plants, dig them after the foliage yellows or before the first fall frost. Cut off the foliage, brush excess soil off the corms, and set them in a warm, dry place for a few hours. Once they've dried a bit, snap or break off the old, withered corm and discard it. You also can save the tiny cormels that form between the two larger ones. Dust the corms with sulfur or another fungicide and store them in a cool (40°F), dry place over winter. (*See* OVERWINTERING) Replant in spring, setting small corms about 3 inches deep and full-size ones about 6 to 8 inches deep.

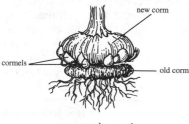

corm and cormels

cormel A small corm that develops around the parent corm. To propagate cormous plants from cormels, separate them from the parent and pot them in flats or pots of growing medium. (Store cormels of nonhardy plants over the winter and pot them up in spring.) Or plant them outdoors in a nursery bed. Set them at a depth of about twice their diameter. Overwinter corms of nonhardy plants indoors as you would full-size ones. They will take several years to reach blooming size.

cormlet A small or secondary cormel.

cormous Bearing corms.

cornell mix Soilless mixes for growing cuttings or plants that consist of peat moss and either vermiculite or perlite. *See* CUTTING MIX, GROWING MIX, SEED-STARTING MIX

corolla The collective term for all the petals of a flower, which are located just inside the calyx (sepals) and make up the inner whorl of the perianth (the corolla plus the calyx). A corolla may consist of separate petals (choripetalous or polypetalous) or petals that are fused together (gamopetalous or sympetalous).

corollaform Resembling a corolla, but not a true corolla.

corolla lobe A rounded segment on a corolla that is sympetalous, meaning the petals have been joined at their edges to form a tubular base.

corolla tube The tube of a corolla that is sympetalous, meaning the petals have been joined at their edges to form a tubular base.

corona A crown or cuplike appendage that often is petal-like, such as the cup or trumpet of a daffodil (*Narcissus* spp.), which is formed from the perianth (collectively the petals and sepals). Milkweed flowers such as those of butterfly weed (*Asclepias tuberosa*) as well as passionflowers (*Passiflora* spp.) also feature coronas.

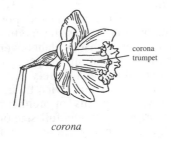

corona
trumpet

corona

corrugated A leaf surface that is heavily textured because of a pattern of wrinkles, puckers, ribs, furrows, and/or folds. Many hostas have corrugated surfaces, including *Hosta sieboldiana* 'Elegans', 'Frances Williams', and *H. tokudama*. Corrugated foliage is more loosely wrinkled than rugose foliage is.

cortex A layer of cells in stems and roots between the epidermis and the vascular tissue, just inside the epidermis.

corymb A type of broad shortened flower cluster, or inflorescence, that is flat or slightly rounded on top. The individual flowers on the outside of the cluster open first, and corymbs are indeterminate, meaning new flowers continue to open and the central stalk continues to elongate after the first flowers open. Corymbs are similar to racemes in structure, but in a corymb the individual flower stalks, or pedicels, are of unequal length, thus creating flat-topped or slightly domed blooms: The flowers of yarrows (*Achillea* spp.), hardy ageratums (*Eupatorium coelestinum*), and sedum 'Autumn Joy' all are corymbs. Bigleaf or florist's hydrangea (*Hydrangea macrophylla*) also bears corymbs. A simple corymb has unbranched flower stalks, while a compound corymb has branched ones.

simple corymb   *compound corymb*

corymbiform Corymblike. A flower cluster (inflorescence) that resembles a corymb but may or may not be a true corymb.

corymbose Corymblike. A flower cluster (inflorescence) that resembles a corymb but may or may not be a true corymb. Also, bearing flowers in corymbs.

costa A single prominent main vein or rib on a leaf or leaflet. This term also is used to refer to the rachis (main stem) of a compound leaf vein on a simple leaf or other plant part.

-costate A suffix referring to a single rib on a leaf, or the main vein on a simple leaf or other plant part. Usually combined with a prefix indicating number. For example, quinquecostate means five-ribbed.

costate Bearing a single, prominent main vein or rib.

cottage garden A style of gardening in which plants are arranged in a colorful, informal, even wild-looking jumble. Cottage gardens feature plants above all, and combine old-fashioned flowers, vegetables, small trees, shrubs, herbs, and any other plants that strike the gardener's fancy. They usually are fairly small, and narrow paths allow passage so plants can be enjoyed up close.

cotyledon Seed leaf. The primary leaf or leaves of a plant embryo, or seed. Germinating seedlings are dependent upon food stored in the cotyledons and endosperm until the first leaves begin to make their own food by the process called photosynthesis. Monocots bear seeds that have one cotyledon; dicots have two cotyledons. The cotyledons of many plants emerge above the soil surface when the seeds germinate (epigeous germination), but in some cases they remain below ground (hypogeous germination). *See* SEED

course In a stone, block, or brick wall, a continuous band or layer of stones, rocks, blocks, or bricks laid side-by-side.

cover crop A crop grown specifically to cover the soil surface. Cover crops protect the soil from erosion by wind or rain, and prevent raindrops from damaging soil structure. Use a cover crop to fill an otherwise unplanted bed, or plant one between rows of vegetables to control weeds and add nitrogen to the soil. Mow or chop it down periodically to keep it from overtaking other plants. A cover crop differs from a green manure crop in that it isn't incorporated into the soil. *See* GREEN MANURE

creeper A plant that grows along the ground and roots as it spreads.

creeping Spreading or growing out, either along the soil surface or just under ground, and producing roots periodically, generally at nodes.

creeping habit

crenate Scalloped, or edged with shallow, rounded teeth. This term is commonly used to describe the edge, or margin, of a leaf or leaflet.

crenate leaf margin

crenulate Finely crenate. Edged with very small rounded teeth, or scallops. This term is commonly used to describe the edge, or margin, of a leaf or leaflet.

crenulate leaf margin

creosote An oily wood preservative that can be toxic to plants. Copper naphthenate is an alternative that is not toxic.

crescent A shape used in flower arranging in which the flowers, leaves, and other plant materials are positioned in a gently curved crescent that rests on top of the container.

crescent arrangement

crescent-shaped *See* LUNATE

crested Bearing a raised, often irregular or toothed ridge, or crest, along the top or back of a surface such as a seed or a petal. Leaves, leaflets, fronds, pinnae, or other leaf segments that end in toothed or forked segments are crested.

crispate, crisped Crinkled, curled, wavy, or crisped in an irregular manner. This term is commonly used to describe the edge, or margin, of a leaf or leaflet. Curley-leaved parsley (*Petroselinum cripsum*) has crispate leaves.

crispate leaf

cristata, cristatus *See* CRESTED

cristate Crested. Bearing a crest or tuft at the top or tip of a plant part. *See* CRESTED

crocus pot A small, decorative container that has four to ten openings in its sides and an opening in its top and is used to force crocuses or other small bulbs.

crop rotation Altering the location where a particular crop is grown from season to season. This technique is most often used in the vegetable garden to keep the soil fertile, make efficient use of soil nutrients, and combat crop-specific soil-borne diseases. One basic principle of crop rotation is not to plant a crop in the same spot it grew the year before. Another is to avoid planting crops that have similar pest and disease problems in the same spot. Since pests and diseases generally attack members of specific plant families, avoid planting crops that belong to the same family in the same spot year after year. Finally, don't plant crops that have similar nutritional needs in the same spot year after year. For example, corn and tomatoes are heavy feeders, while legume crops such as peas and beans actually feed the soil. Many gardeners use the following system to rotate their crops. They group all crops into the following four categories and follow them in the garden: Fruit crops (tomatoes, peppers, eggplants, broccoli, squash, and corn) followed by leaf crops (lettuce, spinach, cabbage, and kale), followed by root crops (carrots, onions, and potatoes), followed by legumes (peas and beans). For best results, work rotation schedules out on paper and keep records of what grew where.

crosier The coiled, emerging leaf of a fern frond, also called a fiddlehead. (The term crosier comes from the name for the crooked or coiled staff carried by an abbot or bishop.) The crosiers of some ferns are tasty eaten hot or cold, and have a flavor something like asparagus. Ostrich fern (*Matteuccia struthiopteris*) crosiers are commonly used for this purpose. Cut them when they are still tightly coiled, gently wash off the scales, and steam lightly. Serve immediately or chill and add to salads. New crosiers and fronds will replace the ones that have been harvested, but it is best to pick only

a few crosiers from each plant to avoid weakening them.

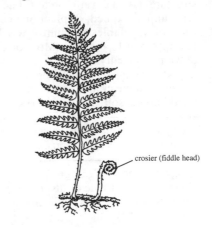

crosier (fiddle head)

cross, crossing A hybrid, or the process of hybridization. *See* CROSS-POLLINATION

cross-compatible, cross-fruitful Two cultivars that can pollinate each other's flowers.

cross-fertilization Fertilization (the union of a male and female gamete) that results from cross pollination.

cross-incompatible, cross-unfruitful Two cultivars that cannot pollinate each other's flowers.

crossing branches Branches that grow from one side of the plant through the center and out the other side. These usually are pruned out because they create unattractive, congested growth, block light and air to the center of the plant, and foster conditions that promote diseases.

cross-pollination The transfer of pollen from the anther(s) of a flower on one plant to the stigma of a flower on another plant. Plants that are naturally cross-pollinated tend to be more genetically diverse (heterozygous) than self-pollinated ones, and cultivars of cross-pollinated plants are more difficult to maintain in uniform populations than self-pollinated ones. In plants that require cross-pollination to set fruit, two individuals of the same clone cannot pollinate one another since they are genetically identical and are technically the same plant. Apples commonly have this requirement: Many apple clones require pollination by a different clone or by a crabapple (*Malus* spp.). *See* SELF-POLLINATION

crotch, crotch angle The angle formed where a branch meets the trunk of a tree. Also called the branch angle. Branches that join the trunk at a wide angle—45 degrees or more—are strongest. Narrow branch angles or narrow crotches commonly cause problems as trees age, because bark becomes trapped in the crotch. The crotch weakens and sometimes splits as a result, or the excess bark provides an entry point for disease or insects. Natural branch angles vary. Many species naturally produce branches that grow at about 45-degree angles, including sweetgum (*Liquidambar styraciflua*), tulip tree (*Liriodendron tulipifera*), and scarlet oaks (*Quercus coccinea*). Others, including dogwoods (*Cornus* spp.), white oak (*Q. alba*), and many pines and firs, bear branches that stick out at 90-degree angles from the trunk, while pin oaks (*Q. palustris*), shingle oak (*Q. imbricaria*), and some spruces (*Picea* spp.) have descending branches. A few species are especially prone to producing narrow branch angles, including elms (*Ulmus* spp.), 'Bradford' pears (*Pyrus callery-ana* 'Bradford'), American yellowwood (*Cladrastus lutea*), Japanese zelkova (*Zelkova serrata*), and poplars (*Populus* spp.). On a young tree with slender branches it's easy to widen a narrow crotch with a simple brace. Cut a light stick or piece of wooden lath to size, notch each end, and insert the brace between the branch and the trunk or the collar of a higher branch. Don't force the branch: Pushing it too far all at once can split the crotch. Leave the brace in place only during the growing season to minimize abrasions to the bark. Another option for widening a narrow crotch angle is pulling the branch down with rope attached to stakes placed around the base of the plant. In this case, to minimize rubbing, run the rope through a short section of hose and place the hose across the branch.

crown This much-used term has several meanings. A crown is the base of a plant, such as a herbaceous perennial, shrub, or tree at ground level where the stems and the roots meet. The crown, which is often woody, is the area that produces new stems and contains resting buds that overwinter—it is something like a very compressed stem. Crown also means corona, the term for the cup or trumpet of a daffodil flower. Although crown refers to the point on a tree or shrub at ground level where roots and trunk meet, crown also is a general term that refers to the branches and foliage of a tree or shrub, and in this sense is commonly linked to an adjective describing its shape—a spreading or weeping crown, for example. Crown can be used to refer to the top of any treelike plant that has a single stem, such as a palm. Finally, crown refers to a piece of rhizome that has roots and a strong bud attached and is used for propagation. Lily-of-the-valley (*Convallaria majalis*) is commonly propagated by crowns, also sometimes called pips. Ferns with ascending rhizomes (*See* RHIZOME) also form crowns.

crown division New plants that form from buds on a crown. Once they have attained sufficient size and root growth, they can be severed from the parent plant and potted up or planted out for purposes of propagation. This term also is used for the simple task of digging up a plant and severing the crown into several pieces with a knife or sharp spade. *See* DIVISION

crown graft A graft union made at the crown of an established rootstock, where the roots and stem join. In this case, the name comes from the location on the plant where the graft is made. The particular grafting technique used is determined by the size of stock and scion. *See* GRAFTING

crown lifting *See* LIMBING UP

crown reduction A pruning technique that can be performed by an arborist to reduce the size and height of a tree or the size of its crown. An expert arborist can accomplish this without destroying the tree's natural shape by combining drop-crotch pruning, which involves cutting branches back to where they meet smaller branches, shortening the longest branches, and selectively thinning to remove excess growth and open up the center of the tree to light and air. *See* CROWN THINNING

crown thinning A pruning technique best performed by an arborist in which branches in the crown are thinned out to reduce congested growth and let light and air into the center of the plant.

cruciate This term refers to a particular pattern of frond division in which each leaflet (pinna) is divided into two forks that stand at right angles to one another. Each fork is generally subsequently divided. Ferns selected for this characteristic, such as lady fern (*Athyrium filix-femina* 'Victoriae') have an overall crisscross pattern.

cruciferous Belonging to the cabbage family (Brassicaceae, formerly Cruciferae).

cruciform Cross-shaped. Plants in the mustard family (Brassicaceae, formerly Cruciferae) such as cabbage and broccoli bear cruciform flowers.

crumb An aggregate of soil particles, also called a ped. The term crumb primarily is used to refer to rounded, porus aggregates found in topsoils that are rich in organic matter.

crustose Hard and brittle.

cryptogram A plant that reproduces sexually by producing spores rather than seeds, as angiosperms and gymnosperms do. Ferns and fern allies (club mosses, spikemosses, quillworts, and horsetails) together with mosses, liverworts, algae, and fungi are all cryptograms. Ferns and fern allies are sometimes called vascular cryptograms because they have vascular tissue that conducts water, nutrients, sugars, or other substances. *See also* ANGIOSPERM, GYMNOSPERM, FERN ALLIES

cucullate Having a hood or shaped like a hood.

culinary herbs Herbs traditionally used in cooking, including basil, thyme, rosemary, oregano, garlic, chervil, tarragon, cilantro, coriander, saffron, dill, mint, marjoram, chives. Culinary herbs can be used fresh, but cooks also use them to make flavored oils and vinegars. *See* HERBAL OILS AND OINTMENTS, HERB VINEGARS, BOUQUETS GARNIS, and HERB PRESERVATION for more information.

culm The stem of a grass plant. Culms are generally hollow except at the nodes, which typically are swollen. Bamboo canes are an easily recognized example of a culm, although even low, tuft- or clump-forming grasses have them. Culms are readily apparent even on low-growing grasses when the flowers or seedheads appear.

cultigen A plant or a group of plants that is only found in cultivation and is presumed to be of cultivated origin.

cultivar A cultivated variety. A particular, distinct form of a plant that originated and is maintained in cultivation by either sexual or asexual propagation. Unlike botanical names, which are latinized words and are set in italics (or underlined) in text, cultivar names are normally in a modern language such as English and are set in roman type. They are either set in single quotes or preceded by the abbreviation "cv." Thus, *Hosta sieboldiana* 'Frances Williams' and *Hosta sieboldiana* cv. Frances Williams are both correct. (When single quotes are used, any punctuation goes outside the single quotes: *Digitalis* 'Foxy'.) In many cases the specific epithet of the botanical name is dropped altogether—*Hosta* 'Frances Williams'. This is especially useful for cultivars that are the result of complex crosses, making parentage hard to trace. The rules dictated in the *International Code of Nomenclature for Cultivated Plants* prevent the same name being applied to cultivars of two different species in a genus. Thus, there is only one cultivar named 'Autumn Joy' in the entire genus *Sedum*. In addition, the *International Code* no longer recognizes latinized words as cultivar names, although some genera such as *Hosta* still retain them— *Hosta fortunei* 'Aurea Marginata', for example. Cultivar names also are called fancy names. *See* VARIETY

cultivating fork *See* BROADFORK

cultivation A general term for the art and science of planting, caring for, and harvesting plants. The phrase "in cultivation" means that a plant is grown in gardens. Also refers to the act of loosening the soil to control weeds, preparing a seedbed, or improving the growing conditions for plants.

cultivator A tool that usually has three or four tines that either have sharpened, diamond-shaped, or straight points. The tines are curved or bent so they can be pulled through the soil to loosen it and pull up small weeds. Sometimes called claw cultivators, these tools also are useful for working organic matter into the soil.

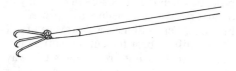

cultivator

cultrate, cultriform Shaped like the blade of a knife.

cultural controls *See* ORGANIC PEST MANAGEMENT

cultural problem A disease-like condition caused by the culture of the plant rather than by a fungus *or* other disease-causing organism.

cuneate Wedge-shaped or narrowly triangular. A base that tapers to a point. At the base of a cuneate leaf the edges, or margins, form an angle between 45 and 90 degrees. While most commonly used to describe a leaf base, this term can be applied to other plant parts such as bracts or the petals of a flower.

cuneate leaf base

cup The round, projecting corona (called a cup or trumpet) of a daffodil *(Narcissus* spp.). The term cup is used when the corona is shorter than the individual petals that surround its base, which are more properly termed perianth segments. When the corona is as long as or longer than the perianth segments, it is called a trumpet.

cupped, cup-shaped A single, semidouble, or double flower that has a rounded, hemispherical shape formed by petals that curve out and up from a relatively flat, open center. Open or broadly bell-shaped. *See also* CAMPANULATE

cupped flower

cupule A dry, cuplike structure that is borne at the base of some fruits. Cupules can be made up of fused, scalelike bracts—the caps of acorns, for example. Some palms bear cupules formed from dry, enlarged flower parts, specifically the calyx (sepals) and corolla (petals).

cushion This term is used to describe a plant that is rounded to slightly flattened, very low-growing, and densely branched, with stems packed together. Many alpine plants, popular in rock gardens, form cushions.

cusp A short, stiff, sharp, abrupt point.

cuspidate Abruptly ending in a short, sharp, inflexible or leathery point called a cusp. While most commonly used to describe a leaf tip, this term can be applied to other plant parts such as bracts (modified petal-like leaves) or the petals or sepals of a flower.

cuspidate leaf tip

cut A general term used to describe leaf margins that have deep or irregular divisions along the edges of the leaf margin. This term is primarily used to describe leaves with divisions that reach from halfway to the midrib of the leaf all the way to the midrib. Cut differs from cleft in that in a cut leaf the divisions between lobes are very narrow.

cutback shrub A shrub that is cut to the ground or nearly to the ground each year, generally in spring. This hard annual pruning encourages the plant to produce new growth that generally flowers better or yields a better foliage display. Plants with ornamental foliage, such as purple-leaved smoke trees (*Cotinus coggygria* 'Royal Purple' or 'Velvet Cloak') are sometimes grown as cutback shrubs because this technique maximizes the foliage display even though it eliminates flowers. In order for cutback shrubs to flower each year, despite their annual spring haircut, they need to be species that bloom on new wood (growth produced in the current year). For example orange-eye butterfly bush (*Buddleia davidii*) is a shrub that blooms on new wood and can reach 10 to 15 feet in warm climates. Many Southern gardeners cut the plants back hard—nearly to the ground—

in spring to encourage new, heavy-blooming wood. Its shoots are killed to the ground over winter from about Zone 6 north (the roots are hardy throughout Zone 5), so Northern gardeners just have to trim out the deadwood in spring. (Shrubs that are killed to the ground each winter sometimes are called dieback shrubs.) Fountain butterfly bush (*B. alternifolia*) blooms on old wood (growth produced the previous summer), and if cut to the ground in spring it won't bloom at all that year because the flower buds have been cut off. It still reaches shrub-size proportions, since its shoots easily reach 5 to 8 feet in a season. Bluebeard (*Caryopteris × clandonensis*) is actually a small shrub, but the shoots are routinely killed to the ground in winter in Zones 4 to 6, and occasionally in Zone 7.

cut flowers, cutting flowers Bringing flowers indoors to use in arrangements is a simple operation, but a few basic techniques will lengthen the vase life of cut flowers. For best results, cut flowers either in the very late afternoon or early evening, after the sun has gone down, or cut them early in the morning, after the dew has dried but well before the sun is very high in the sky. If at all possible, carry a container of water into the garden, and plunge stems into it as you cut them. Most flowers are best cut when the buds are almost ready to open or have just begun to open. Full-blown flowers will have a short vase life. A sharp knife is best for cutting soft stems, because it does not crush stems the way that scissors do; use pruning shears for woody stems. Make cuts just above a node: Cutting above a node is best for the plant, since it encourages branching, but since cutting below a node is usually best for cut flowers, when you recut the stems (see below) recut below a node. Cut hollow stems through a leaf node rather than through the hollow part. Make slanting, rather than straight, cuts, because they heal better on the plant. Cutting flowers is a type of pruning operation. (*See* HEADING CUT) In addition, stems with slanting cuts do not rest flat against the bottom of the vase, thus allowing them to take up water more easily. Once you've brought the flowers indoors, recut the stems under water (this eliminates air bubbles in the stems) and leave them in the water in which they've been recut, because every time you take the stems out of water, new air bubbles form. Slit or pound the stems of woody plants to increase water uptake. For longest vase life, condition cut flowers for 8 hours or overnight. *See* CONDITIONING FLOWERS

cuticle A waxy layer on the surface of the epidermis that helps hold moisture in the plant. This layer, composed of cutin, fatty acids, and cellulose, is found on the outside surfaces of aboveground plant parts such as leaves and herbaceous stems, fruits, or other plant parts. In addition to reducing water loss, it also protects surfaces from invasion by fungi or other organisms.

cutting A portion of a stem, leaf, root, bud, or modified stem (such as a rhizome) that is separated from a parent plant, induced to form adventitious roots, and eventually grown into new plant. Taking cuttings and rooting them is a form of vegetative, or asexual, propagation that duplicates the parent plant exactly. Cuttings provide a relatively fast, easy way to propagate a wide range of plants that produce leafy, branching stems, including tender perennials, hardy perennials, vines, and shrubs. Most plants that grow from basal rosettes, including ornamental grasses, daylilies (*Hemerocallis* spp.), and hostas (*Hosta* spp.), cannot be rooted from cuttings. They need to be propagated by division, although small offsets from these plants are sometimes treated as cuttings if they don't have sufficient roots to grow on their own. The adventitious roots that form on most cuttings are produced by the cambium. On stem cuttings, they arise directly from the stem itself or the wound-healing callous tissue that develops at the base of the cuttings. For information on different types of cuttings, *see* SOFTWOOD CUTTING, SEMI-RIPE CUTTING, HARDWOOD CUTTING, LEAF-PETIOLE CUTTING, BASAL CUTTING, HERBACEOUS CUTTING

cutting back Shortening the branches of trees or shrubs. *See* HEADING BACK Also a general term for shearing or shortening herbaceous plants that have grown too tall.

cutting exchange *See* PLANT EXCHANGE

cutting mix A medium blended specifically for rooting cuttings. Seed-starting mixes generally hold too much moisture for cuttings, causing them to rot before roots form. A mix of equal parts perlite and vermiculite makes a good cutting mix. Premoisten the medium and use it to fill clean containers. Straight sand is also a good medium to use for some types of cuttings, especially evergreens. Use washed sharp builder's sand or plaster sand (not sandbox sand). For a medium that holds a bit more moisture than straight sand, add peat moss, making up to a 50-50 mix depending on the plant being rooted. *See* CUTTING, PREMOISTEN, CLEANING CONTAINERS, GROWING MIX, SEED-STARTING MIX

cutworm These caterpillars, the larvae of brown or grayish moths, are plump and smooth and brown, gray, or green. Cutworms curl around the base of young stems and chew through them near the soil line. Use cutworm collars or apply parasitic nematodes to the soil around young plants.

cutworm collar A barrier that prevents night-feeding caterpillars from severing young transplants right at the soil line and killing them. Cardboard toilet paper or paper towel tubes make fine cutworm collars: Cut them into 3-inch sections and press them an inch or so into the soil surface around small seedlings at transplant time.

cyanthiform Cup-shaped.

cyanthium This type of flower cluster, or inflorescence, is characteristic of spurges (*Euphorbia* spp.). It consists of a single female (pistillate) flower surrounded by several male (stamminate) flowers that together resemble a single flower. Cyanthia usually are borne in clusters that resemble larger inflorescences.

cyclic, -cyclic Arranged in whorls or circles. When used as a suffix, it is usually combined with a prefix that indicates a number. Pentacyclic indicates five whorls, for example.

cylindric, cylindrical Circular, or nearly circular, in cross section.

cymbiform Boat-shaped.

cyme A type of flower cluster, or inflorescence, that is generally flat-topped or rounded. The terminal flower (the one at the tip of the stem) opens first, and flowers that are out from the center of the cluster or down the main stem follow. These secondary flowers are carried on branches that arise from beneath the terminal flower, although their stems may be long enough to carry them above it. Cymes are determinate, meaning the main stem stops elongating after the first flower opens. (A panicle, which a cyme resembles, opens from the bottom to the top and is indeterminate.) Lungworts (*Pulmonaria* spp.), borage (*Borago* spp.), and many other members of the borage family (Boraginaceae) bear their flowers in cymes, as do several species of viburnum. Japanese snowball bush (*Viburnum plicatum*) bears round cymes, while its popular form doublefile viburnum (*V. plicatum* f. *tomentosum*) produces flat-topped ones. There are two main types of cymes. Dichasial cymes produce a terminal flower between pairs of two or more side stems, or branches. Monochasial cymes are branched like dichasial cymes, but one branch in each pair is missing. *See* DICHASIAL CYME, MONOCHASIAL CYME

cyme

cymose Bearing cymes, resembling cymes, or arranged in cymes.

cyperaceous Relating to sedges (*Carex* spp.) or the sedge family, Cyperaceae.

dactyloid, dactylose Fingerlike.

damping off A fungal disease that attacks seedlings, rotting the stems at the soil line and causing them to fall over. Damping off also can rot seeds before they even sprout. Prevention is the best approach to damping off: Sow seeds in a disease-free medium (*See* SEED-STARTING MIX) and sow thinly to avoid overcrowding. Sprinkle a light layer of milled sphagnum moss over sown seeds. Provide seedlings with good air circulation. Water pots from below (by setting them in trays of water until the mix is moist) to avoid wetting the surface.

dandelion fork *See* ASPARAGUS FORK

dappled shade A site in dappled shade generally has patches of sun and shade, usually cast by a tree with a high, tall, somewhat open canopy.

day neutral A plant that does not respond to photoperiod. *See* PHOTOPERIODISM

days-to-maturity The average number of days a plant requires either from sowing or from transplanting to harvest. Days-to-maturity is most often listed in seed catalogs and on seed packets of annuals, vegetables, and herbs, and is a valuable number to know when selecting crops to grow and scheduling seed-sowing dates. (Keep in mind the number of days a particular plant requires will vary from region to region and that this number is an average, not an exact, number.) For crops normally direct-sown outdoors, such as lettuce, spinach, and kale, days-to-maturity is counted from the sowing date. For crops that are normally started indoors such as tomatoes, eggplant, and peppers, it is counted from the transplanting date. To schedule these crops, count back from the transplanting date to determine when to start seeds. Use days-to-maturity

combined with the length of your growing season to select which cultivars to grow as well as to spread out the harvest. In northern areas, fast-maturing crops with fewer days-to-maturity may be the only option for obtaining a crop before frost in fall. For example 'Quickie' sweet corn matures in only 65 days, while 'Silver Queen' takes 91 days. To use days-to-maturity to spread out the harvest, plant a fast-maturing selection for an extra-early harvest along with one or more plants that take a longer season to mature—combine 'Oregon Spring' tomato at 60 days with 'Big Beef', which begins bearing at 70 days, for example. Southern gardeners commonly use days-to-maturity to schedule crops requiring cool temperatures (lettuce and spinach, for example). In this case, they plan time so these crops can mature before hot weather arrives by counting back the number of days-to-maturity from the time hot weather normally arrives (adding plenty of time for harvest) to determine optimum sowing dates. *See* GROWING SEASON

DE *See* DIATOMACEOUS EARTH

deadheading Removing spent blooms before they form seeds. This tends to lengthen bloom season because it encourages many plants to produce more flower buds. Deadheading also prevents self-sowing, which may or may not be a problem depending on what you are growing. To deadhead, pinch flowers between thumb and forefinger or snip them off with pruning shears. Don't tug on the plant, because this can damage the roots and check growth. Plants with an abundance of small flowers can be deadheaded by shearing, in which case hedge clippers or garden shears are the tool of choice. To shear a plant, cut it back by one-third to one-half. To deadhead flowers that bloom in clusters on one main stem, you can remove the first few individual blooms as needed, then cut off the rest of the whole cluster once the remaining flowers are finished blooming.

deadheading

dealbate Covered with white powder. Powdered or whitened.

decay cycle *See* SOIL

deciduous Falling off after a leaf or other plant part is no longer functional. Not evergreen or persistent. Deciduous is most often used to designate trees or shrubs that lose their leaves in fall, but the term also applies to petals or other plant parts that fall off once they have served their function. Whether a plant is deciduous or not isn't necessarily a consistent characteristic however, because some species are deciduous in colder regions and evergreen in warmer ones. Sweet bay magnolia (*Magnolia virginiana*) is a good example: It is deciduous in the North, evergreen in the South, and can be semi-evergreen in areas in between.

declinate, declined Bent or curved down.

decoction An herbal preparation made by simmering herbs—usually bark, roots, stems, large leaves, or other tough plant parts—in water for 15 to 30 minutes or more and then straining the liquid to separate out the plant parts. Use 1 ounce of dried herb to a pint of water.

decompound A compound leaf that has main leaflets that are further divided into smaller leaflets. Two types of decompound leaves are bipinnate, which are twice cut,

and tripinnate, which are cut three times (thrice cut). *See also* BIPINNATE, TRIPINNATE

decumbent Prostrate, lying, or reclining, but with ascending growing tips. This term is commonly used to describe a plant's habit or to describe the position of branches. Recumbent plants lack the ascending growing tips.

decumbent

decurrent A base of a leaf, leaflet, or other plant part that extends down from the point where it is attached to the stem. The base is adnate, meaning it is fused or nearly fused to the petiole (if there is one) and the stem. Bull thistle (*Cirsium vulgare*) has decurrent leaf bases that also are spiny.

decurrent leaf base

decurved Curved downward.

decussate Four-ranked. Pairs of leaves that are borne along a stem, with each pair at right angles to the one above and below it.

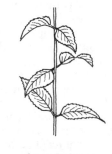

decussate leaves

deep bed method *See* INTENSIVE GARDENING

deep digging *See* DOUBLE DIGGING

deep shade *See* PARTIAL SHADE

deficiency, nutrient *See* NUTRIENT DEFI-
CIENCY

deflexed Bent abruptly downward and
outward, generally at an angle of about 50
degrees. *See also* REFLEXED

defoliate, defoliated With leaves shed.

dehiscent Splitting open at maturity to
release seeds, pollen, or spores. This term
is applied to types of fruit such as capsules, follicles, and legumes that split
open along definite lines to release the
seeds they enclose. It also can be applied
to anthers, which release pollen. Dehiscent fruits can open in several different
ways to release their contents. Follicles
and legumes open along lines on the pod,
follicles along a single line, and legumes
along both sides. Siliques and silicles
also split along their length to release two
walls, or valves, and reveal a papery partition that remains on the plant. There are
four main ways that capsules, as well as
anthers, dehisce: through pores or small
holes (poricidal dehiscence); directly into
seed or pollen-bearing cavities, or locules
(loculicidal dehiscence); in spaces between the cavities, called septa (septicidal
dehiscence); and around their circumfer-
ence (circumscissile dehiscence). Indehiscent fruits are the opposite of dehiscent ones: They do not split open to
release their seeds at maturity.

dehorning *See* TOPPING

deliquescent Disappearing, melting away,
or dissolving, such as the petals of some
plants after they have served their function.
Also, a stem or trunk that branches
frequently and is no longer clearly recognizable.

deltoid Triangular. Roughly the shape of
an equilateral triangle (or the Greek letter

delta), with a flat or nearly flat base,
where the leaf is attached to the stem,
two rounded corners, and a narrower tip
that is pointed or somewhat pointed. A
deltoid leaf is attached at the broad, or
flat, end.

deltoid leaf

dendriform Treelike in shape.

dendritic A treelike branching pattern.
Most often used to describe hairs that have
a forked branching pattern.

dendrology The division of botany devoted to the study of trees and their natural
history.

dentate Toothed. Edged with sharp teeth
that point out, rather than toward the
tip of the leaf. This term is commonly
used to describe the edge, or margin,
of a leaf or leaflet. On a bidentate leaf,
the individual teeth are further divided
into smaller teeth. The teeth on a dentate leaf are shallower and more regular
than the teeth on an incised leaf. *See also*
SERRATE

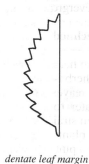

dentate leaf margin

denticulate Finely toothed. Edged with
small, sharp teeth that point out, rather than
toward the tip of the leaf. This term is com-

monly used to describe the edge, or margin, of a leaf or leaflet.

denticulate leaf margin

depauperate Stunted, starved looking, or only partially developed, usually because a plant has adapted to adverse growing conditions.

dependent Hanging down because of the weight of flowers or fruit. *See* PENDULOUS, PENDENT

deplanate Flattened or expanded.

depressed Flattened end-to-end from the top. Sunken.

descending Bent, curved, or pointing down, usually at a gentle angle.

dessicants Substances used to dry or preserve flowers while retaining their three-dimensional condition. Dessicants are especially useful for large flowers that do not preserve well by other methods. (They also can be used to preserve mushrooms.) Flowers dried using dessicants are carefully buried in it—the dessicant needs to be carefully sifted over and around each petal. A large, plastic sweater box is ideal for dessicant drying. To dry flowers using this method, collect them in the morning, after the dew has dried. Spread a layer of dessicant in the bottom of the container you plan to use and arrange a layer of flowers on top of it so they are not touching. Experiment with the position of individual flowers: Some retain the best shape when dried on their sides, while others will crush in this position and are best dried facing up. Carefully sift more dessicant over the top of the flowers, covering them completely, and then add a second layer of flowers and dessicant. Continue adding layers until the container is full. Most plant material dries within a week or less. A variety of substances can be used as dessicants, including: dry, clean beach sand; a mix of 1 part borax to 2 parts beach sand; a mix of 1 part borax to 1 part yellow cornmeal; and uniodized salt. Silica gel is a commercially available dessicating agent (available at craft stores) that is fast and effective, but be sure to use a face mask when using it, as it is harmful if inhaled. You will need to experiment with drying times for various flowers and different agents. Keep records to improve your results. Remove plants from the dessicating agent after they are completely dry. They will be brittle, so handle with care. Dessicating agents are reusable: Sift out excess plant matter and dry them in a warm oven. Store in a tightly sealed container. *See* DRYING FLOWERS

detassel Removing the pollen-producing tassels from a corn plant before the pollen has been shed. This technique is used to produce hybrid seeds. *See* HYBRID

determinate A flower cluster (inflorescence) with a terminal or central flower that opens first, and after the terminal flower opens, the main stem (axis) of the inflorescence stops elongating. Cymes are a type of determinate inflorescence. Plants can be determinate as well. Determinate tomatoes, for example, stop growing once flowers form at the tips of the stems. As a result, they bear most of their fruit all at once, making them good choices if you want a big single harvest for canning. Determinate tomatoes also have short main stems and form fairly compact bushes, unlike indeterminate types, which can reach 5 feet or more. While determinate tomatoes can be staked, because of their shorter stems—from 1 to 3 feet long—they are good choices for growing in cages. Don't remove the suckers that arise in the leaf axils, as this cuts down on fruit production. (One-quarter of tomato cultivars are determinate; three-quarters are indeterminate.) *See* INDETERMINATE

di- A prefix meaning two or twice, for example didymous, meaning borne in pairs.

diamond-shaped *See* RHOMBOIDAL

diatomaceous earth A mineral product that consists of the fossilized shells of diatoms. It is a powderlike substance that contains razor-sharp, microscopic edges that pierce the bodies of insects, causing them to dehydrate. Also called DE, it is dusted on plants, preferably after a light rain. It also can be used as a barrier to keep slugs and snails away from plants.

dibble A small hand tool designed to poke holes in soil for seeds, seedlings, or other small plants.

dibble

dichasial cyme These are cymes that produce a terminal flower between pairs of two or more side stems, or branches. Dichasial cymes exhibit false dichomoty, because the branches are only roughly equal in length; truly dichotomous plants produce pairs of branches that are of equal length. In a simple dichasial cyme (also called a simple cyme), each branch produces a single flower. In a compound dichasial cyme (also called a compound cyme) the side stems also branch at least once. Like the main stem, the side branches are determinate, meaning they stop elongating after the terminal flower opens. Bouncing bet (*Saponaria officinalis*) bears its flowers in condensed dishasial cymes. *See also* CYME, MONOCHASIAL CYME

diachasial cyme

dichasium *See* DICHASIAL CYME

dichogamous A flower that cannot pollinate itself because its pistils and stamens open at different times.

dichotomous Forked or branched into two equal parts. This term can be used to describe branching habits as well as leaf vein patterns.

dichotomous key *See* KEY

dicot A collective term for plants that bear seeds with two cotyledons, have leaves with netlike veining patterns, and bear flowers with flower parts such as petals and sepals in fours and fives, or multiples thereof. Dicots include a vast array of garden plants, including members of the rose family (Rosaceae), buttercup family (Ranunculaceae), and the spurge family (Euphorbiaceae). The stem construction of dicots and monocots also differs. *See* MONOCOT

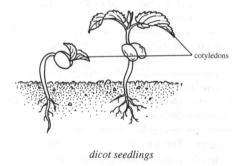

cotyledons

dicot seedlings

dicotyledonous Bearing two cotyledons, or seed leaves. *See* DICOT

didymous Borne in pairs.

dieback A condition in shrubs, trees, and other woody plants in which the ends of the stems or branches die, often progressively back toward the base. Dieback is caused by various problems, including insects, drought, and winter injury. Remove dead wood promptly, cutting back an inch or two into healthy wood.

dieback shrub *See* CUTBACK SHRUB

difficult to transplant This term is used to describe plants that are typically set back or killed outright when grown indoors in containers and transplanted to the garden. Many have taproots that are easily damaged during the transplanting process. (Many perennials that resent being transplanted from one spot in the garden to another also have taproots or unusually deep roots.) Other difficult-to-transplant species may have brittle stems or simply have an easily damaged or sparse root system that make successful transplanting difficult. Outdoor sowing is an option for annuals and perennials that are difficult to transplant, but if handled carefully at transplant time they also can be sown indoors. Many gardeners sow seeds of difficult-to-transplant species into peat pots or other "containers" that can be moved directly to the garden, pot and all. (*See* PEAT POTS, PEAT PELLETS, PAPER POTS, SOIL BLOCKS) Taprooted trees, such as oaks (*Quercus* spp.) and hickories (*Carya* spp.) also are difficult to transplant, but fortunately growers of these species have special systems to handle them. Open-bottomed containers ensure that root tips are exposed to air, which encourages a better-branched, fibrous root system. So-called long pots are another option; these are roughly 4 inches square at the top (larger sizes are available) and 18 or more inches long in order to accommodate a taproot.

digging The most common method used to prepare garden beds. *See* DOUBLE DIGGING, SINGLE DIGGING

digging fork *See* FORK

digitate Palmate. A leaf that has three or more lobes or segments that radiate out from a common point, like fingers on a hand, forming a palmlike or handlike arrangement. (A digitate leaf can be compound, or cut into separate leaflets, or merely lobed.)

dilated Flattened, broadened, or expanded.

dimorphic, dimorphous Having two distinct forms or shapes, either at the same time or at different stages of a plant's development. Many ferns bear fertile and sterile fronds that are dimorphic, including staghorn ferns (*Platycerium* spp.) and flowering ferns (*Osmunda* spp.). English ivy (*Hedera helix*), which bears different types of leaves on juvenile and adult growth, is grown for its lobed juvenile leaves, which are borne on flexible stems. Mature, fruiting plants produce elliptic to ovate foliage and upright, more shrublike stems.

dioecious Bearing separate male (stamminate) and female (pistillate) flowers on separate plants. The flowers on dioecious plants are imperfect, meaning they have either male or female structures (stamens or pistils) but not both. Hollies (*Ilex* spp.) are dioecious, and only the female plants produce the bright berries gardeners—and birds—treasure in fall and winter. In order to have berry-bearing hollies, you need one male plant of the same species growing in the vicinity of about five female plants. Breeders have developed and named improved male and female cultivars. These offer the best insurance of getting plants of both sexes, since seed-grown plants can be of either sex. To identify the sex of unmarked plants in a nursery, you'll need to see (and be able to distinguish) the flowers, or look for berries denoting female plants in late summer and fall. Other plants that are dioecious include spicebush (*Lindera benzoin*).

diploid Having two sets of chromosomes. Most plants and other organisms are diploid.

direct sowing This technique is used for plants that grow so quickly indoor sowing isn't necessary—lettuce, spinach, sunflowers (*Helianthus* spp.), and cosmos (*Cosmos* spp.) are commonly sown right out in the garden where they are to grow, as are lawngrass seeds. Direct sowing also is used for plants that do not transplant well either because they have roots that are easy to damage or the plants tend to languish in the garden if they are disturbed. (*See* PEAT POTS, PAPER POTS, PEAT PELLETS, SOIL BLOCKS for indoor sowing options for plants that are difficult to transplant.) Sowing dates for direct-sown seeds are scheduled according to the last spring frost date just like seeds sown indoors. Warm-weather annuals usually are sown on or just after the last spring frost date. Cool-weather annuals are sown on or before that date. Direct-sown seeds can be planted in rows or by broadcasting. (*See* ROWS, BROADCASTING for more on these methods, as well as HILLING and RAISED BEDS for other options.) Either way, first prepare the soil in the planting site by loosening up the soil, adding a little organic matter such as compost, and raking the surface smooth. To sow in traditional rows, use a board, a hoe, or the edge of a rake to make shallow furrows—generally about $^{1}/_{2}$ inch deep and 6 inches apart, although the best distance will vary according to what you are planting. Vegetable gardeners commonly stretch a string from one end of the garden to the other to ensure straight, evenly spaced rows. To broadcast seeds, sprinkle them thinly over the site. (The thinner you spread them, the less thinning they'll require later on.) Mix a little white sandbox sand in with very fine seeds so it is easy to see where they've already been sown. After sowing in rows or broadcasting, rake the site lightly to cover the seeds with soil, then press the soil down gently with your hands or the back of the rake to ensure good seed-to-soil contact. Keep the seedbed evenly moist until seedlings appear using a fine spray of water from the hose or a sprinkling can. When seedlings are an inch or two tall, you will need to thin them. *See* THINNING

disbud To remove a bud, generally by pinching it between the thumb and forefinger. Disbudding reduces the overall number of buds on a plant and directs the plant's energy into the remaining ones. This technique is used on plants such as roses, peonies, and chrysanthemums to encourage large blooms: The smaller, younger buds are almost always removed in favor of the main flower bud on a stem. (While disbudding is used to produce exhibition-quality flowers, it can shorten the overall bloom time of a plant, because the small buds would have opened after the

large ones.) Disbudding also can be used to remove vegetative buds in order to direct a plant's growth and reduce the number of side shoots it produces. In this case, buds or very young shoots are rubbed off with a thumb or the side of a pruner or other tool. This form of disbudding is frequently used with grapes or other vines that have been trained, as well as with espaliered trees.

disbud

disc, disk An enlarged area or outgrowth of a flower's receptacle near the base of the ovary. The center portion, or "eye" of a flower in the aster family (Asteraceae) that contains the disc florets. Any round, flattened organ, such as the adhesive holdfasts on the ends of the tendrils of some climbing plants, such as woodbines (*Parthenocissus* spp.). The central part of the lip of an orchid flower.

disc floret, disk floret An individual flower in the center or "eye" of a daisylike inflorescence (head) of a plant in the aster family (Asteraceae). Disk florets, also called disk or disc flowers, are generally small and densely packed. In a sunflower (*Helianthus annus*), the disk florets make up the dark center and yield the seeds once they are fertilized.

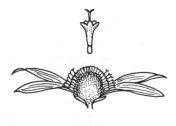

disc floret

discoid Disclike, resembling a disc. This term is used to describe the buttonlike flower heads of aster-family plants (Asteraceae) that lack ray florets, including lavender cotton (*Santolina* spp.). It can also be applied to fleshy, round leaves that have thickened edges, or margins.

discoidal A variegation pattern in which a large, single spot of color appears in the center of another color.

disk *See* DISC

dissected Very deeply cut into many thin segments. The leaves of many popular Japanese maples (*Acer palmatum*) are dissected, as is the foliage of many artemisias, including southernwood (*Artemisia abrotanum*) and silvermound artemisia (*A. schmidtiana* 'Nana'). Ferns with fronds that are exceptionally finely cut also are called dissected or plumose.

distal At or toward the tip, or apex. The end away from where a plant part is attached.

distichous Two-ranked. Leaves, flowers, or other organs arranged in two vertical rows that are opposite one another along the stem. Hemlocks (*Tsuga* spp.) and coastal redwoods (*Sequoia sempervirens*) both have distichous leaves.

distichous leaves

distinct Separate or not attached. Clearly distinguishable. This term is commonly used to describe similar flower parts, such as petals or sepals, that are not attached to one another. *See also* FREE for reference to dissimilar parts that are separate.

diurnal Opening during the daytime or active during the daytime.

divaricate Diverging or spreading very far apart.

divergent Spreading apart, but not as widely as divaricate.

divided Separated into deep segments that either reach the middle or base of a leaf, petal, or other organ or nearly do so. A divided leaf, for example, can be deeply cut, with the indentations (called sinuses) reaching nearly to the midrib. The term divided also is sometimes used to refer to a leaf that is compound, meaning it is separated into individual leaflets. Leaves can be divided either palmately (into finger- or handlike divisions) or pinnately (in a featherlike fashion).

divided leaf

division (botany) The term division has both horticultural and botanical meanings. Botanically, a division is the highest rank in the plant kingdom, Planate. In the 19th century, four divisions were recognized: Thallophyta, Bryophyta, Pteridophyta, and Spermatophyta. Although no longer used by plant taxonomists, these four original divisions gave rise to terms still used today to designate groups of plants. Bryophyte is a common term for mosses and liverworts, for example, and pteridophyte is used to refer to the ferns and fern allies. Today botanists recognize anywhere from 17 to 24 divisions in the plant kingdom. The names of divisions end with the suffix -phyta, and divisions are further divided into classes. (*See* CLASS) Horticulturally, division is a propagation technique (*See* DIVISION, DIVIDING), but it also is used to classify cultivars within large genera, usually those that have been extensively hybridized. Horticulturists recognize nine divisions within the genus *Lilium* for example, including Division I, Asiatic hybrids, and Division VII, Oriental hybrids. Other genera that are similarly divided include *Narcissus* and *Tulipa*.

division, dividing (horticulture) Separating plants by pulling or cutting them apart to make individual pieces or plants that have their own roots and shoots or dormant buds. Gardeners use this technique, which also is called crown division because the crown of the plant is separated into pieces, to increase the number of plants they have, to contain the spread of a plant that has spread too far, and to rejuvenate plants that develop old, woody growth near the centers of the clumps. Most plants are best divided in spring or fall, but the best time to divide varies from plant to plant. Cool and rainy or overcast weather is best, because it reduces stress on the new plants, which have limited root systems that can have trouble supplying top growth with water. Cutting the top growth back by about half can help divisions recover more quickly. To divide a plant, dig around it with a spade several inches away from the base of the stems, and then lift the clump out of the hole. (Very large clumps often are easiest to divide while still in the hole; cut these into manageable pieces before lifting them out.) Pull plants that have fibrous roots into pieces with your fingers. Work clumps of bulbs apart in the same manner. Use a sharp knife to cut apart plants with woody or dense crowns or rhizomes. Cut large clumps apart with a sharp spade or force them apart with two garden forks placed back to back. Ornamental grasses are so dense and woody that a mattock or an ax is required to divide them. If you have difficulty deciding where to cut, wash the soil off the roots with a stiff stream of water from the hose before dividing. Keep the roots moist while the plants are out of the ground by covering them with mulch or a piece of plastic. Discard old, woody growth, and replant the youngest, most vigorous portions of the clumps.

Before replanting, loosen the site and work organic matter into the soil. Water new divisions deeply and if the weather is sunny, shade new divisions with bushel baskets, cardboard boxes propped up on sticks, or burlap for a few days, until they recover from the stress. Plant extra divisions elsewhere in the garden or pot them up and give them away. *See also* BULB, RHIZOME, STEM TUBER, TUBER, TUBEROUS ROOTS

division (horticulture)

dolabriform Mattock- or pickax-shaped. Most often used to describe hairs that are divided in two and attached in the middle. The ends stick out on either side to form a T. Also called malpighian or malpighiaceous.

dormancy, dormant A temporary state during which a plant or seed does not grow and metabolic processes slow down. For established plants, dormancy is a resting phase; deciduous plants shed leaves during dormancy, while many perennials are killed to the ground by freezing temperatures and remain as a crown and/or clump of roots during dormancy. Seeds exhibit dormancy as well, and ones that do not germinate despite optimal conditions (warmth and moisture) are considered dormant. In nature, seed dormancy factors generally prevent seeds from germinating until such time that the seedlings will have the best chance of attaining maturity. A hard seed coat prevents the seed from taking up moisture, thus preventing germination. The seeds of some species have chemicals in the seed coats that must be washed away by a season or more of rain before germination can occur. Some seeds require cycles of warm-moist and/or cool-moist storage in order to break dormancy and germinate. During this period, the embryo undergoes changes that allow it to germinate, a process called afterripening. Seeds that exhibit double dormancy require more than one treatment in order to germinate—a treatment for a hard seed coat followed by a period of moist chilling, for example. Many wildflowers and woody plants commonly require one or more cycles of both warm-moist and cool-moist stratification in order to germinate. *See* SCARIFICATION for information on dealing with plants that have hard seed coats; STRATIFICATION for those that need warm-moist and/or cool-moist storage.

dormant bud *See* LATENT BUD

dormant oil An organic insecticide sprayed during the dormant season to control overwintering insects such as scale, mites, and aphids on fruit trees and a variety of ornamentals. While oil sprays once were heavy petroleum products loaded with impurities (they damaged plant leaves and could only be sprayed during the dormant season), today horticultural oil sprays are lighter, contain fewer impurities, and can be sprayed during the growing season. Dormant oils kill or damage Japanese maples (*Acer palmatum*) and remove the blue "bloom" from blue spruce (*Picea pungens*). *See* HORTICULTURAL OIL

dormant season pruning Also called winter pruning; this is a general term for pruning done any time a plant is dormant. The best time to prune most plants is from late winter to very early spring before growth starts. Pruning cuts heal faster in spring than any other season, so this minimizes the amount of time the plant has unhealed wounds. Another advantage is that you avoid exposing fresh pruning cuts to the most severe winter weather. Dormant-pruned trees and shrubs grow with renewed vigor in spring because they have proportionally more roots and food reserves for their remaining topgrowth. Another advantage of dormant-season pruning is that the plants' framework is clearly visible—on deciduous plants at least—making it easy to see what pruning the plant needs.

dorsal The side of a plant part, such as a leaf, that faces away from the main stem, or axis. The underside of a leaf is dorsal. The same as abaxial.

dorsifixed Attached at the back.

dot plant A British term for a particularly tall or bold specimen plant that is added to a flowerbed to add contrast in form or height.

dotted A variegation pattern in which color is distributed in very small round spots or dots. *See also* SPOTTED

double A flower that has more than the usual complement of petals or petal-like parts is said to be double. Petal-like parts include petal-like stamens (staminodes), such as those found in double peonies (*Paeonia* spp.) such as 'Sarah Bernhardt' or 'Bowl of Cream'. Flowers with staminodes are usually sterile. Flowers in the aster family (Asteraceae), such as sunflowers (*Helianthus* spp.) are double when their flowerheads consist only of ray florets. Flowers with tubular corollas sometimes have a second corolla or one corolla-like calyx inserted inside the other; this form of doubling is commonly called hose-in-hose.

double flower

double cordon A tree, usually a fruit tree, that has two main parallel arms, or branches, and essentially is trained to grow in a single plane. A double cordon is produced by cutting the plant off near its base and selecting two main cordons, or arms, which are trained out from the trunk for 6 or 7 inches on either side. The cordons are then trained to grow upright, thus forming a U-shaped plant. Like cordons, double cordons are supported on wires; however in this case the cordons are trained vertically instead of at an angle. *See* CORDON

double digging Also called deep digging and bastard trenching, this is a tried-and-true technique for preparing soil for garden beds. It makes it possible to improve soil drainage, work plenty of organic matter into the soil, and encourages plants to grow deep, wide-spreading roots. Before double digging, make sure the soil is ready to work—*See* SOIL BUILDING for a simple test to see if it is. To double dig, remove grass and/or weeds from the site, then spread a thick layer of compost or other organic matter over the site, which you will work into the soil surface as you dig. Dig the first trench about 8 inches deep and 1 foot wide along one edge of the planting area. Pile the removed soil on a tarp or in a wheelbarrow. Spread a 1-inch-thick layer of compost or other organic matter over the bottom of the trench, then work it into the soil with a garden fork. Dig a second trench next to the first, turning the soil into the previous trench, and then add more organic matter to the bottom of the new trench and fork it in. Continue this process until you reach the other end of the planting area, then fill the last trench with the soil you removed from the first one.

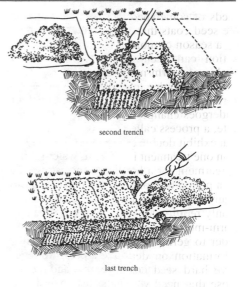

second trench

last trench

double digging

double dormancy *See* DORMANCY

double leader *See* LEADER

double-U cordon *See* FOUR-ARMED CORDON

double working Inserting an interstock between the stock and scion of a grafted plant to separate incompatible stocks and scions or to create some dwarf fruit trees. *See* INTERSTOCK

downy Pubescent. Covered with short, soft hairs.

drainage The movement of excess water through soil. *See* PERCOLATION

draw hoe *See* HOE

drepanium A type of helicoid cyme that has a sickle-shaped main stem, or axis. *See* HELICOID CYME

drift A grouping of plants, especially herbaceous perennials, in a garden bed or border. The term drift usually means that the plants are arranged in a free-form, natural-looking manner, with several clumps making up each drift. Drift also has a more sinister meaning: It is used to refer to pes-

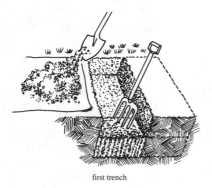

first trench

ticide and herbicide sprays that travel on the breeze, away from their intended target. Applying herbicides on a windy day, for example, can cause them to drift and kill plants unintentionally.

drill A long, relatively shallow trench or furrow into which seeds are sown or transplants are moved.

drip irrigation An efficient, water-saving system for watering plants consisting of a series of hoses or pipes that carry water to the garden under low pressure. The water seeps out of holes in the pipes or specially designed emitters a drop at a time, directly to the roots of the plants. Most drip systems also use a filter and a pressure regulator. Although they take time and money to install—each system is custom designed either by the gardener or by an expert for each garden—they are well worth the effort because of the water savings they deliver. Soaker hoses deliver benefits similar to more sophisticated systems and are easy to move from place to place. *See* SOAKER HOSE

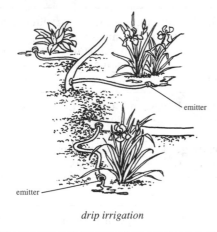

drip irrigation

drip line The line on the soil (either real or imaginary) where rain drips to the ground from the outer edge of the leaves in a tree's canopy.

drip point, drip tip A point on a leaf tip from which water readily drips in wet weather. Acuminate, caudate, and aristate leaves all have drip points.

drip zone *See* DRIP LINE

drooping This term is used to describe an organ that is normally vertical that leans or inclines slightly at the tip.

drop-crotch cut A technique used to reduce the size of a tree's crown by cutting a branch to where it meets a smaller branch, but one that is no less than about one-third the size of the first branch.

drop-forged *See* FORGED

drop layering, dropping A form of layering in which the entire stock plant is set at the bottom of a trench, which is gradually filled in with soil as shoots on the stock plant develop roots. Once established, the layers are severed and potted up.

drupe A stone fruit. A fleshy fruit that does not open at maturity (is indehiscent) and bears a single seed inside a stony casing commonly called a pit or stone. Botanists refer to the pit as an endocarp, an ossiculus, or a pyrene. Fleshy or fibrous outer layers surround the pit. Peaches, nectarines, and almonds all bear drupes. Dogwoods (*Cornus* spp.) also bear small drupes. Walnuts (*Juglans* spp.) and hickories (*Carya* spp.) bear drupes. In this case their nuts are encased inside a fleshy husk; this form of drupe also is called a tryma.

drupe

drupelet A small drupe or stone fruit. This term is commonly used to refer to small drupes borne in clusters. The "berries" of raspberries and blackberries (*Rubus* spp.) are clusters of drupelets.

drying agents *See* DESSICANTS

drying flowers A method used to preserve flowers for dried arrangements and other uses. To dry flowers, strip off the leaves unless you want to use some of them in arrangements, bundle flowers in small bunches, and hang them upside-down in a warm, well-ventilated, dark place as you would for herbs. (*See* DRYING HERBS) The best time for harvesting flowers depends on the species, so either consult a reference with harvesting guidelines, or simply experiment. In general, harvest just as the flowers open fully. *See* EVERLASTINGS for a list of flowers that are especially easy to air dry. Another option is to spread flowers or petals on screens set in a warm, well-ventilated, dark place. To preserve the shape of flat or rounded flowers, try placing them on screens with the stem sticking through the screen and the flower resting on top. Flowers also can be preserved by using dessicants such as silica gel, a white powder that resembles laundry detergent and is available at craft stores. *See* DESSICANTS For another technique used to preserve leaves and flowers, *see* GLYCERIN

drying herbs Gardeners use several drying techniques to preserve maximum flavor, fragrance, and color in herbs. In most cases, herbs and flowers are dried the same way, although some techniques are more suitable for one group of plant or the other. When drying herbs, for maximum flavor and fragrance, harvest them just before they flower. Pick them in the morning, after the dew has dried but before the sun gets hot. The easiest drying technique of all is air drying. Simply bundle herbs in small bunches and hang them upside-down in a warm, well-ventilated, dark place such as an attic. Rubber bands are especially useful for securing the bunches, since they tighten as the stems dry and shrink. Most herbs will be dry within 2 weeks in this manner. If dust may be a problem (especially with cooking herbs), make several ventilation holes in each side of a paper bag by cutting the holes on three sides, leaving the flap attached at the top like an awning over a window. Then cut a hole in the bottom of the bag. Slip the stems through the hole in the bottom of the bag

and hang to dry; the dried seeds will fall into the bag. Another option is to spread culinary herbs on cookie sheets in a warm oven; the oven is a great place to dry chili peppers, too. Leave the oven open and check and stir them periodically. Herbs are dried when they crumble—if they are not complete dry, they will turn moldy in storage. Dehydrators also are effective for drying herbs and chili peppers. Store dried herbs in tightly covered glass jars. For best flavor, don't crumble herbs as you pack them for storage. Instead crumble them as you use them in recipes. Keep dried herbs in a dark place, away from heat to preserve their fragrance.

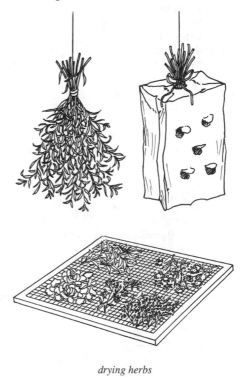

drying herbs

drying seed *See* CLEANING SEED

dry wall, dry-laid wall A stone wall laid without mortar; the stones are simply fitted together.

dry well This structure, used to control water flow and runoff, is a hole filled with coarse stones or rock into which water is directed. A dry well usually is a deep, somewhat cylindrical hole, and water that falls into it seeps slowly into the surrounding soil.

dual leader *See* LEADER

duff The layer of partially decayed leaves, stems, and other organic matter found on top of the soil surface on the forest floor.

dust mulch A shallow layer of dry soil on the surface of garden beds that is maintained by repeated cultivation. The dry layer is thought to help hold moisture in the soil and suppress weeds much like more conventional mulches.

Dutch hoe *See* HOE

dwarf A mutation of a plant that naturally has a compact or small habit. Dwarf plants often are named and propagated vegetatively because they are popular in gardens.

dwarfing rootstock A rootstock used in grafting that will limit the size of the top-growth. Apples and many other fruit trees are grafted onto dwarfing rootstocks to create plants of manageable size.

e-, ex- Prefixes meaning either not, without, deprived of, off, or beyond. For example, ebracteate means without bracts, and eciliate means without cilia.

ear A ripened spike of corn. Also, an auricle, or earlike lobe.

eared *See* AURICULATE

early blight *See* LEAF SPOTS

earthing up Pulling soil up around a plant, usually with a hoe. This technique, also called hilling up, is commonly used to blanch vegetables or to mound layer plants.

earthworms The "intestines of the soil" according to Charles Darwin, earthworms play a vital role in improving soil by burrowing through it, moving nutrients and organic matter from the surface deeper into the soil. In the process they also create tunnels for air and water to pass through. A large population of earthworms is a sign of healthy soil. While most common near the soil surface, earthworms can burrow to depths of 3 to 6 feet. To foster a healthy earthworm population, add plenty of organic matter such as compost to the soil.

echinate Covered with stiff hairs, bristles, or blunt prickles.

ecology The study of plants, animals, and other living organisms in relation to their environment and to each other.

economic botany The study of how plants are used and how the technical and other uses of plants and plant-derived products affect the economy.

ecosystem The complete community of living and nonliving components upon which the lifecycle of any particular living organism is based and with which it exchanges materials or has relationships. Factors that play a role in the ecosystem of a plant include animals or insects that disperse its seeds, pollinate its flowers, feed on its roots or foliage, or affect its environment in a fundamental way. Nonliving elements such as soil, weather, exposure, and other environmental factors also are elements in plant ecosystems.

edaphic Of or pertaining to the soil.

edged A variegation pattern in which one color is surrounded by a very narrow border, or edge, of another color. *See also* BORDERED

edger, edging knife A tool designed to cut clean, neat edges in the lawn along beds, borders, sidewalks, and driveways. It features a straight handle, a semicircular, knifelike blade, and a tread to stand on the blade to push it into the soil.

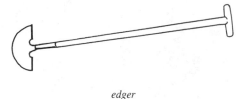

edger

edging This term refers to the tedious task of trimming grass with shears around the edge of a lawn as well as slicing through grass roots to create neat straight edges using an edger or edging knife. It also is used to refer to barriers that prevent the spread of grass (*See* EDGING STRIP). Finally, plantings of low, mounding plants along beds and borders also are called edgings. An edging resembles a low hedge because the plants are spaced fairly close together. Some edgings consist of all one plant;

others may form a pattern by alternating foliage or flower colors, for example. Lilyturf (*Liriope* spp.), low-growing lavender (*Lavandula* spp.), and lavender cotton (*Santolina* spp.) are three popular edging plants. Foliage annuals such as Joseph's coat (*Alternanthera ficoidea*) or beefsteak plant (*Iresine herbstii*) also make handsome edgings.

edging strip A barrier designed to prevent the spread of plants—usually lawn grasses or groundcovers—beyond a specified area. Edging strips are commonly installed along the edges of flower beds or borders to prevent lawngrass from spreading. This reduces the need to weed out invading grasses or other plants, maintains a neat-looking edge, and reduces the time required to trim lawn edges. Plastic edging strips are common, but aluminum ones also are available. Bricks or flagstone edging strips are expensive and time-consuming to install, but are quite handsome. Set the top of the edging strip just barely above the soil surface, but low enough so that you can run over it with your lawn mower. Keep a mulched strip just inside the edging strip so you can run one wheel of your mower in the bed and trim along the edge of the grass all at one time.

edging strip

edible flowers Used to add color and visual appeal to food, edible flowers are added fresh to salads, either whole or as petals. They also can be arranged as garnishes on plates, and sometimes are cooked in dishes—daylily (*Hemerocallis* spp.) flower buds can be added to stir fries, for example. Edible flowers include pinks (*Dianthus* spp.), pansies and violets (*Viola* spp.), marigolds (*Tagetes* spp.), pot marigolds (*Calendula officinalis*), roses (*Rosa* sp.), honeysuckle (*Lonicera* spp.), sweet peas (*Lathyrus odoratus*), cornflowers (*Centaurea* spp.), and glads (*Gladiolus* spp.). While most edible flowers add more color than flavor, both the flowers and foliage of nasturtiums (*Tropaeolum majus*) add spicy flavor to salads. Many herbs have edible flowers as well, including basil (*Ocimum basilicum*), borage (*Borago officinalis*), lavender (*Lavandula* spp.), oregano (*Origanum vulgare*), and thyme (*Thymus* spp.). When using edible flowers, be absolutely sure that you know the correct identity of the plant from which they were gathered.

edible landscaping A style of gardening in which edible plants—vegetables, fruits, herbs, and nuts—are incorporated throughout the landscape.

eelworms *See* NEMATODES

egg A fertile female reproductive cell. Female gamete. *See* GAMETE, FERTILIZATION

elaiosome An appendage on a seed that secretes oil or a process that attracts ants to seeds to aid in their dispersal. An aril is a type of elaiosome. *See also* ARIL, MYRMECOPHYTE

elliptic Ellipse-shaped. An elliptic leaf has the shape of an ellipse or a narrow oval, and its base and tip are narrower but regularly rounded. In shape, elliptic leaves are halfway between oval and oblong ones.

elliptic leaf

elongate To lengthen or stretch out.

emarginate Notched. A tip or base with a pronounced notch. An emarginate leaf is rounded or blunt, and has a notch that reaches from one-sixteenth to one-eighth of the distance to the midpoint of the leaf blade. While most commonly used to describe a leaf base or tip, this term can be applied to other plant parts such as bracts (modified petal-like leaves) or the petals or sepals of a flower.

emarginate leaf tip

emasculation Removing the anthers of a flower before the pollen is ripe in order to prevent self-pollination. This technique is used in plant breeding when the breeder intends to fertilize the flower with pollen from another plant.

embracing With the base of a leaf or other plant part clasping the stem.

embryo The immature or rudimentary plant contained within a seed.

emergent, emersed Standing or rising out of the water. This term is commonly used to describe aquatic plants that have leaves or flowers that are held above the water's surface. Water lilies (*Nymphaea* spp.) commonly have emergent flowers, while lotuses (*Nelumbo* spp.) have emergent leaves.

empty glume *See* GLUME

endemic Native to or found only in a particular region, usually a small, restricted one. Many endangered native plants, for example, are found only on sites that have a particular soil type or are characterized by other environmental conditions. Hawaii has the largest number of endangered endemic plants in the United States.

endo- A prefix meaning within or inner. For example, endocarp is the innermost layer of the pericarp, which is the wall of a seed or ripened ovary.

endocarp *See* PERICARP

endophyte A type of fungi contained in some grasses that repels a variety of lawngrass pests, including various aphids, armyworms, webworms, and cutworms. While grasses that contain endophytes can cause serious illness in cattle, lawngrass breeders have developed and released several strains of improved, insect-resistant grasses that contain these bug-fighting fungi, which were first discovered in perennial ryegrasses and are passed from generation to generation in the seeds. There are endophyte-enhanced cultivars of perennial ryegrasses as well as turf-type tall fescues.

endosperm The tissue around an embryo, consisting of starches and oils, that fuel the germination process. Germinating seedlings are dependent upon food stored in the endosperm and the cotyledons until the first leaves begin to make their own food by the process called photosynthesis. Endosperm also is called the albumen.

ensiform Sword-shaped. Ensiform leaves have an acute point (less than 90 degrees) at the tip. Many irises (*Iris* spp.), including bearded irises and Japanese iris (*I. ensata*), have ensiform leaves.

ensiform leaf

entire Smooth and unbroken by lobes, teeth, spines, or other features.

entire leaf margin

entomophagous Insectivorous. Insect-eating.

entomophilous Pollinated by insects.

EPDM Fish-grade EPDM is a rubber used to make the best quality water garden or pond liners available. It is long-lived, and is more elastic and more resistant to ultraviolet light than PVC liners, and also more resistant to tearing or puncturing. EPDM rubber liners are more expensive than PVC, but also are longer-lived, and generally have at least 20-year warranties. EPDM bonded to a geotextile (GeoPond and UltiLiner are two brands) are 60 mm thick and usually come with a lifetime guarantee. Don't use roofing grade EPDM, as it contains chemicals that are toxic to fish. *See* WATER GARDEN LINERS, UNDERLAYMENT

ephemeral Fleeting. Lasting only a short time, generally only a day. The individual flowers of daylilies (*Hemerocallis* spp.) and spiderworts (*Tradescantia* spp.) are ephemeral. The term ephemeral also is used describe the lifecycles of some plants. Spring ephemeral is a general term for plants that produce foliage and flowers early in spring, often before the trees above them leaf out. They set seed, and their leaves ripen and die back to the ground very early in the season—by late spring or early summer. Many native woodland wildflowers fall into this category, including Virginia bluebells (*Mertensia virginica*) and spring beauties

(*Claytonia virginica*). The term annual ephemeral is sometimes used to describe short-lived annuals commonly found in warm, dry regions that flower in spring, if rains allow, then quickly set seed and die before adverse conditions return. In years with little rain, annual ephemerals may not appear at all—they survive harsh conditions as seeds.

epi- A prefix meaning on, above, or over. Epipetalous means growing on or arising from the petals, for example.

epicalyx A whorl or involucre of bracts attached outside and below a true calyx. A false calyx.

epicormic shoot A shoot that grows from a latent or adventitious bud located under the bark of a tree or shrub. They frequently appear just below a pruning cut on tree trunks and branches.

epicotyl In a seed or on a seedling, the portion of the stem that is above the cotyledons. The growing point of the stem.

epidermal Relating to the outer layer of cells on leaves or other plant parts. The epidermis.

epidermis The outer layer of cells on leaves, stems, fruits, or any plant part.

epigenous Growing on the surface. Some fungi can be described as epigenous because they grow on the surface of leaves.

epigeous germination In this type of germination, the portion of the stem below the cotyledons, called the hypocotyl, elongates and raises the cotyledons above the soil surface. Many plants germinate in this manner, including tomatoes (*Lycopersicon* spp.) and peppers (*Capsicum* spp.). *See* HYPOGEOUS GERMINATION

epigynous Borne or attached on top of the ovary. An epigynous flower has petals, sepals, and stamens attached to the top of the ovary, making the ovary inferior. Irises (*Iris* spp.) and bellflowers (*Campanula* spp.) along with squash and pumpkins (*Cucurbita* spp.) have epigynous flowers.

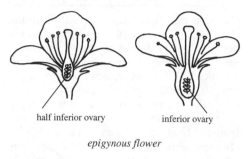

half inferior ovary   inferior ovary

epigynous flower

epilithic Growing on rocks.

epiphyte, epiphytic A plant that grows on another plant—often attached to the bark or among its branches—but does not take water or nutrients from it. Members of the bromeliad (Bromeliaceae) and many members of the orchid family (Orchidaceae) are epiphytes. A parasite takes nutrients and water from its parent plant. *See also* PARASITE, SAPROPHYTE

epiphyte mix Epiphytes require fast-draining potting media rich in organic matter. Orchids, bromeliads, and other epiphytes can be grown in pots filled with chunks of osmunda fiber or in bark chips packaged especially for this use. For epiphytes such as bromeliads, try a mix of 1 part coarse peat moss, 1 part shredded osmunda fiber, and 2 parts coarse sand, perlite, or crushed granite. Substitute well-rotted sawdust for the osmunda fiber and leaf mold for the peat moss, if desired. You can mix in chunks of bark packaged for orchids to increase drainage. *See* FERN POTTING MIX for a recipe for epiphytic ferns.

epithet Any word in a two-part (binomial) botanical name that is not the name of the genus. Thus, in the common name of Sacramento rose, *Rosa stellata* var. *mirifica*, *stellata* is the specific epithet and *mirifica* is the varietal epithet.

equitant This term is used to describe folded (conduplicate) leaves that overlap one another in two opposing ranks to form a fan. Many irises (*Iris* spp.) have leaves arranged in this fashion.

eramous Bearing unbranched stems.

erect Vertical, upright. Not curved or spreading.

ericaceous Belonging to the heath family (Ericaceae), which includes azaleas and rhododendrons (*Rhododendron* spp.), mountain laurels (*Kalmia* spp.), blueberries (*Vaccinium* spp.), and heaths or heathers (*Erica* spp.). Many members of this family prefer acid soil that is rich in organic matter, evenly moist, yet well-drained, and the term ericaceous is often applied to plants that require these conditions. Also, resembling heaths or heathers (*Erica* spp.).

erinous Prickly. Covered with sharp points.

erose Gnawed. Irregularly indented or jagged, as if gnawed. This term is commonly used to describe the edge, or margin, of a leaf or leaflet.

erose leaf margin

escape A non-native cultivated plant that has become naturalized in a particular area. *See* NATURALIZED

espalier A tree or shrub that has a vertical central trunk and horizontal branches that have been trained to grow in a single plane. Espalier patterns can be simple or complicated, but all espaliered plants require regular maintenance. Frequent tying, pinching, and pruning are required to keep the pattern of the plant visible and keep the plant from overrunning its space. A south-facing wall is ideal for an espalier, because the fruit and the plant will get plenty of sunshine. Apples, pears, peaches, plums, apricots, and nectarines are all candidates for espaliers, as are some citrus and other tender fruits. Gooseberries and currants have long been espaliered in Europe. For information on specific espalier patterns, *see* CORDON, DOUBLE CORDON, FOUR-ARMED CORDON, FAN. Espaliers are pruned throughout the season, rather than in late winter. Your fingers are the best tools for the job, because most "pruning" consists of removing buds and pinching out shoots. Rub off unwanted or misdirected buds in early spring. During the growing season, pinch off unwanted growth as it appears. In midsummer, prune for fruit production by snipping back shoots near the base of the branch to four or five buds to encourage the formation of fruiting buds for the next season. Most espaliers take several years to establish; when they reach the desired height, maintain them there by cutting them back uniformly as needed.

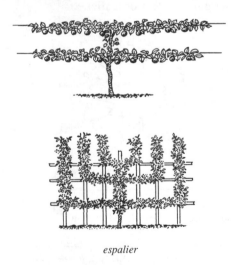

espalier

essential elements Substances that plants require to grow and complete their lifecycles. Scientists recognize two types, macronutrients and micronutrients.

essential oil Oil used to make perfumes and flavorings that have the fragrance and/or flavor characteristic of the plant from which they are made.

ethnobotany The study of the relationship, use, and lore of plants, especially as it pertains to a particular race or community.

etiolated White because of a lack of chlorophyll. Etiolated growth develops because a layer of mulch or soil or another type of covering keeps stems or other plant parts from the light. In addition to turning white, etiolated stems are longer and thinner than normal and generally lack leaves or have poorly developed ones. Etiolated growth is actually a gourmet treat in some cases: Leeks, celery, endive, and asparagus are commonly covered to exclude light and create white, or blanched, growth. *See* BLANCHING for more information.

etiolation layering *See* TRENCH LAYERING

eu- A prefix meaning true, real, or good.

evanescent Fleeting. Lasting only a short time.

even pinnate A compound leaf divided in a featherlike fashion (pinnate), with pairs of leaflets attached along a main stem, or rachis, and ending with a pair of leaflets at the tip. Honeylocust (*Gleditsia triacanthos*) has even-pinnate leaves. *See also* ODD PINATE

even pinnate leaf

evergreen Retaining green leaves through the winter, the opposite of deciduous. Plants that are evergreen in some regions may not be evergreen in others. For example, sweet bay magnolia (*Magnolia virginiana*) is evergreen in southern zones, deciduous in the North. Evergreen also is a general term for conifers such as pines (*Pinus* spp.), spruces (*Picea*), yews (*Taxus* spp.), and arborvitaes (*Thuja* spp.) that retain their needles all year. While true evergreens hold leaves for 2 or 3 years, the term evergreen is commonly used in a very general way when referring to herbaceous plants such as perennials and ferns. In this case, evergreen usually means a plant has leaves that stay green through most of the winter, but the leaves turn brown and/or die before or as new leaves emerge in spring. Hellebores (*Helleborus* spp.), European wild ginger (*Asarum europaeum*), and Christmas fern (*Polystichum acrostichoides*) all behave in this manner. Some gardeners refer to plants with this cycle as wintergreen. Many perennials commonly described as evergreen only stay green over winter in very mild climates and are generally deciduous up north—epimediums or barrenworts (*Epimedium* spp.) fall into this category. Plants that routinely are evergreen in England (and thus reported as evergreen in British gardening books) are often completely deciduous or at best semi-evergreen in this country. The term evergreen also is applied to plants with foliage that turns red over winter.

everlastings A collective term for plants that have papery petals, practs, or other plant parts that hold their color and form well after being dried. Everlastings, sometimes called immortelles, dry easily and quickly, and are ready for harvest just before they are fully open. Simply cut the stems when they are dry—late morning after the dew dries is a good time—bundle 6 or 8 stems together with string or rubber band, then hang them upside down in a warm, dry place. Some everlastings have sturdy enough stems to dry right side up (statice, *Limonium* spp., is an example). Place them in a vase with a small quantity of water and let them dry in place. Do not replace the water after it is depleted the first time. Everlastings include pearly or winged everlasting (*Ammobium alatum*), cockscomb (*Celosia* spp.), gomphrena or globe amaranth (*Gomphrena* spp.), strawflower (*Bracteantha bracteata*, formerly *Helychriysum bracteatum*), and immortelle (*Xeranthemum* spp.).

evolute Unfolded.

excluded Extending beyond or not enclosed. Stamens that extend or project beyond the corolla of a flower are excluded. *See also* INCLUDED

excrescence An abnormal or irregular growth.

excurrent Extending beyond the tip of the leaf, such as the short, sharp, abrupt point at the tip of a mucronate leaf. Also, a growth habit with a clearly recognizable main trunk, or axis, and secondary side branches. Spruces (*Picea* spp.) exhibit this type of form.

exfoliate To peel or shred off, either in thin layers or small plates. Many popular trees are grown for their handsome, exfoliating bark, including sycamores (*Platanus* spp.), paperbark maple (*Acer griseum*), and lace-bark pine (*Pinus bungeana*).

exo- A prefix meaning outward. Exocarp is the outermost layer of the pericarp.

exocarp *See* PERICARP

exotic Non-native. A plant that is native to another country. This term usually is used to describe non-native plants growing in gardens, but is applied to non-native plants that have escaped cultivation. *See also* INTRODUCED, NATURALIZED

exposure The direction a site faces, which affects growing conditions there. A site with a south-facing exposure along a building or wall will warm up earlier in spring and generally stay warmer in winter, for example. South-facing exposures often are not the best spots for broad-leaved evergreens, because in winter they receive the most sunshine: On sunny winter days, the foliage can warm up and begin to transpire water, but since the soil is still frozen the roots are unable to take up more water. This leads to a condition commonly known as winterburn (*See* WINTERBURN). A north-facing exposure tends to be cooler and warm up more slowly than a south-facing one. A site close to the east side of a house may receive morning sun and afternoon shade, making it cooler than one on the west side, which is exposed to the hot afternoon sun. In some areas, exposure to prevailing winds has a profound effect on growing conditions.

exserted Protruding. Sticking out or projecting beyond the surrounding parts. Not included. Stamens that stick out beyond the corolla are exserted.

extra- A prefix meaning outside or beyond. For example, extrafloral means outside the flower.

exudate A substance that oozes out slowly.

eye The center of a flower that is colored differently than the rest of the petals or corolla. For example, a peach-colored daylily (*Hemerocallis* spp.) flower with a maroon spot in the center has an eye. The undeveloped buds on tubers such as potatoes also are called eyes. The center of a daisylike flower, more properly called an inflorescence, also is called an eye. Sunflowers (*Helianthus* spp.) and other members of the aster family (Asteraceae) bear flowers with eyes. Bare-root peonies are commonly sized and sold by the number of eyes on each division—three- to five-eye clumps are most common. In propagation, a stem cutting that has a single bud is sometimes called an eye.

eye socket construction A method for attaching the metal head of a tool to its handle by means of a round or oval opening, or eye, forged in the blade. Eye sockets are used for attaching handles on picks, mattocks, axes, and other similar tools, and make it possible to replace the handle as necessary.

F₁ hybrid A plant that is the result of cross-pollination between two distinct lines of parent plants, which are recrossed each time to create hybrid seed for the next generation. F₁ hybrids are very uniform in appearance but genetically very diverse. As a result, seed collected from them usually does not result in plants that resemble the parents. *See* HYBRID

F₂ hybrid A plant that is the result of cross-pollination between two F₁ hybrids. They are less uniform in appearance than their parents. Crosses made beyond the F₂ generation are less vigorous, more variable, and generally of poor quality. *See* HYBRID

facultative Able to exist without, unrestricted. The opposite of obligate.

falcate Sickle-shaped, curved, or hooked. Daylilies (*Hemerocallis* spp.) commonly have falcate leaves.

falcate leaf

fall One of the outer "petals" of an iris (*Iris* spp.) or other related plant. Falls normally are drooping or spreading and frequently are broader than the upright standards. Technically, falls are petal-like sepals. *See also* SEPAL, STANDARD

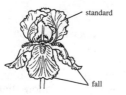

fall frost date *See* FROST DATES

fallow The practice of leaving an area unplanted for a period either to improve soil structure or to reduce the level of soil-borne pathogens.

false indusium *See* INDUSIUM

family A group of plants with similar characteristics within an order. Families are further divided into genera, although large families may be organized into subfamilies and tribes, which then contain genera. The scientific names of families end in the suffix -aceae and usually are derived from the genus used to determine the basic characteristics of the family. Unlike species, which are set in italics, family names always are set in roman type. Most families also have common names. For example: the rose family, Rosaceae; the aster family, Asteraceae; the mallow family, Malvaceae. (Since the suffix -aceae means family, it is redundant to use the word family with the scientific name; thus "the Rosaceae family" is incorrect.) A few commonly used family names do not conform to the -aceae suffix, although horticultural references are beginning to use the correct terms. The following list gives the correct name followed by the former, but still commonly used one and the common name of the family in parenthesis: Arecaceae (Palmae, the palm family); Brassicaceae (Cruciferae, the cabbage family), Poaceae (Gramineae, the grass family), Fabaceae (Leguminosae, the pea family), Apiaceae (Umbelliferae, the parsley or carrot family), Lamiaceae (Labiatae, the mint family). Botanists continue to redefine (and disagree about) the size and scope of plant families: One trend is to break up enormous, relatively ill-defined families such as Liliaceae, which contains up to 240 genera. While some experts prefer a broad view of this family, others break it into three or more individual families. For example, depending on the source, ornamental onions (*Allium* spp.) belong to the amaryllis family, Amaryllidaceae or the lily family, Liliaceae.

fan A plant that has been pruned and trained so that its main branches emerge from a short trunk and radiate out in a fan shape arranged in a single plane. To produce a fan, cut the plant off near its base and select two main arms, or branches, to train out at a 45-degree angle from the ground. Sideshoots or lateral branches that arise from the two main arms are also trained to grow parallel to the main branches, so that the tree is essentially growing in two dimensions. The branches are supported on wires. Apples, pears, plums, sour cherries, peaches, and apricots are some of the fruit trees that can be trained as fans.

fancy A flower that has petals of a single, uniform color that are striped or flecked in a contrasting color. Pinks (*Dianthus* spp.) come in fancy patterns.

fancy name *See* CULTIVAR

fan-shaped *See* FLABELLATE

farinose Mealy, granular, or powdery in texture, with surfaces covered with a mealy or powdery coating, called farina. Leaf surfaces and stems are most commonly described as farinose. Several species of saltbush (*Atriplex* spp.) have leaves and stems that are farinose or scurfy, which means covered with tiny scales. There also are primroses that have farinose leaves and/or flowers. *Primula farinosa* is one example, but auricula primroses, which are grown in rock gardens and alpine houses, often have farinose foliage and flowers.

-farious A suffix meaning ranked, or arranged, in vertical rows. Quadrifarous means arranged in four ranks, for example.

fasciate, fasciated Bundled or grown together. This term is used to describe two or more very congested stems or other plant parts that have grown very closely together lengthwise in an abnormal fashion. It also can refer to a single stem or plant part that has been flattened or misshapen in such a way that it looks like several stems that have been fused together.

fascicle A compact bundle of leaves, flowers, stems, or other plant parts. The needles of pines (*Pinus* spp.) are borne in fascicles.

fastigiate Strongly erect with densely clustered branches and a narrow crown. This term is primarily used to describe the habit of various trees and shrubs that bear dense clusters of branches that are nearly vertical and parallel to the main stem. Fastigiate, or columnar, trees are popular choices for planting along streets because of their narrow crowns and the fact that their upright branches don't block sidewalks. Most are cultivars—Lombardy poplar (*Populus nigra* 'Italica') is well-known but disease-prone and short-lived. 'Armstrong' and 'Columnare' are two columnar or fastigiate forms of red maple (*Acer rubrum*).

father plant The parent in a cross from which the pollen was collected.

faveose, faveolate Honeycombed.

feathered maiden A small tree, or whip, that is in its first year after grafting or budding and has a slender main stem and several lateral branches. This term primarily is used in reference to fruit trees.

feather-veined A leaf with a single midrib and veins that arise from the center vein in a pinnate, or featherlike, fashion.

felted-tomentose Very woolly. Covered with short, soft, woolly hairs that are very matted down and tangled together. *See* TOMENTOSE

fenestrate Bearing windowlike or translucent openings.

fern Ferns are ancient plants that have been in existence for more than 300 million years. Botanically speaking, they are pteridophytes, meaning plants that reproduce by spores and have roots, stems, leaves, and vascular tissue. On the evolutionary scale, ferns are a step above mosses and liverworts, collectively called bryophytes, which lack true roots and specialized vascular tissue. For gardeners, ferns are essential plants for the shade garden, where they add lush color and delicate texture. They also are beloved houseplants. In general, they grow in partial to full shade (but good light) with evenly moist, well-drained soil that is rich in organic matter. An acid pH is best for most species. Some species will grow in sun while others will grow in drier or wetter soil. *See* FERN LIFECYCLE for details on growing ferns from spores.

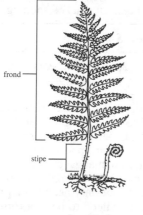

fern frond

Fern Age Another name for the Carboniferous Period (the Coal Age), when ferns were the dominant vegetation on Earth.

fern allies A collective name for fernlike plants that primarily belong to four genera: club mosses (*Lycopodium* spp.), spike mosses (*Selaginella* spp.), quillworts (*Isotes* spp.), and horsetails (*Equisetum* spp.). Ferns and fern allies also are sometimes called pteridophytes. *See also* CRYPTOGRAM, PTERIODOPHYTE

fern lifecycle Ferns reproduce sexually from spores, not seeds, and have a lifecycle with two distinct generations: sporophyte and gametophyte. The ferns

grown in gardens are the sporophyte generation. They produce dustlike spores in sporangia, sometimes called spore cases, which are usually arranged in clusters, called sori. Spores can be borne under the leaves or on specialized fertile fronds. The sporangia open when they are ripe to release the spores. If a spore lands in suitable conditions it grows into a small, heart-shaped prothallus, which is the gametophyte or sexual stage of the lifecycle. Spores require constant moisture and shade to germinate, and the prothallus cannot withstand too much competition from other plants. The prothallus bears male and female structures on the underside (soil side) called antheridia (male) and archegonia (female), which produce sperm and eggs on the same plant. The sperm swim on a film of water to reach the eggs; fertilization cannot occur if conditions are too dry because the sperm cannot reach the eggs. Once fertilized, the eggs grow into the sporophyte, or spore-producing, generation, which is sometimes called a sporeling when still very small. The sporelings grow into the ferns treasured by gardeners. Some ferns appear to conform to this lifecycle, but actually bypass sexual reproduction altogether. *See* APOGAMY for details. *See* FERN SPORES for information on growing ferns from spores.

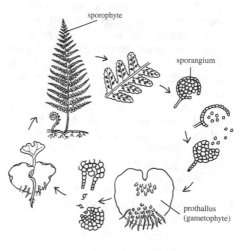

fern lifecycle

fern, mother *See* MOTHER FERN

fern potting mix Most ferns require soil that is evenly moist and rich in organic matter. To grow most ferns in containers, combine 2 parts leaf mold, well-rotted compost, or other organic matter with 1 part clean topsoil or commercial potting soil, and 1 part perlite or coarse sand. For ferns that require dryer conditions, use 2 parts perlite or sand. For epiphytic ferns such as staghorns (*Platycerium* spp.) combine 1 part osmunda fiber, 1 part pine bark or commercial orchid bark, and 1 part coarse sand. Add a small quantity of charcoal (the kind sold for aquarium filters, not cooking). If the mix dries out too quickly, add sphagnum moss. Sphagnum moss also is useful for packing in on top of the mix if you are attaching the plants to a basket or tree.

fern spores The basic unit of reproduction of a fern. To grow ferns from spores, wash pots in a 10 percent bleach solution (1 part bleach to 9 parts water) and fill them with a mix of 1 part potting soil, 1 part coarse sand, and 2 parts peat moss. Pour boiling water over the filled pots to sterilize the medium, then cover them loosely with plastic as they cool. Sprinkle the spores (*See* SORUS for directions on collecting them) onto the medium and set the pots in plastic bags to provide high humidity. Place the pots in a north or east window, or under plant lights. Keep the soil evenly moist, but not wet. In 2 to 10 weeks the spores will grow into heart-shaped prothalli and eventually you'll see tiny fronds that indicate the new sporophytes, which can be carefully moved on to individual pots—sterilize pots and medium as before. Keep the new plants enclosed in plastic until they are established in individual pots. Then gradually expose them to lower humidity by opening the bag a bit more each day.

fern, walking *See* MOTHER FERN

ferruginous Rust colored. Red-brown.

fertile Bearing seed that is viable, meaning it will germinate and grow. The term fertile also can be used to describe flower parts that are viable—anthers that have viable pollen, pistils that are able to produce seeds, for example. A fertile shoot produces flowers and fruit.

fertile frond A frond that bears sporangia and spores. This term is most commonly used to refer to ferns that are dimorphic, meaning they bear separate fertile and sterile fronds. Flowering ferns (*Osmunda* spp.) all exhibit this characteristic. Some fertile fronds contain almost no leafy tissue, only veins and sporangia; the brushlike, red-brown fertile fronds of cinnamon fern (*O. cinnamomea*) are a good example. Interrupted fern (*O. claytoniana*) bears fertile fronds that have normal leaflets above and below a section in the center of the frond that has brownish-black leaflets consisting of veins and densely packed sporangia.

fertile glume *See* GLUME

fertile shoot A shoot that bears a flower or flowers.

fertility Soil that is rich in nutrients that plants need to grow has good fertility or is called fertile. Green plants absorb nitrogen, phosphorus, sulfur, potassium, calcium, magnesium, iron, manganese, zinc, copper, molybdenum, boron, and chlorine from the soil. Nutrients not only need to be present in the soil, they need to be in a form that plants can use. Soil pH is one factor that affects nutrient availability. The most reliable way to determine a soil's fertility is to test a soil sample in a lab or to test a sample at home. (*See* SOIL SAMPLE) A report from a soil-testing lab will indicate the availability of major nutrients and most also will make recommendations on fertilizer and other amendments. Home test results usually are less accurate than laboratory results. *See* SOIL, pH

fertilization The union of a male and female gamete, which is a fertile reproductive cell of either sex, to produce a fertilized egg, called a zygote.

fertilizer Any material that provides nutrients to plants. *See* ORGANIC FERTILIZER,

CHEMICAL FERTILIZER, INORGANIC FERTILIZER, SOIL AMENDMENT

fertilizer analysis The percentage of elements in a bag of fertilizer that are immediately available, usually expressed as the NPK (nitrogen-phosphorus-potassium) ratio. A fertilizer with a 5-10-5 ratio contains 5 percent nitrogen by weight, 10 percent phosphate (a form of phosphorus), and 5 percent potash (a form of potassium). The remainder of the material in the bag consists of filler or other elements in the compounds with the nitrogen, phosphorus, and potassium that are not immediately available to plants. Because organic fertilizers release their nutrients slowly, they contain a significant amount of nutrients that will be released over time—from months to years depending on the material—but that are not immediately available and thus are not included in the NPK ratio.

fertilizer, balanced *See* BALANCED FERTILIZER

festoon An ornamental garland strung from point to point. Vines can be trained as festoons if they are grown on strings, wires, or chains that run between posts, columns, or trees. The term festooning also refers to bending shoots or branches over so they are in a more horizontal position in order to control vigor or induce flowering. In this technique, also called bending, the branches are held in place with weights or ties.

fetid Having an unpleasant odor. Carrion flowers (*Stapelia* spp.) are pollinated by flies and bear fetid blooms to attract them.

fibers *See* SCLERENCHYMA

fibrous Having a somewhat woody but threadlike texture. Containing fibers.

fibrous roots A branched, wide-spreading root system in which all of the branches are more or less the same size. Fibrous-rooted plants are especially effective for erosion control, because they branch heavily and help hold the soil in place. They can have thin roots or thick, fleshy ones. Grasses and lettuce are two examples of fibrous-rooted plants.

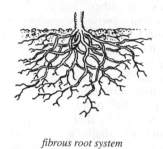

fibrous root system

fiddlehead The coiled, emerging leaf of a fern frond. Also called a crosier. The fiddleheads of some ferns are edible. *See* CROSIER

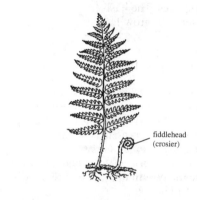

fiddlehead (crosier)

fiddle-shaped *See* PANDURATE

-fidus A suffix meaning deeply cut, or cleft. It is usually combined with a prefix indicating a number. Bifidus means twice cut, for example.

filament The threadlike stalk that supports an anther, which is the pollen-bearing portion of a flower. Together, a filament and anther make up the stamen, which is the male reproductive organ of a flower.

filamentous Made up of or bearing filaments.

filiform Threadlike, or resembling a filament. Filiform leaves are round or rounded in cross section and are flexible rather than rigid. Love-in-a-mist (*Nigella damascena*) has filiform leaf segments, which give the foliage a feathery appearance. *See also* FILAMENT

fimbriate Fringed. Edged or fringed with hairs or hairlike structures (called fimbrilla), which are extensions of the leaf blade. This term is commonly used to describe the edge, or margin, of a leaf or leaflet. The bracts (modified scalelike leaves) that are borne around the base of bachelor's buttons (*Centaurea dealbata*) have fimbriate-pectinate (comblike) edges.

fimbriate leaf margin

fines herbes A mix of fresh, chopped herbs consisting of chervil, parsley, thyme, and tarragon. *Fines herbes* are used in egg dishes and cheese sauces, and are added at the very last minute, just before the dish is served.

finished compost *See* COMPOST

fire blight A bacterial disease that causes leaves to turn brown, die, and cling to branches, and stem tips to suddenly turn black and wilt. Afflicted stems develop oozing, reddish brown stem cankers that later turn brown and dry. Fire blight attacks many rose-family plants, including apples, firethorns (*Pyracantha* spp.), and pears, and spreads quickly in warm wet weather. After planting resistant cultivars, pruning is the best control. Prune out and destroy diseased shoots as soon as you see them, cutting at least 6 inches below the visibly damaged area. Disinfect shears in a bleach solution (1 part bleach to 9 parts water) between cuts. Cut down and destroy severely infected

plants in winter. To prevent problems, spray with bordeaux mix when the tree is dormant or with streptomycin just prior to bloom and when plants are in full bloom.

first fall frost *See* FROST DATES

first frost date *See* FROST DATES

fish emulsion An organic fertilizer consisting of filtered, stabilized fish solubles, which are by-products of fish protein concentrates used by makers of animal food. It contains between 4 and 5 percent nitrogen, 1 percent phosphate, and 1 percent potassium.

fish meal An organic fertilizer consisting of dried, pulverized fish parts. It contains about 5 to as much as 10 percent nitrogen, 5 to 15 percent total phosphate, and 2 to 3 percent total potassium.

fishtail weeder *See* ASPARAGUS FORK

fissile Splitting open easily.

fistulose Cylindrical or tubular and hollow. The leaves of many onions (*Allium* spp.) are fistulose.

fixative A plant or animal substance that keeps essential oils from evaporating and thus helps keep potpourris, sachets, and pomanders fragrant. Orris root, the ground rhizomes of *Iris germanica* var. *florentina*, is a common fixative. Other plant-derived fixatives include benzoin, rose attar, dried and ground rosemary, sandalwood, storax, sweet flag, tonka beans, and vetiver root. Animal-derived fixatives include ambergris, civet, and musk.

flabellate Fan- or broadly wedge-shaped. Ginkgo trees (*Ginkgo biloba*) have flabellate leaves.

flabellate leaf

flaccid Limp, flabby, or weak.

flagellate Bearing long, slender runners. Sarmentose.

flagelliform Whiplike. Long, thin, and flexible.

flaming A relatively new organic technique for controlling weeds by searing them with a flame from a propane torch specially adapted for garden use. Flaming is best on young, soft-stemmed weeds, and is especially useful for controlling weeds in paved areas or in gravel. Garden flamers are available from several mail-order companies.

flange A rim or edge that sticks out of another surface.

flat A shallow tray that holds pots. Flats can be open at the bottom, to allow water to drain away, or they can hold water. Flats are commonly used to hold pots of seedlings or cuttings that are rooting, but also can be filled with soil and directly sown or filled with cuttings. Traditionally, flats were constructed of wood or wood with a hardware cloth bottom in various sizes. Today, the most common flats are made of plastic, and the standard size is roughly 12 inches wide by 20 inches long.

flathead rake *See* RAKES

flavescent Nearly yellow or becoming yellow.

flea beetles Tiny, dark beetles that jump quickly, somewhat like fleas, when disturbed. The adults chew tiny holes in leaves, and are especially problematic early in the season. The tiny grubs feed on roots. To prevent these pests from damaging plants, protect vegetable crops with floating row covers until midsummer. Spray seriously infested plants with neem, pyrethrins, or rotenone. Apply parasitic nematodes to the soil to control larvae.

fleshy Firm, but soft and juicy. Easy to cut. This term is commonly applied to fruits, but also is used to describe the leaves of succulent plants. It is also used to describe storage organs or roots of plants that grow from bulbs, corms, thick rhizomes, tubers, or tuberous roots. *See* SUCCULENT

flexous, flexuose Bent in alternate, opposite directions. This term is used to describe a stem with a zig-zagged shape.

floating-leaved plants A general term for all plants that grow in a water garden with the leaves floating on the surface. Some grow in the soil (or in containers) at the bottom of the pond; others float on the surface. Floating-leaved plants include water lilies (*Nymphaea* spp.), floating heart (*Nymphoides* spp.), and four-leaved water clover (*Marsilea mutica*).

floating row covers *See* ROW COVERS

floccose Covered with tufts of dense woolly hairs that give a feltlike texture. The hairs are easy to rub off and come off in clumps.

flora A collective term for all the plants of a particular region or era. A published work that systematically covers all the plants of a particular region also is called a flora. Flora is also the Roman goddess of flowers.

floral diagram A schematic diagram used by botanists to show the arrangement and number of the parts in a flower. Floral diagrams are drawn looking at a flower from the top and show its composition, not its shape. These diagrams use standard symbols for the basic parts (sepals, petals, stamens, and pistils) and also show bracts or other parts that may be part of the flower. Lines are drawn between parts (such as petals) that are fused together, and the ovary is commonly shown in cross section to indicate the position of the carpels.

floral envelope A collective term that refers to the calyx, or sepals, and the corolla, or petals, of a flower. The perianth.

floral foam A water-absorbing product used in flower arrangements to hold flowers in place that can be cut to fit any container, and that stems can penetrate easily. It can be jammed into a container or secured with tape. Oasis is the most common brand of floral foam. There also are products that are similar but designed to be used with dried arrangements.

floral formula A shorthand method that botanists use to record the parts of a flower. A floral formula lists the basic plant parts in the following order: calyx, corolla, androecium (stamens), gynoecium (pistil or carpels). These formulas can be listed in numbers only—5-5-10-1 indicates a flower with five sepals, five petals, ten stamens, and one ovary, for example. Or, letters can be used to indicate each plant part as follows: K = calyx, C = corolla, A = androecium, and G = gynoecium. In that case, the floral formula for the flower in the example would be K5, C5, A10, G1. A variety of other symbols can be used to indicate other characteristics, such as ovary position, whether the flower is actinomorphic, and so forth.

floral pick A thin, 2- to 4-inch-long piece of wood, sharpened at one end, with a length of thin wire at the other end. These are attached to short stemmed flowers by wrapping the wire around the stem. They are especially useful with dried flowers, which often have brittle stems that break off. Stab the sharp end into the base of the arrangement.

floral pick

floral preservative Chemicals added to the water in flower arrangements that help prolong the vase life of cut flowers. Commer-

cial preservatives are available at florists and craft stores that carry florist's supplies. For a homemade preservative, combine 3 heaping teaspoons of sugar and 2 tablespoons of white vinegar per quart of water. Some gardeners simply add lemon-lime soda (not diet soda) to water in arrangements instead.

floral shovel *See* SHOVEL

floral tube The long, tube-shaped base of a perianth, which is the collective term that refers to the calyx, or sepals, and the corolla, or petals, of a flower.

flore pleno Double flowered.

floret A very small flower. This term is most commonly used to refer to the flowers that make up a head or daisylike inflorescence of members of the aster family, Asteraceae. *See also* RAY FLORET, DISK FLORET, HEAD

floricane A second-year shoot or cane of a bramble fruit such as blackberry or raspberry (*Rubus* spp.), which bears flowers and fruit. The term floricane is for second-year canes only; they are called primocanes during their first season, when they do not flower. Since floricanes die after they have fruited, cut them to the ground soon after harvest. *See* BRAMBLES

floriculture The science and art of growing flowers, including cut flowers and pot plants.

floriferous Strictly speaking, this term means flowering bearing, but it is commonly used to indicate a plant that bears flowers in abundance.

florist's tape *See* TAPING

florist's wire *See* WIRING

-florus A suffix referring to flowers. Uniflorus means bearing one flower, for example.

flower The reproductive part or organ of a plant, which consists of pistils (the female reproductive organs) and/or stamens (the male reproductive organs). A flower with both pistils and stamens is called a perfect or bisexual flower. One with only female reproductive organs is a pistillate flower; with only male reproductive organs, it is a staminate flower. Typically, flowers also have a calyx (sepals) and a corolla (petals), collectively called a perianth. A flower that has all four parts—pistils, stamens, calyx, corolla—is called a complete flower.

flower bed *See* BED

flower border *See* BORDER

flowerhead A short, dense cluster of flowers, or inflorescence, that has individual flowers, or florets, attached to a common point on the flower stem. *See also* HEAD

flowering glume *See* GLUME

flowering plant *See* ANGIOSPERM

flower pick *See* FLORAL PICK

fluid extract A concentrated herbal preparation that is similar to a tincture but considerably more potent. Fluid extracts are made by combining herbs with alcohol and are sold commercially.

flush This term is used to refer to flowers, fruit, or new shoots that are produced in abundance over a short period of time. Many roses, for example, produce a main flush of bloom in early summer followed by several smaller flushes or intermittent bloom later in the season.

flute budding A technique similar to patch budding, but the patch of bark removed from the stock reaches nearly around the stem, leaving a small section of bark intact. The patch from the budstick is cut to match and otherwise treated like a patch bud. *See* patch bud, budding

fluted Having grooves or furrows on the surface.

focal point, focus The center of attention in a design. The eye of the viewer is drawn first to a design's focal point, and then moves out to take in the rest of the composition. Effective focal points should be clear and unambiguous, and should set the tone of the design. In a garden, the focal point could be a birdbath or sundial at the center of a formal garden or a particularly bold plant. In a flower arrangement, the focal point usually is a cluster of flowers that commonly fall just at or above the top of the container.

foliaceous Leaflike. Bearing leaves or pertaining to leaves.

foliage A collective term for all the leaves of a plant.

foliar Pertaining to leaves.

foliar feeding A technique for applying dilute fertilizer in which the material is sprayed onto the leaves of the plant. Foliar feeding is used to give plants a quick nutritional boost during the growing season.

foliate, -foliate Bearing leaves. Also a suffix referring to leaves. It is usually combined with a prefix indicating a number. Bifoliate means two-leaved, for example.

foliolate Bearing leaflets. Often the number of leaflets is added as a prefix, as in trifoliate, for example.

foliose Leafy.

follicle A dry fruit that opens at maturity (is dehiscent) along a single line and is derived from one carpel, which is the organ containing the ovules where seeds develop once the flower is fertilized. Milkweeds (*Asclepias* spp.) bear follicles, which commonly are called pods.

follicle

folly A garden structure that has no function and is designed only to catch the eye of garden visitors. They are often odd-looking and can take many forms, including towers, pyramids, or artificial ruins.

forb Any herbaceous plant other than grass. This term is commonly used to refer to the plants in a meadow or prairie other than grass. It is also used to categorize green manure or cover crops.

forcing The process of inducing a plant to grow and flower or produce fruit by manipulating its environment. Hardy spring bulbs are especially easy to force, and forcing is a great way to enjoy these plants indoors in winter. To force bulbs, start with healthy, top-size bulbs, a selection of clay bulb pans or azalea pots (both of which are shallower than normal pots), and potting soil. Cover the hole in the bottom of each pot with a curved pot shard so water can drain out but the potting medium stays in. Spread a layer of potting medium on the bottom of the pots, and then set the bulbs so their tips will be just at or slightly above the surface of the medium. Pack the bulbs in next to one another for the best show. Fill the pots almost to the rim with medium and water them thoroughly. The bulbs then require a 3 $1/2$- to 4-month-long period of cold, but above-freezing temperatures (35 to 40°F) to grow roots. During this period the medium should remain moist but not wet. Set the pots in a cold frame, an unheated garage, a root cellar, or even a refrigerator for this period. After that, bring them indoors and set them in a dark, cool place (55 to 60°F) for about a week. Then force them either under lights or on windowsills in a cool place (65°F days and 60°F nights). If you plan on moving forced bulbs to the garden, feed them every other time you water. After they have bloomed, set the pots in a sheltered corner outdoors after the last spring frost date. Once the foliage has turned yellow, plant the bulbs in the garden. Forced bulbs may take a season or two to resume blooming. Stems of woody plants also can be forced. Early-blooming species like forsythias, apples, pussy willows, some azaleas, and flowering cherries are easiest.

Cut branches in mid- to late winter (the best time depends on the plant you are forcing) and slit or crush the ends of the stems. Stand them in a deep container of water at room temperature (70°F or so) for 24 hours, and then move them to a cooler spot (60°F) until the flowers begin to open. Replace the water every few days, and recut the stem ends weekly. Misting every other day also helps keep the forced branches plump.

forged A construction technique used in making high-quality gardening tools in which a solid steel bar is rolled over dies, or molds, to shape it. This ensures that the part of the tool that receives maximum stress is thickest and allows the metal to be tapered down where a thin, sharp blade is required. Also called tempered, heat-treated, or drop-forged. Forged tools are much stronger than stamped tools: Quality digging, cultivating, and cutting tools all are made of forged construction. Forged tools do cost more than stamped ones, but are much longer lasting. With proper care, they should last a lifetime.

forged socket construction *See* SOLID SOCKET CONSTRUCTION

fork A tool designed for digging, scooping, or both depending on the design, that has from two to ten or more tines, or prongs. The sturdiest of the digging-type forks is an English garden fork, which has four tines that are square in cross section with pointed tips. They are ideal for digging in clay soil (an advantage forks have over spades in this regard is that clay soil doesn't stick to the tines), double digging, and harvesting root crops. Spading or digging forks are lighter in weight and feature less heavy-duty construction than English garden forks, but still are useful digging tools for turning over garden beds. They have four tines that taper to a point and are either oblong or triangular in cross section. Of these, spading forks are somewhat lighter in weight than digging forks, and often are made of stamped construction. A border fork is about two-thirds the size of a standard fork, and is ideal for gardeners of small stature. Forks designed for scooping materials such as hay, manure, or compost have rounded tines: Historically hay forks had only two or three tines, but standard models have from four to six today. They are ideal for turning compost, spreading straw mulch, and also harvesting root crops.

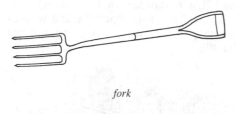

fork

forked Divided or branched into two equal branches; also referred to as crested, it is used to describe ferns that have frond tips and/or the tips of the primary leaflets (pinnae) divided or cut one or more times. The forked tips can be fairly flat or they can be congested to create a tassel-like appearance. Gardeners have selected and named many of these forms.

fork hoe *See* HOE

forking Digging soil, moving materials, such as compost, or incorporating materials into the soil with a fork.

-form A suffix meaning having the form of, similar to. Racemiform means bearing flowers that resemble racemes but do not have the true structure of a raceme, for example.

form, forma A taxonomic category distinguishing a group of naturally occurring plants sharing minor characteristics that set them apart from other individuals in the species but do not make them distinct enough to be recognized as a botanical variety. Forms usually are sporadically distributed in the wild—a white-flowered plant in a group of pink-flowered ones, for example. Like botanical varieties, forms are given latinized names, and the name of a form is set in italics and preceded by the abbreviation "f" or the word forma. For example, *Digitalis purpurea* f. *albiflora* is a white-flowered form of common foxglove (*Digitalis purpurea*).

formal garden A garden design style that features a clearly patterned, strongly visible layout using geometric shapes such as squares, rectangles, circles, and ovals. Paths are laid out in straight lines or along classic curves. Garden elements, and even plants, are symmetrically balanced—with matched flower beds or plants on either side of a central walkway arranged in a mirror-image fashion, for example, or with matching blocks or clumps of a particular plant repeated at predictable intervals. Hedges are commonly sheared to form geometric shapes. While most formal gardens use different elements sparsely—building materials and plants, for example—they are repeated throughout the design to give it unity. Formal gardens commonly feature classic materials such as brick, cut stone, and crushed gravel, as well as details such as stone benches, sundials, or statues. A formal design is balanced and restful to look at. *See also* INFORMAL GARDEN

formal hedge A hedge sheared into a geometric shape such as a rectangle or ball. When shearing a formal hedge (or pruning any hedge, for that matter) keep in mind that the hedge should be slightly wider at the bottom than at the top so that light can reach the lower branches. Otherwise, they tend to die out at the base. Privets (*Ligustrum* spp.) and boxwoods (*Buxus* spp.) can be maintained as formal hedges.

foundation planting A planting along the foundation of a house originally used to hide the unattractive foundations of modern-day houses. Typical foundation plantings consist of evergreens sheared into unattractive, gumdrop-like shapes. For a more natural, lower maintenance option, consider a mix of deciduous and evergreen trees and shrubs (dwarf cultivars are best because they will not outgrow their site) along with groundcovers, perennials, and annuals.

four-armed cordon Also called a "double-U cordon," this is a tree, usually a fruit tree, that has four main parallel arms, or branches, and essentially is trained to grow in a single plane. A four-armed cordon is trained the same way a double cordon is, but during the first or second season, a second arm is selected and trained on either side of the trunk to form a pair of U-shaped arms on either side.

four-ranked *See* DECUSSATE

foveate Covered with small pits, called fovea.

frame saw *See* PRUNING SAW

framework The permanent branch structure of a tree, especially fruit trees. Also, the elements of a garden and where they are located. *See also* BONES

free Separate or not attached. This term commonly is used to describe dissimilar plant parts that are not attached, such as the filaments of anthers that are not attached to the petals. The term distinct is used to refer to similar plant parts that are separate.

free draining *See* SHARP DRAINAGE

freeze-free period *See* GROWING SEASON

French intensive gardening *See* INTENSIVE GARDENING

French layering Also called continuous layering, this is a variation of mound layering (*See* MOUND LAYERING) in which shoots are mounded over and induced to produce roots, but not the entire plant. To mound layer, select a stem in spring, and fasten along the soil surface with U-shaped wire pins. Mound loose soil over the stem as you would for a mound layer up to a depth of 6 inches. Check in late summer or early fall for signs of roots and either sever and dig them up or rebury and check again in spring.

friable Soil with a crumbly structure that holds together if compressed but crumbles easily is said to be friable, or to have good tilth. *See* TILTH, SOIL STRUCTURE

fringed *See* FIMBRIATE

frog To florists and flower arrangers a frog isn't necessarily a water-loving amphibian; it's a useful tool that's set in the bottom of an arrangement to hold flowers in place. Frogs are made of heavy metal and consist of a base with pins that stick up and hold flower stems in place. Also called a pinholder. In toolmaking parlance, a frog is the open-backed tube of a stamped tool that is bent around the handle.

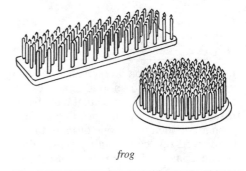

frog

frond A leaf of a fern. Also commonly used to refer to any large compound leaf, such as a palm frond.

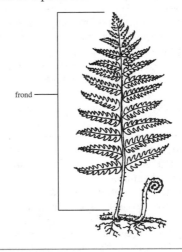

frond

frost dates Gardeners mark time by the last spring and the first fall frosts of each season. They are the keys to scheduling seed-sowing and transplant dates. If you don't know your frost dates, which are average dates based on data collected by the National Climatic Data Center, ask your local Cooperative Extension agent.

The last spring frost date, also called the last frost date or the spring frost date, is the average last date gardeners can expect freezing temperatures. It is important to remember this is an average date. During a cool spring, frost can happen after this date; during a warm or early spring, the last frost can occur days and even weeks earlier. The first fall frost date, often simply called the first frost or the fall frost date, is the average date when freezing temperatures first damage or kill frost-sensitive crops such as basil or peppers. This, too, is an average. The actual frost date can occur before or after this date. Growing season length is the average number of days between these two dates. A killing frost occurs when temperatures drop low enough to kill even cold-tolerant perennials and vegetables. Seeds for most annuals are sown in relation to the date of the average last spring frost. To determine the sowing date for a particular plant, count back the recommended number of weeks (on the seed packet or in a reference book) from your average spring frost date. Marigolds and tomatoes are sown indoors 6 to 8 weeks before that date and transplanted outdoors after it, for example. Petunias and geraniums, which take longer from seed, are sown indoors 10 to 12 weeks before the last frost. Other annuals are sown outdoors on or before that date. Count back from the first fall frost date to schedule sowing dates for fall crops of vegetables that tolerate cool weather or to schedule when to transplant biennials or perennials. They should generally be in place 4 to 6 weeks before the first frost date to give them time to put down roots before the onset of winter. To keep track of what you want to sow when, jot the names of plants to sow on a particular date on a calendar. Note outdoor sowing dates as well as dates when you think plants will be ready for transplanting. Keep track of when you need to sow biennials or fall crops of vegetables on the same calendar—early- to midsummer are common times to start these seeds. *See* GROWING SEASON

frost-free period *See* GROWING SEASON

frost heaving Alternate cycles of freezing and thawing that cause plant crowns and roots to be pushed up out of soil over winter. Newly planted specimens are most susceptible. Try to finish planting about 6 weeks before the first fall frost to give plants time to grow roots that will help them withstand frost heaving. Mulch at planting time to keep the soil warm; this allows roots to grow longer into the fall. Inspect the garden regularly over winter during warm spells to look for signs of frost heaving. Cover plants have heaved up with loose soil or mulch, or simply re-plant them.

frost pocket An area that characteristically has later spring frosts and earlier fall frosts than the surrounding area. Cold air sinks and it will collect at the bottom of a slope or on the uphill side of a hedge, building, or fence, creating a frost pocket. In spring and fall this sinking air can create a localized area of below-freezing temperatures that can damage susceptible plants. When peaches or other fruit trees with tender buds are planted at the bottom of a slope where frost collects, they are easily damaged in spring, even when plants on higher ground (up the slope) are not. A vegetable garden located in a frost pocket will have a shorter season that one that is not.

fruit An ovary that has ripened along with any parts that are attached to it. The seed-bearing organ of a plant.

fruit picker Essentially a cloth bag fastened on a rim that holds the bag open and attaches to a long pole. A fruit picker makes it easy to harvest out-of-reach tree fruits without resorting to a ladder. For a homemade option, attach a small basket or can to a pole. Fill the fruit-catching container partway with a soft rag to cushion the fall of the fruit.

frutescent, fruticose Shrubby or becoming shrubby. Bearing stems and branches but lacking a main trunk.

fry Baby fish

fugacious Ephemeral, transitory. Withering or falling off quickly.

full-blown A flower that is fully open.

full sun Ideally, this means 10 hours or more per day of direct, uninterrupted sunlight, although many plants recommended for full sun will perform very well with 8 hours of direct sun daily.

fulvous, fulvid Tawny or yellow-brown in color.

fungicide A substance used to control disease-causing fungi. Baking soda spray is a safe, effective homemade fungicide. Mix teaspoon baking soda per quart of water, and add a teaspoon of liquid dish soap to make the solution stick to foliage. Antitranspirants have fungicidal properties, but actually act as barriers (or physical controls) on plant leaves. *See* SULFUR, BORDEAUX MIX, COPPER for more on organically acceptable fungicides.

fungus, *pl.* **fungi** Beneficial or disease-causing plants that lack chlorophyll. Beneficial fungi help break down organic matter in soil as well as in compost. (*See* SOIL MICROORGANISMS) Disease-causing ones are responsible for black spot, molds, mildews, and a host of other garden problems.

funiculus, funicle The stalk by which the immature seed is attached to the placenta in an ovary.

funnelform Funnel-shaped. A flower that is narrow and tube-shaped at the base and widens into a flaring, funnel-like shape. Morning glories (*Ipomoea tricolor*) and petunias (*Petunia × hybrida*) have funnelform corollas (petals).

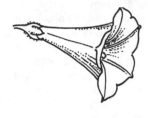

funnelform flower

furcate, -furcate Forked, with prong-like lobes. Also a suffix meaning branched or forked. Trifurcate means divided into three forks or branches, for example.

furfuraceous Covered with soft, flaky scales.

furrowed Veins that are sunken into the surface.

fuscous Blackish or dusky in color.

fused This term is used to describe parts that are joined together but normally are separate.

fusiform Spindle-shaped. Swollen in the middle and tapered at both ends.

galeate Helmet-shaped. Bearing a hollow, arched, or domed petal called a galea. The flowers of monkshoods (*Aconitum* spp.) are galeate.

galeate flower

gall Essentially a tumor, swelling, or other abnormal growth. Galls can infest leaves, stems, crown, roots, and other plant parts and come in many shapes, sizes, and colors. They are common symptoms of diseases spread by insect vectors. Plants also form galls in response to insects that lay eggs in stems or leaves.

gallery Also called a tunnel, a gallery is a series of arches over which vines or other plants are trained to create a tunnel-like effect. Galleries usually are fairly light structures built of metal or lath, but also can be constructed of wood.

gallery

gamete A fertile reproductive cell of either sex that contains half the number of chromosomes in a normal cell (is haploid) and is capable of uniting with another gamete to produce a fertilized egg, called a zygote. The zygote has the original number of chromosomes, and is capable of developing into a new individual.

gametophyte The gamete-producing generation or stage in a plant's lifecycle. This generation is haploid, meaning it contains half the number of chromosomes in a normal cell and consists of male and female gametophytes. Once the male gametophyte fertilizes the female, it creates the diploid sporophyte generation, which has the full component of chromosomes. In flowering plants (angiosperms) the gametophyte generation takes place within a single flower: Pollen grains form pollen tubes, which produce the male gametes, and the embryo sac within a flower's ovule(s) produce the female gametes. Once the male and female gametes are united through fertilization, they produce a diploid zygote, which develops into a seed. In nonflowering plants such as ferns, the haploid gametes grow on their own. In ferns, they develop into a small ($^1/_4$-inch-wide) heart-shaped plant called a prothallus. The prothallus bears male and female structures on the underside (soil side) called antheridia (male) and archegonia (female) that produce sperm and eggs on the same plant. The sperm swim on a film of water to reach the eggs (this is why high humidity is so important when growing ferns from spores). Once fertilized, the eggs grow into the sporophyte, or spore-producing, generation, which are the ferns we know and grow in gardens. The term gametophyte also is used to refer to the heart-shaped prothallus itself.

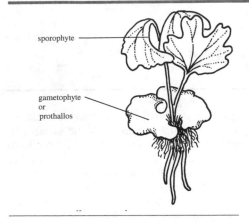

sporophyte

gametophyte
or
prothallos

gamo- A prefix meaning the uniting or joining of parts that are alike.

gamopetalous With petals that are united, or at least partially joined by their edges, or margins, to form a tubular or funnel-shaped base. Petunias (*Petunia* × *hybrida*), flowering tobacco (*Nicotiana alata*), and trumpet vine (*Campsis radicans*) all bear gamopetalous flowers. Also called sympetalous.

gamopetalous flower

gamophyllous Bearing leaves or leaflike plant parts that are united, or at least partially joined by their edges, or margins.

gamosepalous Bearing sepals that are united, or at least partially joined by their edges, or margins.

gardener's gold *See* COMPOST

garden fork *See* FORK

garden house Any garden building that is designed solely for ornament or enjoying the garden at leisure.

garden room *See* OUTDOOR ROOM

garden shears *See* SHEARS, GARDEN

gator A sleevelike bag used to slowly water newly planted trees. Gators are fastened around the base of the trunk and filled with water, which drips slowly out of a few small holes in the bottom.

gazebo A freestanding structure that has a roof, open sides, and offers a comfortable, shady place in which to sit. Traditionally the term gazebo has been used for any structure designed to command a view of the landscape, including a separate garden house, a turret, or even a balcony or window projecting from a house.

geitonogamy Fertilization between two flowers that are on the same plant.

gelatinous Jellylike.

geminate Borne in pairs.

gemma A budlike, vegetative reproductive organ that detaches from the parent plant. Clubmosses (*Lycopodium* spp.) bear gemma, which are somewhat flaplike in appearance and are borne near the tips of the stem. These can be removed before they drop from the parent plant and grown in sphagnum moss for propagation.

gene A segment of a chromosome that functions as a hereditary unit.

-geneous A suffix meaning of a particular type or kind. Homogeneous means all the same kind, for example.

geniculate Having abrupt bends, like a knee.

geniculum A sharply bent kneelike joint.

genotype The genetic makeup of a plant or other organism. For information on two terms plant breeders commonly use to characterize the genotype of a particular plant, *see* HOMOZYGOUS, HETEROZYGOUS. *See also* PHENOTYPE

genus, *pl.* **genera** A group of plants with similar characteristics within a family. A genus can contain a single, very distinctive species such as ginkgo (*Ginkgo biloba*). More often, it contains a group of species that share similar characteristics. In text genus names always are capitalized and set in italics or underlined, for example, *Nandina, Narcissus, Papaver*. The generic, or genus, name is an essential part of any binomial and can be used alone or linked with a specific epithet or the name of a cultivar—*Nandina domestica* or *Nandina* 'Harbor Dwarf', for example. Genus names also can be abbreviated in text, usually the second time the name is used, for example, *Dicentra canadensis, D. eximia*.

geotextile A synthetic, woven or nonwoven fabric through which water can flow relatively freely. In the landscape, geotextiles are used to prevent erosion and as underlayment (*See* UNDERLAYMENT) to protect water garden liners from being punctured. They also are used as mulch. *See* MULCH

geotropism The movement of a plant or other organism in relation to gravity.

germ cell A cell that is primarily devoted to reproduction. This term is especially used to refer to sperm and egg cells, or gametes.

germination The process by which a seed grows into a seedling. To germinate, a seed first absorbs water, which softens cells and tissues within the seed coat and causes them to expand. Eventually, the seed coat breaks open, which allows even more water, as well as oxygen, to reach the embryonic plant inside. Stored food (starches, proteins, and fats) inside the seed is converted to sugars and amino acids that the embryo needs to grow. These substances are delivered to the meristematic tissue, which begins to lengthen. The seedling's root pushes down first, anchoring the plant and beginning to take up water and minerals by a process called osmosis. After that, the first shoot emerges from the soil, ending the germination process. For more information on seed sowing and germination, *see* EPIGEOUS GERMINATION, HYPOGEOUS GERMINATION, SEED, SEED SOWING

germination testing This technique is used to determine whether seeds are viable and will germinate, and also is useful for determining whether you should sow more thickly than usual to compensate for seed that has low viability. Germination testing works best on annuals and vegetables, which tend to sprout quickly. For most perennials, which tend to take longer, it is often easier to simply sow the seeds and see what comes up. To test the germination of a batch of seeds, spread 10 seeds on a damp paper towel, keeping them about 1 inch apart. Roll or fold up the paper towel, place it in a loosely closed plastic bag, and set the bag in a warm place. Use a separate bag for each type of seed and enclose a label with the name of the plant and the date "sown" or place several towels in a single bag and fold a label into each towel. After the normal number of days to germination (see the seed packet for this information; if you're not sure, begin checking in about a week), begin checking daily or every two days for signs of sprouting by unrolling or unfolding the towel. If more than seven of the seeds sprout, sow at the normal rate recommended on the seed packet. If less than that sprout, sow more thickly than usual. If no seedlings have sprouted several weeks after the normal germination time, the seed probably is no longer viable, or capable of germinating.

germ plasm A general term for the hereditary materials in cells (including chromosomes, genes, and other self-propagating tissue) that are transferred to offspring via reproductive cells. This term also is used to refer to the potential genetic resources of an entire population of plants, or a crop or species.

gibbous Swollen, enlarged, or pouched on one side, usually at the bottom. The term ventricose means the same thing, but is used to indicate a more pronounced swelling.

girdle, girdling Removing the bark all the way around the trunk of a tree or the stem of a shrub. Girdling interrupts the flow of nutrients through the phloem, and can stunt growth as well as damage and/or kill the plant. Rodents such as mice and voles can girdle plants, especially when mulch is piled up against the base of the trunk. Repeatedly ramming into a tree trunk with a lawnmower also causes girdling; thin-barked trees can be girdled with string trimmers. Mulching or covering the area around trees with groundcovers eliminates the need to trim close to trunks, thus keeping these implements away from tree trunks and avoiding this problem.

girdling root A root that spirals around the base of a trunk rather than extending outward. As the trunk expands, the girdling root tightens, pressing more closely against the trunk each year. Eventually, the trunk cannot expand any more and the root compresses the bark, limiting movement of nutrients and formation of new phloem tissue. Girdling roots usually are caused by improper container culture at the nursery or careless transplanting. Sometimes a girdling root is visible near the soil surface. Another telltale sign is a trunk that flares gracefully on one side but goes straight down on the other. Use a mallet and chisel to remove the offending root. Of course, the ideal time to prune girdling roots is at planting time, when it is easy to clip off all circling roots.

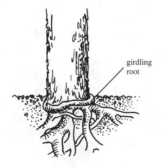

girdling root

glabrate, glabrescent Nearly hairless or becoming hairless at maturity.

glabrous Hairless, smooth. Most often used to describe leaf surfaces.

gladiate Swordlike or sword-shaped.

gland A small, often warty-looking plant part that sticks out from the surrounding surface and secretes a sticky or oily substance.

glandular Bearing glands, which are small, often warty-looking plant parts that secrete sticky or oily substances. Glandular hairs have glands at the tips that secrete such substances. Flowering tobaccos (*Nicotiana* spp.) and spider flowers (*Cleome hassleriana*) have glandular-hairy or glandular-pubescent leaves. Hay-scented ferns (*Dennstaedtia punctilobula*) have glandular hairs on their fronds that give them their characteristic haylike scent.

glasshouse A greenhouse glazed with glass. *See* GREENHOUSE

glaucous Covered with a whitish, blue-gray, or gray bloom, which is a waxy or powdery covering. On a glaucous leaf or other surface, the bloom can be rubbed off easily. Many blue-leaved hostas, including *Hosta sieboldiana* 'Elegans', 'Hadspen Blue', and 'Blue Umbrellas' have glaucous leaves, which are generally most pronounced in spring. The leaves gradually loose their blue hue as the season progresses and rains wash away the bloom.

globular, globose Spherical, or nearly so. This term is commonly used to describe three-dimensional organs such as fruits, but also can be used to describe the shape of a leaf. Also, globular is used to describe a double flower with a round or globelike shape formed by petals that curve inward. Also called spherical.

globular flower

glochidate Bearing barbed hairlike spines or bristles, called glochids, which are hooked down or backward at the tip. Many cacti, including prickly pears (*Opuntia* spp.) are glochidate. The glochids are often carried in clumps on areoles, which are small, well-defined areas on leaves or the surface of a cactus.

glomerate Densely or compactly clustered.

glume A papery or chaffy bract borne in pairs at the base of a grass or sedge spikelet, which is the basic unit of the flower clusters of members of the grass family (Poaceae) and the sedge family (Cyperaceae). The term is used for bracts that are sterile, meaning they are borne at the base of the spikelet but not directly under a flower. The bract that is borne directly under a flower is called the lemma or a fertile or flowering glume. The palea is an even smaller bract borne above the lemma on the stalk of the individual flower. The lemma partially encloses the palea, and together they enclose the individual flowers until the spikelet opens so it can be pollinated by the wind. The lemma and palea are forced apart by microscopic structures called lodicules. A spikelet is made up of two glumes plus one or more florets, which consist of a lemma, a palea, and the flower.

glume — glume

glutinous Sticky, gluey, or gummy. Covered with a sticky or gummy exudate.

glycerin A substance that can be used to preserve leaves and some types of flowers. Plant parts preserved using glycerin remain supple, but often change color; color will vary depending on when the material was collected. This method is most effective on leaves, and can be used to preserve colorful fall leaves, as well as some flowers, including bells-of-Ireland (*Moluccella laevis*), hydrangeas (*Hydrangea* spp.), as well as heaths and heathers (*Erica* spp. and *Calluna* spp.). To preserve stems, stand them in a solution of 1 part glycerin to 2 parts water for 2 or more weeks until glycerin begins to ooze out of the edges of the leaves. (Glycerine gradually replaces the water in leaves and flowers during this process.) During this time, occasionally wipe leaves with a damp cloth or one dipped in glycerine. Before standing woody stems in glycerin solution, crush the bottom 2 inches of the stems with a hammer to increase the amount of solution absorbed. You can also preserve individual leaves by immersing them in a 1-to-1 solution of glycerin and water. After about 2 weeks, blot up excess glycerine by pressing leaves preserved in this manner between sheets of newspaper topped by weights. Glycerin is available from biological supply companies and may also be available at craft stores or your local pharmacy. Glycerin-and-water solutions can be reused indefinitely.

goni-, gonia, -gonous A prefix or suffix meaning angled or angular. Goniocarpus means bearing angled fruits. Trigonous means three-angled, for example.

good bones *See* BONES

gooseneck hoe *See* HOE

gootee An Indian name for air layering. *See* AIR LAYERING

gourd A fleshy fruit that has one chamber, or locule, and many seeds. Gourds are characteristic of many species that belong to the gourd family (Cucurbitaceae). Bottle gourds (*Lagenaria* spp.) are large, vining plants that bear gourds that come in many different shapes and can be dried to make birdhouses or other objects.

graft chimera, graft hybrid A chimera formed by grafting two plants together that produce tissues that intermingle between stock and scion to create a "hybrid" with characteristics of both plants. The names of graft chimeras are preceded by a plus sign (+): +*Laburnocytisus* is created by grafting *Laburnum* and *Chamaecytisus*.

graft incompatibility *See* INCOMPATIBILITY

grafting Joining plants or plant parts together in such a way that the individual parts will unite and continue to grow as a single plant. Grafted plants consist of the upper portion, called the scion, and the lower portion, called the rootstock, stock, or understock. Grafting offers various benefits. It offers a way to propagate plants that do not root easily or reliably from cuttings. Scions that offer outstanding fruit or flowers may not have vigorous or adaptable root systems, and grafting makes it possible to improve on them. Depending on the species being grafted, rootstocks are available that tolerate heavy clay soil, resist soilborne diseases, or simply offer more vigor to speed the growth of a particular plant or ensure that it has a wide-spreading, vigorous root system. Fruit trees, especially apples, are commonly grafted onto dwarfing rootstocks that limit the mature size of the plant. (Rootstocks can be grown from seedlings or maintained as clones by vegetative propagation. *See* SEEDLING ROOTSTOCK, CLONAL ROOTSTOCK) Grafting also can be used to change the cultivar of fruit produced by a single tree. (*See* TOP-WORKING) Grafting commonly is used to create special forms of plants—weeping cherries or conifers, for example, as well as to propagate special cultivars of woody plants such as Japanese maples (*Acer palmatum*). Finally, grafting can be used to repair damaged plants. (*See* INARCHING, BRIDGE GRAFTING) Essentially, a graft union is a healed wound, and meristematic tissue is essential to making successful unions. To make a graft, the cambium of the scion is next to the cambium of the rootstock in such a way that it is held immobile. (Proper polarity is essential to forming a successful union; a scion inserted upside down will not graft to the stock. *See* POLARITY for details.) Temperature and

humidity around the joined surfaces need to be maintained to keep the exposed cells growing. When the graft union begins to heal, the outer exposed cells of both stock and scion produce parenchyma cells that intermingle to form callus tissue. (Cambium layers do not have to be exactly "matched" or placed directly against one another to form a successful union; they only need to be close enough together so that the parenchyma cells formed when they begin to heal can intermingle.) Next, some of the interlocking parenchyma cells differentiate to form new cambium cells that interlock stock and scion, and these new cells form vascular tissue to allow water and nutrients to pass between the two parts. Once that occurs, growth resumes in the scion. A few factors prevent the formation of a successful graft union. Some plants are easier to graft than others: Apples and pears are easy to graft and yield a high percentage of successful unions, while oaks (*Quercus* spp.), beeches (*Fagus* spp.), and hickories (*Carya* spp.) are difficult to graft and generally yield a high percentage of failures. Closely related plants are easiest to graft. A scion from a fruit or nut tree usually will graft easily onto another plant of the same clone or a different clone. Grafting within members of a species also is successful in many cases—oranges, grapefruit, and other citrus trees (*Citrus* spp.) can be grafted onto one another, for example, and apricots (*Prunus armeniaca*) and plums (*P.* × *domestica* and *P. salicina*) onto peaches (*P. persica*). Smooth cuts made in a single stroke with a sharp knife are essential to success because they ensure good contact between the cambium layers of stock and scion. Temperature and humidity also affect success. Turgid cells in well-watered plants form callus tissue more effectively than ones that are wilting, and temperatures that are too hot or too cold also affect callus formation. Temperatures above 40°F and below 90°F favor callus formation. Grafts usually are waxed or wrapped to keep them from drying out during the healing process. In most cases, scions are dormant when they are grafted; they are normally collected in winter and stored. *See* SCION for information on selecting, storing, and using scions. In general, the best time to graft plants is in spring, from just before buds begin to swell to during the time they break, or open, because callus tissue forms most quickly then. Scions or rootstocks infected with viruses, fungi, insects, or other pests or pathogens also will prevent or delay the formation of a strong graft union. Graft incompatibility is a potential problem. *See* INCOMPATIBILITY for details. After grafting, remove shoots that arise from the stock. For information on individual grafting techniques, *see* APPROACH GRAFTING (spliced), BARK GRAFTING, BRIDGE GRAFTING, CLEFT GRAFT, BUDDING, CHIP BUDDING, DOUBLE WORKING, SIDE GRAFTING, SIDE-TONGUE GRAFT, SIDE-VENEER GRAFT, SPLICE GRAFT, INARCHING, INLAY APPROACH GRAFT, PATCH BUDDING, TONGUED APPROACH GRAFT, WHIP-AND-TONGUE GRAFT. *See also* SCION, GRAFTING KNIFE, GRAFTING WAX, NURSERYMEN'S ADHESIVE TAPE, RUBBER BUDDING STRIPS

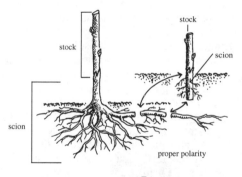

proper polarity

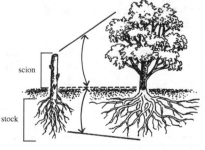

grafting

grafting knife A knife that has a straight, very sharp blade and is used for making cuts in grafting.

grafting, natural *See* NATURAL GRAFTING

grafting wax Special wax used to seal newly cut graft unions in order to hold in moisture and protect newly forming callus tissue in both stock and scion. Grafting wax also seals out disease-causing organisms such as fungi. There are commercially available formulations of grafting wax designed to be applied hot as well as cold; hand waxes, which are pliable are available as well (hot and cold waxes are in liquid form when applied).

graft union The point on a stem where stock and scion were joined. The graft union usually is a knobby place on the trunk. When buried below the soil, roots may form on the scion, above the union. Shoots that form from the stock, which emerge from below the union, should promptly be removed at their point or origin.

grain A collective term for cereal crops such as wheat, barley, or sorghum. Botanically, grains are the type of fruit called a caryopsis, meaning they are dry fruits that bear a single seed that doesn't open along definite lines when ripe and has a seed coat that is fused to the wall of the fruit inside.

granular Having very small granules or grains. Grainy in texture.

granular fertilizer A fertilizer sold in dry, or granular, form. Granular fertilizers are easy to apply by broadcasting or top-dressing.

grass, cool season *See* COOL-SEASON GRASS

grass shears A tool designed to trim grass around rocks, trees, and along sidewalks and other edges to produce a neat, manicured cut. Modern models have various features that reduce pressure on the wrist, so experiment with them. Long-handled versions are available, too, making it possible to trim without stooping.

grass, warm season *See* WARM-SEASON GRASS

gravitational water Water that moves through soil in response to gravity. It either drains away completely or becomes capillary water once it reaches a layer where the soil is not saturated.

gray mold This fungal disease, also known as botrytis blight, produces gray-brown spots or streaks on leaves, buds, and flowers that may have visible woolly fungal growth. Fruits develop a fuzzy gray mold, then rot. To control gray mold, remove and destroy infected plant parts. Thin crowded stems and space new plants properly for good air circulation. Handle fruit gently to prevent bruising.

greenhouse A structure designed for the cultivation of plants and large enough for a gardener to walk in. A greenhouse is covered, or glazed, with either glass or various plastics.

green manure A crop that is grown and then dug or tilled into the soil to increase soil fertility and organic matter. Green manure crops that are sown in fall protect the soil over winter, essentially acting as cover crops. Common green manure crops include alfalfa, clovers, vetches, soybeans, annual ryegrass, buckwheat, and winter rye. Sowing times vary depending on the crop, but there are green manure crops for spring and fall sowing (some can be sown either time). Plan to till or dig under the plants from 3 to 4 weeks before you transplant vegetables or other plants.

greensand An organic fertilizer that is a mined mineral deposited on ancient seabeds. It contains about 7 percent potassium and many other minerals. Greensand also is useful for loosening clay soil.

greenwood cutting A cutting taken from very lush, soft tips of new growth, immediately after the flush of spring and early summer growth has slowed down. They are treated like softwood cuttings, and the terms often are used interchangeably. *See* SOFTWOOD CUTTING

grex A collective name for all plants derived from crossings between the same species, usually the same two species, but sometimes more. This term is used almost exclusively by orchid hybridizers and grex names are set in roman type with a capitalized first letter, *Paphiopedilum* Maudiae, for example. A specific cultivar name can be attached to the name of a particular grex—*P.* Maudiae 'Coloratum'.

grid A design device that uses a grid of squares of a unique dimension to guide and establish a garden or landscape design. The exact dimension of the grid squares is determined by a unique feature of the house or property. The grid square for a given project usually is taken from a measurement on the house—the width of the central entryway, an ell at the back of the house, or the width of a porch bay, for example. The grid is laid over the plot plan, much like a sheet of graph paper, and lined up in a pleasing, logical way with the house. Its squares are then used as the basis for establishing elements in the landscape or garden design. Using a grid ensures that house and garden are closely linked in a design because its dimensions spring from and are oriented to the house. A grid also ensures a pleasing sense of proportion between house and garden: Elements such as patios, lawn areas, or garden beds occupy one, two, or more grid spaces. Landscapes and gardens designed with a grid don't necessarily feature squares and rectangles; the grid squares also are useful as a guide for drawing curves and other free-form shapes.

grotto An ornamental, usually artificial, garden feature designed and constructed to resemble a cave (although a grotto can be an aboveground structure). Grottoes often were quite fanciful and elaborately decorated with rocks, statues, and fountains.

ground cover Plants used to cover the soil surface, ideally densely enough to prevent weeds from germinating. Ground covers protect the soil surface from compaction by raindrops, and their matted roots prevent erosion. They also are low-maintenance alternatives to lawn grasses. In a landscape, sweeping beds of ground covers unify elements and can be used to soften hard edges. Ground covers usually are low growing—from completely prostrate up to about 3 feet or so in height. Most good ground covers spread by suckers, rhizomes, or stolons to cover an area densely. They are usually perennials or shrubs, but annuals can be used as temporary ground covers, and vines can be trained horizontally as ground covers as well.

ground layering A general term for layering techniques that involve bending stems to the ground and covering them with soil. *See* MOUND LAYERING, FRENCH LAYERING, SERPENTINE LAYERING, TIP LAYERING, TRENCH LAYERING

ground water Water located below the soil surface and the water table, where the soil remains saturated. Ground water supplies wells and springs.

group A term used to distinguish plants within a species to collectively identify similar cultivars, similar hybrids of uncertain origin, or a range of individuals that share enough characteristics to make them an identifiable unit. Groups are commonly used in large, diverse genera such as *Clematis*, which is divided into three groups that identify plants with similar blooming habits and pruning requirements. *Brassica oleracea*, commonly known as wild cabbage, is typically broken into eight groups: Acephala Group contains kale, collards, and ornamental cabbage; Capitata Group contains cabbages; Gemmifera Group, Brussels sprouts.

growing mix A medium blended specifically for growing seedlings, rooted cuttings, or plants. Growing mixes usually are lighter than seed-starting mixes and hold more air; they hold more water than typical cutting mixes. In addition, they can contain nutrients for the plants as well. To make your own home-blended growing mix for seedlings or rooted cuttings, combine 2 parts peat moss, 1 part perlite, and 1 part vermiculite. Ideally, add a small quantity of lime (5 tablespoons per bushel of mix) to neutralize the acidity of the peat moss. It's best to premoisten growing media before filling containers. *See* PREMOISTEN, POTTING MIX

growing point The tip of the stem. *See* MERISTEM

growing season Most often, when gardeners talk about the growing season they are referring to the period of time from the last spring frost until the first fall frost in any given area. When measured from frost date to frost date, growing season length is expressed in terms of the number of freeze-free or frost-free days. Your local Cooperative Extension agent will know the average number of freeze-free days in your area. This number is useful for selecting and scheduling seed-sowing dates for frost-sensitive plants such as annuals, herbs, and many vegetables, including marigolds, zinnias, basil, tomatoes, and peppers. In International Falls, Minnesota, where the freeze-free period is a brief 86 days, long-season vegetables need to be started indoors and fast-maturing cultivars are the best bet. In areas with a long growing season—such as Athens, Georgia, with 204 freeze-free days—sowing indoors and selecting fast-maturing crops may not be necessary. Crops that need cool temperatures to grow well may need to be started indoors so they have time to mature before hot weather sets in, however. *See* DAYS-TO-MATURITY for more information. Gardeners also refer to growing season as the period from when the first flowers of spring appear to the last hard, killing frost of late fall or even early winter.

growing season pruning This is the best time to prune plants that bloom on old wood, but pruning during late spring and summer has other advantages. It is easy to direct new growth with a minimum of stress on a plant at this time of year simply by pinching out shoot tips to encourage branching. It also is a good time to remove excessively twiggy growth to direct a plant's energy into developing its main scaffold branches. Pruning during the growing season tends to reduce a plant's vigor, so this is a good time to tackle a plant if you want to reduce its size. Summer is also the best time to remove unwanted growth such as watersprouts and suckers.

growing tunnel *See* TUNNEL, ROW COVER

grow on To place seedlings, rooted cuttings, or other young plants in a protected environment where they will receive optimum care until they grow large enough and become well enough established to be moved to permanent sites. Plants being grown on can be grown in a nursery bed or planted in pots set in a protected location.

growth habit *See* HABIT

growth ring *See* TREE RING

grub knife *See* WEEDERS

grubs A larval, or immature, stage of a beetle. Grubs are plump, whitish, usually C-shaped creatures that live in the soil and generally range from $1/2$ to $1 1/2$ inches long. They feed on roots, weakening plants and causing wilting or death. The presence of skunks, birds, or moles digging in the grass often indicates grub infestations. To control them, apply milky disease (a microbial insecticide) to the lawn with a fertilizer spreader. It may take several seasons to produce a noticeable effect, but once the spores build up, they will provide long-term control. For faster results, apply parasitic nematodes to affected areas.

grub

guano An organic fertilizer consisting of dried aged bird excrement. It contains about 15 percent nitrogen and 10 percent phosphate.

guard cells A pair of cells that open or close the pores (stomates) in the outermost layer of cells (the epidermis) of a leaf or stem. *See* STOMATE

gum A thick adhesive substance extruded from stems that hardens when it comes in contact with air.

guttaring *See* TAPING

gymnosperm One of the two major types of seed-bearing plants, a gymnosperm lacks flowers and bears naked seeds that are not enclosed in an ovary. Examples include conifers, such as pines (*Pinus* spp.), spruces (*Picea* spp.), ginkgo (*Ginkgo biloba*), and cycads (including *Cycas* spp., and *Zamia* spp.). Gymnosperms bear their naked seeds on scales, which are most often arranged in cones. In contrast, angiosperms, the other major type of seed-bearing plant, produce flowers and bear seeds enclosed in an ovary.

gynodioecious Bearing perfect flowers (with both pistils and stamens) on some plants and pistillate (female) flowers on others.

gynoecium The female reproductive portion of a flower. A collective term for all the pistils or carpels of a flower.

-gynous A suffix referring to pistils or styles of a flower, usually combined with a prefix that indicates a number. Octogynous means having eight pistils or styles, for example.

habit The general appearance or characteristics of a plant, including what general type of plant it is—herbaceous perennial, shrub, or tree—as well as other important characteristics such as its size or shape, its means of spreading, and/or its branch position.

habitat The area or type of conditions in which a plant grows naturally.

haft The base of a petal or other plant part when it is narrow or constricted. The term haft most often is used to refer to the narrow bases of iris (*Iris* spp.) falls.

ha-ha, ha-ha wall A retaining wall, designed to separate the garden from the landscape beyond, that was sunk in the side of a slope or along one side of a long ditch so that it is not visible from the garden. A ha-ha kept cattle and other farm animals out of the garden yet gave the impression that there was no separation between it and the surrounding landscape.

hair On plants, hairs are linear structures that emerge from the epidermis, the outermost layer of cells on leaves or other plant parts. They consist of only one cell or a row of cells, but they are only one cell wide.

halberd-shaped Hastate. Roughly arrowhead- or spear-shaped, but with the two lobes at the base pointing out. This term is used to refer to the overall shape of a leaf or just the base.

half-hardy annual An annual that tolerates a light freeze but will be stunted, damaged, set back, or killed outright by continued exposure to freezing weather. Half-hardy annuals thrive in cool weather and are excellent choices for areas with cool, rainy springs. Sometimes combined with hardy annuals under the heading cool-weather annual. *See* COOL-WEATHER ANNUAL for growing information.

half-inferior ovary A flower with a cup-shaped base, called an hypanthium, that is fused to the lower part of the ovary, making it seem as if the sepals, petals, and stamens are arising from about the middle of the ovary.

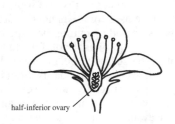

half-inferior ovary

half-ripe wood Also called semi-ripe wood. A shoot of the current year's growth that has become somewhat firm and mature as it develops woody tissue, and thus is no longer soft and succulent. *See* SEMI-RIPE CUTTING

halophyte, halophytic A plant that thrives in soil with high salt content. Many plants native to the desert Southwest tolerate saline soils, including species of saltbush (*Atriplex* spp.).

hamate Hooked at the tip.

hand-pollination Moving pollen from one flower to another, usually for purposes of plant breeding or to produce fruit. Pollen can be transferred by picking one flower and rubbing it on the stigma of another. Or the transfer can be made via a paintbrush, or by picking an anther to transfer the pollen.

hand pruners An essential, hand-held pruning tool that comes in two basic designs: Bypass and Anvil. Bypass pruners cut like scissors—a sharp convex cutting blade slides past a blunt concave hooked blade that supports the stem being cut. Also called bypass and blade-and-hook pruners as well as secauters, these cut when the broader, sharpened blade passes the narrower anvil one. Anvil shears cut like a knife on a cutting board: A straight blade cuts against a soft metal surface, the anvil, which also supports the stem. Bypass shears tend to damage a stem less than anvil shears; they're also better able to reach into tight spots. Anvil shears, however, are the more powerful of the two tools. Avid gardeners will probably want a pair of each type. Bypass pruners are designed for pruning small stems of woody plants (up to about $^3/_4$-inch thick; for thicker stems, use loppers), and also can be used for all manner of other garden tasks, including cutting back perennials and taking cuttings. Look for models with replaceable, carbon steel blades (Felco and Sandvik are two top-quality brands). Anvil pruners especially are useful for removing deadwood: Ratchet-action anvil models are available. These increase cutting force dramatically with minimum effort from the user. They make it possible to cut stems up to 1 $^1/_2$ inches in diameter. They, too, are best for removing deadwood.

hand pruners

hand weeders *See* WEEDERS

hapaxnanthic Flowering once, or having only one flowering period.

haploid Bearing half the normal number of chromosomes within each cell. Reproductive cells of either sex (gametes).

hardcore Crushed stone.

hardened off This term is used to describe new growth that has finished its main annual growth spurt. Hardened-off growth has fully expanded leaves and shoots that are firmer and less flexible than new rank growth—they snap instead of bend over when bent.

hardening off The technique used to gradually expose seedlings, cuttings, or other plants to the conditions they will encounter outdoors in the garden. Plants grown indoors under ideal conditions—with optimum light, temperature, humidity, soil moisture, and air circulation—are seldom ready to cope with the harsher conditions outdoors. Full sun, fluctuating temperatures, and drying winds can stunt growth or even kill plants that have not been exposed to them gradually. To harden off plants, about 2 weeks before they are scheduled to go into the garden, stop fertilizing and cut back on watering. A week before transplanting, set them outdoors in a sheltered spot such as a shady, protected spot on the north side of the garden for about 2 hours. Over the next few days, gradually increase the number of hours they spend outside and move them to an increasingly brighter spot each day until they can withstand being outdoors all day long. After that, they're ready for transplanting. If you work away from home, start the process on Friday afternoon or Saturday and leave them out in a protected spot all day Monday.

hardiness zones Climactic zones established for the purpose of classifying plant hardiness. The most commonly used hardiness zone system is the USDA Hardiness Zone Map, which is based on average minimum low temperatures. See USDA Hardiness Zone Map in Appendix. (The Arnold Arboretum Hardiness Zone Map is similar, but minimum low temperatures vary between it and the USDA version, so it is important to determine which map a given source is using.)

hardpan A dense, nearly impenetrable layer of soil below the topsoil. Hardpans usually result in poor drainage in the upper layers of the soil. Double digging is one option for dealing with hardpan. Or, consider building raised beds on the site.

hardscape A general term for the nonliving elements of a landscape, including stone and brick walkways, patios, terraces, walls, curbs, and so forth.

hard to wet *See* PREMOISTEN

hardwood Oaks (*Quercus* spp.), maples (*Acer* spp.), and other trees that are angiosperms are called hardwoods. Hardwoods transport water in xylem tissue composed of vessels, while softwoods transport it in tracheids. *See* SOFTWOOD, XYLEM

hardwood cutting A cutting taken from fully mature hardened growth on a woody, usually deciduous, shrub or other plant. Gather hardwood cuttings in from fall to midwinter, at least 2 to 3 weeks after the plants have dropped their leaves. Vigorous, pencil-thick shoots from wood of the current year's growth (first-year shoots) usually root best, but second-year or older growth may root as well. Cut stems at least 8 inches long (one long stem can yield several smaller cuttings). Trim 1 or 2 inches off the tip. Cut hardwood cuttings into 4- to 8-inch lengths, with at least two buds on each piece. Make a straight cut about $^1/_2$ inch above a bud at the top end of each piece (the end that was closest to the shoot tip) and a sloping cut about $^1/_2$ inch below the bud at the base. Cuttings planted upside down won't root, and this system keeps track of which end is which. (*See* POLARITY) In areas with mild winters (roughly Zone 6 south), plant hardwood cuttings immediately, either directly in a nursery bed or into pots. Before sticking them, dip the base of each cutting in a rooting hormone to encourage roots to form. Insert them vertically into moistened, loose soil, leaving only one or two buds above ground, and lightly firm the soil. Mulch the soil around the cuttings after the ground freezes to prevent rapid thawing and refreezing, which can damage the tender new roots. In the North, store hardwood cuttings for early spring planting. Storing protects them from extreme cold and promotes the formation of callus tissue at the base of each cutting, which increases the chance the cuttings will root successfully. (*See* CALLUS) To store them, treat the base of each cutting with rooting hormone, gather them into bundles with the top ends all facing in one direction, and secure them with rubber bands. To keep them cool and moist over the winter, bury them outdoors in a well-drained spot filled with sandy soil, sand, or sawdust; place the bundles horizontally, 6 to 8 inches deep or vertically but upside down, with the bases 3 to 4 inches from the soil surface. (The latter, seemingly unlikely, position keeps the bases slightly warmer to encourage callus formation and the tips cooler, encouraging the buds to remain dormant.) Or store them in boxes of moist sand, sawdust, or peat moss in an unheated room or garage or in the refrigerator. In early spring, plant the stored cuttings outdoors in moist, well-prepared soil deep enough to cover all but the top one or two buds. Space them roughly 4 to 6 inches apart. Hardwood cuttings may take several months to a year to root. Once they have rooted, set them in a sheltered spot or in a cold frame for the winter instead of transplanting them right away. Feed them after new growth starts in spring, then move them to individual pots about 2 to 4 weeks later. In mid- to late summer, transplant them to a nursery bed, then move them to the garden the following spring or fall.

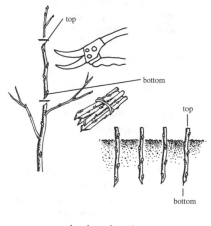

hardwood cuttings

hardy annual An annual that will withstand a reasonable amount of frost. The seeds of many hardy annuals will overwinter, even in northern climates, and will germinate in the spring. The seedlings are able to withstand the rigors of fluctuating spring temperatures. Some hardy annuals germinate in fall and overwinter as small plants before blooming the following spring. Sometimes combined with half-hardy annuals under the heading cool-weather annual. *See* COOL-WEATHER ANNUAL for growing information.

hardy, hardiness The ability of a plant to survive cold temperatures without winter protection. Hardiness varies from plant to plant, and some species fail to survive over winter because of conditions other than cold temperatures. A species that is perfectly hardy in a northern zone where it is protected by a winter-long blanket of snow may die farther south because of cold wet soil conditions (winter rain rather than snow) that cause the crown to rot and/or alternate periods of freezing and thawing that heave the plant out of the soil. Most gardening books and catalogs have assigned hardiness ratings to perennials, shrubs, and other hardy plants. As gardeners continue to experiment with growing plants at the northern limit of their zones, these ratings change. Gardeners experimenting with growing plants at the northern limit of their hardiness often depend on winter protection to see them through the cold months. *See* WINTER PROTECTION, HARDINESS ZONES, FROST HEAVING

harmonious colors Most gardeners use this term to mean any two or more colors that are pleasing to the eye. In terms of the color wheel, harmonious colors are adjacent to one another and thus have a pigment in common—blue and violet, for example, because violet contains blue.

harmony A design principle that means all the individual elements of a garden or flower arrangement fit together to make a pleasing whole. A formal garden with a scarecrow at its center isn't in harmony, nor is a flower arrangement with delicate spring wildflowers set against huge tropical foliage. Obviously personal taste and aesthetics figure into whether a composition is harmonious.

harvesting herbs *See* HERB PRESERVATION

hastate Roughly arrowhead- or spear-shaped. On a hastate leaf, the two lobes at the base point out, rather than down as they do in a sagittate leaf. This term is used to refer to the overall shape of a leaf or just the base. Sheep sorrel (*Rumex acetosella*) has hastate leaves. *See also* SAGITTATE

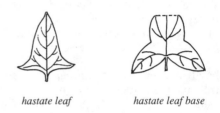

hastate leaf   *hastate leaf base*

head A short, dense cluster of flowers, or inflorescence, that has individual flowers, or florets, that are attached to a common point on the flower stem called a receptacle. Also called a capitulum. The florets are either stalkless (sessile) or nearly so (subsessile). Clovers (*Trifolium* spp.) and members of the aster family (Asteraceae) produce their flowers in heads. The best known aster-family plants bear daisylike heads, including sunflowers (*Helianthus* spp.), asters (*Aster* spp.), and purple coneflowers (*Echinacea* spp.). They usually are composed of two types of florets: Densely packed disk florets, which make up the "eye" or center of the daisy; and showier ray florets, which are commonly called petals. Gayfeathers (*Liatris* spp.) also belong to the aster family but bear fuzzy, buttonlike heads carried in dense spikelike clusters. *See also* DISK FLORET, RAY FLORET

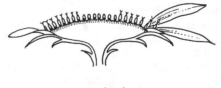

head

heading back Using a series of heading cuts to cut back all or most of the main branches of a tree, shrub, or perennial. Heading cuts induce branching, so use this technique to promote dense growth and flowering, or to cut damaged or diseased growth back to healthy wood. Always cut back to a bud facing in a direction you wish growth to develop (usually out from the center of the shrub). Pinching or cutting off growing tips is also a form of heading back. (*See* PINCHING) Heading back also is used in an attempt to reduce the size of a plant, but since heading cuts induce growth, this isn't an effective technique for size control: Thinning cuts are the best option, and also are the best choice for eliminating crossing or crowded branches, opening up the center of a plant to light and air, and reducing structural stress from weight or wind. *See* HEADING CUT, THINNING CUT

heading cut A pruning cut made across a branch to remove the stem tip. To make a proper heading cut, cut just above a bud or a side branch, and ideally make the cut at a 45-degree angle away from the bud. Make flat cuts on plants with opposite leaves. Since buds grow in the direction they are pointing, in most cases prune just above a bud that points to the outside of the plant to encourage a spreading habit and keep the center of the plant open. (On plants with opposite leaves, just rub off the bud that is pointing into the center of the plant.) If a shrub needs more growth in the center, prune above an inward-pointing bud. Heading cuts stimulate growth and encourage branching along the stem. (They remove the dominant tip bud, eliminating its effect on apical dominance. *See* APICAL DOMINANCE) Pinching as well as shearing are both forms of heading cuts. Don't use heading cuts to try to control the size of a plant; use thinning cuts instead. *See* THINNING CUT

healing, wound *See* NATURAL BARRIER

heart-shaped *See* CORDATE

heartwood The wood at the center of a tree trunk, consisting of secondary xylem tissue that has darkened and no longer conducts water. *See* XYLEM

heating mat *See* PROPAGATION MAT

heat-treated *See* FORGED

heavy soil A soil that has a high proportion of clay. Clay soils tend to be dense and are especially weighty when they are wet. *See* CLAY

hedge *See* FORMAL HEDGE, INFORMAL HEDGE

hedge shears A pruning tool with long, sharp blades that pass one another with a scissor-like action. Long- and short-handled models are available. In addition to trimming hedges, hedge shears are useful for cutting back perennials, a task that often can be accomplished in a single swipe. Electric hedge trimmers have a single blade that cuts by moving rapidly back and forth.

heel cutting A cutting that has been pulled or cut off of the main stem and has a small strip of bark and wood from that stem at its base. The heel helps promote rooting, and heel cuttings are most commonly used for propagating evergreens such as rhododendrons and azaleas (*Rhododendron* spp.). Heel cuttings usually are gathered and treated as semi-ripe or hardwood cuttings.

heel cutting

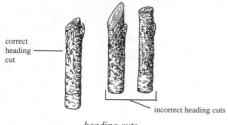

correct heading cut

incorrect heading cuts

heading cuts

heeling in Temporarily storing plants that cannot yet be moved to the garden, usually because their permanent site isn't prepared or because it is too cold or wet for planting. Any type of plant can be heeled in, including bare root specimens, new divisions, and container-grown plants. To heel in perennials, plant them in a protected, shady location with loose, rich soil. Shrubs, roses, and trees usually are placed in a trench for heeling in and laid at an angle. Either way, cover the roots with loose soil and water thoroughly to settle them. Move heeled-in plants to their permanent locations as soon as possible.

heirloom This term is used to describe cultivated forms of plants that originated before 1940; hybrids only became common after World War II. Heirloom vegetable crops are open pollinated and can be perpetuated by saving seeds from year to year, as can heirloom annuals and some perennials. Other heirlooms, including fruit and rose cultivars, are propagated by cuttings or other asexual techniques.

helicoid cyme This type of cyme, sometimes called a bostryx, has a curled or spiraled main stem, or axis, with branches that all appear on one side. It somewhat resembles a raceme, but the flower at the bottom of the iflorescence, which opens first, terminates the main axis, making this a deterimnate inflorescence. (A raceme is indeterminate.) *See also* CYME

helicoid cyme

heliophilic Thriving in light and sun.

heliophobic Thriving in shade.

helophyte A plant that grows in mud permanently or in mud that is present seasonally.

herb A plant that does not have woody stems that persist above ground over the winter. Also, a plant valued for its flavor, fragrance, or medicinal value, such as basil (*Ocimum basilicum*), lavender (*Lavandula* spp.), or thyme (*Thymus* spp.).

herbaceous Not woody. A plant that is herbaceous dies back to the ground in winter. This term also is used to refer to plant parts that are leafy or leaflike in color and texture.

herbaceous border A border planted primarily with perennials. *See* BORDER

herbaceous cutting This term sometimes is used to distinguish cuttings taken from herbaceous perennials and tender perennials such as coleus (*Solenostemon* spp., formerly *Coleus* spp.), geraniums (*Pelargonium* spp.), and chrysanthemums (*Dendranthema* spp., formerly *Chrysanthemum* spp.) and soft-stemmed cuttings taken from new growth on shrubs. Herbaceous cuttings are taken and rooted just like softwood cuttings. *See* SOFTWOOD CUTTING

herbaceous perennial A perennial, meaning a plant that persists for more than 2 years, that does not have any woody growth. Since gardeners generally use the term perennial specifically to refer to nonwoody, or herbaceous, species that are killed to the ground each winter, herbaceous perennial and perennial can be used interchangeably.

herbal A book that describes the medicinal and culinary uses of plants.

herbal oils and ointments Preparations that preserve the active ingredients of herbs in oil or a mixture of oil and a thickener such as wax. Herbal oils can be prepared for medicinal or culinary use. Commercial medicinal oils are made by distilling active ingredients by steam and are very concentrated. For homemade medicinal oils, combine 2 ounces of crushed, dried herbs or 4 ounces of finely chopped fresh herbs with a pint of olive, safflower, or pure vegetable oil. Set the mix in a warm place for several days, then strain and bottle. You can also make herbal oils by combining the herbs, as above, and heating them slowly, uncovered. Don't allow the temperature of the oil to exceed 200°F. To thicken medicinal oil to make an ointment, add 1 to 1 ½ ounces of melted beeswax. To make flavored oil for cooking, place springs of herbs in a glass jar, then slowly heat olive, peanut, or other vegetable oil. Pour the heated oil over the herbs, and then let the mixture cool before covering it tightly. You'll need about three sprigs of oil and/or a clove of garlic or a chili pepper for each cup of heated oil. Store culinary herbal oils in a cool, dark place, where they will last for up to 6 months. A good starter recipe for herbal oil is oregano, thyme, and garlic in olive oil. Or try basil and garlic in olive oil.

herbal syrup An herbal preparation made by combining honey or sugar with herbs. To make an herbal syrup, place 2 ounces of dried herbs or 4 ounces or fresh herbs in a pot with 1 quart of water. Using a glass, ceramic, or enameled container, boil it down until the volume of the liquid equals 1 pint, then add 1 to 2 tablespoons of honey or another sweetener to sweeten to taste. Store syrups in the refrigerator for up to a month.

herbarium A collection of plants that have been dried, mounted, and labeled so they can be used in scientific study.

herbicides Substances that kill weeds. For organic gardeners, commercial soap-based herbicides are the product of choice. These work best on young weeds, and older weeds may need several treatments.

herb preservation While cooks and gardeners alike swear by the flavor of herbs picked fresh from the garden, various techniques can be used to preserve the flavor and fragrance of herbs. Whatever the preservation method, for maximum flavor and fragrance, harvest herbs just before they flower. Pick them in the morning, after the dew has dried but before the sun gets hot. Store bundles of fresh herbs for up to 2 weeks in the refrigerator by placing them in a jar with an inch or two of water in the bottom. Loosely cover the foliage with plastic wrap. Freezing herbs is effective and easy; it is the best method for preserving herbs like basil, which do not retain much flavor or fragrance when dried. To freeze whole leaves or whole springs of herbs, space them out on a cookie sheet and place them in the freezer. When they have frozen completely, gather them up and place them in plastic bags. To use, chop or add whole, directly from the freezer, just as you would fresh herbs. Herbal ice cubes are another handy option and make it easy to process and preserve quantities of herbs. Fill a food processor with clean herb leaves and add water or a bit of oil before chopping them up. Pack the mixture into ice cube trays and freeze. Move the herbal cubes to plastic bags after they have frozen solid and add them to soups, stews, or other dishes a few minutes before serving. You can make herbal cubes of one herb—basil, for example—or mix them. Consider combining basil, thyme, parsley, and garlic for seasoning cubes ideal for Italian dishes. For other herb preservation techniques, *see* DRYING HERBS, HERB VINEGARS, HERBAL OILS AND OINTMENTS.

herb vinegars These are easy-to-make, easy-to-use flavored vinegars used in salad dressings and any recipe that calls for vinegar. To make herbal vinegars, place fresh springs or leaves of herbs in a clean jar or bottle with a tight-fitting lid. You also can add garlic cloves or chili peppers to vinegars. Heat the vinegar, but don't boil it, and pour it into the jar or bottle over the herbs. (Experts prefer using a glass, ceramic, or enameled container for heating.) You can use white vinegar, white wine vinegar, rice vinegar, red wine vinegar, or apple cider vinegar depending on the herbs you plan to use. You'll need about two springs of herbs per cup of vinegar. Let the vinegar cool before capping the jar or bottle tightly. Store in a cool, dark place, where it will last for up to a year. A starter recipe for flavored vinegar combines garlic, parsley, and fennel leaves in white wine vinegar. For a spicier mix, try garlic, chili peppers, and oregano in apple cider vinegar.

hermaphroditic flower *See* PERFECT FLOWER

hesperidium A fleshy fruit with obvious partitions, or septa. Oranges, grapefruits, lemons, and other citrus fruits bear this type of fruit.

hesperidium

hessian The British term for burlap. *See* BURLAP

hetero- A prefix meaning different or other.

heterogamous Bearing two different types of flowers, such as the ray and disk florets of a daisy or other aster-family plants (Asteraceae).

heterogeneous Not uniform, variable. Bearing or containing dissimilar parts.

heteromorphic Having different forms or shapes during different parts of a plant's development or its lifecycle. Ivies (*Hedera* spp.) are heteromorphic because they have juvenile and adult stages that exhibit distinct habits and leaf shapes.

heterophyllous Bearing two or more different leaf forms on the same plant, either at the same time or at different times during a plant's development. Mulberries (*Morus* spp.) and sassafras (*Sassafras albidum*) bear different-shaped leaves at the same time, while English ivy (*Hedera helix*) bears different types of leaves on juvenile and adult growth.

heterosis *See* HYBRID VIGOR

heterosporous Bearing two kinds of spores: Megaspores, which develop into the female gametophyte, and microspores, which develop into the male gametophyte.

heterozygous A plant that has a high proportion of genes that do not match on its chromosomes (usually there are two). Whether self-pollinated or pollinated by a seemingly similar parent, a heterozygous plant yields offspring that do not necessarily resemble the parent(s). Particular traits may not be passed from one generation to another, and the resulting seedlings can be extremely variable. Clones are heterozygous plants that are maintained by asexual propagation and most start with one plant that exhibited some outstanding characteristic. *See* HOMOZYGOUS

hexa- A prefix meaning six. A plant that is hexaploid, for example, has six sets of chromosomes in each cell.

hexamerous Bearing flower parts or other organs in sixes or multiples of six.

hibernaculum An overwintering body produced by some species consisting of a tight rosette of reduced leaves, with very few roots, that resembles a bud. Butterworts (*Pinguicula* spp.) produce these.

hibernal Borne in or flowering in winter.

high pH soil *See* ALKALINE SOIL

hilium Seed scar. The scar on the seed that marks the point where it was attached to the ovary. When scarifying seeds to encourage germination, it is important not to sand or clip into the hilium.

hill A group of several seeds, seedlings, or plants that have been planted in mounds or rows of soil. (Crops planted in clumps over a flat or relatively flat area of soil are still said to be planted in hills.) Squash, pumpkins, melon, and watermelon traditionally are grown in hills of rich soil, because hills provide the rich, well-drained conditions these crops require. To make a hill, loosen the soil, pile several shovelfuls of well-rotted compost over the site, and then cover with ordinary garden soil. The finished site should measure about 1 foot high and 2 to 3 feet wide. Tamp the hill down gently, water, and plant.

hilling, hilling up Pulling soil up around a plant, usually with a hoe. This technique, also called earthing up, is commonly used to blanch vegetables or to mound layer plants. Potatoes are planted in trenches and then hilled up as they sprout to keep the tubers covered with soil. *See* BLANCHING

hip The leathery, rounded "fruit" of a rose (*Rosa* spp.), which actually consists of a fleshy, urn- or vase-like hypanthium (sepals, petals, and stamens that are fused at the base) and encloses achenes, which are the true fruits. Many roses bear handsome hips that ripen to shades of red or orange-red and thus add color and interest to the garden in late summer and fall. Roses with attractive hips include rugosa roses (*Rosa rugosa*), eglantine rose (*R. eglanteria*, formerly *R. rubiginosa*), red-leaved rose (*R. glauca*, formerly *R. rubrifolia*), Scotch briar (*R. spinosissima*), and many modern shrub roses. Hips are produced after the flowers have been pollinated, so to enjoy them in the garden in the fall, don't remove the flowers as they fade.

hip

hippocrepiform Horseshoe-shaped.

hirsute Covered with long, relatively stiff, somewhat coarse hairs that are more or less erect. Most often used to describe leaf or stem surfaces. The stems of winter squash (*Cucurbita maxima*) range from setose to hirsute.

hirtellous Infinitesimally or minutely hirsute.

hispid Covered with stiff bristles that are somewhat less sharp than the bristles on a setose surface. Can be used to describe leaf surfaces as well as flower buds, pods, or other organs. The leaves of pumpkins (*Curcurbita pepo*) and alkanets or buglosses (*Anchusa* spp.) are hispid. Okra (*Abelmoschus esculentus*) plants can range from hispid to hirsute-bristly, although some cultivars are glabrate, or nearly hairless.

hoary Covered densely with short white or gray hairs. Incanous.

hoe A multipurpose tool designed for cultivating the soil and/or cutting off weeds that takes many different forms. Essentially, a hoe consists of a cutting blade held at an angle to the handle. The common garden hoe, also called the American pattern hoe and the draw hoe, has a broad, straight blade with a sharpened lower edge and a rounded top. The blade is attached at about a 70-degree angle to the handle, which can vary in length from 50 to 70 inches or more. To use a hoe while standing upright, and thus lessen strain on your back, hold it like you would a broom, with thumbs up, and pull it toward you. Use a common garden hoe for chopping clods of soil, digging furrows, weeding, and cultivating. A swan-neck hoe—also known as a Stalham hoe and a gooseneck hoe—resembles a common garden hoe but has a long, curved neck that allows you to stand up straighter while you pull the blade toward you. A collinear hoe has a narrow, rectangular blade and is designed to be used while the gardener remains standing upright in the "thumbs up" position. A warren hoe has a pointed, arrowhead-shaped blade and is ideal for digging furrows, grading, and backfilling soil over newly planted seeds. An oscillating hoe is designed primarily for weeding: Its hinged, stirrup-like head moves as it is pushed and pulled across the soil surface while the sharpened blade cuts off weeds. Oscillating hoes also are known as stirrup hoes, hula hoes, and action hoes. A scuffle hoe—also called a Dutch, push, or cavex hoe—is similar to an oscillating hoe and is designed for weeding. It doesn't have a hinged blade, but the blade is set parallel to the soil surface and is designed to cut on the push stroke. Many variations of the scuffle hoe are available, with blade shapes that can be crescent-shaped, rectangular, or triangular, often with blades sharpened on more than one edge. *See* SWOE for another version of a scuffle hoe. One more common variation of the hoe (there are many more) is the tined or fork hoe, which has pointed tines (usually four) rather than a blade and is handy for digging up weeds, loosening soil, and working compost or other organic matter into the soil surface. *See also* WHEEL CULTIVATOR

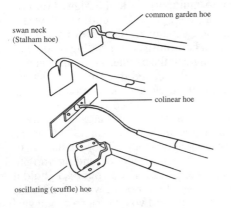

common garden hoe

swan neck
(Stalham hoe)

colinear hoe

oscillating (scuffle) hoe

hoes

hogarth curve A shape used in flower arranging in which the flowers, leaves, and other plant materials are positioned to form an open, free-form S shape. The curved S can be arranged more or less vertically or horizontally.

hogarth curve arrangement

holdfast A structure that holds a plant to another object. Gardeners commonly use this term to refer to the aerial roots or the discs produced by vines that allow them to climb flat surfaces such as brick or stone walls and wood fences. Tendrils and twining leafstalks also can serve as holdfasts. Aerial roots and discs are both adhesive, meaning they stick directly to the surface on which they climb. As a result, plants with adhesive holdfasts aren't suitable for planting along walls that require periodic maintenance, such as painting. They are difficult to remove from any surface and also can damage mortar in brick walls. For a surface that requires painting or other maintenance, a trellis mounted a couple of inches out from the wall or fence is best to allow access.

holding area *See* NURSERY BED

homo- A prefix meaning the same. A homochromous flower, for example, is all one color. Homomorphic means having the same shape.

homochlamydeous A flower that has tepals, which means the sepals (calyx) and petals (corolla) cannot be distinguished from one another.

homogamous Bearing one kind of flower, either bisexual flowers or flowers of the same sex. Also, a flower that can pollinate itself because its pistils and stamens open at the same time.

homogeneous Uniform, not variable. Bearing or containing similar parts.

homophyllous Bearing leaves that are all alike.

homosporous Bearing only one kind of spores.

homozygous A plant that has a high proportion of genes that match on its chromosomes (usually there are two). When self-pollinated or pollinated by a genetically similar parent, homozygous plants will "come true," meaning the offspring will resemble its parent(s) because they will be genetically similar. Particular traits are usually passed from one generation to another and the resulting seedlings are fairly uniform. *See* HETEROZYGOUS

hood, hooded A nontechnical term for an arched, dome-shaped petal, such as those borne by monkshoods (*Aconitum* spp.). *See* CUCULLATE, GALLEATE

hoof-and-horn meal An organic fertilizer consisting of ground hooves and horns from slaughterhouses. It contains about 12 percent nitrogen and 2 percent phosphate.

hoop house A greenhouse-size plastic tunnel that is unheated. Hoop houses are useful for extending the season in the vegetable garden, and even growing vegetables over the winter in mild climate areas. They also are useful for protecting plants that are not quite hardy in a particular region. A hoop house can be built to cover an entire garden bed. The simplest ones consist of PVC pipe arches to which clear plastic has been stapled. Ventilation is crucial in sunny weather, as heat can easily build up underneath the plastic. Either open the ends of the "house" or slit the plastic.

horizon, soil A layer of soil with characteristics that distinguish it from layers above and below it. Horizons run roughly parallel to the surface of the land and are created by differing soil-building processes.

horizontal line A shape used in flower arranging in which the flowers, leaves, and other plant materials are positioned in a gently curved, horizontal line or mass that is parallel to the surface on which the container rests.

horizontal line arrangement

horn-shaped *See* CORNUTE

horticulturalist The British spelling for horticulturist.

horticultural oil Organic insecticides made of purified petroleum oil that kill pests such as scale, mites, and aphids by smothering them. Originally called dormant oils, these once were heavy petroleum oil sprays that were loaded with impurities. Since they damaged plant leaves, they could only be sprayed during the dormant season. (*See* DORMANT OIL) Today horticultural oils are lighter, contain fewer impurities, and can be sprayed either when plants are dormant or during the growing season. (Bottles of horticultural oil will provide two dilutions, growing season and dormant, so be sure to read the label carefully.) The new oils are called superior oils, summer oils, or supreme oils, and are very effective insecticides that can be used on a variety of plants (read the label for restrictions), including many houseplants.

horticultural variety *See* VARIETY

horticulture The science and art of growing fruits, vegetables, herbs, flowers, and other plants.

horticulture, ornamental *See* ORNAMENTAL HORTICULTURE

horticulturist An individual who studies or practices horticulture.

hose-in-hose A type of double flower with a corolla (petals) that usually is tubular and is inserted in the throat of a second corolla or a corolla-like calyx (sepals).

host A plant or animal that nourishes a parasite.

hot bed Traditionally a structure similar to a cold frame that was heated with a layer of manure in the bottom. Today, hot beds are much more likely to be heated with a heating cable installed in the bottom.

hotcap A small, disposable cloche made of waxed paper. *See* CLOCHE

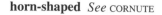

hot colors Red, orange, and yellow—the colors of fire—are commonly known as hot colors. While hot pink and magenta are hot colors, pale pink is considered a cool color. Exciting, cheerful, and vibrant in a garden, hot colors tend to look closer to the eye than cool colors. *See also* COLOR TEMPERATURE, HOT COLORS

hot composting *See* COMPOSTING

hue A color such as red, yellow, or blue.

hula hoe *See* HOE

humidity The amount of water vapor in the atmosphere.

humifuse Creeping or spreading along the soil surface.

humus Created by soil-dwelling organisms such as bacteria and fungi, humus is a beneficial component of soil that is composed of decayed organic matter— primarily hard-to-decompose plant parts such as waxes and lignins—along with gums and starches generated by soil-dwelling organisms. Humus, which is generally black or dark brown, is very effective in holding nutrients and water in the soil (it can hold 80 to 90 percent of its weight in water). It also improves soil structure, thus making it easier to work, by holding soil particles together, and allowing space for air and water. Although the terms organic matter and humus are sometimes used interchangeably, true humus is stable—it is the end product of the decomposition process that organic matter goes through—and it does not decompose readily. Active, or effective, humus is still in the process of being decomposed by soil-dwelling organisms. *See also* ORGANIC MATTER, SOIL, SOIL STRUCTURE

humus, peat *See* PEAT MOSS

husk The outer covering of some types of fruit, such as nuts, walnuts (*Juglans* spp.) for example. In nuts, the husk is derived from the pericarp, meaning the wall of the ripened ovary. The term also is used for the inflated, papery coverings of ground cherries or husk tomatoes (*Psysalis* spp.). In this case the husk is an enlarged calyx. Botanically speaking, the "husks" that cover ears of corn (*Zea mays*) actually are spathes.

hyaline Thin and transparent or translucent. This term is usually applied to leaf and bract margins.

hybrid A plant that is the result of cross-pollination between two genetically different parents or genetically different lines. Hybrids can result from natural causes (by bees pollinating different plants, for example) or by plant breeders deliberately transferring pollen from one plant to another. They can involve crosses between different forms of the same species, between different species, and even between plants in different genera. A multiplication sign (×) in the botanical name of a plant between the genus name and the specific epithet indicates that the plant is a hybrid created by crossing two species. For example, the botanical name of Shasta daisy is *Leucanthemum* × *superbum*; goldflame honeysuckle, another hybrid, is *Lonicera* × *heckrottii*. When a plant is the result of a cross between plants in two genera, the "×" appears before the genus name. For example, × *Heucherella tiarelloides* is the result of a cross between *Heuchera* × *brizoides* and *Tiarella cordifolia*. To produce hybrid seed, plant breeders maintain distinct lines of parent plants (either as inbred lines or asexually propagated clones). These original parents are crossed each time to create hybrid seed for the next generation. Crosses either can be made manually or by planting alternating rows of the parent plants that have been altered so that one always provides the pollen and the other produces the seeds. In corn, for example, the pollen-producing tassels can be removed from the seed (female) parent so that the pollen always comes from the pollen (male) parent. Breeders also have developed seed- parent lines that exhibit male sterility to ensure that pollen for a hybrid comes from a selected pollen parent. Plants from the first generation of crosses between lines of parent plants are called F_1 hybrids. Despite the fact that F_1

hybrid plants are very uniform in appearance, genetically they are very diverse. As a result, seed collected from them usually does not result in plants that resemble the parents. (If you are planning to save seeds, look for the word "hybrid" or "F_1," on the seed packet. If you aren't sure whether a plant is a hybrid, save some seeds and see what results!) F_2 hybrids are created by crossing two F_1 hybrids. They are less uniform in appearance than their parents. Crosses made beyond the F_2 generation usually are less vigorous, more variable, and generally of poor quality. Hybrids can be propagated by asexual techniques such as cuttings.

hybridization The processes by which hybrids are created.

hybrid vigor This term is used to refer to the robust growth, yield, or improved characteristics of some hybrids. Also called heterosis.

hydrophyte A plant that grows in water.

hydroponics Growing plants in a liquid medium, which contains all of the nutrients they require.

hypanthium A ring-, cup-, tubular, or vase-like structure that seems to carry the sepals, petals, and stamens of a flower. Actually the hypanthium consists of sepals, petals, and stamens, as well as sometimes a portion of the flower's receptacle, that are fused at the base. A rose hip is actually a hypanthium rather than a true fruit. The term calyx tube is sometimes substituted for hypanthium, but a calyx tube consists of fused sepals only. *See* HIP

hypertufa A material used to make troughs in which to grow alpine and other small plants. Hypertufa consists of 2 parts Portland cement, 3 parts sieved peat moss, and 3 parts perlite. Some experts add acrylic bonding agents or fiberglass or plastic reinforcing fibers to the mix, along with coloring powders. Hypertufa is then molded in a form (or over damp sand piled in the desired shape). Making hypertufa troughs is a time-consuming but rewarding activity. Consult a reference book on rock gardening for complete directions as well as suggestions for suitable plants. *See* TROUGH

hypo- A prefix meaning below, beneath, or under.

hypocotyl The portion of an embryonic stem that is below the cotyledons. The hypocotyl elongates upon germination and either raises the cotyledons above the soil surface (epigeous germination) or it elongates but remains underground (hypogeous germination). The radicle, or rudimentary root, develops from the hypocotyl.

hypogeous germination In this type of germination, the portion of the stem below the cotyledons, called the hypocotyl, elongates but does not raise the cotyledons above the soil surface. Instead, the portion of the stem above the cotyledons, called the epicotyl, elongates and rises above the soil surface and the stem and cotyledons remain below the soil surface. Peaches and sweet peas (*Lathyrus odoratus*) germinate in this manner. *See* EPIGEOUS GERMINATION

hypogynous Borne or attached beneath the ovary. This term describes the petals, sepals, and stamens of a flower with a superior ovary, where these parts are attached to the receptacle and the ovary is above them. Poppies (*Papaver* spp.) have hypogynous flowers.

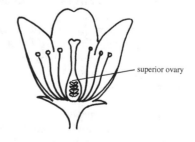

hypogynous flower

hysteranthous Bearing leaves that develop after the flowers. *See* PRECOCIOUS

IBA *See* ROOTING HORMONE

I-budding A technique that is something like a combination of patch budding and T-budding. Prepare the stock by making a vertical cut, as well as cuts at the top and the bottom. To prepare the scion, cut a square patch as for a patch bud. Gently loosen the flaps of bark on the scion and slip the patch under them. Otherwise, wrap and treat like a patch bud, taking care to fasten down the flaps of bark. *See* PATCH BUDDING, BUDDING

ichneumon wasp *See* BENEFICIAL INSECTS

idioblasts Specialized cells in the epidermis (surface layer) of leaves or other organs that exude gum or slime.

Ikebana The Japanese art of flower arranging in which elements of the design reflect earth, man, and heaven in specific portions of the design. Ikebana arrangements are deceptively simple, and use just a few flowers and a minimum of foliage or other natural elements such as driftwood or rocks.

illegitimate, nomen illegitimum This term is used to describe names for plants that have been published but violate rules in the *International Code of Botanical Nomenclature* or *International Code of Nomenclature for Cultivated Plants.*

imbibition The process by which a germinating seed absorbs water. *See* GERMINATION

imbricate Overlapping, like shingles or roof tiles. Commonly used to describe leaves or bracts (modified scalelike leaves) that overlap in a discernible pattern.

immersed Growing under water; submerged.

immortelles *See* EVERLASTINGS

imparipinnate Odd pinnate.

imperfect A flower that has either male or female structures (stamens or pistils) but not both. Unisexual.

implicate Intertwined or twisted together.

impressed Sunken into the surface.

improving soil *See* SOIL BUILDING

inarching A grafting technique used to join two separate plants both growing on their own roots. In this case, a small scion is grafted onto a tree to augment the established plant's root system. In addition to strengthening the root system of an established plant, inarching can be used to repair plants with trunks damaged by lawnmowers, mice or other rodents, or even by cars running or backing into them. This type of graft is best made in early spring, just as the established tree begins growing and the bark "slips" easily, but can be attempted at other times as long as the plant is actively growing. For rootstock, select seedlings or rooted cuttings that are $1/4$- to $1/2$-inch thick at the top, and plant them around the tree (the scion) at a spacing of about 5 to 6 inches. When you are ready to graft (the seedlings or cuttings can be planted any time during the previous fall or winter; prepare and graft them one at a time), make a long, shallow, 4- to 6-inch-long cut along the seedlings next to the tree (scion), cutting through the bark, and remove some of the wood. At the tip of the seedling, make a short, $1/2$-inch-long cut to create a sharp wedge at the tip. To prepare the scion, cut a long, narrow slot in the trunk that is exactly the width of the seedling rootstock and the same length as the cut you made in it. Leave a small flap of bark at the top of the slot. Fit the top of the seedling into the slot, slipping the tip under the flap of bark. Then use wire nails to nail the scion in place as you would for bark grafting; be sure to nail through the flap of bark and to nail down any loose bark. Then coat the entire area with grafting wax. Repeat the procedure with each rootstock to be grafted. As the graft union forms, cut back the tips of any shoots that appear on the rootstocks, and after it has healed, remove any shoots that appear on them.

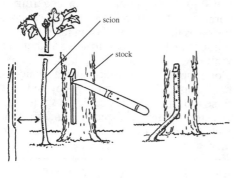

inarching

inbred line A line of plants created by enforced self-pollination of a species that normally cross-pollinates. Inbred lines are used as parent plants for hybrids and are recrossed for each new generation of seeds.

incanous Covered densely with short white or gray hairs, or pubescence. Hoary.

incised Deeply cut, toothed, or slashed, generally in an irregular fashion. This term is commonly used to describe the edge, or margin, of a leaf or leaflet. The teeth on an incised leaf are deeper and more irregular than those on a dentate leaf. On an incised leaf the indentations are shallower than on a lobed one. A lobed leaf also has rounded rather than sharply cut indentations.

incised leaf margin

inclining Abruptly leaning or bending down. Reclining abruptly. *See* RECLINATE

included Enclosed within, or not projecting beyond. Stamens that do not extend beyond the corolla are included. *See also* EXCLUDED

incompatibility A grafting term that refers to the inability of two individual plants to form a successful graft union. A graft between incompatible plants may fail completely right from the start, but incompatibility often takes longer to manifest itself. A graft may form initially, and the scion(s) may grow for a time, but develop symptoms of delayed incompatibility: The scion(s) can die or break off cleanly at the graft union even years after they were joined. Incompatibility also can cause the phloem to degenerate, affecting nutrient flow and eventually girdling the plant. In some cases, inserting an interstock that separates stock and scion can solve the problem. Viruses in either stock or scion also can cause graft incompatibility symptoms. Signs of graft incompatibility include complete failure of the union, yellowing foliage and early leaf drop on the scion from mid- to late in the season, shoot dieback on the scion, stock and scion that grow at decidedly different rates, and early death of grafted trees. *See* GRAFTING

incomplete This term is used to refer to flowers that lack one or more of the four whorls of a complete flower: The sepals, petals, stamens, or pistils.

incomplete metamorphosis *See* META-MORPHOSIS

incumbent Folded in and lying on or against another organ, but not fused or united to it. Used to refer to unlike plant parts such as seed leaves (cotyledons) that lie against the rudimentary root (radicle) in a seed. Cotyledons are incumbent when they are arranged with the radicle lying along one side. They are accumbent when the radicle lies along the edge, rather than the side.

incurved Curved inward, either toward the tip or base of the stem or axis.

indefinite Apparently capable of unlimited growth. This term is used to describe a plant that can spread widely.

indehiscent Not splitting at maturity. This term is applied to types of fruit, such as achenes, berries, drupes, and pomes, that do not split open to release the seeds they enclose. Dehiscent fruits are just the opposite: They split open to release their seeds at maturity.

indeterminate A flower cluster (inflorescence) with a main stem (axis) that continues to elongate after the first flowers open. Plants can be indeterminate as well. Indeterminate tomatoes are large, sprawling plants that have stems ranging from 6 to as much as 20 feet. (Three-quarters of tomato cultivars are indeterminate; the rest are determinate.) Indeterminate tomatoes continue producing flowers and fruit all season long, until they are cut down by frost. For best fruit production—and to keep them from sprawling and occupying too much garden space—indeterminate types need to be staked with 5- to 7-foot-long stakes or contained in a large, tall cage. They also need to be pruned, because otherwise they put too much energy into producing leaves and stems. To prune, snap off some or all of the suckers that emerge from the leaf axils. *See* DETERMINATE

Index Kewensis A published listing of all genera and species of flowering plants throughout the world. *Index Kewensis* was first published in 1893 and the Oxford University Press, in conjunction with the Royal Botanical Gardens, Kew, issues supplements every five years.

indigenous Native to a particular area. Not introduced.

indolebutyric acid (IBA) *See* ROOTING HORMONE

indument, indumentum This term refers to the covering of hairs or scales on a plant.

It is most often used as a general term for "hair."

induplicate Folded or rolled inward. Petals or sepals that are rolled or folded so their edges run parallel or alongside one another are induplicate.

indurate Hardened.

indusium A separate structure that functions like a specialized flap covering a sorus on a fern frond to protect the spores inside as they develop. The indusium either withers or bends back to release them at maturity. Ferns that bear sori arranged along the edge of leaflets, such as maidenhair ferns (*Adiantum* spp.) are covered by a false indusium. In this case, the spores are covered by a specialized leaf margin that rolls or bends over to cover the sori. *See also* SORUS

inerm, inermous Without spines, thorns, or teeth. Unarmed.

inferior Attached or borne beneath. A flower with an inferior ovary has petals, sepals, and stamens attached to the top of the ovary. Irises (*Iris* spp.) and bellflowers (*Campanula* spp.) have inferior ovaries.

inferior ovary

infertile Sterile. Unable to produce viable seed.

infiltration The process by which water soaks or percolates down into the soil.

inflated Swollen, blown-up, or bladder-like. Urceolate (pitcher- or urn-shaped) flowers such as blueberries (*Vaccinium* spp.) are inflated.

inflexed, inflected Flexed or bent toward the main stem, or axis.

inflorescence The flower cluster of a plant or the flowering part of a plant. Also, the arrangement of the individual flowers on a plant.

inflorescence

informal garden A garden design style that features an unstructured, dynamic layout using curving lines, free-form shapes, and asymmetrical balance. Paths and garden beds are laid out in sinuous curves that can wind through the landscape or run in straight lines, depending on the site and the whim of the gardener. Instead of the brick or stone used to mark paths in a formal design, paths in an informal garden may be covered by shredded bark or randomly placed stepping stones. Garden elements and plants usually are asymmetrically balanced—a large shrub may be offset by a cluster of three smaller ones, for example. Symmetrical balance, when it exists, is subtle: A pair of shrubs that mark a pathway may be surrounded by different plants, for example, or a pair of beds that are the same size could be filled with a different mix of plants. Informal gardens may or may not use repeating elements, and they certainly don't feature them in the predictable manner found in formal gardens. Materials, elements, bed sizes, and plants can all vary, creating a feeling of change and movement in the garden. *See* FORMAL GARDEN

informal hedge A hedge in which the plants are pruned selectively in order to maintain their natural, rounded shape. When flowering shrubs are used in hedges, they are best in informal ones because the shearing required to maintain a formal hedge removes their flowers. Rhododendrons and azaleas, old-fashioned weigela (*Weigela florida*), and mock orange (*Philadelphus* spp.) all make handsome informal hedges.

infra- A prefix meaning below. For example, infrastaminal means below the stamens. Infraspecific means any taxon below the rank of species, including subspecies, varieties, and forms.

infusion A type of herbal tea made by brewing herbs in water from 15 minutes to as much as several hours. Leaves and flowers usually are used to make infusions. To make an infusion, use a glass, ceramic, or enameled container that can be covered tightly, and combine about 1 ounce of dried herb per pint of water; use 2 ounces of fresh herbs per pint. Pour near-boiling water over the herbs, and steep, covered. Infusions usually are made in fairly large quantities to be consumed over the course of a single day. *See also* TEA, TISANE

inlay approach graft A type of approach graft used to unite two separate plants when the stock is considerably thicker than the scion. To make an inlay approach graft, select the stock and scion as you would for a spliced approach graft. (*See* APPROACH GRAFTING) Then to prepare the stock, make a narrow, 3- to 4-inch-long slot that is exactly as wide as the scion. To prepare the scion, make a long, shallow cut in the stem where it will join with the stock. This cut should go through the bark and slightly into the wood. Then fit the cut portion of the scion into the slot cut in the stock. Hold it in place with small, flat-head wire nails, and then coat the entire area with grafting wax.

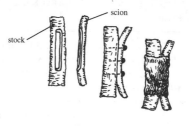

inlay approach graft

innate Borne at the apex, or tip, of an organ.

inoculant A treatment for seeds of plants that have beneficial relationships with nitrogen-fixing bacteria, allowing them to transform atmospheric nitrogen (a gas plants can't use) into nitrates (a nutrient plants need for growth and can readily absorb). Inoculants are crop-specific, so buy one for the particular crop—beans, peas, and other legumes—that you are growing.

inorganic fertilizer Fertilizers made from nonliving sources such as rocks as well as chemical salts. Technically, inorganic fertilizers can be of organic origin—rock powders such as limestone and greensand fall here. Chemical salts and rock powders treated with acids to make them more soluble are considered to be chemical or synthetic and are not used in organic gardens.

inrolled Rolled or curled inward. *See also* INVOLUTE, REVOLUTE, VOLUTE

insecticidal oils *See* DORMANT OIL

insecticidal soap Organic insecticides consisting of solutions of fatty acids that kill a variety of pests, including aphids, mites, and white flies. These paralyze the pests, which then die of starvation. To make a homemade insecticidal soap spray, mix 1 to 3 teaspoons of household soap (not detergent) with a gallon of water.

insecticides Substances that kill insects. Microbial insecticides are biological controls containing disease-causing organisms that attack pests. Organic insecticides are chemical controls made from natural substances. *See* ALCOHOL, INSECTICIDAL SOAP, SABADILLA, SULFUR, NICOTINE, ROTENONE, RYANIA, PYRETHRIN, NEEM

insectivorous Insect-eating. A plant that traps and digests insects such as Venus's-flytraps (*Dionaea muscipula*) or pitcher plants (*Sarracenia* spp.).

inserted Attached to, growing out of, or placed upon.

insertion The point of attachment or the manner in which a plant part, such as a leaf, is attached to its support. A leaf insertion is the point on the main stem where it is attached, for example.

insipid Flavorless or tasteless.

integrated pest management A system for managing pests on plants by monitoring pest populations and taking steps to control them if damage reaches unacceptable levels. Also called IPM, this is not an organic system, since synthetic pesticides may be the control measure of choice. IPM practitioners use a combination of preventive techniques and control measures to keep damage at acceptable levels. *See* ORGANIC PEST MANAGEMENT

intensive gardening Gardening systems that use a variety of techniques designed to maximize harvests by making the best use of available space. Most intensive systems grow crops in raised beds and use close spacing between individual plants. They also use succession planting and crop rotation, and pay special attention to building soil and maintaining soil fertility. A well-planned, well-cared-for intensive garden can produce from four to ten times the harvest of a conventional vegetable garden planted in rows. The French intensive and bio-dynamic gardening systems are best known. *See* BIO-DYNAMIC GARDENING

inter- A prefix meaning between or among. An intergeneric plant is the result of a cross between plants in two different genera and an interspecific plant results from a cross between two different species.

inter-breeding *See* HYBRIDIZATION

intercalary meristem *See* MERISTEM

intercropping Growing two crops together in the same bed or in alternate rows in a field. *See* INTERPLANTING

intermediate stem section *See* INTERSTOCK

intermediate stock *See* INTERSTOCK

internodal cutting A stem cutting that is severed above and below a node. Internodal cuttings are gathered and treated as either softwood or semi-ripe cuttings and generally consist of a single node, with stem above and below it, along with a single leaf. Clematis (*Clematis* spp.) can be propagated by internodal cuttings, which make extremely efficient use of propagating material. *See* SOFTWOOD CUTTING, SEMI-RIPE CUTTING

internode The section of stem between two nodes.

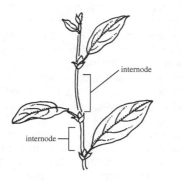

internode

internode

interplanting A technique used to maximize the use of garden space by planting two crops together in the same row or bed. Two crops that mature at different rates can be interplanted successfully. For example, when fast-maturing lettuce is interplanted with slow-to-mature cabbage, the lettuce is ready for harvest well before the cabbage plants have gotten large enough to fill up the space available. Two crops with different root systems also are good inter-planting candidates: Planting beans, which have fairly deep, spreading root systems, works well with shallower-rooted onions, for example. Warm-weather and cool-weather crops also can be interplanted: Try interplanting peas with tomatoes. The spring-planted peas go into the garden well before the tomatoes, and when the pea harvest is finished the vines can be pulled up and used to mulch the tomato plants.

interrupted Not continuous. Most often used to refer to small leaflets or other seg-

ments inserted between others. Interrupted fern (*Osmunda claytonia*) bears fronds that are interrupted in the center with pairs of spore-bearing pinnae (leaflets) that are brown on the bottom and drop off early in the season, leaving a space in the center of the front. A leaf that is interruptedly pinnate has leaflets of various sizes.

interstem *See* INTERSTOCK

interstock A section of stem inserted between the stock and scion of a grafted plant, using a technique called double working. Interstocks are used to separate incompatible stocks and scions. They also are used to create some dwarf fruit trees: A dwarfing interstock can be inserted between a vigorous stock and scion.

interveinal chlorosis *See* CHLOROSIS

intra- A prefix meaning within or inside. Intraspecific means within a species.

introduced, introduction A non-native plant deliberately brought from another area. Used to describe plants, especially garden escapees, that have been introduced from another region or country and are now found growing in the wild. Orange daylily (*Hemerocallis fulva*), which now grows wild in the United States, is originally native to China and Japan. From there it was introduced to Europe, and European settlers introduced it to this country. *See also* NATURALIZED

introrse Facing inward or turned inward toward the main stem, or axis.

invalid A plant name that was not published validly, meaning it was not accompanied with the required information, such as description. Invalid is also used incorrectly to mean illegitimate. *See* ILLEGITIMATE

invasive A plant that spreads very quickly, usually by wide-spreading roots, and is difficult to keep under control in a garden. Invasive plants spread quickly to areas where they are not wanted, both inside the garden and beyond its bounds, and are usually very difficult to eradicate.

inventory, site *See* SITE INVENTORY

inversely heart-shaped *See* OBCORDATE

inversely lance-shaped *See* OBLANCEOLATE

inverted Upside-down or reversed.

inverted T-budding A technique used in rainy climates to reduce the amount of moisture that seeps into a bud union. To make an inverted T-bud, follow the directions for T-budding, but make the horizontal cut on the stock at the bottom of the vertical one. Cut the bud off opposite as well, with the horizontal cut at the bottom. Insert the bud from the bottom and treat as you would a T-bud. *See* T-BUDDING

involucel A small or secondary involucre. Carrot-family plants such as Queen Anne's lace (*Daucus carota*) and dill (*Anethum graveolens*) bear involucels under the secondary flower clusters in their compound umbels.

involucral Forming an involucre. Bracts that make up an involucre are referred to as involucral bracts. *See* INVOLUCRE

involucrate Having or borne with an involucre. *See* INVOLUCRE

involucre One or more whorls or spirals of bracts (small modified leaves) borne beneath a flower or flower cluster (inflorescence) or other organ. Flowers borne by members of the aster family (Asteraceae) have involucres: The scaly bracts on the back of a sunflower (*Helianthus annuus*) and at the base of cornflowers (*Centaurea cyanus*) both consist of involucral bracts. Several species of dogwoods, including flowering and kousa dogwoods (*Cornus florida* and *C. kousa*) have an involucre of showy petal-like bracts. Sea hollies (*Eryngium* spp.) bear an involucre of silver-gray, spiny bracts. In spurges (*Euphorbia* spp.) the involucre

is cup-shaped and forms an inflorescence called a cyanthium. In some grasses, bristles (short stiff hairs), make up the involucre. *See also* BRACT, CYANTHIUM

involucre

involute Rolled or curved inward toward the top, as in a leaf whose edges curl in over the upper surface.

IPM *See* INTEGRATED PEST MANAGEMENT

Irishman's cuttings This is actually a form of division used to propagate plants with loose crowns such as some asters (*Aster* spp.), basket-of-gold (*Aurinia saxatilis*), moss phlox (*Phlox subulata*), catchflies (*Silene* spp.), and speedwells (*Veronica* spp.). These plants produce individual stems that have adventitious roots at the base. To use them for propagation, simply pull them apart gently or cut them with a sharp knife. Pot them up immediately, and treat them as a softwood or semi-ripe cutting that has not quite rooted.

Irishman's cuttings

Irish spade *See* SPADE

irregular flower A flower that is asymmetrical, meaning it lacks the radial symmetry of a regular (actinomorphic) flower. This term is most commonly used in reference to zygomorphic flowers, which are bilaterally symmetrical and can be divided into two mirror-image halves along only one plane or line. Cannas (*Canna* spp.), however, bear irregular flowers that are *not* zygomorphic. *See also* REGULAR FLOWER, ZYGOMORPHIC, BILATERAL SYMMETRY

irregular flower

island bed Usually installed in the center of a lawn, these are islands of plants surrounded by lawn and usually are designed to be viewed from all sides. They can consist entirely of perennials or may surround existing trees and/or shrubs. Island beds also can be designed as mixed plantings. They should look like natural features, with smoothly curving shapes, much like water pooling on a lawn. Plants normally are arranged with the tallest plants in the middle and drifts of shorter plants surrounding them.

isopropyl alcohol *See* ALCOHOL

Japanese-form, Japanese A single or semidouble flower with one or more whorls of petals (called guard petals) surrounding a dense cluster of narrow petal-like structures (actually petaloids or staminodes) in the center. Also called an anemone. *See* ANEMONE-FORM

Japanese pruning shears *See* SHEARS, GARDEN

jardiniere An ornamental stand or container used to grow plants, especially houseplants.

joint Node. The point on a stem where one or more leaves or branches are attached. This term especially is used to describe the clearly defined, somewhat swollen nodes on grass stems.

jointed Having nodes or points of articulation, either real or apparent, that are narrow enough to make separation easy. *See* ARTICULATE

jugate Paired. Also used as a suffix to indicate organs arranged in pairs, and in this case usually combined with a prefix indicating a number. Quinquejugate means arranged in five pairs, for example.

juvenile A term that refers either to the foliage or to the growth habit of some species in which the appearance of immature individuals differs from that of mature or adult plants. For example, the popular English ivies (*Hedera helix*) grown in gardens are all juvenile forms: Mature plants have a shrubbier habit and less attractive foliage.

keel A prominent ridge that runs lengthwise down the center of a structure such as a leaf or petal. The two lower petals of a papilionaceous flower are joined at the

base to form a sheath, called a keel, that covers the flower's stamens and pistils.

keiki A small plant that appears at the node of an orchid stem. Keikis are adventitious plants and develop roots while still attached. To use them for propagation, sever them when a good root system has formed and pot them up.

kelp meal An organic fertilizer consisting of dried, ground seaweed. It contains about 2.5 percent potassium along with some nitrogen, a wide variety of micronutrients, some vitamins, and amino acids.

kernel The inner portion of a seed, inside the seed coat(s), or the entire seed, as in a corn kernel.

key A device used to identify plants or other unknown objects. A key employs a sequence of statements that are mutually exclusive and are arranged in a series. The most common types of keys are dichotomous, meaning forked or branched, and present the user with pairs of statements. Keys sometimes provide three or even four choices, depending on the plants they are distinguishing among. To identify or "key out" a plant, you select the answer that applies to it in the first pair of choices, which leads to a second pair, and so forth. By making a series of successive choices, you eventually narrow down the selection to identify the plant in question.

key out To use a key to identify a plant, animal, or other unknown object.

kidney-shaped *See* RENIFORM

killing frost *See* FROST DATES

kitchen garden A garden devoted to edible plants including all manner of vegetables and herbs. Such a garden may also include flowers for cutting.

knees The woody, upright projections of the root systems that arise around the trunks of some species of trees, such as bald cypress (*Taxodium distichum*), when they are growing in wet soil conditions. They are thought to have an aerating function.

knobbed *See* CAPITATE

knot garden A style of garden popular in the 16th and 17th centuries in which beds were laid out in intricate, almost mazelike, patterns edged with closely clipped hedges of shrubs. The shrubs—boxwood (*Buxus* spp.) and lavender cotton (*Santolina* spp.) are two traditional choices—were chosen to create color contrast. The areas inside the clipped hedges were either filled with flowers, which were changed annually or even seasonally, or were mulched with gravel or other materials. The designs normally were intended to be viewed from above. Because of the constant clipping necessary to keep the hedges neat-looking,

knot gardens are high-maintenance undertakings. If you want to try a knot garden, for the hedges consider dwarf cultivars of traditional boxwood, lavender cotton, or green-leaved santolina (*Santolina virens*), a dwarf lavender (*Lavandula angustifolia*) such as 'Hidcote', or germander (*Teucrium* spp.). For a temporary knot garden, try an annual such as Joseph's coat (*Alternanthera ficoidea*) or beefsteak plant (*Iresine herbstii*). Mulch the areas between the hedges with gravel or fill them with mounding annuals.

knot garden

labellum Lip. This term is primarially used to describe the enlarged lower petal of an orchid flower, which is often pouched or otherwise distinctive in appearance.

labiate Having a lip or lips. Used to describe flowers that have the calyx (sepals) and/or corolla (petals) divided into upper and lower lip-shaped segments. Members of the mint family (Lamiaceae, formerly Labiatae) such as mint (*Mentha* spp.) or salvia (*Salvia* spp.) have bilabiate (two-lipped) flowers. Also used to refer to any member of the mint family (Lamaiceae).

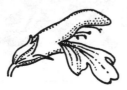

labiate flower

labium The lower lip of a flower that is bilabiate, such as a snapdragon (*Antirrhinum* spp.) or salvia (*Salvia* spp.).

lace bugs Small, flat, square insects with lacy, transparent wings. The adults and tiny, spiny, wingless larvae feed on the underside of leaves, sucking plant juices and producing a yellow or whitish stippling on the foliage. Lace bugs are a common problem on azaleas grown in full sun, but these pests attack many other plants. To control them, spray leaves thoroughly with insecticidal soap or neem. Treat serious infestations with pyrethrins or rotenone.

laced A variegation pattern in which a flower of one color has a scalloped border of another color around its edges. Pinks (*Dianthus* spp.) come in picotee patterns.

lacerate Torn looking, or irregularly cut or cleft. This term is commonly used to describe the edge, or margin, of a leaf or leaflet.

lacerate leaf margin

lacewings *See* BENEFICIAL INSECTS

lacinate Slashed or irregularly cut into narrow, pointed lobes. This term is commonly used to describe the edge, or margin, of a leaf or leaflet.

lacinate leaf margin

lactiferous Containing or producing latex. Figs (*Ficus* spp.) are lactiferous, and exude milky latex from cut stems or roots as well as wounds.

lacunose Pitted. Pockmarked or pitted with deep holes or depressions. Most often used to describe leaf surfaces.

ladies' spade *See* SPADE

lady beetles *See* BENEFICIAL INSECTS

laevigate Polished-looking, lustrous, or shining.

lageniform Flask-shaped.

lamellate Having, or made up of, thin, flat plates or scales.

lamina The expanded portion of a leaf, called the blade, or of a petal.

lanate Woolly. Covered with long, soft, usually matted hairs. Lamb's ears (*Stachys byzantina*) has lanate leaves, while cotton (*Gossypium* spp.) has lanate seeds.

lanceolate Lance-shaped. A lanceolate leaf is longer than it is wide (from three to six times longer than wide), and has a pointed tip and a rounded base. The widest part of the leaf is below the middle of the blade.

lanceolate leaf

landscape fabric *See* MULCH

langbeinite Also called sulfate of potash-magnesia or sul-po-mag, this is an organic fertilizer that is either mined or produced as an industrial by-product. (Langbenite ore is mined.) It contains 22 percent potassium, 22 percent sulfur, and 11 percent magnesium, all of which are highly soluble and thus readily available to plants. Use it carefully, since it can burn plants because of its high solubility.

language of flowers The practice of assigning specific meanings to individual flowers, which dates back to classical times: Romans crowned poets with laurel leaves. Shakespeare also referred to the meaning of flowers—in *Hamlet*, Ophelia says "There's pansies, that's for thoughts."

The practice of assigning specific meanings to individual flowers reached its peak during the sentimental Victorian age, however, when bouquets of carefully chosen flowers became coded love letters. Floral dictionaries helped keep track of the meanings—every flower had a meaning, and presentation and positioning also were crucial to conveying a message correctly. For example, a flower presented stem first had the opposite meaning of one presented flower first. There even was a method for specifying dates and times with leaves and flowers.

languinose Woolly or downy. Covered with soft, usually matted hairs that are somewhat shorter than those on a lanate surface.

lanulose Minutely woolly. Covered with short, soft, usually matted hairs.

larva, *pl.* **larvae** An immature stage of an insect such as a caterpillar.

last frost date *See* FROST DATES

last spring frost *See* FROST DATES

-late A suffix meaning having or bearing. Aculeolate means covered with very small prickles, for example.

latent bud A bud that does not develop during the season in which it forms and remains dormant. It may be stimulated to grow in subsequent years; pruning often can cause latent buds to begin growing.

lateral A side shoot or side branch. Borne on or to the side of the main stem, or axis, of an inflorescence, leaf, or other organ.

lateral meristem *See* CAMBIUM, MERISTEM

lateral vein A secondary vein branching from the main vein, or midrib, of a leaf.

latex White, milky-looking sap.

lath house A simple structure constructed of lath or slats of wood and designed to shade plants. Lath houses can be used to grow tropical plants outdoors year-round; they also are used to summer houseplants outdoors or to provide a protected spot for valuable plants, such as bonsai, that are kept outdoors year-round even in the North.

lavender wand Also called lavender sticks or lavender bottles, these are bunches of lavender flowers woven in such a way that the flowers themselves end up inside the stems, which are woven with ribbon. They are used as sachets to add fragrance to sweaters and linens. To make a lavender wand, start with an odd number of fresh lavender flowers picked with long stems. Harvest them (usually 13 to 19 stems) in the morning after the dew has dried, and remove any leaves at the bottom of the stems. Tie the bundle just under the flowers with string or florist's wire. (You may want to put the flowers in a glass before tying and also fold the stems around the edges of the glass, as shown.) Then fold the stems down over the flowers one by one in an umbrella-like fashion. The lavender needs to be freshly picked for this to work; otherwise the stems break. Using a $1/4$-inch-wide satin or velvet ribbon that is 3 to 5 yards long, begin to weave the ribbon in and out between the stems. Once you've completed a couple of rows, fold the stems all the way down, forming a bottle-shaped bundle with stems on the outside and flowers on the inside. Use a toothpick or crochet hook to straighten out and tighten the ribbon, then continue weaving until the flowers are entirely covered by a basket-weave pattern. Pull the ribbon snugly, but not so tight that the juice from the stems stains the ribbon. Once the stems are covered by 4 or 5 inches of woven ribbon, wrap the remainder of the ribbon around the stems and fasten it carefully with a pin. Then set the nearly finished wand in a warm, dry, dark, well-ventilated place for about 2 weeks until the flowers and stems are dried. Then tighten up the ribbon again, wrap the rest of the ribbon around the base of the bottle, and sew it in place with thread. You can finish the bottle with a bow of matching ribbon. Even up the

stems at the base of the wand for a neat, finished look.

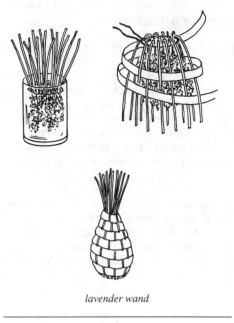

lavender wand

lax Loose and spreading or widely spaced. The opposite of compact or congested.

laxpendant Hanging loosely.

layering A vegetative or asexual propagation technique in which a shoot(s) is caused to form roots by covering it with soil while it is still attached to the parent plant. The rooted portions, which produce both roots and shoots at the nodes, are then severed from the parent plant and grown on. Shoots being layered often are cut or otherwise wounded to induce the formation of roots. Plants can be layered either by bringing shoots to the ground and covering them with soil or by mounding soil up over the plants themselves; excluding light is one factor that promotes the formation of roots. Many plants, including strawberries, layer naturally by sending out runners that root where they touch the ground; others, including brambles (*Rubus* spp.), root when stem tips touch the ground. Simple layering, the most common technique used, can be used to propagate many shrubs, vines, and perennials. To make a simple layer, in late winter or early spring select a long, low, flexible stem that you can easily bend to the ground. (Year-old shoots are best; older growth is less likely to produce roots.) Loosen the soil and work in compost or other organic matter in the area where the stem will touch, to a depth of about 4 or 5 inches. Pick off all the leaves from the stem to be layered except those at the tip. Then use a sharp knife to wound the stem at a leaf node (leaves indicate where these are located) by slicing into it to form a thin 1- to 2-inch-long flap or tongue of bark on the bottom of the section that will be buried. Take care not to cut too deep. Place a toothpick or thin sliver of wood in the wound to keep it open. Then bury the wounded section about 3 inches deep in the area where you improved the soil. Pin it down with a U-shaped wire pin if necessary (these are easy to make from cut sections of coat hangers). Stake the tip, which remains above ground. Keep the soil moist all summer. The following fall or spring, check for roots and cut apart and pot up or move the new plant. Keep it evenly moist and partially shaded until it is well established. For information on other layering techniques, *see* AIR LAYERING, MOUND LAYERING, FRENCH LAYERING, SERPENTINE LAYERING, TIP LAYERING, TRENCH LAYERING

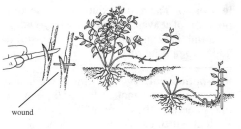

wound

layering

layering, Chinese *See* AIR LAYERING

leach, leaching The process by which water removes nutrients that are dissolved in it from the soil.

leader The main, terminal shoot or trunk of a tree or the terminal shoot of a branch. Many prized shade trees feature a single, strong trunk, but when the leader of a young tree forks, it creates two competing leaders, called a double or dual leader. If both mature, the tree won't have its distinctive shape, and the resulting narrow crotch is extremely weak and may break under stress, thus disfiguring the tree. To correct a double leader on a conifer simply remove the second leader at its base. On other trees, remove the second leader entirely or cut it back to a bud about halfway down its length, forcing it to send out side shoots. To replace a damaged or missing leader select a healthy branch from below the point of damage and tie it to a vertical splint made of wood or bamboo. Attach the splint to the trunk and new leader with twine. (If the trunk alone won't support it easily, tie the splint to a stout stake driven into the ground.) Trim off the old leader just above the new one. Leave the splint in place until the new leader can support itself, which may take a year or two.

leaf An expanded organ borne on a shoot or stem of a plant that is usually green. Using the chlorophyll contained in leaves, plants are able to covert the energy from light into food through a process called photosynthesis.

leaf axil *See* AXIL

leaf blade *See* BLADE

leaf bud *See* BUD

leaf-bud cutting A type of semi-ripe cutting that consists of a short portion of the main stem, a single bud, and a leaf. *See* SEMI-RIPE CUTTING

leaf, compound *See* COMPOUND LEAF

leaf cutting A cutting that consists of a leaf, a portion of a leaf, or a leaf with its attached leafstalk. This technique is most often used with tropical plants such as houseplants. Leaf cuttings require much the same conditions as softwood cuttings do. Most can lose water and wilt rapidly, so before you collect them it's best to fill pots with premoistened rooting medium and set up a system for maintaining high humidity around the cuttings. (*See* HUMIDITY) Collect leaf cuttings any time, although they are best gathered when plants are in active growth. Select healthy, turgid leaves; wilted or water-stressed ones are not likely to recover and root well. Hold leaves in a plastic bag to keep them from drying out, and keep them out of direct sun. If you can't plant them immediately, wrap them in a moist paper towel and keep them in the plastic bag in a cool, shady spot. Stick leaves that have leafstalks attached—such as those taken from African violets (*Saintpaulia* spp.)—with the base of the leafstalk in the cutting mix. (African violets also root in water.) Leaves of rex begonias (*Begonia rex*) and various gesneriads such as Cape primrose (*Streptocarpus* spp.) can be cut or scored to cause them to produce plantlets at the base of leaf veins. Slash a rex begonia leaf across several veins and pin it to the surface of a cutting mix with U-shaped wire pins. Cut Cape primrose leaves lengthwise, eliminating the midvein, then bury the cut edge in a moist cutting medium with the margin of the leaf pointing up. Plantlets will appear at the base of the veins. Cut portions of rex begonia leaves—squares or V-shaped pieces—will root provided they have a main vein. Pin them down with U-shaped pieces of wire. Sections of sansevieria (*Sansevieria* spp.) leaves also can be rooted; cut them across the leaf and pot them up. Use a separate container for each type of plant, since roots form at different rates. Label each container with the name of the plant and the date, and water thoroughly. Then treat the leaf cuttings as you would softwood cuttings. When transplanting, you may need to gently tease apart individual plantlets, as they commonly form in clusters. *See* SOFTWOOD CUTTING, TRANSPLANTING

leaf cutting

leafhoppers Small, wedge-shaped insects that hop quickly when disturbed. Leafhoppers may be green or brown or may have bright bands of color on their wings. Nymphs look similar to the adults but lack wings. Both adults and nymphs feed by sucking plant juices from stems and the undersides of leaves, causing discoloration and stunted or distorted growth. They also exude a sticky honeydew on leaves and fruit and may also transmit plant diseases. To control them, spray with insecticidal soap or or pyrethrins; use rotenone or sabadilla as a last resort. Protect crops with floating row covers.

leaflet A leaflike division on a compound leaf. The small individual "leaves" that make up a compound leaf.

leafminers The larvae of tiny wasps, leafminers are small, wormlike creatures that tunnel between the upper and lower surfaces of leaves, feeding and producing papery blotches or meandering tunnels that turn yellow or brown. To control them, remove and destroy badly infested leaves. To prevent damage in the future, protect vegetable crops with floating row covers from planting to flowering or harvest.

leaf mold The end product of the decomposition of leaves, a dark brown, powdery material that can be used to improve soil or added to potting mixes.

leaf-petiole cutting A cutting that consists of the leaf and attached leafstalk, or petiole; generally these are referred to simply as leaf cuttings. African violets (*Saintpaulia* spp.) and peperomias (*Peperomia* spp.) are commonly propagated by leaf-petiole cuttings. *See* LEAF CUTTING

leaf primordia *See* MERISTEM

leafrollers Small, yellowish to pale green caterpillars that feed on leaves at night and hide in leaves during the day, which they roll up and fasten with webbing. Serious infestations can defoliate plants. To control them, pick off and crush rolled leaves.

leaf scar The mark or scar that remains on a twig after a leaf falls. Generally found directly below a bud or buds, the scar shows the outline of the base of the petiole, or leaf stalk, as well as the bundle scars, which mark where the vascular tissue entered the leaf. Leaf scars, together with the shape and appearance of dormant buds and twigs, can be used to identify trees, shrubs, and other woody plants in winter, because their appearance varies from species to species.

leaf scorch A cultural condition found on plants growing in dry, hot sites, especially those exposed to heat reflected from walls and paving. The edges of leaves turn yellow and then brown and crispy. They also may roll inward. Leaves or whole plants may wilt and affected plants may be stunted. Because leaf scorch is caused by drought and excessive heat, water susceptible plants regularly to minimize damage. Mulching also helps keep the soil moist and cool. Select plants that tolerate hot, dry conditions when planting difficult sites, and work plenty of organic matter into the soil before planting.

leaf, simple *See* SIMPLE LEAF

leaf spots Various fungi and and bacteria cause leaf spots, which can differ widely in appearance. Anthracnose produces dark, sunken lesions, often with pinkish spore masses. Bacterial spot leads to small, circular, light green spots that later turn brown; there may be angular, purplish areas around the spots. Early blight produces small, circular, yellow spots that expand and turn brown with a grayish center; late blight forms fast-spreading, purplish or brown-black areas, sometimes with pale halos. Leaf spot diseases also cause sunken lesions on stems, stunted growth, and spotted or deformed fruit. Prevent problems with leaf spot diseases by growing resistant cultivars as well as spacing and pruning plants to ensure good air circulation. To control these diseases, pinch off and destroy infected parts. Clean up dropped leaves. A sulfur- or copper-based fungicide, applied every 7 to 10 days, may prevent the spread of fungal leaf spots, but destroy severely infected plants.

leaf stalk *See* PETIOLE

leaf trace The vascular bundle running from the petiole into the main vascular tissue (stele).

leaf, true *See* TRUE LEAF

lean A general term used to describe soil that drains quickly, is poor in nutrients, and has a low organic matter content.

leathery *See* CORIACEOUS

legitimate This term is used to describe names for plants that have been properly published according to the rules in the *International Code of Botanical Nomenclature* or *International Code of Nomenclature for Cultivated Plants*.

legume A dry fruit that opens at maturity (is dehiscent) along two lines and is derived from one carpel, which is the organ containing the ovules where seeds develop once the flower is fertilized. The fruits of peas and beans, which are commonly called pods, are legumes. Asparagus beans (*Vigna unguiculata* var. *sesquipedalis*) bear particularly long legumes, which can reach 2 to 3 feet or more in length. Legume also is used to refer to any member of the pea family (Fabaceae, formerly Leguminosae).

legume

lemma A papery or chaffy bract borne at the base of a grass flower. *See* GLUME

lenticel A rounded, somewhat raised, and slightly corky area on the surface of a stem on on bark. Lenticels are actually pores through which gases such as oxygen can pass to reach the living portions of the wood beneath. Many cherries (*Prunus* spp.) have prominent, dark ornamental lenticels on their bark.

lenticular Lens-shaped. Nearly flattened and rounded in outline, but with convex sides.

lepidote Covered with tiny scales that are attached in a peltate fashion, with a stem-like attachment in the middle of each scale. Most often used to describe leaf surfaces.

liana A woody, climbing vine.

lifting Digging a plant from the ground.

light shade *See* PARTIAL SHADE

lignification The process whereby woody, or lignified, tissue develops in the new growth of trees, shrubs, and other woody plants. New growth, or softwood or greenwood, becomes firmer as it ripens, or lignifies, and semi-ripe cuttings are taken from this firmer wood.

lignified, ligneous Woody or woody-textured.

lignin A tough, woody substance found in walls of plant cells. Cells that contain lignin provide support for the plant. (Lignin combines with the cellulose in the cell wall and hardens, or lignifies, making the cell wall inelastic.) Lignins are a principal component of woody plant stems; xylem (water-conducting) cells contain lignin.

ligulate, ligule Tongue- or strap-shaped. This term can be used for any strap-shaped plant part or body, called a ligule. When used to describe leaves it is applied to ones that are narrower than lorate leaves, which also are strap-shaped. Society garlics (*Tulbaghia* spp.) have ligulate leaves. The "petals" (actually ray florets) of many aster family plants (Asteraceae) such as oxeye daisies (*Leucanthemum vulgare*) are ligulate in shape.

ligulate flower

ligulate leaf

limb The flaired or expanded and flattened part of a petal or leaf, or the expanded part of a corolla if the petals are united. Limb also refers to a larger branch on a tree.

limbing up Removing the lower branches on a tree to make it possible to walk beneath it. Evergreens are generally grown with branches that extend all the way to the ground—they usually are quite unattractive if limbed up. Most shade trees, on the other hand are limbed up to provide room under them to enjoy the shade they cast. Limbing up also makes it easy to tend grass or grow groundcovers or perennials under shade trees. Deciduous trees that naturally produce descending branches, including pin oak (*Quercus palustris*) and shingle oak (*Q. imbricaria*), often look awkward when limbed up; plant these species away from walkways and let the branches sweep the ground for a natural, low-maintenance effect. Do not remove the lower branches for the first few years after planting a new tree, because they help the tree develop a thicker trunk. In about the fourth year of growth, begin removing the branches from the ground up at a rate no faster than the rate that new branches are being formed at the tree's top. Work up from the bottom, thinning out whorls of branches over 2 or 3 years. It's best to cut back the lowest side branches by about one-third (to a point where a smaller side branch joins it) the first year; the next year, remove those pruned branches entirely and head back the next tier of branches by one-third. Continue this process for several years until the lowest branches are growing at the desired height.

lime A general term for several substances that contain calcium, which primarily are used to raise the pH of acid soils. *See* ACID SOIL

limestone Rock formed by dissolved calcium and magnesium carbonate solution that settled on the ocean floor. Ground limestone is used to raise the pH of acid soils. *See* ACID SOIL

liming Adding lime to raise the pH of an acid soil. *See* ACID SOIL

line A general term for a group of plants that has been systematically selected over several generations to create plants that have similar characteristics and come true from seeds. Plants in each generation that do not exhibit the particular characteristics selected are rouged out (pulled up or destroyed) and seed is saved from the best individuals.

linear Long and slender, like a line. The edges of a linear leaf are parallel, or nearly parallel, and linear leaves are at least 12 times longer than they are wide. Torch lilies (*Kniphofia* spp.) and crocuses (*Crocus* spp.) have linear leaves.

linear leaf

lined *See* STRIATE

line out To plant bedding annuals, vegetables, cuttings, or other plants outdoors arranged in straight rows to grow them on until they reach a desired size.

liner A young plant produced in a small container that has been planted or is ready to be planted in its first full-size pot.

linnaean system *See* BINOMIAL NOMENCLATURE

Linnaeus, Carolus (1707–1778) Also known as Carl Von Linné, a Swedish botanist who founded the system of binomial classification still used today by taxonomists to classify plants, animals, and other organisms.

lip The upper or lower segment of a corolla (petals) that is divided into two segments.

Members of the mint family (Lamiaceae) such as mint (*Mentha* spp.) or salvia (*Salvia* spp.) bear flowers that are two-lipped (bilabiate). Also used for the the enlarged lower petal, or labellum of an orchid flower, which is often pouched or otherwise distinctive. Plants in the ginger family (Zingiberaceae) also bear flowers with lips; in this case, the lip is a staminode, a modified, petal-like stamen.

liquid fertilizer A fertilizer that is designed to be dissolved in water. The concentrated form either can be liquid (fish emulsion) or dry (kelp meal). Liquid fertilizers are especially useful when plants are already showing signs of nutrient deficiencies because they are in a form that plants can take up immediately through their leaves or roots. Manure and compost tea are two liquid fertilizers that are easy to make at home.

lithophyte A plant that grows on rocks or poor, rocky soil and obtains nutrients from the atmosphere rather than the soil.

little bulbs A general term for the smaller species of hardy plants that grow from bulbs, corms, or similar structures that bloom in spring, summer, or fall. This includes crocuses (*Crocus* spp.) as well as species and cultivars of daffodils (*Narcissus* spp.) and tulips (*Tulipa* spp.) that are small in stature. A wide variety of other small, hardy bulbs are commonly referred to as "little bulbs," including ornamental onions (*Allium* spp.), bulbous anemones or windflowers (*Anemone* spp.), glory-of-the-snow (*Chionodoxa* spp.), hardy cyclamen (*Cyclamen* spp.), bluebells (*Hyacinthoides* spp., formerly *Endymion* spp.), winter aconites (*Eranthis* spp.), dogtooth violets (*Erythronium* spp.), fritillaries (*Fritillaria* spp.), snowdrops (*Galanthus* spp.), bulbous irises (*Iris* spp.), snowflake (*Leucojum* spp.), grape hyacinths (*Muscari* spp.), stars of Bethlehem (*Ornithogalum* spp.), squills (*Puschkinia* spp.), and scillas (*Scilla* spp.). Autumn crocuses (*Colchicum* spp.) and autumn daffodils (*Sternbergia* spp.) also are commonly called "little bulbs," along with many rarer species.

littoral Growing on the seashore.

loam A medium-textured class of soils that have moderate amounts of all three particles—sand, silt, and clay—and are ideal gardening soils. *See* SOIL TEXTURE

-lobate A suffix referring to lobes, which are rounded segments of an organ such as a leaf or petal. Trilobate means divided into three lobes, for example.

lobe A rounded segment of an organ such as a leaf or petal.

lobed Having an edge, or margin, that is divided into segments, which are generally rounded. The segments, called lobes, are separated from one another by indentations, called sinuses, that extend from one-quarter to almost one-half of the distance to the middle or base of the leaf, petal, or other organ. The terms cleft and parted are used to distinguish between lobes and deeper divisions. Leaves can be lobed either palmately (into divisions arranged in a finger- or handlike fashion) or pinnately (divisions arranged in a featherlike fashion). *See also* PALMATELY LOBED, PINNATELY LOBED, CLEFT, PARTED

lobed leaf margin

lobulate Bearing lobules.

lobule A small lobe, or a small, lobelike division of a lobe.

-locular A suffix referring to locules, usually combined with a prefix indicating a number. Octolocular means having eight locules, for example.

locule A chamber or cavity within an ovary, an anther, or a fruit.

loculicidal dehiscence *See* DEHISCENT

locusta A grass spikelet.

lodicule Microscopic structures on the florets of a grass spikelet that are sensitive to changes in water pressure. The lodicules swell when conditions are suitable for pollination and cause the florets to open. *See* GLUME

loment A type of legume (a dry fruit that opens at maturity along two lines) that is narrowed or constricted between the seeds and breaks apart across the pod at the points of constriction. Tick trefoils or beggar's-ticks (*Desmodium* spp.) bear loments.

long-day plant A plant that flowers when nights are getting shorter and days longer. *See* photoperiodism

longitudinal Lengthwise. Along the axis (length) of a leaf, seed, petiole, or other organ.

long pot *See* DIFFICULT TO TRANSPLANT

loopers *See* CATERPILLARS

lop, lopping Cutting back shoots or branches drastically or removing them entirely.

loppers A handheld pruning tool with long handles and two curved blades that bypass one another with a scissorlike action. Anvil-style loppers, with a flat blade that is pressed down into a flat anvil, also are available. Loppers resemble large hand pruners, but are designed to tackle branches up to about 3 inches in diameter (for larger branches, use a pruning saw). They have handles that range from about 15 inches up to 36 inches, making it possible to reach higher up or deeper into a plant for pruning. Because of their longer handles, loppers offer considerable leverage for cutting. Ratchet-style loppers also are available: These make it quite easy to cut branches, because each time you press the handles together, the ratchet mechanism brings them closer together with minimum effort. Ratchet loppers are difficult to maneuver in tight spaces and will tear or crush branches if used on stems that are too thick.

loppers

lorate Strap-shaped. Lorate leaves are generally wider than ligulate ones, which also are strap-shaped.

lorate

lower vascular plants *See* FERN ALLIES

low pH soil *See* ACID SOIL

lunate Crescent-shaped. A lunate leaf forms a half circle in outline. The two outer corners of the leaf, on either side of the stem, form acute angles (less than 90 degrees). The base of the leaf is more or less flat or curved outward, rather than indented as it is in a reniform leaf.

lunate leaf

lustrous Shiny or glossy. Most often used to describe leaf surfaces.

luteous, lutescence Yellowish or greenish yellow.

lyrate A type of pinnatifid leaf, meaning it is has pairs of lobes or segments along the midrib. In this case the leaf has a large lobe at the tip and one or more pairs of smaller lobes closer to the base. *See also* PINNATIFID

lyrate leaf

maceration A method of preparation used for herbs whose active ingredients would be damaged by high temperatures. To make a maceration, place herbs in water in a glass, ceramic, or enameled container that can be covered tightly, and steep them at room temperature for 12 hours. Then strain or press the liquid to separate out the plant parts. To prepare a standard maceration, combine 1 part herb to 5 parts water.

macro- A prefix meaning large.

macrofauna Larger soil-dwelling animals such as earthworms millipedes, centipedes, pill bugs, snails, spiders, ants, and many other kinds of insects. A few, such as root-attacking grubs, are pests, but the vast majority are beneficial. These creatures feed on living and dead plant parts, on bacteria and fungi, and on each other. They also help mix the soil by tunneling through it, both vertically and laterally. They open passages for air and water in the process.

macronutrients Elements plants require in relatively large amounts for healthy growth. These are: Calcium, carbon, hydrogen, magnesium, nitrogen, oxygen, phosphorus, potassium, and sulfur. Plants take up carbon, hydrogen, and oxygen from the air. The other elements all normally are taken up from the soil (foliar feeding is an exception); to be available to plants they need to be dissolved in the soil solution and are thus taken up by plant roots.

macropore *See* PORE SPACE

macrospore *See* MEGASPORE

macula A spot or blotch of color.

maculate Marked with large blotches of color.

maggot A larva, or the immature stage, of a fly.

maiden A young tree the first year after being budded or grafted. This term is primarily used in reference to fruit trees.

malacophyllous Having soft leaves.

mallet cutting A cutting that has a short section of the main stem from which it was cut still attached at its base. Mallet cuttings are usually collected and treated as semi-ripe cuttings. The mallet encourages rooting, and this type of cutting is especially useful for plants that have pithy or hollow stems, because the mallet seals the base of the cutting, helping to prevent fungal diseases from invading it.

mallet cutting

malodorous Ill-smelling.

malpighian, malpighiaceous *See* DOLABRIFORM

mammillate, mammillate Bearing nipple-like bumps or knobs called mammilla.

manicate Thickly hairy. Covered with thick, interwoven hairs.

manna The dried, sugary exudate that oozes out of some trees, especially flowering or manna ash (*Fraxinus ornus*).

manure An organic fertilizer and soil amendment that can be used to add nutrients and organic matter to soil. It also can be added to the compost pile. Whether it comes from a cow, chicken, horse, rabbit, or zoo animal, manure contains nitrogen, potassium, and phosphorus, as well as bacteria. The analysis varies, depending on the source of the manure. Do not apply fresh manure to plants because it can burn them. Composted manure—or manure collected from a well-aged manure pile—is safest to use. Do not use droppings from cats or dogs in the garden, as they can transmit disease organisms.

manure fork *See* FORK

manure tea A dilute liquid fertilizer that is easy to make at home. To make manure tea, place a shovelful of manure in a burlap sack or old pillowcase, tie the top closed, and let the sack soak in a tub or large bucket of water for several days. When the water looks dark, remove the "tea bag" and toss the contents on the compost pile. Add enough water to dilute the remaining liquid to the color of weak tea. Apply manure tea to the soil around plants with a watering can or sprinkle it onto the leaves. Strain it through a piece of nylon stocking if you want to spray it on the foliage.

marbled A variegation pattern that resembles marble. The color is distributed in irregular, often sinuous, bands of color.

marcescent Withering but persisting.

marcot A branch that has rooting medium tied or otherwise bound to it in order to air layer it.

marcottage *See* AIR LAYERING

margin Edge or border. Used to refer to the edge of a leaf.

marginal Borne on the edge or border of another organ. Spines on the edge of a leaf are marginal, for example. This term also refers to plants that grow at the water's edge, such as cattails (*Typha* spp.). *See* MARGINAL PLANTS

marginal plants Often sold as bog plants, these are species that require constantly moist soil to thrive and usually will grow in standing water up to a certain depth—some tolerate only 1 to 2 inches of water over the crowns of the plants, while others will grow in up to a foot of water. Many marginals are very fast growing and can quickly take over a pond, especially an earth-bottomed one. Some even have sharply pointed rhizomes that are capable of piercing flexible liners. In water gardens, these plants normally are confined to containers sitting in the water on ledges designed for their cultivation. Marginal plants include sweet flags (*Acorus* spp.), flowering rush (*Butomus umbellatus*), pickerel weed (*Pontederia cordata*), golden club (*Oronitum aquaticum*), lizard's tail (*Saururus cernuus*) arrowheads (*Sagittaria* spp.), cattails (*Typha* spp.), and some species of iris, including blue flag (*Iris versicolor*) and yellow flag (*I. pseudacorus*).

marginate Having a distinct margin.

maritime Native to a coastal area or belonging to the sea.

market pack A molded plastic container that contains four or six "cells" in which seedlings or cuttings are grown and sold.

mass planting A planting that consists of a large clump or drift of a single plant or is made up of large clumps of several different plants, usually ones that are easy to grow.

mast The nuts of trees used for food, especially for animals, such as acorns and beechnuts.

master plan *See* SITE PLAN

match the plant to the site A useful guideline for plant selection that means select plants that will grow well in the sun, soil, and weather conditions available in your garden. Plants selected because they thrive in the conditions available inevitably look better, bloom better, and have fewer problems with pests and diseases than ones that have to struggle to survive. They also will require less maintenance. To match plants to the site, study the existing conditions carefully, by looking at sun and shade pattern, learning about the soil, and so forth. Then choose plants that naturally thrive in those conditions.

mattock A hand tool useful for digging new garden beds and cutting through roots. Several sizes are available, from small hand-size tools that weigh about 1 $\frac{1}{2}$ pounds to both intermediate and large models that can weigh 8 pounds or so. (Look for a tool supplier that offers more than one size of mattock so you can try out the different sizes.) A mattock has a two-ended metal blade with a handle inserted through an eye socket in the middle. One end of the blade ends in an axlike blade at right angles to the handle, while the other end also has an axlike blade that cuts parallel to the handle. A mattock is used by swinging it over your shoulder.

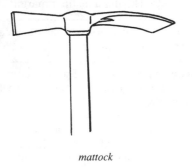

mattock

maturation The period in the development of a fruit immediately before it is ripe.

matutinal Functioning in the morning. Some flowers open only in the morning.

meadow garden A perennial planting that has a free-form, natural-looking design and features native grasses planted with wildflowers such as goldenrods (*Solidago* spp.), asters (*Aster* spp.), coneflowers (*Echinacea* spp. and *Rudbeckia* spp.). Naturalized plants such as Queen Anne's lace (*Daucus carota*) and oxeye daisies (*Leucanthemum vulgare*) also make fine additions to a meadow garden.

mealy Farinose. Crumbly, granular, or powdery in texture.

mealybugs Insects that suck sap from stems and leaves. The adult females are small, white, oval, soft-bodied insects. Males are tiny, winged insects, while nymphs resemble the adult females. Mealybugs cluster in leaf axils and their feeding causes stunted, off-color plants. They are common houseplant pests, but also attack outdoor plants. To control them outdoors, attract beneficial predators. (*See* BENEFICIAL INSECTS) On small plants, touch individual mealybugs with a cotton swab dipped in isopropyl alcohol. Discard severely infested plants. Spray larger plants with insecticidal soap or pyrethrins.

median, medial Located in the middle or relating to the middle. The median leaflet of a compound leaf is the leaflet at the midpoint. This term also is used to describe sori on a fern frond that are located halfway between the edge of the leaflet and the midvein.

medicinals, medicinal herbs Herbs traditionally used to make herbal medicines. Medicinal herbs range from safe species that are commonly used in teas, such as mints (*Mentha* spp.), feverfew (*Tanacetum parthenium*), and Roman chamomile (*Chamaemelum nobile*), to quite potent plants that can be extremely toxic and are best appreciated for their historical use in herbal medicine or administered by an expert in medicinal plants. Examples of toxic plants that have a history of medicinal use include monkshood or aconite (*Aconitum* spp.) and foxglove (*Digitalis purpurea*). Medicinal herbs are prepared in several different ways—*see* DECOCTION, MACERATION, INFUSION, TEA, TISANE, POULTICE, PLASTER, COMPRESS, HERBAL SYRUP.

medium A mixture of ingredients used to fill containers for germinating seeds, rooting cuttings, or growing plants. Also commonly called potting mix or potting soil, although many commercial potting media no longer contain any actual soil. *See* POTTING MIX

mega- A prefix meaning large. For example, megaphyllous means large-leaved.

megasporangium A sporangium, or spore-producing body, that bears megaspores.

megaspore The larger of the two types of spores borne by a heterosporous plant. Megaspores develop into female gametophytes.

megasporophyll In nonflowering plants, a leaf that bears megaspores. In flowering plants (angiosperms), a carpel.

membranous Thin, flexible, and translucent or more or less translucent.

mericarp Half of a schizocarp. *See* SCHIZOCARP

meristem An area of undifferentiated cells that actively divide and differentiate, ultimately giving rise to the various organs and specialized tissues in a plant. There are two types of meristems: apical and lateral. Apical meristems, sometimes simply referred to as growing points, are located in shoot and root tips. As apical meristem cells divide, they give rise to what is called primary growth, especially by lengthening stems and roots. Damaged meristems cannot be regenerated, so they are carefully protected by other plant structures. In roots, the apical meristems are protected by root caps; in shoot tips, they are protected by tiny primordial leaves that are folded over them. At the base of each leaf primordium is a bud primordium that will grow into a branch if the plant stimulates it to grow. Lateral meristems are located along the length of stems and roots. As lateral meristem cells divide, they cause stems and roots to thicken and better support the plant, giving rise to what is called secondary growth. The cambium in the trunk or branches of a tree is lateral meristem. Grasses have a layer of meristem, called intercalary meristem, that is located between the leaf blade and the rhizome, rather than at the top of the plant; that's why lawngrasses can be cut repeatedly

without damaging the growing points. Monocots such as palms also have a thickening meristem, responsible for the thickening of woody parts such as the trunk. (*See* MONOCOT) The term meristem was once used for a propagation technique now most often referred to as tissue culture. *See* CAMBIUM, TISSUE CULTURE

meristematic Relating or pertaining to the meristem.

-merous A suffix meaning parts of a set, usually combined with a prefix indicating a number. Pentamerous means arranged in multiples or sets of five, trimerous, sets of three, for example.

mesic Moist.

mesicape A garden or landscape designed for a region that receives relatively dependable amounts of rain yet incorporates various water-saving features. *See also* XERISCAPE

meso- A prefix meaning middle. For example, mesophyll is the tissue in the center of a leaf, between the upper and lower epidermis.

mesocarp *See* PERICARP

mesophyte A plant that grows in average soil conditions (halfway between hydrophytic and xerophytic).

metamorphosis A change in the form or structure of an insect during its development or lifecycle. There are two types of metamorphosis: complete and incomplete. In complete metamorphosis, the larval stage of the insect is transformed during a resting stage, and when it emerges, it resembles an entirely different organism. Caterpillars and butterflies exhibit this type of metamorphosis. In some cases, one stage is a pest while another is harmless. For example, parsleyworms are the caterpillars of black swallowtail butterflies. Insects that exhibit incomplete metamorphosis progress from larvae to adults without a resting stage. The larva, called a nymph, sheds its skin several times as it grows and each time it more closely resembles the adult.

micro- A prefix meaning small.

microbial insecticide A general term for organic insecticides that are biological controls containing disease-causing organisms—bacteria, fungi, viruses, and protozoa—and that kill specific pest insects. BT (*Bacillus thuringiensis*) probably is the best known of these substances, but there are others. (*See* BACILLUS THURINGIENSIS) Milky disease (*Bacillus popilliae* and *B. lentimorbus*) infects grubs of Japanese beetles. Beneficial nematodes also can be used as microbial insecticides. These are applied to the soil where they parasitize grubs and other larvae.

microclimate A spot with growing conditions that vary from the surrounding area. Expert gardeners use microclimates to find spots for plants with special requirements or to coax unusually early or late bloom from various species. For example, a spot on the south side of a wall warms up earlier in spring and if it is sheltered may be perfect for overwintering plants that are not quite hardy in your area. South-facing sites also are ideal for planting with early spring bulbs or other plants, since they are warmer and encourage early bloom. A site on the north side of a wall has the opposite effect—it remains cooler later, but can be used to encourage unusually late bloom. A low spot may create a moist, even marshy area, while a high spot (especially if the soil is amended with crushed granite) may be perfect for rock-garden plants, which require perfect drainage.

microfauna Microscopic soil-dwelling animals such as nematodes, protozoa, and rotifers. *See* MICROORGANISMS

microherd A general term for the beneficial microorganisms that break down materials in compost or soil. *See* SOIL MICROORGANISMS

micronutrients Elements plants require in very small amounts for healthy growth.

These are: Boron, chlorine, copper, iron, manganese, molybdenum, and zinc.

microorganisms, soil *See* SOIL MICROORGANISMS

micropore *See* PORE SPACE

micropropagation *See* TISSUE CULTURE

microsporangium A sporangium, or spore-producing body, that bears microspores.

microspore The smaller of the two types of spores borne by a heterosporous plant. Microspores develop into male gametophytes.

microsporophyll In nonflowering plants, a leaf that bears microspores. In flowering plants (angiosperms), a carpel.

mid- A prefix that means middle or central. The midvein is the central vein on a leaf, for example.

midrib The center or primary vein of a leaf or leaflet. The midrib usually runs down the center of the leaf, extending the leaf stalk, or petiole.

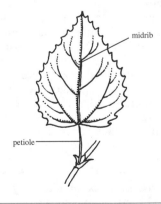

midvein The center vein of a leaf or leaflet.

mildew Fungal diseases—powdery mildew and downy mildew are most common—that cause white to grayish patches on plant leaves, stems, buds, and flowers. Downy mildew also produces light green patches on upper leaf surfaces or cottony, purplish lesions on leaves and stems. To prevent mildews, grow resistant cultivars of plants, space plants properly, avoid overhead watering, and avoid handling wet plants (fungal spores are easily transported from plant to plant when foliage is wet). To control these diseases, pick off infected leaves and thin crowded stems to ensure good air circulation. Or spray with a sulfur- or copper-based fungicide every 7 to 10 days. Destroy seriously infected plants.

milky disease *See* MICROBIAL INSECTICIDE

milled sphagnum *See* SPHAGNUM MOSS

minor bulbs A general term for less well-known hardy plants that grow from bulbs, corms, or similar structures and usually bloom in spring or fall. Daffodils (*Narcissus* spp.), tulips (*Tulipa* spp.), hyacinths (*Hyacinthus* spp.), and crocuses (*Crocus* spp.) usually are not considered minor bulbs. Summer-blooming bulbs are commonly referred to simply as summer bulbs. Minor bulbs include anemones (*Anemone* spp.), ornamental onions (*Allium* spp.), Jack-in-the-pulpit (*Arisaema* spp.), quamash (*Camassia* spp.), glory-of-the-snow (*Chionodoxa* spp.), hardy cyclamen (*Cyclamen* spp.), bluebells (*Hyacinthoides* spp., formerly *Endymion* spp.), winter aconites (*Eranthis* spp.), dogtooth violets (*Erythronium* spp.), fritillaries (*Fritillaria* spp.), snowdrops (*Galanthus* spp.), bulbous irises (*Iris* spp.), snowflake (*Leucojum* spp.), grape hyacinths (*Muscari* spp.), stars of Bethlehem (*Ornithogalum* spp.), squills (*Puschkinia* spp.), and scillas (*Scilla* spp.). *See* SUMMER BULBS

mites Very tiny, golden, red, or brown spiderlike pests, often called spider mites, that may spin fine webs around leaves or between leaves and stems, especially at the tips. Mites suck plant juices from the undersides of leaves, producing a light-colored stippling on leaf surfaces. Whole leaves become pale and dry and may drop. Seriously infested plants may have webbing and stunted growth. Outdoors, mites feed through the growing season; indoors, they feed all year. To control them, rinse or spray leaves regularly with water to suppress populations. Outdoors, attract beneficial predators (*See* BENEFICIAL INSECTS). Spray serious infestations with insecticidal soap, horticultural oil, neem, or pyrethrins.

mixed border *See* MIXED PLANTING

mixed planting A planting that contains a variety of different plant types, typically herbaceous perennials combined with a mix of hardy bulbs, shrubs, trees, woody vines, annuals, and other plants such as herbs and even vegetables.

modified open center A pruning and training technique, similar to a central leader, that creates a tree with a series of strong scaffold branches but without a central leader at maturity. Height control is the main advantage of this style of training, which is often used on standard-size apple trees. In addition to apples, it is also a good choice for cherries, pears, and some upright plums. To create a modified open-center tree, train as you would for a central-leader tree (*See* CENTRAL LEADER), then when the tree reaches the desired height, remove the central leader to check the tree's upward growth. Then train the tree, which usually has five or six scaffold branches by this time, somewhat like an open-center tree.

moist chilling *See* STRATIFICATION

moisture-loving plants Plants that thrive in evenly moist soil. While some also will grow in standing water, others prefer moisture-retentive, but well-drained soil for best growth. Plants that prefer rich, evenly moist, but well-drained conditions include goatsbeard (*Aruncus dioicus*), astilbes (*Astilbe* spp.), turtlehead (*Chelone* spp.), Siberian and Japanese irises (*Iris sibirica* and *I. ensata*), cardinal flower (*Lobelia cardinalis*), royal fern (*Osmunda regalis*), Japanese primroses (*Primula japonica*), and rodgersias (*Rodgersia* spp.).

mold, gray *See* GRAY MOLD

mono- A prefix meaning one or once. For example, a monocarpic plant flowers and sets fruit only once before dying. Monanthous means one flowered and monomorphic means having one shape or form. Monocephalous means having only one head.

monocarpic species A species that blooms once, sets its seed, and then dies. Archangel (*Angelica archangelica*) and *A. gigas* are monocarpic.

monochasial cyme These are cymes that produce a terminal flower and are branched like dichasial cymes, but one branch in each pair is missing, so they often look as if they have a single stem, or axis. Tomatoes (*Lycopersicon esculentum*) bear their flowers in monochasial cymes. There are two types of monochasial cymes: Helicoid, which has a coiled axis, and Scorpioid, which has a zigzag axis. *See also* CYME, DICHASIAL CYME, HELICOID CYME, SCORPIOID CYME

monochasium *See* MONOCHASIAL CYME

monoclinous flower *See* PERFECT FLOWER

monocot A collective term for plants that bear seeds with one cotlyedon, have leaves with parallel veins, and bear flowers with flower parts such as petals and sepals in threes or multiples thereof. Monocots include members of the grass family (Poaceae), iris family (Iridaceae), lily family (Liliaceae), orchid family (Orchidaceae), and palm family (Aracaceae) among others. The stems of monocots and dicots also differ. While both have clusters of vascular tissue called vascular bundles, in monocots they are scattered irregularly through the stem; in dicots, they are arranged in a ring. Monocots lack the lateral meristem tissue called cambium that is responsible for the thickening and stiffening of the trunk and branches of dicots, and for this reason monocot stems also do not develop annual rings. The trunks of treelike monocots such as palms consist of many scattered vascular bundles formed by a diffuse mass of meristematic cells called a thickening meristem. The vascular bundles pushed to the outside of a monocot trunk dry out and form the outer "bark" or "cork" layer. *See* DICOT

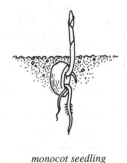

monocot seedling

monocotyledonous Bearing one cotyledon, or seed leaf. *See* MONOCOT

monoecious A plant that bears separate male and female flowers on the same plant. The flowers on a monoecious plant are imperfect, meaning they have either male or female structures (stamens or pistils) but not both. Begonias (*Begonia* spp.) are monoecious, and they generally bear male and female flowers in the same inflorescence. The female flowers have a prominent three-angled ovary at the base of the flower. Corn (*Zea mays*), castor bean (*Ricinus communis*), and oaks (*Quercus* spp.) also are monoecious.

monogeneric A family or higher-ranking taxon that contains only one genus. The ginkgo family, Ginkoaceae, contains only the genus *Ginkgo* and is monogeneric.

monopetalous Bearing a single petal. This term is also used to refer to flowers with petals that are fused together (gamopetalous or sympetalous).

monophyllous Bearing a single leaf or having simple leaves.

monopodial A type of growth in which a stem or rhizome grows indefinitely from the bud at the tip, but rarely produces branches. *See* SYMPODIAL

monospecific A term sometimes used to designate a genus that contains only one species. Monotypic is more commonly used in this case.

monotypic The term used to designate a taxon that contains only one representative or individual—a genus that contains only one species, for example. The genus *Callistephus* is monotypic because it contains only one species, the popular annual China aster (*C. chinensis*). *Kirengeshoma* and *Platycodon* are two other monotypic genera. While this term is most often used to refer to a one-species genus, it also can be used to designate a family with only one genus, or any other taxon that contains only one representative. Since the ginkgo family (Ginkoaceae) contains only the genus *Ginkgo*, and *Ginkgo* in turn contains only the species *G. biloba*, both are monotypic.

-morphic, -morphous A suffix meaning having a particular or specified form. Dimorphic means having two forms, while polymorphic means having many forms.

morphology In botany, the study of plant structure.

moschate Musky smelling.

moss peat *See* PEAT MOSS

mother ferns Ferns that develop plantlets or bulblets on their fronds that sprout into plants once they touch the soil. Two species of spleenworts that are commonly called mother ferns—*Asplenium bulbiferum* and *A. daucifolium*—have this characteristic, as does Oriental chain fern (*Woodwardia orientalis*). Other ferns produce pealike bulblets that actually can weigh down the leaf until they touch the soil and sprout, or that sprout once the leaf has died and rests on the soil. Bulblet bladder fern (*Cystopteris bulbifera*) bears large numbers of bulblets that easily fall from the fronds when they are jarred loose. Other ferns have an unusually long rachis (the main stem of the frond) that produces a plantlet at the tip where it touches the

soil. These are commonly called walking ferns and include *Camptosorus rhizophyllus* and *Polystichum lepidocaulon*. Mother ferns produce plants vegetatively, or asexually, so the plantlets are exact copies of the parent plant. *See also* VEGETATIVE GROWTH

mother plant A plant used to provide cuttings, divisions, or other plant material for use in vegetative propagation techniques, which yield genetically identical plants. Also called a parent plant. In hybridizing, a mother plant also is the seed parent.

mottled Blotched or spotted with color.

mound layering Also called stooling, this type of layering involves mounding loose soil or other media over the top of a plant to encourage the production of many new plants. It is especially useful for propagating plants with stiff or short shoots that are difficult to bend to the ground, and is commonly used on shrubby herbs such as thymes (*Thymus* spp.) and lavenders (*Lavandula* spp.), as well as lavender cottons (*Santolina* spp.) and artemisias (*Artemisia* spp.). Mound layering also can be used to renew these plants, which tend to get woody and less attractive and productive as they age. Mound layer plants in spring by piling 3 to 5 inches of loose, sandy soil or mulch mixed with compost over the top of the plant. Leave the 3 or 4 inches of each shoot tip exposed. Be sure to sift soil around the base of the stems; roots won't form if there are air pockets. Water gently to moisten the soil but avoid washing it away. Keep the mound evenly moist and replenish the sandy soil/mulch as necessary. In late summer or early fall, gently brush it away to see if roots have formed. If they have, sever the stems, taking as many roots as possible with each piece. Pot up the individual plants or move them to a nursery bed or another spot in the garden. If roots haven't formed, recover the plant and check again the following spring or early summer. Most gardeners replace the parent plant, which can be

unsightly, with one of the new plantlets.
See LAYERING

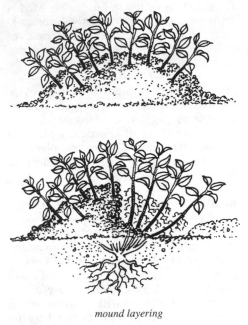

mound layering

mucilaginous Wet, slimy.

mucronate Ending with a short, sharp, abrupt point, called a mucro, which is an extension of the midrib. The point has a length-to-width ratio of 3-to-1 or less. While most commonly used to describe a leaf base or tip, this term can be applied to other plant parts such as bracts (modified petal-like leaves) or the petals or sepals of a flower.

mucronate

mucronulate Ending with a very short mucro, which is a sharp, abrupt point. The point has a length-to-width ratio of 1-to-1 or less. While most commonly used to describe a leaf tip, this term can be applied to other plant parts such as bracts (modi-

fied petal-like leaves) or the petals or sepals of a flower.

mucronulate leaf tip

mugs A colloquial term, popular among rock gardeners, used to describe the summertime combination of high heat and high humidity, which is often fatal to alpine plants.

mulch A protective soil covering that controls weeds, holds in moisture, and offers protection from erosion by wind and rain. Gardeners use two general types of mulch—organic and inorganic. Organic mulches include compost, shredded bark, chopped leaves, pine needles, grass clippings, ground corncobs, cocoa bean hulls, and newspaper (use a layer several sheets thick as a weed-suppressing barrier under another mulch such as shredded bark). Unlike inorganic mulches, organic mulches add a small but steady supply of organic matter to the soil: As they decompose, soil-dwelling organisms such as earthworms move this organic matter down into the soil. Inorganic mulches include plastic, crushed stone, gravel, and landscape fabric. Black plastic is most often used in vegetable gardens, and is especially useful for warming the soil for heat-loving crops such as melons and peppers. Install plastic mulch a week or two before planting, weighting down the edges with soil. (It's a good idea to install a soaker house under plastic mulch, because water can't penetrate it; otherwise, you'll have to water by hand to make sure plants don't go dry.) Poke holes in the mulch to plant. The best time to install mulch is in late spring, once the soil has warmed up and is no longer sopping wet from spring rains. Be sure the soil is moist before you mulch, however, because mulch may soak up water before it can seep through to the soil. Water before installing mulch if the soil is dry, and weed, too, because mulch won't kill existing weeds. Mulch new gardens anytime, as soon as you are finished planting them. Avoid piling mulch around the base of plants—keep it about 1 inch away from annual stems, 2 to 3 inches away from perennial stems, and 4 to 6 inches away from shrub stems and tree trunks. Just say no to mulch volcanoes! Mulch piled in a volcano-like mound around the base of a tree invites damage to bark by diseases and pests and also reduces the amount of air that reaches tree roots. In all cases, for best results, feather out the thickness of the mulch layer as you get closer to the crown or stems of the plant. Many gardeners remove and compost mulch in late fall and replace it each spring. Other gardeners leave mulch on their garden year-round, although mulch can encourage rodents to spend the winter dining on the crowns of plants.

multi- A prefix meaning many. For example, multifid means cut into many parts. Multiplicate means folded many times or repeatedly.

multigeneric This term is used to describe hybrids that are the result of crosses between several different genera. Orchid hybrids commonly have such complex parentage.

multiple cordon A trained cordon that has three or more vertical stems. *See* CORDON

multiple fruit A dense cluster of separate fruits commonly referred to as a single fruit, all derived from separate flowers. Mulberries (*Morus* spp.) and pineapples (*Ananas comosus*) bear multiple fruits. *See also* SYNCARP

muricate Rough-surfaced, due to many small hard bumps or sharp projections. Most often used to describe leaf surfaces.

muriculate Finely rough-surfaced, due to many very small hard bumps or sharp projections. Most often used to describe leaf surfaces.

mutation A change in the genes or chromosomes of a cell that results in a change that can be inherited by the descendants of the cell that carry the altered gene. In plants, mutations commonly affect only a segment of tissue and become apparent only if the affected tissue produces a shoot. Many popular garden plants are the result of mutations. When a mutation results in a noticeable change in a clone—a different flower or leaf color, for example—the altered portion of the plant can be selected for further propagation (vegetative, or asexual, only) to develop a new clone if the new characteristic is a good one. Or the mutated growth can be rogued out to maintain the uniformity of the existing clone. In their search for new plants, hybridizers may use chemicals and other treatments (colchicine and X rays, for example) to induce mutations. For information on two types of mutations, *see* CHIMERA, BUD SPORT

muticous Blunt at the tip, without a point or spine.

mycorrhizae A group of fungi that form beneficial, symbiotic relationships with some plants, including pines and beeches. They live partly inside a plant's root hairs and take carbohydrates from the host plant. In return, the mycorrhizal fungi extract nutrients from soil and rock particles, thus making them available to plants. They also are thought to protect roots from pathogens.

myrmecophyte, myrmechorous A plant that has a symbiotic relationship with ants. Plants that bear arils on their seeds are usually myrmechorous. *See also* ARIL

nacreous Having a pearly luster. Pearlescent.

naked Lacking hairs, scales, or other appendages that typically are present. A naked bud is not covered with protective scales, for example.

napiform Turnip-shaped.

narrow crotch *See* CROTCH, CROTCH ANGLE

nascent Starting to develop but not fully formed.

natant Floating on the water or immersed in it.

native Indigenous. A plant that grows naturally in a particular area. *See also* INTRODUCED

natural barrier A plant's natural defense against wounds or disease. The plant transports chemicals to the site of a wound, including a pruning wound, that essentially wall off the damaged tissue from the rest of the plant and create a barrier to wood-rotting organisms. Eventually, the barrier becomes both air- and watertight, and the walled-off tissue dries out and falls off. Cells in the cambium divide rapidly to form callus (scar tissue) that eventually covers the surface of the wound. Damaged cambium tissue, which can be caused by a branch that has broken off or a bad pruning cut, slows the healing process. Wound paint, once thought to be beneficial, also slows this process. To aid the natural healing process, always make proper pruning cuts that do not leave stubs or cut into the branch collar, which plays a role in the healing process. Make the smallest pruning cuts possible. For large branches always make three-step cuts. Remove dead and diseased wood, but if the healing process has begun do not cut below the natural barrier (look for callus tissue that has begun to form). For storm-damaged trees, recutting broken branches to make clean cuts outside the branch collar will help the healing process. *See* HEADING CUT, THINNING CUT, BRANCH COLLAR, THREE-STEP CUT

natural fertilizer Any fertilizer derived from a natural source such as mineral deposits or animal by-products.

natural grafting Grafts formed between branches or roots that have grown together naturally after having been pressed together for a long time. Natural grafts aided the spread of Dutch elm disease, which was passed from tree to tree up and down streets by natural root grafts. Oak wilt also is passed in this manner.

naturalize To use a planting technique in which bulbs, wildflowers, or other plants are arranged in the landscape in such a way that they appear to be growing naturally. Spring-blooming bulbs such as daffodils and crocuses are commonly planted in this fashion. In most cases, the plants continue to spread and reproduce as if they grew there naturally.

naturalized Alien, non-native. Used to describe plants, often garden escapees, that have been introduced from another region or country and are now found growing in the wild. Queen Anne's lace (*Daucus carota*) and oxeye daisies (*Leucanthemum vulgare*) are two common "wildflowers" that actually are naturalized plants. *See also* INTRODUCED

natural landscape An informal design style that is inspired by nature and emphasizes natural materials such as native stone walls. It usually features plants that are native to the region or at least look as if they are. *See* INFORMAL GARDEN

natural layering *See* LAYERING

nautiloid Spiral-shaped.

navicular Boat-shaped. The glumes (papery or chaffy bracts borne in pairs at the base of grass or sedge spikelets) of many grasses are navicular in shape.

nebulose Fine and indistinct.

neck The narrowed, upper part of a bulb, where the leaves and flowers emerge.

nectar A sweet, sticky secretion produced by many plants that is attractive to pollinators.

nectar guides Spots or lines on a flower that guide pollinators toward the nectar-bearing glands of the flower. Nectar guides often are visible only in ultraviolet light.

nectariferous Bearing nectaries and nectar.

nectary Nectar gland. A gland that secretes nectar.

needle A leaf that is slender, needle-shaped (acicular), and usually stiff. Conifers such as pines (*Pinus* spp.) and spruces (*Picea* spp.) bear needles.

needle-shaped. *See* ACICULAR

neem An organic insecticide extracted from the seeds, leaves, bark, flowers, and wood of neem trees (*Azadirachta indica*). Neem is an oil that kills a wide variety of insects. It also acts as a repellent and an antifeedant, disrupts the growth of some species, and sterilizes others. Neem can be applied as a soil drench or a spray on foliage.

nematodes Threadlike microscopic soil animals that can be beneficial or harmful. Beneficial nematodes break down soil organic matter or attack other soil-dwelling

organisms. Nematodes also can be parasites: Those that attack plants cause diseaselike symptoms such as yellowed leaves and stems, stunted growth, and distorted leaves, stems, or flowers. Rotating crops, solarizing the soil, and planting marigolds and then digging them into the soil are all techniques that help control nematodes. Working organic matter into the soil also is benefical because it encourages fungi that feed on nematodes. Parasitic nematodes also can be beneficial, because many species parasitize pest insects: Available from mail-order companies and well-stocked garden centers, these are applied to the soil.

nephroid Reniform or kidney-shaped.

nervation *See* VENATION

nerve A prominent vein or rib on a leaf or other organ.

nerved, nervose Having prominent veins or ribs (nerves).

netted *See* RETICULATE

net-veined *See* RETICULATE

new American garden A modern, informal style of garden that features mass plantings of easy-to-grow plants. A new American garden might feature ornamental grasses, coneflowers (*Rudbeckia* spp. and *Echinacea* spp.), and sedums in sunny areas. In shady areas, plantings might consist of drifts of hostas, ferns, and astilbes.

newspaper pot *See* PAPER POT

new wood Growth produced during the current season. Plants that bloom on new wood form flowers on the shoots that emerge in spring, and for this reason they usually flower from mid-summer onward. Shrubs that bloom on new wood are pruned during the dormant season, usually in late winter or very early spring. Hybrid tea and grandiflora roses bloom on new wood, as do butterfly bush (*Buddleia davidii*), and beauty-berries (*Callicarpa* spp.).

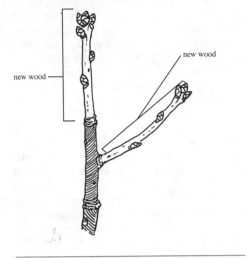

nicking A training technique used to inhibit the development of a dormant bud on a fruit tree, especially one that is not located in a favorable position for the training method being used on that plant (on a tree that is being trained flat against a wall, you might nick a bud pointing out from the wall, for example). A small semicircle or triangle of bark is removed directly beneath the bud, thus restricting its supply of nutrients. The bud may develop into a flower or a small shoot, but most of the plant's energy is directed toward a bud that is in a better position (one facing parallel to the wall, for example). (*See also* NOTCHING) Nicking also is a technique used for the germination of some seeds. *See* SCARIFICATION

nicotine An organic insecticide extracted from tobacco plants (as well as cigarettes and other tobacco products). Nicotine is an extremely toxic alkaloid that is absorbed by plant leaves and remains active for several weeks. (Don't use it the last month before harvest in the vegetable garden.) Use nicotine as a spray as well as a soil drench to control root aphids or other soil-dwelling pests.

nigrescent Blackish.

nitid Shiny or lustrous.

nitrogen A macronutrient that is a major component of plant cells and a component of chlorophyll. Organic sources of nitrogen include manure and blood meal. Because they can fix atmospheric nitrogen and make it available to plants, legumes grown as green manure crops also are a good source of nitrogen. Nitrogen deficiency symptoms include lower leaves that turn yellow, a plant that is yellowish or pale green overall, and stunted growth.

niveous White.

nocturnal Opening or functioning at night.

nodal Borne on or related to a node.

nodal cutting A cutting that has a leaf node at its base. The cut is made just below the node, because roots are most likely to form there. Most softwood, semi-ripe, and hardwood cuttings are nodal.

nodding Bent to one side and pointing downward. This term usually is used to describe flowers. Snowdrops (*Galanthus* spp.) and cyclamen (*Cyclamen* spp.) bear nodding flowers.

node The point on a stem, or axis, where one or more leaves, shoots, branches, or flowers are attached. In members of the grass family (Poaceae) the nodes typically are swollen.

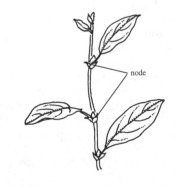

nodiferous Bearing nodes.

nodose Bearing many closely packed nodes that result in a knobby appearance.

nodule A small, nearly round bulge or swelling.

nodulose Covered with very small nodules.

nomenclature The scientific naming of plants, animals, or other organisms in order to establish a worldwide standard of reference that scientists and other interested individuals can use. Rules in the *International Code of Botanical Nomenclature* and the *International Code of Nomenclature for Cultivated Plants* govern the nomenclature as it applies to plants. Specialist organizations have their own rules for governing the naming of plants in large taxa such as orchids (the International Orchid Commission publishes the *Handbook on Orchid Nomenclature and Registration*, for example).

nomen illegitimum *See* ILLEGITIMATE

noncalcareous Lacking lime. This term is used to describe soil or rock that does not contain lime. Soil that is noncalcareous is usually acid, or sour, in pH. *See* pH

non-tunicate bulb *See* BULB

nose The top, or pointed end, of a bulb.

nosegay A small bouquet or bunch of flowers.

notate Marked with spots or lines.

notched *See* EMARGINATE, RETUSE

notch grafting *See* SAW-KERF GRAFTING

notching A training technique used to encourage the development of a dormant bud on a fruit tree. Cutting out a shallow semicircle or triangle of wood above a bud will stimulate it to grow. *See also* NICKING

NPK ratio *See* FERTILIZER ANALYSIS

nucamentum *See* CATKIN

nuciferous Bearing nuts.

nudicaul Having bare or leafless stems.

numerical plan *See* FLORAL FORMULA

nurse-root grafting A grafting technique sometimes used to encourage a difficult-to-root cutting to form its own roots. This kind of graft is temporary, because steps are taken to ensure that the stock will die once the scion has rooted successfully. To make a nurse-root graft, start with a section of a seedling rootstock or a rooted cutting and a scion that are roughly the same size. Use a whip-and-tongue or splice graft to unite them. However, graft the rootstock on upside down so it will eventually die. Or tie a rubber budding strip around the base of the scion, above the graft, and bury the base of the scion so the rubber is below the soil surface. Eventually, the rubber will girdle the stem, severing the nurse root from the scion.

nursery bed A special growing area for seedlings, new divisions, rooted cuttings, or other plants that are too small or not well enough established to move to garden beds and borders. Grouping new plants in a nursery bed makes it easy to give them the extra care they require to thrive, such as regular watering and weeding. It also ensures that they won't be overtaken by more robust bedfellows. To make a nursery bed, select a sunny, protected site that is within easy reach of a hose. Since a nursery bed is a production area, and won't necessarily be ornamental, an out-of-the-way site is best. A spot with rich, well-drained soil is best. Loosen the top 12 inches of soil and add plenty of well-rotted organic matter to ensure optimum conditions for plant roots. Creating a raised bed is a good idea, especially if soil drainage is a problem. Use a nursery bed for direct sowing seeds, planting out cuttings, or growing on small plants or divisions. Planting in rows makes it easy to weed and care for the plants. As plants become large enough to move to the garden proper, transplant in spring or fall.

nursery-grown A term used in reference to wildflowers that have been grown in a nursery for a year or two; nursery-grown plants may be collected from the wild. *See* NURSERY-PROPAGATED, WILD-COLLECTED

nurserymen's adhesive tape A special adhesive tape developed for grafting. The tape holds stock and scion secure and also keeps cut edges from drying out. Grafts covered with nurserymen's tape do not need to be waxed.

nursery-propagated A term used in reference to wildflowers that have been grown from seeds or propagated by an asexual technique such as division. Not to be confused with nursery-grown. *See* NURSERY-GROWN, WILD-COLLECTED

nursery spade *See* SPADE

nut A hard, woody, or brittle one-seeded fruit that does not open at maturity (is indehiscent). Hazelnuts (*Corylus* spp.), beeches (*Fagus* spp.), and oaks (*Quercus* spp.) all bear nuts. Walnuts produce nuts, but bear them within a husk that resembles a stone fruit, or drupe.

nut

nutant Drooping or nodding. This term is most often used to describe an inflorescence (rather than individual flowers) with a curved or drooping flower stalk (peduncle). *See also* CERNUOUS

nutlet A small nut. A nutlet resembles an achene, but has a hardier, woodier casing. Forget-me-nots (*Myosotis* spp.), verbenas (*Verbena* spp.), and most members of the mint family (Lamiaceae) produce nutlets.

nutrient deficiency A condition caused by insufficient amounts of a particular nutrient in a form that is available to plants. Signs of nutrient deficiencies vary, but chlorosis and stunted growth are two common symptoms.

nutrients, plant *See* MACRONUTRIENTS, MICRONUTRIENTS

nyctanthous Flowering at night.

nyctigamous Opening at night.

nymph An immature stage of an insect that undergoes incomplete metamorphosis and does not form a pupa.

oasis A water-absorbing product used in flower arrangements to hold flowers in place. Oasis can be cut to fit any container, and stems penetrate it easily. It can be jammed into a container or secured with tape. There also are similar products designed to be used with dried arrangements.

ob- A prefix meaning inverted or in a reversed position. For example, a cordate leaf is heart-shaped, with the stem attached at the rounded end, while an obcordate one is just the reverse, with the stem attached at the pointed end.

obclavate Club-shaped and attached at the broad, rather than the pointed, end.

obconic, **obconical** Cone-shaped and attached at the narrow, rather than the broad, end.

obcordate Inversely heart-shaped. The outline of an obcordate leaf is rounded in an egg-shaped fashion, like an ovate leaf, but has rounded lobes and a deep indentation, called a sinus, at the tip of the leaf. The depth of the sinus is from one-eighth to one-fourth the distance to the midpoint of the leaf blade. The base of the leaf, where the stem is attached, is pointed. The widest point of the blade is at the tip. The term retuse is used for a leaf that has a very small notch, or sinus, at the tip (less than one-sixteenth of the distance to the midpoint of the leaf blade). Emarginate is used to designate a leaf that lacks lobes but has a sinus about the size of an obcordate leaf.

obcordate leaf

obcuneate Wedge-shaped or narrowly triangular, but attached by the broad, rather than the narrow, end.

obelisk A tall, four-sided structure that tapers from a wide base to a pyramidal point at the top. Traditionally, obelisks were constructed of stone or concrete, but they also can be built of wood. In French, they are called a *tuteur*, or trainer. Wood obelisks can be used as supports for vines, which are trained up the center.

obelisk

obhastate Roughly arrowhead- or spear-shaped, but with the triangular lobes at the tip rather than at or near the point of attachment.

oblanceolate Inversely lance-shaped. An oblanceolate leaf is longer than it is wide (from three to six times), has a rounded tip, and a tapering base. The widest part of the leaf is above the middle of the blade.

oblanceolate leaf

obligate Restricted to or unable to exist without. The opposite of facultative. Parasitic plants such as the native wildflower pinedrops or giant bird's-nest (*Pterospora andromedea*) and mistletoes (*Phoradendron serotinum*, the species harvested for Christmas decorations, along with other members of the mistletoe family, Loranthaceae) are obligate, because they cannot survive without their host plant.

oblique Asymetrical or uneven. A leaf base that has uneven or unequal edges, or margins, on either side of the leaf stem, or petiole. Begonias (*Begonia* spp.) have oblique leaf bases. While most commonly used to describe a leaf base, this term can be applied to other plant parts such as bracts (modified petal-like leaves) or the petals of a flower.

oblique leaf base

oblong A leaf that is much longer than it is wide (from two to four times) and has sides that are more or less parallel. An oblong leaf has either blunt or rounded tips and bases.

oblong leaf

obovate Reverse egg-shaped. An obovate leaf is rounded like an upside-down egg, with a wide arching tip and a somewhat narrower base. The widest point of the leaf is near the tip.

obovate leaf

obtuse A tip or base that gradually ends in a blunt or rounded shape. The edges, or margins, of an obtuse leaf are straight or convex, and they come together at the tip or base at an angle of more than 90 degrees. While most commonly used to describe leaves, this term can be applied to other plant parts such as bracts (modified petal-like leaves) or the petals or sepals of a flower.

obtuse leaf tip   *obtuse leaf base*

obvolute This is a type of venation (the arrangement of leaves in a bud) with two leaves overlapping in a bud in such a way that half of each leaf is on the outside and half is on the inside.

ocellated A variegation pattern in which a large spot or blotch of one color has a spot of a different color inside it.

ocellus An eyelike spot on a petal or other organ, such as a rounded blotch of one color surrounded by a similar-shaped blotch of a contrasting color.

ocrea A tubular or inflated sheath formed around a stem by stipules, which are leaflike appendages at the base of the leaf stem, or petiole. Members of the buckwheat family (Polygonaceae) including old-fashioned annual kiss-me-over-the-garden-gate (*Persicaria orientale*, formerly *Polygonum orientale*) have ocrea. Some palms have ocrea that are formed by the expansion of the leaf sheath.

ocreate Bearing ocrea, or stipules that form a sheath around the stem.

ocreola The tiny ocrea (stipular sheaths) at the base of stems in an inflorescence. They are characteristic of members of the buckwheat family (Polygonaceae).

octa-, octo A prefix indicating eight. Octopetalous means bearing eight petals and octosepalous, eight sepals, for example.

odd pinnate Imparipinnate. A compound leaf divided in a featherlike fashion (pinnate), with pairs of leaflets attached along a main stem, or rachis, and ending with a single leaflet at the tip. Sumacs (*Rhus* spp.) and most walnuts (*Juglans* spp.) have odd-pinnate leaves; black walnuts (*Juglans nigra*), are often missing the end leaflet, however, making them even-pinnate. *See also* EVEN PINNATE

odd pinnate leaf

odoriferous Having a distinct odor.

officinal, officinalis Having commercial value, especially pertaining to herbs used in medicine, herbal preparations, or cooking. This term, first used by herbalists, has been used to derive the botanical names of several herbs, including common or culinary sage (*Salvia officinalis*), comphrey (*Symphytum officinale*), and vervian (*Verbena officinalis*).

offset A small, often prostrate, shoot or plant produced from the base of the main stem of a parent plant. Offsets, also called offshoots, are produced asexually and are usually easy to detach from the parent with a sharp knife. In some woodier species, a hatchet or mattock may be the tool of choice. If an offset has roots, it can be potted up and grown on immediately; if it doesn't, either layer it or pot it up in rooting medium and treat it as a cutting. (*See* LAYERING, CUTTING) Offset is most often used to refer to bulbs and rosette-forming plants, but also is applied to small clumps of shoots that appear around loosely joined clumps of fibrous-rooted plants. Removing the main stem of a plant is a technique sometimes used to encourage the production of offsets for purposes of propagation.

offshoot A shoot or branch produced at the base of a parent plant. *See* OFFSET

oil *See* HERBAL OILS AND OINTMENTS, ESSENTIAL OILS

oil, dormant *See* DORMANT OIL

oil sprays *See* HORTICULTURAL OIL

old wood Growth produced during the previous season or seasons. Plants that bloom on old wood usually bloom from spring to early summer, and they form flower buds for the next year shortly after the current season's blooms fade. Prune them in late spring or summer, no more than a month after they flower; otherwise, you risk cutting off all of next year's blooms. Most popular spring-blooming shrubs fall into this category, including azaleas and rhododendrons, forsythia, and mock oranges (*Philadelphus* spp.). Old wood also is a general term for growth that no longer is growing vigorously and/or producing flowers. *See* RENEWAL PRUNING

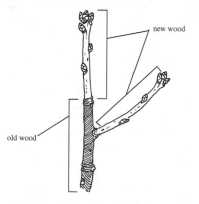

new wood

old wood

oleaginous Oily or producing oil.

oligo- A prefix indicating few or less than typical. Oligophyllous means bearing few leaves, oligospermous, bearing few seeds, and oligopetalous, few petals.

once-cut Pinnate. A compound leaf divided in a featherlike fashion, with pairs of smaller leaflets attached along a main stem, or rachis. *See* PINNATE

once-cut leaf

OP *See* OPEN-POLLINATION

open center A pruning and training technique used to develop a tree that has three or four scaffold branches, spaced more or less evenly around the trunk and that lacks a central leader. Once the central leader is removed, energy is diverted into the formation and growth of scaffold branches lower down. Peaches, nectarines, plums, sour and sweet cherries are commonly trained in this fashion. To train an open-center tree, start with an unbranched whip, and the first growing season select four main branches, which will become the scaffold branches. (Some nurseries sell small trees that already have undergone some training and have scaffold branches; in this case, start with second-year pruning.) The scaffold branches should emerge from different sides of the trunk and be separated vertically by 4 to 8 inches. Cut off all the other branches and also cut off the central leader (the tip of the unbranched whip). Spread branches to widen crotch angles as needed. (*See* CROTCH, CROTCH ANGLE) The second year in winter or early spring, and in subsequent years, head back the tips of the scaffold branches

by one-third to one-half to encourage side branches to form. Remove secondary branches from the scaffolds that arise within 6 to 8 inches of the trunk to keep the center of the plant open. During the growing season, thin as necessary to maintain a clear, open framework.

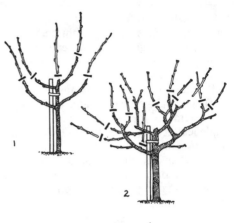

open center pruning

open-pollination Freely pollinated, usually by wind, bees, or other insects without intervention by a gardener or plant breeder. This term is primarily used to describe cultivated forms of plants—especially vegetables—that are allowed to freely cross-pollinate. The designation OP is used to indicate that a particular plant is open-pollinated. Many gardeners save seeds from open-pollinated crops from year to year because they will grow into plants for next year's garden that resemble their parents. Keep in mind that if you grow two cultivars of an open-pollinated plant, they will cross and seed saved from them will not come true. If you want to maintain pure strains, isolate the plants intended for seed-saving by planting them in different parts of the garden (recommended distances vary from plant to plant). Another option is to grow plants under floating row covers until seed sets; in this case, you will need to pollinate by hand because row covers will exclude most pollinators. Finally, you can isolate individual flowers and hand-pollinate them to ensure seed comes true. For best results, always save seeds from the best-looking fruit and/or plant; heirloom crops, which are open-pollinated, were developed by generations of such selections. *See* HYBRID, HEIRLOOM

open socket A method for attaching the metal head of a tool to its handle by means of folding two flaps of metal around the handle to create a collar and holding them in place with a pin or rivet. This creates a lighter-weight, but very weak, connection and is not used in top-quality tools. *See* TOOLS

OPM *See* ORGANIC PEST MANAGEMENT

opposite Leaves that are borne in pairs at the nodes on the opposite sides of a stem. The term opposite also can be used to describe other organs such as pedicels (the stalks of individual flowers in a flower cluster) or branches that are borne in pairs on opposite sides of a stem or axis.

opposite leaves

oppositiflorus Having opposite pedicels (the stalks of individual flowers in a flower cluster) or peduncles (flower stalks).

oppositifolious Having opposite leaves.

orbicular Rounded. Circular, or nearly so, in outline.

orbicular leaf

orchioid Orchidlike.

order, **ordo** A group of plants, or subdivision, that all share common characteristics within a class. The names of orders commonly end with the suffix -ales, and orders are further divided into families of plants. The order Ranales, for example, contains such plant families as Magnoliaceae (the magnolia family), Ranunculaceae (the buttercup family), and Berberidaceae (the barberry family). Botanists disagree on the classification of plant families at this level, and depending on the authority consulted, Ranales contains from 12 to 23 or more families of plants. *See* FAMILY

organ A plant part that has a specific function, such as a petal, stamen, or leaf.

organic fertilizer Fertilizers made from plant or animal residues or by-products such as manure, bonemeal, wood ashes, bloodmeal, dried sewage sludge, and fish emulsion as well as from natural inorganic compounds mined from natural deposits. Natural inorganic compounds also are acceptable to organic gardeners. These include rock phosphate, limestone, greensand, and granite meal, which are ground into a fine powder but are used in the same chemical form in which they are mined. Organic fertilizers release their nutrient content slowly, because they have to be broken down by soil organisms before they are available to plants. As a result, they are less likely to burn plant roots and less prone to be lost by leaching than synthetic or chemical fertilizers. Some materials are found both on lists of fertilizers and soil amendments because they provide nutrients to plants and also improve soil structure. *See* CHEMICAL FERTILIZER, SOIL AMENDMENT

organic gardening A system of gardening that uses natural systems and cycles to care for plants without the use of synthetic chemical pesticides, herbicides, fungicides, or fertilizers. "Feed the soil and let the soil feed the plants" is an organic gardening adage pointing to the fact that soil-building techniques are at the heart of organic gardens. Organic gardeners use animal manures, green manures, and crop rotation along with techniques such as double digging and mulching to build and maintain rich soil to support their crops. When they do fertilize, they use natural rock powders and materials such as seaweed, fish emulsion, and compost or manure tea rather than synthetic fertilizers to provide nutrients without harming beneficial soil-dwelling organisms. Keeping plants healthy—with rich soil and good care—also helps reduce problems with pests and diseases, because vigorously growing plants are less susceptible to problems than ones that are struggling to survive. Fostering natural biological diversity also plays a key part in an organic pest-control program. This encourages rich population of beneficial insects and other organisms, which reduces the need for artificial pest control. For more on organic methods, *see* SOIL, ORGANIC PEST MANAGEMENT, ORGANIC FERTILIZER, BENEFICIAL INSECTS, BENEFICIAL ANIMALS

organic matter In soil, organic matter consists of everything from roots and living organisms to decomposing plant and animal residues. Adding organic matter to soil—in the form of compost, chopped leaves, well-rotted manure, or grass clippings—improves structure and increases the activity of beneficial soil organisms. It also has a moderating effect on pH: Adding organic matter tends to bring soils that have both alkaline and acid pH values closer to neutral. You can dig or till organic matter into the soil (double and single digging are good options), or simply mulch with it (compost makes a good mulch) and soil organisms will work it into the soil for you. Another option is to grow green manure crops. *See* SOIL, SOIL STRUCTURE, DOUBLE DIGGING, SINGLE DIGGING, GREEN MANURE, SOIL BUILDING

organic mulch *See* MULCH

organic pest management Also called OPM, this is a system for managing pests and diseases organically by using basic organic gardening techniques to keep plants healthy and thriving, along with a variety of control measures to prevent problems or keep them in check. Control measures are ranked according to how they affect the entire garden—the populations of beneficial insects and other organisms there—as well as the environment as a whole. The safest, least toxic controls are used first, because these have little or no effect on nontarget organisms such as beneficial insects, pets, or humans. In an OPM system use controls in the following order, from least to most toxic or invasive: Cultural controls, Physical controls, Biological controls, and Chemical controls (organically acceptable sprays and dusts). Cultural controls are easy steps to take when planning and planting a garden that will make plants better able to withstand attack by pests or will interfere with the lifecycle of pests. These include planting resistant plants, keeping plants healthy with good care so they are less susceptible to attack, rotating crops (*See* CROP ROTATION, COMPANION PLANTING), cleaning up and disposing of insect- or disease-infested plants promptly, solarizing the soil (*See* SOLARIZATION), and not working among plants when they are wet (this can spread fungal diseases on tools and clothing). Physical controls include using traps and barriers to keep insects from reaching pests as well as techniques like handpicking to remove insects from plants. Barriers include cutworm collars (*See* CUTWORM COLLAR), tree bands that prevent caterpillars from climbing tree trunks, and dust barriers (*See* DIATOMACEOUS EARTH). Floating row covers also can be used as barriers (*See* ROW COVERS). Sticky traps will attract a variety of insects: Red balls covered with a sticky substance like Tanglefoot will trap apple maggot flies and prevent them from laying eggs on real apples, for example. Pheromone traps also are effective physical controls (*See* PHEROMONE). Knocking Japanese beetles into a can of soapy water or blasting aphids or mites off plants with a stream of water from the hose also are physical controls. Pruning is a form of physical control, too: Clipping or sawing off insect- or disease-infested branches or stem tips often is an easy, effective control measure. Biological controls include attracting beneficial insects and animals and using organisms that cause diseases in pest insects (*See* BENEFICIAL INSECTS, BENEFICIAL ANIMALS, MICROBIAL INSECTICIDE). Use chemical controls as a last resort, when other, less toxic control measures have not provided adequate control. (*See* INSECTICIDES, FUNGICIDES)

organisms, soil *See* MICROORGANISMS, MACROFAUNA

ornamental horticulture The art and science of growing ornamental plants such as perennials, annuals, trees, shrubs, and vines.

ornithophilous, ornithophily Pollinated by birds.

orophilous Growing in mountainous regions.

ortho- A prefix meaning straight. Orthocladous means having straight branches, for example, while orthostichous means borne or arranged in straight rows.

orthopterous Straight-winged. Ash fruits (*Fraxinus* spp.) have straight samaras, a type of seed or fruit.

orthotropic Having a straight, vertical growth habit.

oscillating hoe *See* HOE

osseous Bony.

ossiculus *See* DRUPE

outdoor living space *See* OUTDOOR ROOM

outdoor room A garden space designed for a particular purpose and usually set apart either physically or just visually from other parts of the landscape. Outdoor rooms can be formal and quite obvious, such as those outlined by tall hedges on all sides, with an arch to serve as an opening. More often, they are semi-enclosed—a terrace with a flower bed along two sides or a

small sitting area surrounded on three sides with low shrub borders, for example. Even a low mound of edging plants can mark the boundaries of an outdoor living space, or it can be simply a clearing along a woodland path. Like indoor rooms, outdoor rooms are furnished—with a table and chairs, a bench, or simply rustic stones to sit on—so they invite garden visitors to linger and enjoy the space outdoors.

outdoor sowing *See* DIRECT SOWING

oval (botany) Broadly elliptic or ellipse-shaped. An oval leaf is broadest in the middle and has a rounded tip and base. In shape, an oval leaf is slightly more rounded than an elliptic one.

oval leaf

oval (design) A shape used in flower arranging in which the main flowers, leaves, and other plant materials are positioned so that the tips of the materials in the main part of the arrangement outline an imaginary oval.

oval arrangement

ovary The base of the pistil or carpel, which is the basic unit of the female reproductive organ of a flower, and the part that contains the ovules, where the seeds develop once the flower is fertilized. Ovary position is commonly used to describe and classify plants. If the petals, sepals, and stamens of a flower are attached beneath the ovary, it is a superior, or hypogynous, ovary. If the petals, sepals, and stamens are attached to the top of the ovary, it is inferior, or epigynous. A half-inferior or sub-inferior ovary has sepals, petals, and stamens that seemingly are borne around the middle of it. *See* HYPOGYNOUS, EPIGYNOUS, HALF-INFERIOR OVARY

ovate Egg-shaped. An ovate leaf is rounded, with a wide base and a somewhat narrower tip, much like an egg. The widest point of the blade is near the base, where the leaf is attached to the stem.

ovate leaf

overseeding A technique used to rejuvenate an unhealthy, ragged-looking lawn, or to add a new, improved grass cultivar without replacing the entire lawn. To overseed, cut the lawn very close to the ground—as low as $1/_2$ inch—then heavily rake the soil, removing any thatch and roughing up the exposed soil. Spread the seed at about one and one-half times the recommended rate on the package, then rake the area lightly and topdress with a very thin layer of sand or topsoil. Water well, and keep the area evenly moist until grass seedlings appear. Keep off the lawn until the seedlings are well established. For large areas, consider renting a tool called a verticutter, which resembles a lawnmower with blades set on end that slice through thatch and into the soil. To thoroughly cut up the soil, run the verticutter over the area in one direction and

then repeat at right angles to the first pass. Then seed as above. A slice seeder is another rental option: It cuts into the soil and seeds in one pass.

overwintering Holding tender plants over winter by keeping them in a frost-free spot. Gardeners have several options when it comes to overwintering plants. Taking and rooting cuttings in late summer to early fall is easy and efficient. For best results, take cuttings before cool weather sets in, because cold temperatures can damage plants. Or dig entire plants and pot them up. Container-grown plants are easy to bring indoors over winter. Some gardeners keep tender plants in containers and then "plant" them in the garden each spring by sinking them—pot and all—in the soil. During the winter months, most plants grow very slowly, if at all, so water sparingly and do not feed them until growth resumes in late winter or early spring. While the best temperature will depend on the plant you are trying to overwinter, in general set overwintering plants in a sunny, cool (60 to 65°F) spot. Be sure to harden them off in spring before moving them back to the garden. To overwinter tender bulbs, tubers, and other structures, dig the plants after the first light frost in fall and cut off the tops. Dry the structures in a warm, dry spot, then brush off excess soil. Discard any bulbs or corms that show signs of rot, and cut off any rotted spots on tubers or tuberous roots. Dust the cuts with sulfur or another fungicide. (Some gardeners lightly dust all such structures to be overwintered.) Store them in dry sawdust, vermiculite, or peat in a cool (40 to 50°F), dark spot over winter. Bulbs and corms also can simply be placed in open-mesh bags and hung over winter. Whichever method you use, be sure to label each group of bulbs so you can identify them in spring. Check periodically and discard any that show signs of rot; mist tubers or tuberous roots lightly if they begin to shrivel. Replant in spring.

ovoid An egg-shaped, three-dimensional organ.

ovulate Producing ovules.

ovule An immature seed. The megasporangium, or spore-producing case or body, in a seed plant.

oxygenators *See* SUBMERGED PLANTS

oxylophyte A plant that grows in acid soils.

pachy- A prefix meaning thick. Pachy-cladous means having thick branches; pachycarpous means having a thick fruit wall.

painted A variegation pattern in which the color is distributed in streaks of varying intensity.

palate The lower lip of a personate flower, which is a two-lipped flower with a closed throat. The palate is raised somewhat and appears to close the throat. *See* PERSONATE

palea A papery or chaffy bract borne at the base of a grass flower. *See* GLUME

paleaceous Chaffy textured. Covered with small, chaffy bracts or scales, called palea. Most often used to describe leaf surfaces.

palmate A leaf that has three or more lobes or segments that radiate out from a common point, like fingers on a hand, forming a palmlike or handlike arrangement. (A palmate leaf can be compound, or cut into separate leaflets, or merely lobed.) The term palmate also is used to describe veins in a leaf, when three or more veins radiate out from the tip of the leaf stalk, or petiole, in a fingerlike fashion.

palmate

palmate venation Leaf veins that radiate out from a common point, like fingers on a hand, forming a palmlike or handlike arrangement.

palmate venation

palmately compound A compound leaf with leaflets that radiate out from a common point, in a fingerlike fashion. Buckeyes (*Aesculus* spp.) have palmately compound leaves.

palmately lobed A leaf that is divided into lobes that radiate out from a common point, like fingers on a hand. The indentations between lobes, called the sinuses, all point to the tip of the leaf stalk, or petiole. The sinuses can either be shallowly or deeply cut, so a palmately lobed leaf can be lobed, cleft, parted, or divided depending on the depth of the indentations. Most maples (*Acer* spp.) along with sycamores (*Platanus* spp.) and sweet gums (*Liquidambar* spp.) have palmately lobed leaves.

palmately lobed

palmate-pinnate A compound leaf with leaflets arranged in a palmate fashion and then further divided into leaflets arranged in a featherlike (pinnate) fashion.

palmatifid Divided or cut into segments that radiate out from a common point, like fingers on a hand. The indentations, called sinuses, between the segments reach from halfway to the tip of the central leafstalk to nearly the tip. On a palmatifid leaf, the sinuses do not reach all the way to the midrib, and the individual lobes or segments are not separated into individual leaflets.

palmatisect Divided or cut into segments that radiate out from a common point, like fingers on a hand. The indentations, called sinuses, between the segments reach to the tip of the leafstalk or nearly so. On a palmatisect leaf, although the sinuses may reach all the way to the tip of the leaf stalk, the individual lobes or segments are not separated into true leaflets. Palmatisect leaves also have narrower lobes or segments than palmatifid leaves do.

paludose Growing in damp meadows or in marshes.

pampinus *See* TENDRIL

pandurate, **panduriform** Fiddle-shaped. A leaf that is rounded at both ends with a shallow indentation or constricted area near the middle. One end of the leaf, either the base or the tip, is markedly larger than the other. A pandurate leaf can have a single constricted area in the center, but also can have additional shallow lobes along the edges.

pandurate leaf

panicle A type of flower cluster, or inflorescence, with a single main stem and branched side stems. (A raceme, which it resembles, has unbranched side stems.) The flowers open from the bottom to the top of a panicle, and panicles are indeter-

minate, meaning the main stem continues to elongate after the first flowers open. Lilacs (*Syringa* spp.), panicle hydrangea (*Hydrangea paniculata*), and oakleaf hydrangea (*H. quercifolia*) bear their flowers in panicles. Astilbes (*Astilbe* spp.) bear plumelike panicles. Devil's walking stick (*Aralia spinosa*) bears panicles divided into racemose branches that in turn carry umbels of flowers.

panicle

paniculate, **paniculiform** Paniclelike. A flower cluster (inflorescence) that resembles a panicle but may or may not be a true panicle.

pannose, **panniform** Feltlike. Covered with short, dense woolly hairs that give a feltlike texture. Most often used to describe leaf surfaces.

papaveraceous Poppylike. Belonging to the poppy family (Papaveraceae).

paper pot Also called newspaper pots because they are generally made from this material, these are a homemade alternative to peat pots made from strips of newspaper. (Avoid glossy paper; ordinary black-and-white newsprint is best.) Two-piece molds are available to make paper pots; simply roll a strip of newspaper of the length and width specified ($3\frac{1}{2}$ to 4 inches by the width of a two-page section of newspaper works well) around the mold and crush the bottom of the "pot" into the bottom section of the mold. Then fill with premoistened medium. The pots don't need taping to stay together, but are best fit snugly into a flat; moistening the paper after the pot has been formed also helps hold it together. To make larger pots, or to make them without a mold, simply wrap strips of newspaper around cans or other containers. Large paper pots may need taping; they are especially useful for dealing with large seedlings that benefit from a head start indoors yet are hard to transplant, such as gourds (*Lagenaria* spp.), squashes, and pumpkins. Move seedlings to the garden, pot and all. There's no need to tear off the top of the pots (as with peat pots), which won't wick water out of the soil. Once in the garden, the paper decomposes rapidly.

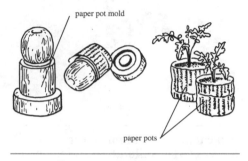
paper pot mold

paper pots

papery *See* PAPYRACEOUS

papilionaceous A five-petaled, butterfly-like flower with a large, upright petal, called a banner or standard, and two side, or wing, petals. The two lower petals are joined at the base and form a sheath, called a keel, that covers the flower's stamens and pistils. Papilionaceous flowers are characteristic of many members of the pea family (Fabaceae) including garden peas (*Pisium sativum* subsp. *sativum*), sweet peas (*Lathyrus odoratus*), and wisteria (*Wisteria* spp.)

papilionaceous flower

papilla, papillae A soft pimplelike or nipplelike lump.

papillate Covered with soft pimplelike or nipplelike lumps, called papillae, in various sizes. Most often used to describe leaf surfaces. Livingstone daisies (*Dorotheanthus* spp.) have fleshy leaves covered with crystal-like papillae.

papillose Bearing very small papillae.

papillose-hispid Bearing stiff hairs or bristles that arise from papillae.

pappiferous, **pappose** Bearing pappus.

pappus The modified calyx of flowers in the aster family (Asteraceae). The pappus is borne at the top of the ovary and consists of small scales, bristles, awns, or hairs that are separate or united.

papyraceous Papery or tissuelike in texture and color.

parallel-veined Veins that are parallel to the edges, or margins, of the leaf as well as parallel to one another. Most monocots, including grasses, irises (*Iris* spp.), and lilies (*Lilium*), have leaves with parallel veins.

parallel-veined leaf

paraphysis, *pl.* **paraphyses** A hair, or sometimes a scale, borne on a fern frond among the sporangia in a sorus.

parasite A plant or other organism that grows on another plant and takes some or all of its nutrients and/or water from that parent. Members of the mistletoe family (Loranthaceae) and pinedrops or giant bird's-nest (*Pterospora andromedea*) are parasites. An epiphyte lives on another plant but does not take any nutrients or water from it. Insects can be parasites as well—mosquitoes and fleas are two examples. Insects that parasitize other insects, called parasitoids, are sometimes used to control pests in the garden. *See also* EPIPHYTE, SAPROPHYTE

parasitized Hosting a parasite.

parasitoid An insect that parasitizes another insect. Some are used to control pests in greenhouses and gardens. For example, whitefly parasite (*Encarsia formosa*) lays eggs on greenhouse whiteflies, and their larvae feed on and kill the host.

parenchyma Tissue composed of thin-walled, undifferentiated cells that make up a large portion of most plants. The "typical" plant cell.

parent plant A plant used to provide cuttings, divisions, or other plant material for use in vegetative propagation techniques, which yield genetically identical plants. Also called a mother plant.

paripinnate *See* EVEN PINNATE

parted Divided into deep segments that reach from halfway to the middle of the leaf, petal, or other organ to nearly its middle or base. On a parted leaf, for example, the indentations (called sinuses) extend from more than one-half the distance to the midrib almost to the midrib. (The individual lobes or segments are not separated into individual leaflets.) Leaves can be parted either palmately (into fingerlike divisions) or pinnately (in a featherlike fashion). *See also* CLEFT, LOBED

parted leaf

parterre A level area in a garden that is filled with ornamental flower beds in vari-

ous shapes and sizes. Typically, the individual beds were edged with closely clipped shrubs and filled with flowers arranged in a pattern.

parthenocarpy, parthenocarpic The development of fruit without either fertilization or the development of seeds.

parthenogenesis The development of a seed from an egg cell without fertilization.

partial shade This is a general term for a site that receives shade for part of the day and direct sun for the rest of the day. Sites in partial shade differ greatly, depending on what is casting the shade—a high, open tree canopy, or a building, for example—as well as how many hours of sun or bright, indirect light the plants receive. Some sources use the term light shade if a site receives from about 5 to 8 hours of sun and is shaded the rest of the day, but there is by no means a standard definition or usage. A site in full shade usually receives no direct light—sites on the forest floor are in full shade, for example. The term deep shade is reserved for sites under evergreens, where no sun ever reaches the ground, making it difficult to garden at all. (Sites under deciduous trees are sunny in spring, making them perfect for hardy spring bulbs and many wildflowers that bloom in spring and disappear by early summer.) Sites on the north side of buildings or walls also tend to be in deep shade.

parti-colored Variegated.

-partite A suffix referring to parts, usually combined with a prefix indicating a number. Quinquepartite means five-parted, for example.

pastel colors *See* TINT

pasteurization Destroying disease-causing organisms in potting media with heat. With very tiny seeds, as well as with fern spores, it is a good idea to pasteurize even soilless mixes to prevent fungi from overtaking the tiny plants. An easy way to treat germinating mixes is to fill pots with premoistened medium and pour boiling water over the top of the medium. Immediately cover the pots with plastic wrap and let them cool. You can repeat the process for an extra measure of security, or sow. Always wait for the soil to cool to sow, and never pour boiling water over seeds. To pasteurize soil for use in potting mixes, add water so it is moist but not soggy, and spread it in a large, covered pan, such as a broiler. Add a meat thermometer, then set the broiler in the oven set on either "warm" or 200°F. Heat the soil until it reaches 140°F, then keep it at that level for 30 minutes. Cool and use. (Some sources recommend maintaining temperatures between 150 and 180°F, but the slightly lower temperature allows some beneficial soil organisms to survive, and these help keep pathogens in check if the mix is recontaminated. Also, the lower temperature reduces problems with toxicity from released ammonia and nitrites.) Baking soil has an unpleasant smell; try pasteurizing outdoors on a grill if you can't stand it.

patch budding A budding technique suitable for thick-barked plants, including walnuts and pecans. Select stock and budsticks that are both slipping and are $1/2$ to 1 inch in diameter. To prepare the stock, make two parallel horizontal cuts and two parallel vertical cuts through the bark to remove a square, 1- to $1\,3/8$-inch patch about 2 to 10 inches above the soil surface. To prepare the bud, cut a patch the same size from the budstick; slide it off the budstick rather than pry it off so a small core of wood remains on the back, beneath the bud. (Professionals use special double-bladed knives and patch-budding tools to perform these cuts.) Then fit the bud patch onto the patch on the scion. Fasten the bud and bark flaps in place with a rubber budding strip or a piece of raffia. Do not cover the bud. Rubber budding strips will drop off soon after the graft union has formed; gently cut away raffia or other materials used to tie the bud in place before they constrict the stem. *See* BUDDING, T-BUDDING, RUBBER BUDDING STRIP

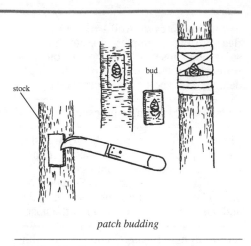

patch budding

pea brush *See* PEA STAKES

pea stakes Also referred to as pea brush, brushy twigs, and twiggy brush, pea stakes are a traditional staking method used for peas and some other vegetables as well as flowers. Pea stakes are generally better for smaller, lighter-weight plants, such as catmint (*Nepeta* spp.). Start with well-branched twigs cut from shrubs that ideally have a fairly straight section at the bottom. Push the stakes into the soil around the clumps. Break the tips of the twigs and point them toward the center of the clump to provide added support, or leave them upright. Keep in mind that twigs from some shrubs will root when stuck back in the garden. Try cutting them several weeks before you need them and leave them in the sun. Even then, watch for leaves or other evidence that the pea stakes are rooting.

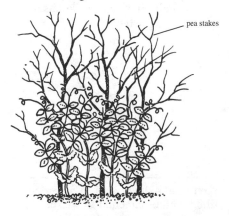

pea stakes

peat, **peat moss** Partially decomposed remains of aquatic, bog, and marsh vegetation. The most common form of peat is usually sold as peat moss, and it is the decomposed remains primarily of sphagnum moss and/or other species of moss found in bogs. Sometimes called moss peat, peat moss ranges from light to dark brown in color and has extremely high moisture-holding capacity—it can hold up to ten times its dry weight in water—and is quite acidic. Average pH ranges from 3.8 to 4.5. Red-brown to black reed sedge peat is composed of the decomposed remains of grasslike sedges, reeds, and other bog plants. Its pH varies from 4.5 to 7.0, and it is not considered as good a potting soil amendment as peat moss. Peat humus is dark brown to black in color and consists of such extremely decomposed material its origin is impossible to determine. Peat humus has very low moisture-holding capacity. Peat moss is a common ingredient in seed-starting and potting mixes because of its water-holding capacity. (It contains very few nutrients.) It always should be premoistened before use. Never use it as a mulch because it will form an impenetrable crust that causes water to run off, rather than percolate into, the soil. Peat is sometimes used as a soil amendment to acidify soil. Since it is a mined product that is not readily renewed, and mining operations have raised environmental concerns in various parts of the globe, many gardeners avoid using peat altogether.

peat humus *See* PEAT, PEAT MOSS

peat pellet A compressed cylinder of peat contained in mesh netting designed to function as a "container" for germinating seeds. To use peat pellets, soak them for several hours in water so they expand (from about $1/_4$-inch tall to $2 1/_2$ inches). Then sow seeds in the top. Seedlings grown in peat pellets can be transplanted to the garden "pot" and all, making these a good option for germinating seeds that are difficult to transplant.

peat pot A container made of compressed peat moss and designed for germinating seeds or growing seedlings up to transplanting. Roots easily can penetrate a moist peat pot and are traditionally used to start seeds that are difficult to transplant because the seedlings can be planted right in the garden pot and all, thus minimizing transplant stress. However, roots cannot penetrate a dry peat pot, so when transplanting seedlings grown in peat pots to the garden, be sure to tear off the top part of the pot. If the top is left exposed to the air, the entire pot will dry out (the peat acts as a wick, pulling moisture right out of the soil), preventing the seedlings' roots from spreading into the surrounding soil. For other options for "pots" that can be moved to the garden plant and all, *see* PAPER POT, PEAT POT, SOIL BLOCKS.

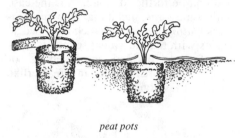

peat pots

pebble tray A shallow, watertight tray filled with 1 or 2 inches of pebbles that are covered with water in order to increase the relative humidity for houseplants.

pectinate Comblike. Thin, evenly spaced segments—leaflets, hairs, or thin, narrow segments, which are extensions of the leaf blade—that are arranged along a stem or axis like the teeth of a comb. If the segments, or lobes, are thin and closely spaced, a pectinate leaf also is pinnatifid. The term pectinate also can be used to describe thin, closely spaced leaves arranged along a stem in a comblike fashion, such as those of bald cypress (*Taxodium distichum*).

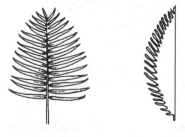

pectinate leaf   *pectinate leaf margin*

ped An aggregate of soil particles such as a crumb or block. Soil scientists differentiate between natural soil aggregates and those caused by digging or other disturbance. Clods of soil are caused by digging or cultivating heavy, or clay, soils when they are wet.

pedate A palmate leaf (which is divided into lobes or segments radiating out from a common point, like fingers on a hand) that has two outer lobes or segments further lobed or divided. Lenten roses (*Helleborus* × *hybridus* and *H. orientalis*) have pedate leaves. The segments on a pedate leaf can be further divided, as is the case with some ferns, including many maidenhairs (*Adiantum* spp.), which have pedate leaves with the individual segments (pinna) further divided into leaflets or pinnules that are arranged in a featherlike (pinnate) fashion.

pedate leaf

pedately lobed A leaf that is palmately lobed (meaning it is divided into lobes radiating out from a common point, like fingers on a hand) with two outer lobes that are further lobed or divided.

pedately lobed leaf

pedatifid Pedately lobed or cleft.

pedicel The stalk of an individual flower in a flower cluster, or inflorescence.

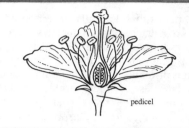

pedicel

pedicellate Having a pedicel.

peduncle The stalk that supports an inflorescence, including the stalk of a single flower. The main stem of a branched inflorescence, which is an extension of the peduncle, is commonly referred to as the rachis, while the stalks of the individual flowers in it are called pedicels.

pedunculate Having a peduncle.

peel The skin or rind of a fruit.

pegging A training technique in which the stems or canes of floppy-stemmed shrubs are bent down against the soil surface and held in place, usually with U-shaped pieces of wire. Pegging creates an arching, fountainlike look and increases bloom—it is commonly used on roses that have floppy habits—because horizontal stems produce flowers all along their length. Peg stems in spring; new shoots are the best candidates, so gradually cut out the older shoots on roses or other plants to encourage new growth.

pelletized seed Seed that has been coated with an inert material to make it easier to handle when sowing. Very small seeds like petunias often are pelletized. The material used to pelletize seeds may contain pesticide.

pellicle A thin, skinlike or membranelike covering. A pellicle usually is not made up of cells.

pellucid Transparent or translucent.

peltafid Peltate but with the leaf or bract divided into lobes or segments.

peltate A leaf or bract that is round or rounded in outline and has the stem attached near the center. Water lilies (*Nymphaea* spp.), nasturtiums (*Tropaeolum majus*), and May apples (*Podophyllum* spp.) all have peltate leaves.

peltate leaves

pendent Hanging down or drooping. This term is not used to refer to stems that are bent because of the weight of flowers or fruit, but rather ones that hang down naturally.

pendulous Hanging down or drooping because a stem or other support is weak. Stems that are bent because of the weight of flowers or fruit are called pendulous, or sometimes dependent.

penicil A tuft of short hairs that is brushlike.

penicillate Bearing a brushlike tuft of short hairs called a penicil.

penjing The ancient Chinese art of creating and growing miniaturized trees in containers as well as entire landscapes on trays or in shallow containers. Penjing emerged in China at least 800 years before it was passed to Japan, where it is called bonsai. While cultural methods are similar, the Chinese depend on pruning more heavily to achieve the desired shape than the Japanese, who also use wiring extensively to position branches. *See* BONSAI

penta- A prefix indicating five. For example, pentadactylous means divided into five fingerlike lobes or segments, and pentapetalous means five-petaled.

pepo A berrylike fruit that contains many seeds inside a single cavity, has fleshy or pulpy flesh, and a hard, leathery rind that does not open at maturity (is indehiscent). Members of the gourd family (Cucurbi-

taceae), including gourds, pumpkins, and squashes, all bear pepos. Pepos are formed from inferior ovaries, a fact to remember when looking at a pumpkin or squash plant to see if it has begun fruiting: The female flowers have a prominent ovary just beneath the flower, whereas the male flowers do not.

pepo

percolation The flow or movement of water through soil. The percolation rate of soil is a measure of the rate at which water passes through it, usually expressed in minutes per inch. Water moves quickly down through sandy soils, which tend to be droughty, spreads evenly through loam soils (both down into the soil and laterally), and in clay soils tends to be held tightly near the soil surface. Adding organic matter such as compost helps hold water in sandy soil and helps it spread through clay soil. To perform a simple percolation, or perc, test dig a 1-foot-deep, 6-inch-wide hole, fill it with water, then let the water drain away completely. Then fill it again and time how long it takes for the water to drain out of the hole. Soils that take more than 8 hours to drain need to be improved. *See* SOIL STRUCTURE

perennate To survive for more than one year. This term is most often used to refer to plants that overwinter by producing resting buds (turions) or plantlets that survive the parent.

perennial A plant that persists for more than two years. Technically, shrubs, trees, and woody vines are perennials, but gardeners and horticulturists generally use this term specifically to refer to nonwoody, or herbaceous, species. A short-lived perennial is one that only lives for two or three years. Gardeners grow many of these as biennials or even annuals because they flower best the first season or two. *See* BIENNIAL

perennial bed *See* BED

perennial border *See* BORDER

perennial island *See* ISLAND BED

perfect, **perfect flower** A flower with both male and female structures (pistils and stamens). Also called a bisexual, monoclinous, or hermaphroditic flower.

perfoliate A base of a leaf or bract (a modified petal-like leaf) with lobes that are united and completely surround the stem, making it appear as if the stem is inserted through the leaf. A perfoliate leaf is sessile, meaning it has no stalk. Perfoliate bellwort (*Uvularia perfoliata*) and great merrybells (*U. grandiflora*) bear perfoliate leaves.

perfoliate leaf

perforate Having holes or perforations.

pergola A tunnel-like series of arches over which plants are grown. Pergolas usually are constructed of vertical pillars and horizontal beams to create a flat-topped structure. The term gallery is commonly used for structures with rounded arches. *See* GALLERY

pergola

peri- A prefix meaning surrounding. Peripterous means surrounded by a wing or border, for example.

perianth A collective term that refers to the calyx (sepals) and the corolla (petals) of a flower. It is most often used when the two are similar in appearance.

perianth segments Petal-like parts of a flower that has a calyx and corolla that are similar looking. The "petals" of a daffodil are an example. *See also* PERIANTH

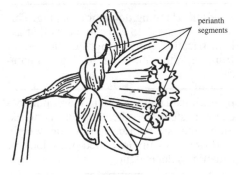

perianth segments

perianth whorl A collective term for either the calyx (sepals) or the corolla (petals) of a flower.

pericarp The wall of a fruit or a ripened ovary. The pericarp sometimes has three distinct layers: In this case, the outer layer is called the exocarp, the middle layer the mesocarp, and the inner layer the endocarp.

periclinium *See* INVOLUCRE

peridroma The main stem, or rachis, of a fern frond.

perigynous A flower with sepals, petals, and stamens united at the base and borne on a cup-shaped base, called an hypanthium, that is attached below the ovary. The ovary of a perigynous flower is superior, and the sepals, petals, and stamens are carried on a cup-shaped rim around it, so they are neither above nor below the ovary. Roses (*Rosa* spp.) bear perigynous flowers. *See* HYPANTHIUM

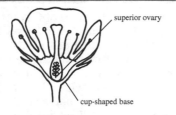

perigynous flower

period garden A garden that is designed using the plants, materials, and techniques characteristic of a particular historical era. A medieval garden might feature traditional herbs surrounded by a wattle fence. A colonial period garden, for example, could include the herbs, vegetables, and fruits used before the Revolutionary War arranged in a pattern characteristic of that time.

perlag *See* PERLITE

perlite Small white pellets of volcanic rock that have been popped like popcorn. Perlite is added to various potting mixes to improve aeration and drainage. Also called perlag.

permeability The ability of soil to convey or move water or air, usually measured in the number of inches per hour of water that can flow through soil.

pernicious Harmful or destructive. This term is often used to indicate extremely weedy plants that spread with abandon and/or crowd out native species in natural areas. Purple loosestrife (*Lythrum salicaria*) is a pernicious weed in wetlands in North America.

persistent Remaining attached to a plant longer than other similar organs, especially after an organ's function has been completed. Purple bell vine (*Rhodochiton atrosanguineus*) bears handsome, bell-shaped calyxes that persist on the plant even after the flowers drop off.

personate A two-lipped (bilabiate) flower with a closed throat. The throat is closed by a prominent lower lip called a palate.

Snapdragons (*Antirrhinum majus*) have personate flowers.

personate flower

perula A scale covering a leaf bud.

perulate Having scales. Usually used to describe buds that have scales.

petal One segment of the corolla. Petals are brightly colored or white.

petal-like Petaloid. A plant part that looks like a petal but is not a true petal. Poinsettias have colorful, petal-like bracts that are actually modified leaves. Sepals and other flower parts also can be petal-like.

petal lobe The lobe of a flower with fused petals. The petal lobe is the remaining free portion at the top of each petal.

petalody A condition that causes various parts of a flower to become petal-like in appearance. Many double flowers exhibit this condition. For example, double peonies have petaloid or petal-like stamens.

petaloid Petal-like in color and texture. The small "petals" at the center of many peony flowers are actually petaloid stamens or carpels. An individual potaloid organ is termed a petalode.

-petalous A suffix referring to petals, usually combined with a prefix indicating a number. Octopetalous means bearing eight petals, for example.

petiolar Relating to or growing from a petiole.

petiolate Having a petiole.

petiole Leaf stalk.

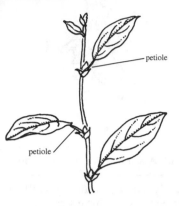

petiolule The stalk of an individual leaflet in a compound leaf.

pH A measure of the acidity or alkalinity of soil that determines which nutrients can dissolve in the soil water and are thus available to plants. The pH also has an influence on the activity of soil organisms. Soil pH and soil water are closely related. Water is made up of two hydrogen atoms and one oxygen atom (H_2O). Although these atoms normally cling together in soil, they can come apart, or ionize, into hydrogen ions and hydroxyl ions. It is the relative numbers of hydrogen and hydroxyl ions that determine the acidity or alkalinity of the soil solution. Soil that is acid has more hydrogen ions than hydroxyl ions in the soil solution, while soil that is alkaline has more hydroxyl ions than hydrogen ions. When numbers of hydrogen and hydroxyl ions are the same, the solution is neutral. Scientists use the pH scale, which runs from 0 to 14, to rate acidity and alkalinity. A pH of 7 indicates neutral pH. When pH numbers range from 0 to 7, the soil solution is more acid (the concentration of hydrogen ions increases). As numbers increase from 7 to 14, the solution is more alkaline (the concentration of hydroxyl ions increases). Each number on the scale differs from the preceding one by a factor of 10. That means a pH of 5 is 10 times as acid as a pH of 6, and a pH of 4 is 100 times as acid as a pH of 6. A pH range near neutral (roughly 6.5 to 7.0) is considered ideal for most garden plants. Within this range, most nutrients are in forms plants can use. At more acid or alkaline pH, some nutrients bond with others to form compounds that are not available to plants because they will not dissolve in water. You can determine the pH of your soil by taking a soil sample and doing a home test kit or sending it out to a lab. *See* ACID SOIL, ALKALINE SOIL

phenology The study of the timing of biological events as they relate to one another and to climate. The biological events can include when the buds of certain flowers open, when a certain insect emerges, when birds migrate, or when certain plants germinate or begin growing after winter's dormant period. The old saying, "Plant corn when oak leaves are the size of a squirrel's ear," is an example of how these events can be linked and used in the garden.

phenotype The outward characteristics or observable appearance of a plant or other organism. Phenotype is the result of the genetic makeup of the plant (its genotype) and the way traits are inherited. Environmental conditions such as the characteristics of the site, the soil, the climate, or other factors, also play a role in the outward appearance or growth habit of a plant, thus affecting its phenotype. Phenotypes linked to a specific gene are fairly easy to trace from generation to generation, but the inheritance of traits usually is quite complex. *See* GENOTYPE

pheromones Hormonelike chemicals produced by insects and other animals to communicate with other members of their species. Pheromones are highly specific, meaning each one attracts a specific species of insect. They are organically acceptable and are used to bait traps for pest insects such as peachtree borers, codling moths, corn earworms, and Japanese beetles. Pheromone-baited traps are used to monitor pest populations, to determine if other control measures are in order. They also can be used to simply confuse insects;

hanging a large number of pheromone-baited traps can prevent insects from finding mates or plants of choice.

phloem The food-conducting tissue of both woody and herbaceous plants, which moves food made in the leaves down to the roots. It consists primarily of elongated, thin-walled cells called sieve elements. Fibers, such as those used to make linen, are derived from phloem tissue. Phloem tissue also constitutes the inner layer of bark on a tree. Unlike xylem, which conducts water, phloem cells are alive when mature, but they usually get crushed or otherwise destroyed as woody stems grow. *See also* XYLEM, VASCULAR BUNDLE, CAMBIUM

phosphate, colloidal *See* COLLOIDAL PHOSPHATE

phosphorus A macronutrient that is a major component of genetic material in plants and is used in various biochemical processes. Bonemeal and rock phosphate are organic sources of phosphorus. Plants that are deficient in phosphorus have red, purple, or very dark green lower leaves and stunted growth.

photoperiod The relative exposure to daylight that an organism receives as a function of the total number of hours of darkness and light in an entire day, or 24-hour period.

photoperiodism, photoperiodic The ability of a plant or other organism to respond to the length of the photoperiod, or the number of hours of darkness and light. Florist's chrysanthemums are photoperiodic plants that bloom when they are exposed to long nights (hours of darkness). They bloom naturally in fall when days get shorter and nights get longer. Poinsettias also are photoperiodic. When grown as greenhouse crops, both are covered at night to exclude light and thus provide the hours of darkness they require to set flower buds. Photoperiod, specifically shorter days and longer nights, also can signal plants to get ready for the dormant season by dropping leaves and/or slowing down growth.

photosynthesis The process by which green plants convert carbon dioxide, water, and nutrients into food, consisting of complex organic molecules.

phototropism The movement of a plant in response to light. As anyone who has grown houseplants knows, plants grow toward the light.

phyllary A bract on the back of an aster family (Asteraceae) flower that is part of the involucre, which is the series of bracts beneath the flowerhead.

phylloclad, phylloclade A flattened stem or branch that functions like a leaf. Prickly pear cacti (*Opuntia* spp.) and celery pine (*Phyllocladus* spp.) bear phylloclads.

phyllode An expanded petiole that has taken over the function of a leaf. Some species of mimosa or wattle (*Acacia* spp.) bear phyllodes.

physic garden A garden devoted to medicinal plants and herbs. First established in 16th- and 17th-century Europe in conjunction with medical facilities, physic gardens are considered the precursors to modern-day botanical gardens.

physical controls *See* ORGANIC PEST MANAGEMENT

pick, pickax A hand tool useful for digging in rocky or clay soil and for removing rocks. A pick weighs about 7 or 8 pounds and has a two-ended metal blade with a handle inserted through an eye socket in the middle. One end of the blade ends in a point, while the other end is a very short, axlike blade. A pick is used by swinging it over your shoulder. Use a crowbar to remove large rocks and a mattock for cutting through roots.

picking flowers *See* CUTTING FLOWERS

picotee A flower that has petals of one color that are edged in a contrasting color. Pinks (*Dianthus* spp.) come in picotee patterns.

piece-root graft *See* ROOT GRAFTING

pillar A narrow, ornamental column often constructed of forged metal and used to support vines and climbing roses. The term pillar also is used to refer to a plant trained to form a narrow column.

pillar

pilose Covered with long, straight hairs that are soft in texture. Most often used to describe leaf or stem surfaces. The old-fashioned annual kiss-me-over-the-garden-gate (*Persicaria orientale*, formerly *Polygonum orientale*) bears pilose-hairy leaves.

pilosulose Covered with very short, straight hairs that are soft in texture. Most often used to describe leaf surfaces.

pinch pruning Pruning and shaping a plant's growth by repeatedly pinching the stem tips.

pinching Removing stem tips to encourage branching and denser, more compact growth or simply to shorten soft stems. To pinch a plant, snap off the tip of each shoot just above a set of leaves with thumb and forefinger. If the growth is too hard to remove with fingers, use pruning shears, garden shears, or a pocket knife. Pinching a plant often results in more, although smaller, flowers and is best used on bushy, multistemmed perennials and annual. It won't work on plants with unbranched

stems (such as lilies) or basal foliage (such as daylilies).

pinching

pinetum An arboretum or collection of plants devoted mainly to evergreen conifers, especially pines (*Pinus* spp.), but also including other evergreen conifers such as spruces (*Picea* spp.) and junipers (*Juniperus* spp.), as well as deciduous conifers such as larches (*Larex* spp.). *See also* CONIFER

pinholder A useful tool used by florists and flower arrangers that's set in the bottom of an arrangement to hold flowers in place. Pinholders are made of heavy metal in several shapes and sizes and consist of a base with pins that stick up and hold flower stems in place. Also called a frog.

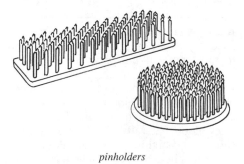

pinholders

pinna, *pl.* **pinnae** A primary leaflet of a pinnately compound leaf, meaning one that is attached along the main stem, or rachis. The term most often is used to refer to the leaflets of a fern frond. Pinnae can be entire (with a continuous, unbroken edge, or margin), or they can be further lobed or cut. *See also* FROND, PINNATE, PINNULE

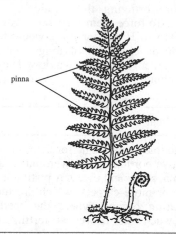

pinna

pinnate Featherlike. A compound leaf that has a main stem, or rachis, with pairs of smaller leaflets running along it in a featherlike fashion. Walnuts (*Juglans* spp.) and honeylocusts (*Gleditsia* spp.), along with many ferns including Christmas fern (*Polysticum acrostichoides*) have pinnate leaves. If the leaflets are divided again, the leaf is bipinnate, or twice-cut. Leaves that are divided three times are tripinnate, or thrice-cut. The term pinnate also is used to describe veins in a leaf that have a featherlike arrangement. *See also* ODD PINNATE, EVEN PINNATE, BIPINNATE, TRIPINNATE.

pinnate

pinnately compound *See* PINNATE

pinnate-pinnatifid Once-cut pinnatifid. A compound leaf divided in a featherlike fash-

ion (pinnate) with leaflets attached along a main stem, or rachis. The leaflets are pinnatifid, meaning they are further divided (cleft or parted) into pairs of segments arranged in a featherlike (pinnate) fashion, with the indentations, called sinuses, cut about halfway to the middle of the midrib of the leaf, but not all the way to the midrib.

pinnate-pinnatifid

pinnate venation Featherlike. Leaf veins arranged in a featherlike fashion, with a main central vein or midrib and side veins arranged along it in a featherlike fashion.

pinnate venation

pinnatifid Divided or cut into pairs of segments arranged in a featherlike (pinnate) fashion. The indentations, called sinuses, between the segments reach from halfway to the midrib of the leaf to nearly the midrib. On a pinnatifid leaf, the sinuses do not reach all the way to the midrib, and the individual lobes or segments are not separated into individual leaflets, as they are in a pinnate leaf.

pinnatifid leaf

pinnatipartite *See* PINNATIFID

pinnatisect Deeply divided or cut into pairs of segments arranged in a featherlike (pinnate) fashion. The indentations, called sinuses, between the segments reach all the way to the midrib of the leaf, or nearly so. On a pinnatisect leaf, although the sinuses may reach all the way to the midrib, the individual lobes or segments are not separated into individual leaflets. Pinnatisect leaves also have narrower lobes or segments than pinnatifid leaves do.

pinnatisect leaf

pinnule The smallest divisions or leaflets of a leaf or frond that is at least bipinnate (twice-cut) or tripinnate (thrice-cut). The pinnules are the leaflets or segments of the pinna, which are the leaflets that line the main stem, or rachis, of the leaf. *See also* FROND, BIPINNATE, TRIPINNATE

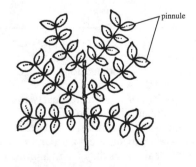

pinnule

pip A single crown. A piece of rhizome that has roots and a strong bud. Lily-of-the-valley (*Convallaria majalis*) plants are commonly divided into these small pieces for propagation and sale. Fall or late winter/early spring are good times for planting them. Pips also can be potted up and forced for flowering in winter. Either start with pips that have received a period of cold storage, or pot them up in fall and store them outdoors in a protected location before bringing them indoors in midwinter. To force them, first set pots in a dark, 60 to 70°F spot for 1 to 2 weeks to ensure the development of long stems. Then move them to a sunny window. They will take about 3 or 4 weeks to come into flower.

piriform Pear-shaped.

pistil The traditional name for the female reproductive portion of a flower, made up of a stigma, style, and ovary. A pistil contains one or more carpels, which are the ovule-bearing organs, where the seeds develop when the flower is fertilized. (Technically, the stigma, style, and ovary are part of the carpel.) A simple pistil contains one carpel, and in this case, the carpel makes up the entire simple pistil. A compound pistil bears two or more united carpels, in which case each carpel makes up a separate section of the pistil. Botanists use the term gynoecium to refer collectively to all the carpels or pistils of a flower. *See also* CARPEL

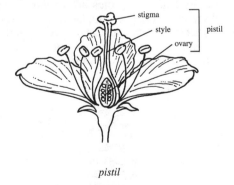

stigma
style
ovary
pistil

pistil

pistillate flower A female flower. A pistillate flower has a pistil or pistils (female reproductive organs), but no stamens (male reproductive organs).

pit house A greenhouse built with the side walls underground.

pitch The resin exuded by conifers such as pines (*Pinus* spp.) or spruces (*Picea* spp.).

pith The spongy tissue in the center of the herbaceous stems and roots of many plants. Pith is composed of thin-walled, undifferentiated cells, called parenchyma. *See* PARENCHYMA

---

pitted *See* LACUNOSE

---

plant bug Flattened, fast-moving insects that suck plant juices, causing sunken, brown or black spots on leaves and deformed leaves, buds, and shoots. They may also feed on fruit, producing scarring, swellings or depressions, and distorted growth. Four-lined plant bugs are greenish yellow, with four black stripes on the back, and their nymphs are reddish with black dots. Tarnished plant bugs are greenish to brownish, with brown or black mottling on the back. The wingless nymphs are smaller and pale yellow with black dots. Stink bugs are $^{1}/_{2}$-inch-long, green, gray, or brown, triangular-shaped bugs. Chinch bugs have white wings with a black triangular spot on the outer edge. To control them, handpick adults and nymphs in early morning (while they are still sluggish) and drop them in a container of soapy water. Attract beneficial predators (*see* BENEFICIAL INSECTS). Treat serious infestations with neem, sabadilla, or rotenone. To prevent damage to future crops, clean up garden debris in fall and spring to remove overwintering sites for adults. Use floating row covers to prevent plant bugs from attacking vegetable crops. Lawn grasses that contain endophytes (*see* ENDOPHYTES) repel chinch bugs.

plant bug

---

plant exchange Many plant societies organize exchanges or sales of plants and/or cuttings between members, and these present an excellent way to obtain unusual plants from other members. While cuttings are relatively easy to exchange through the mail, plant exchanges/sales are usually local in nature. To find organizations that offer plant or cutting exchanges (as well as plant and cutting exchanges) look through the Horticultural Societies list in *Gardening by Mail*, by Barbara Barton (Houghton Mifflin, 1997) for organizations specializing in plants that interest you. Also consult local botanical gardens, arboreta, gardening groups, plant societies, and conservation organizations; they often hold plant sales as fund raisers. *See* SEED EXCHANGE

---

plant supports *See* STAKING

---

planting A cool, cloudy, or even rainy day in spring or fall is the best time to plant container-grown plants and balled-and-burlapped ones. To plant a container-grown perennial or annual, dig a hole large enough to accommodate the roots, tip the plant out of its pot, set it in place, and firm the soil over the root ball. If the plant has roots that wind around the inside of the pot, use a knife to score them on each side before planting to encourage the roots to extend out into the surrounding soil. Set plants at the same depth at which they were growing in the pot, or position them slightly higher to allow for settling. For shrubs and trees, digging a deep hole and amending the soil with peat moss, compost, and/or fertilizer is no longer the recommended planting procedure. Studies have shown that trees and shrubs planted in this manner rarely send their roots out beyond the confines of the original hole. Instead, they wind them around and around in the amended soil as if it were a container, eventually becoming as potbound as if they actually were growing in a pot. Trees planted this way actually can blow over, a problem called windthrow, because the topgrowth isn't supported by wide-spreading roots. Instead, dig a wide, shallow hole, that is two to three times as wide as the root ball. Loosen the soil on the sides of the hole, then set the plant in place and check to make sure it will be at the same depth it was growing in the nursery.

A straight board laid across the hole from rim to rim works well for this. Refill without amending the soil. (*See* PLANTING SITES for the best approach to planting several trees, shrubs, or other plants.) Form a broad saucer of soil around the plant that will collect and direct water. Then flood the soil around newly planted shrubs to settle it and eliminate air pockets. Finally, mulch with shredded bark or other organic matter, keeping it an inch or two away from the stems of the plant. Then water again, and continue watering regularly—1 inch of water every 10 days to 2 weeks—for the first season to give plants a good start and encourage a vigorous, widespreading root system. If the weather is warm or windy, cover new plants with burlap, bushel baskets, or spun-bonded row covers for a few days to help them recover. For information on planting bare-root plants, *see* BARE ROOT

planting pocket A restricted area, either among stones or roots, used to grow one or more plants. Planting pockets can occur naturally, or they can be created by the gardener by digging and amending the soil. When creating planting pockets around trees, select deep rooted species such as oaks (*Quercus* spp.) and take care to damage as few roots as possible.

planting sites An ideal approach to planting areas with a mix of shrubs, trees, perennials, and groundcovers by preparing the soil over a wide area. Mark off the area to be planted, remove any grass or weeds, and then work compost, well-rotted manure, or other organic matter as deeply into the soil as possible—12 inches is fine. Then plant the entire area (*see* PLANTING), mulch, and water deeply. Since the entire site has amended soil, roots are encouraged to spread widely. Although this approach requires more work up front, it makes it easy to underplant with ground covers and is great from a maintenance standpoint because one large planting is easier to trim around than several individual plants. A large planting also is more attractive from a design standpoint than a mix of shrubs and trees dotted in the lawn.

planting wall A wall designed and built with pockets of soil between the stones that are designed to accommodate plants.

plantlet A small plant that has leaves and often roots and is produced naturally on a larger plant. Plantlets commonly arise from a runner, stolon, rhizome, or other organ. Plantlets can be severed from their parent and potted up or moved elsewhere in the garden for purposes of propagation. This also is a general term for small plants produced by division or other propagation techniques. *See* OFFSET, VIVIPAROUS

plaster A pulplike or pastelike herbal preparation, similar to a poultice, made by combining chopped fresh herbs or crushed or powdered dried herbs with a little bit of hot water or hot herbal tea. The mix is placed between the folds of a cloth or bandage, which is then placed on the skin. A plaster should be as hot as is bearable. Replace as necessary.

plastic mulch *See* MULCH

pleaching A pruning and training technique in which the branches in a row of trees are trained and woven together to form a dense but narrow screen, arch, or tunnel of foliage above a line of clear trunks. The plants are trained to a frame initially, and all growth that sticks out from the surface is pruned back to a bud that faces sideways. Shoots of ajacent plants are woven together and tied in place as they grow. A row of pleached trees can take 10 to 15 years to establish, and is maintained much like a hedge once the plants are trained.

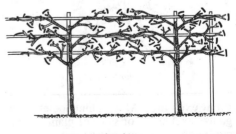

pleaching

pleated *See* PLICATE

plicate Folded lengthwise like a fan.

plot plan A map that is drawn to scale and indicates the boundaries or property lines of a particular lot, existing rights-of-way, sidewalks, setbacks, and easements.

plug A small seedling that has been produced in specially designed flats with individual, closely spaced openings that are roughly cylindrical or tapered in shape. The individual cells are filled (usually mechanically) with medium and sown. Plants grown in this manner, including annuals and many perennials, are transplanted into individual containers when they have two to three leaves and are then grown on until they reach garden size. Plugs are most often produced for the wholesale market, but are sometimes available to homeowners. They require more care than finished plants, but offer a good way to acquire large quantities of a single plant at a good price. Ground covers are good plants to buy as plugs. Some lawn grasses are commonly sold as plugs, especially asexually propagated ones such as zoysia grass. To plant plugs over a large area, prepare the soil, and set them at regular intervals. Keep the soil evenly moist until the plants resume growing actively.

plugging The process of planting plugs.

plume, plumelike Airy, featherlike flower clusters, such as those borne by astilbes (*Astilbe* spp.) are commonly described as plumes or plumelike. The term also is occasionally used to describe leaves or fronds, such as those of ostrich fern (*Matteuccia struthiopteris*)

plumose Very finely dissected. This term is commonly used to describe ferns that have very finely cut fronds.

plumule The stem, or axis, of a plant embryo or of a seedling.

plunge To set a flowerpot up to its rim in water, soil, or sand. Tender perennials that are kept in containers for easy overwintering can be plunged into garden beds over the summer. (Plants treated in this manner require less watering than containers kept above ground.) Alpine plants are commonly plunged into beds of sand, which helps keep the soil in the containers cool, yet provides the very well-drained conditions these plants require.

plur-, pluri- Prefixes meaning many.

pod Any type of dry fruit that splits open at maturity (meaning it is dehiscent). This term is most commonly used to refer to follicles and legumes.

pointed *See* ACUTE

polarity This term is of importance to plant propagators and grafters alike, and refers to the fact that stems and roots have an intrinsic orientation that determines where shoots and roots will form. On a stem cutting, shoots always form at the tip, or distal end, and roots always form at the base, or proximal, end. This is true even if the cutting is stuck upside down (in that case, roots and shoots may not form at all). Root cuttings form shoots at the end of the cutting that was nearest the crown of the plant. Most propagators have a system for keeping track of polarity when taking cuttings or grafting; simple systems for determining "which end is up" are covered in the individual definitions in this dictionary where proper polarity is essential. Polarity also determines the orientation that will create a successful graft union. Grafted material that is inserted upside down will not form a successful union: The basal, or proximal, end of the scion must be joined to the top, or distal, end of the stock if they are to join successfully. *See* GRAFTING

pole pruner A pruning tool on a long handle that has a lopperlike cutting blade operated by a lever or a long string. Some models have pruning saws that can be attached. Pole pruners reach from 6 to about 14 feet high, making it possible to prune without balancing on a ladder.

pollard, pollarding A tree that is regularly cut back to the top of the main trunk to maintain a head of ornamental new growth. Pollarding is used much like coppicing to enhance stem and foliage color and also requires a tree that tolerates heavy pruning. (*See* COPPICE, COPPICING for suggestions.) After the plant is established and the trunk is between 4 and 5 inches in diameter, cut the trunk off at a height of 4 to 6 feet in late winter or early spring, just above the lowest branches. Cut the remaining branches back to a length of 2 to 3 inches. After that, cut the branches that arise from the top of the trunk back to the main trunk every 1 to 3 years in late winter or early spring. Cut them off from $\frac{1}{2}$ to $\frac{3}{4}$ inch from the trunk, but do not cut into the top of the main stem. Remove excess shoots as necessary.

pollen Dustlike pollen grains are the male gametophytes, borne on the anthers of flowering plants (angiosperms) and the male cones of gymnosperms. Pollen grains are haploid, meaning they contain half the number of chromosomes in a normal cell, and have two cells. When they land on a receptive stigma, one cell develops into a pollen tube, while the other divides to form sperm cells, which fertilize the flower. *See* GAMETOPHYTE

pollination The transfer of pollen from an anther to a stigma. Pollen can be transferred by insects, birds, or other pollinators, as well as by wind. *See* FERTILIZATION, CROSS-POLLINATION, SELF-POLLINATION, OPEN-POLLINATION, WIND-POLLINATION, HAND-POLLINATION

pollinator An insect or other organism that transfers pollen from one flower to another. Honeybees are perhaps the best-known pollinators, but many insects also move pollen, as do birds, such as hummingbirds. Other pollinators include bats, flies, and moths. This term also refers to a tree or shrub planted specifically to provide pollen for another plant. Many fruit and nut trees need a second tree of the same or a different cultivar to pollinate them if they are to set fruit. Trees that need pollinators include sweet cherries, pears, Japanese plums, most apples, some apricots, some avocados, pecans, and walnuts. Usually specific pollinators are suggested for each cultivar, since it is essential that both plants be in bloom at the same time for pollination to occur.

poly- A prefix meaning many. Polystichous means arranged in many or several rows, for example. Polymorphic means variable or having many or several forms.

polygamo-dioecious A species that is polygamo-dioecious is primarily dioecious, meaning male and female flowers are on separate plants, but plants produce some perfect (bisexual) flowers as well. Thus, some individuals will bear male (staminate) flowers and perfect flowers; others female (pistillate) flowers and perfect flowers. Black tupelo (*Nyssa sylvatica*) and honeylocust (*Gleditsia triacanthos*) are polygamo-dioecious.

polygamo-monoecious A plant that is primarily monoecious, meaning it bears separate male and female flowers on the same plant, but also produces some perfect (bisexual) flowers.

polygamous Bearing both imperfect (unisexual) and perfect (bisexual) flowers on the same plant. A polygamous plant produces staminate and pistillate flowers as well as perfect flowers, which have both pistils and stamens. Smoke trees (*Cotinus* spp.) are polygamous.

polygonal Having many angles.

polymorphic Variable. Having more than two different forms or shapes. This term is used to describe species that have several very closely related forms within the species. It also is applied to plants that have variable habits or bear variable organs; sassafras (*Sassafras albidum*) bears leaves in various shapes, for example.

polypetalous Bearing separate petals, rather than ones that are fused together. Roses (*Rosa* spp.) and buttercups (*Ranunculus* spp.) are both polypetalous. Also called apopetalous, choripetalous.

polyploid Bearing three or more sets of chromosomes within each cell.

pomander Historically, pomanders were small bags or boxes filled with aromatic plant parts and other ingredients. They were worn to cover the stench of unsanitary living conditions as well as to protect against disease. Today, pomanders typically are made from oranges and cloves: They are a popular gift that is easy for a child to make. Simply cover the surface of an orange, lemon, lime, or other citrus fruit with cloves by sticking the stems into the surface of the fruit. For longest life, dust the clove-encrusted orange with powdered orris root or another fixative (*See* FIXATIVE). You also can dust the surface with powdered spices such as cinnamon. Set the pomander in a dark, well-ventilated spot for a month to age and to let the fragrances meld. Set pomanders in drawers, display them in bowls, or add a hanger by piercing them with a large needle and thread. Add a ribbon for decoration.

pome A fleshy fruit, characteristic of apples, pears, hawthorns (*Crataegus* spp.), and crab apples (*Malus* spp.). Pomes have several chambers, or locules, and are formed from flowers with inferior ovaries.

pome

pomology The science and practice of growing fruit.

pompon A small, round or nearly round, fully double flower that has masses of small petals. Pompons usually are borne in clusters.

pore A small opening that is usually more or less circular.

pore space The spaces between soil particles, called aggregates, which can be filled with water or air. When it rains or when you water your garden, the water runs, or percolates, into the soil and down through the larger pores, which fill with air. Large pores are called macropores or aeration pores. (*See* PERCOLATION) The water usually clings to the soil particles themselves and also is held in the smaller pores, called micropores or capillary pores. While gravity pulls water down, adhesion to particles slows its movement. This process is why sandy soils, which have a large percentage of coarse particles and large pore spaces, tend to drain quickly. Since clay soils have tiny particles that fit together closely, leaving tiny pore spaces, they hold water very tightly and have very little space for air (poor aeration). One reason that repeatedly walking or, worse yet, driving on soil is so damaging is that it compacts soil pores, thus affecting the amount of air and water they hold. *See* SOIL, SOIL STRUCTURE

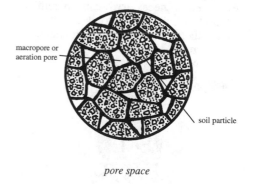

macropore or aeration pore

soil particle

pore space

poricidal dehiscence *See* DEHISCENT

potager An ornamental garden with a formal design that combines vegetables, herbs, fruits, and even edible flowers. Commonly, potagers are divided into a series of small beds separated by lawn or mulched paths to make cultivation and harvesting easier, and the beds are either at ground level or raised. Vegetables and other plants are arranged in various patterns and combined for maximum visual effect.

potassium, potash A macronutrient that is found in plant proteins, carbohydrates, and chlorophyll. Greensand and granite meal are organic sources of potassium. Plants that are deficient in potassium are weak-stemmed and develop lower leaves that have yellowish tips and edges that eventually turn brown.

potbound A container-grown plant that has filled all of the available space with roots. Potbound plants dry out much more quickly than ones that are not, and this condition eventually stunts growth. Tipping a potbound plant out of its container reveals a dense mat of roots circling the root ball; roots sticking out the bottom of the pot also are a sign of a plant that has been in the same pot too long. When planting potbound specimens, score the sides of the root ball with a sharp knife or trowel and tease out roots to encourage them to spread into the surrounding soil. Inspect container-grown trees especially carefully for girdling roots that are developing, and sever them. If necessary, wash any remaining soil off the roots so it is easier to inspect them carefully and prune them.

potbound plant

pot grown *See* CONTAINER GROWN

pot herb An edible herb or herblike plant that is used for culinary, rather than medicinal, purposes.

pot layering *See* AIR LAYERING

pot, long *See* DIFFICULT TO TRANSPLANT

potpourri, pot-pourri A mixture of dried flower petals, flower buds, leaves, and other plant parts mixed with spices and other ingredients. Potpourris are used to scent rooms or clothes. The basic ingredients are dried flowers, flower buds, petals (especially rose petals), and leaves combined with a fixative, which keeps the essential oils in the potpourri ingredients from evaporating and thus helps it hold its fragrance. (*See* FIXATIVE) Most recipes call for a drop or two of essential oil to add additional fragrance. There are countless recipes for potpourri, or you can experiment with your own mixes. Combine plants and plant parts with scents that appeal to you—lavender, mints, rose petals, or lemon balm, thyme, and nutmeg. Be sure all the ingredients are thoroughly dry, or mold will form on them. Add about 1 tablespoon of fixative and 1 or 2 drops of essential oil per quart of dried herbs. Stir the mix gently and place it in a wide-mouthed jar with a tight-fitting lid. Set the jar in a cool, dry place for about 6 weeks to let the fragrances blend. Shake or stir the mix weekly. Display potpourris in jars, baskets, bowls, or other containers. Moist potpourris are made with fresh rather than dried ingredients to which scented oils are added. The mix is then layered into a wide-mouthed jar with uniodized salt and stirred daily for several weeks. After that, it is pressed under a weighted plate for 2 weeks until it begins to ferment and forms a cake. Finally, the cakes are scented with essential oils and a fixative, then stored for a few more weeks before they are used.

pot shard A broken piece of a clay pot. These are commonly used to cover the bottom of containers so that soil mix doesn't fall out the bottom. Always use a curved piece or several pieces so that the hole isn't blocked by a single, flat piece. A layer of pot shards in the bottom of a container doesn't improve soil drainage, as some gardeners believe. Substitute a piece of screening for pot shards if you don't have them to keep potting medium in the containers. (Screening also prevents most pests from crawling up into the pots.)

potting mix, potting soil, potting medium A mixture of ingredients used to fill containers to grow plants. Commercial potting mixes can contain a variety of ingredients, including real soil (generally pasteurized), compost, composted bark, peat moss, vermiculite, perlite, and sand. Some contain fertilizers, too. To make a good, general home-blended potting soil, combine 1 to 2 parts commercial potting soil or good (loamy, disease-free) garden soil, 1 part washed builders sand or perlite, and 1 part peat moss, well-rotted compost, or leaf mold. Add 1 tablespoon bonemeal per quart of mix. For plants that require especially rich soil, use 2 parts peat moss, compost, or leaf mold. For cacti and succulents, which require drier, well-drained soil, add up to 2 parts sand or perlite. To make a soilless mix that is especially useful for large containers, combine 1 part peat moss or well-rotted compost, 1 part pulverized or composted pine bark, and 1 part perlite or vermiculite. Since a soilless mix contains no nutrients, add a balanced organic fertilizer according to the package directions or plan on feeding at least weekly. It's best to premoisten soilless mixes before filling containers, and moisten very dry mixes before planting to avoid damaging plant roots. *See* PRE-MOISTEN, CUTTING MIX, GROWING MIX, SEED-STARTING MIX, EPIPHYTE MIX, FERN POTTING MIX

potting on Moving a container-grown plant from a smaller pot to a larger one. This term is also used to refer to seedlings or cuttings that are being moved from seed trays or pots into individual containers.

potting up Moving seedlings or cuttings from seed trays or pots into individual containers. Also called potting on.

poultice A pulplike or pastelike herbal preparation made by combining chopped fresh herbs or crushed or powdered dried herbs with a little bit of hot water or hot herbal tea. The mix is placed directly on the skin, and should be as hot as is bearable. Cover the poultice with a warm cloth or strips of gauze, and replace as necessary.

praemorse Ending abruptly. A leaf tip that is squared off, but ragged, as if it was bitten or chewed. A truncate leaf is squared off, but smooth. While most commonly used to describe a leaf tip, this term can be applied to other plant parts such as bracts (modified petal-like leaves) or the petals or sepals of a flower.

praemorse leaf tip

prairie garden A perennial planting that has a free-form, natural-looking design and features native North American prairie species—various grasses along with species such as *Rudbeckia maxima*, cup plant (*Silphium* spp.), and asters (*Aster* spp.)

pre- A prefix meaning before. Prevernal means before spring, for example.

precocious Appearing or developing unusually early. Deciduous magnolias (*Magnolia* spp.) and some spring-blooming shrubs such as forsythia (*Forsythia* spp.) have precocious flowers, which open before the leaves appear.

predator An insect or other animal that hunts, attacks, and feeds on other insects or animals. Many beneficial insects are pretadors, including lady beetles and ground beetles.

preformed pools *See* WATER GARDEN LINERS

pregerminating Sprouting seeds before planting them is a technique that gardeners use if they want extra control over the germinating process, especially with expensive or hard-to-find seeds. Also called presprouting, pregerminating is much like germination testing: To pregerminate, place seeds on a moist paper towel, fold the towel, and place it in a loosely closed plastic bag set in a warm spot. Either use a separate bag for each type of seeds and enclose a label with the name of the plant and the date "sown" or place several towels in a single bag and fold a label into each towel so you don't lose track of which plant is where. Check every few days to look for sprouting seeds. (*See* GERMINATION TESTING for more information.) Carefully remove sprouted seeds and pot them up in containers filled with premoistened mix. (*See* PREMOISTEN) Refold the towel and continue checking and potting up until most or all have sprouted. Remoisten the towel if it begins to dry out, and spread the seeds on a new towel if mold appears. This technique is handy for seeds that have complicated dormancy requirements: Some seeds need alternating cycles of warm and cold temperatures in order to sprout, and keeping them on towels in plastic bags saves space and time because you don't have to pot up all the individual seeds. *See* DORMANCY and STRATIFICATION

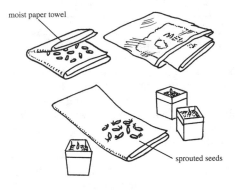

moist paper towel

sprouted seeds

pregerminating seeds

preliminary design *See* SITE PLAN

premoisten Growing, seed-starting, and cutting mixes, along with soilless media in general, can be very difficult to wet, especially once they are in containers. (Dry mixes actually can float on the surface of the water, while the water pours right out the bottom of the containers.) Premoistening eliminates this problem, and once these types of mixes are wet, they retain water well and are easy to keep evenly moist. To premoisten, place a quantity of dry mix in a 5–gallon bucket and add warm

water. Either let the mix sit overnight or stir with your hands while adding more water until it is evenly moist, but not wet (like a damp sponge that has been wrung out). Fill containers and let excess water drain away before sowing seeds or sticking cuttings. Another option is to fill containers with dry medium and set them overnight in a flat filled about halfway with water. The medium should soak up the water. Premoistening also has important benefits for the plants. Dry mix can actually pull water out of plant roots—especially those of tender seedlings—causing permanent damage or even death. Transplanting into premoistened medium eliminates this problem.

preservatives *See* FLORAL PRESERVATIVES

preserving herbs *See* HERB PRESERVATION

presprouting *See* PREGERMINATING

pressing flowers A preservation process in which flowers, leaves, and other plant parts are held flat between absorbent layers of paper. The simplest way to press flowers is simply to insert them between the pages of a book, but this can damage the book and doesn't give consistent results. Fast drying is the key to pressed flowers that still have bright colors and a plant press provides the best results. To make a simple plant press, start with two pieces of thick plywood—12 inches by 18 inches is a good standard size and will neatly accommodate folded sections of newspaper, which are used for absorbing moisture. Cut several pieces of corrugated cardboard the same size as the newspaper (roughly 11 inches by 13$\frac{1}{2}$ inches). Then lay a piece of cardboard or a folded section of newspaper down on the plywood to determine where you will need to drill holes to fasten the top and bottom of the press together. Drill in the four corners, immediately outside the newspaper/cardboard so you can insert long bolts and wing nuts in the corners. (You also can hold the top and bottom layers of the press together with straps.) To press flowers, leaves, and other plant materials, you will need a stack of folded sections of newspaper as well as a stack of blotter paper, recycled paper, or newspaper upon which to arrange plant materials. To fill the press, place the bolts face up in the corners of the bottom piece of plywood, then add a piece of corrugated cardboard and a section of newspaper. Top this with a piece of blotter paper, recycled paper, or newspaper. Arrange flowers and leaves to be pressed on top of this layer, making sure they do not touch. Use materials of similar thickness in each layer, so that they will receive even amounts of pressure. Top the flowers with another layer of blotter paper, recycled paper, or newspaper and another section of newspaper. Then repeat the process until the press is filled, finishing with a section of newspaper and a piece of corrugated cardboard. Put the top piece of plywood on the press and tighten down the corners until they are firm. Most flowers and leaves will be dry within 2 weeks, although thicker materials may take longer. Handle pressed flowers with care, as they are quite brittle. Store them on the pieces of paper in which they were dried, layered between sheets of corrugated cardboard to ensure adequate ventilation and discourage mold. To use dried flowers, glue them to a sturdy backing sheet—shirt cardboard or very stiff card stock are ideal. Brush glue on the backing sheet to attach background plants; dab it on the backs of flowers or other materials with a toothpick or cotton swab. Tweezers are handy for handling pressed materials. Don't be afraid to glue on layers of flowers and foliage to create the desired effect. *See also* SKELETONIZED LEAVES, which can be used with dried flowers

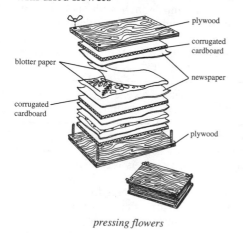

plywood

corrugated cardboard

blotter paper

newspaper

corrugated cardboard

plywood

pressing flowers

pretreating seeds Some seeds require special treatments to allow them to break dormancy and germinating. *See* SCARIFICATION, STRATIFICATION

pricking out, pricking off Digging up very small seedlings from a seedbed or container and moving them to flats or other containers. A plastic label or a pocketknife works well for digging up tiny seedlings. Always water thoroughly before pricking out seedlings and move them to premoistened medium.

prickle A small, sharp-pointed structure that is an outgrowth of the bark or the epidermis, which is the outermost layer of cells on a stem. A true prickle does not have vascular tissue. The familiar "thorns" of roses are actually prickles. *See also* SPINE, THORN

primary First. The leaflet at the tip of a compound leaf is the primary leaflet, for example.

primary colors Red, blue, and yellow. These are not made by mixing other colors. *See* COLOR WHEEL

primary phloem *See* PHLOEM

primary xylem *See* XYLEM

primocane A first-year shoot or cane of a bramble fruit such as blackberry or raspberry (*Rubus* spp.), which produces only foliage. The term primocane is for first-year canes only; they are called floricanes during their second season, when they produce flowers and fruit. *See* BRAMBLES

priority This is a nomenclatural rule designating that the first validly published name for a plant is the accepted name.

procumbent Lying flat on the ground or trailing loosely across it without producing roots at the nodes. Creeping and shore junipers (*Juniperus horizontalis* and *J. conferta*) are procumbent.

proliferating, proliferous Bearing small plants (plantlets), bulbs (bulblets), or offshoots. This term is especially used to refer to buds or offshoots produced by unusual organs or in an unusual manner, such as plantlets from leaves or shoots that arise from flowers. Piggy-back plant (*Tolmiea menziesii*) bears plantlets on the leaves, where the blade is attached to the petiole. Mother fern (*Asplenium bulbiferum*) bears small bulblets on its leaves that sprout into plantlets, while leaves of walking ferns (including *Camptosorus rhizophyllus* and *Polystichum lepidocaulon*) have an extended rachis that yields a plantlet once it comes in contact with the soil. Spider plants (*Chlorophytum* spp.) often bear plantlets in the flower clusters or instead of flower clusters.

prominent Raised or standing out from the surface. Ribs or veins that stand out from a leaf are called prominent, for example.

prop root A root that emerges from the stem of a plant above ground and helps to support the plant. Corn (*Zea mays*) produces prop roots. Many species of fig or banyon trees (*Ficus* spp.) produce prop roots as well, enabling mature specimens to cover large areas.

propagate, propagation To cause new plants to be produced from existing ones. This term is often used to refer only to vegetative propagation methods, but seed sowing (sexual propagation) is properly included here. Gardeners use many different techniques for propagation. *See* CUTTING, DIVISION, LAYERING, GRAFTING, SEED SOWING

propagation box, propagation case A box that has plastic or glass walls and is used for germinating seeds or rooting cuttings. Such boxes provide high humidity and can be set on a heat mat to provide bottom heat, which spurs rooting; fancy models come with heating cables installed. You can make a simple propagation box by draping or stapling lightweight plastic over a wire or wood frame. A plastic sweater box and even an old aquarium makes a good propagation box.

propagation mat A specially designed electric mat designed to raise the soil temperature in containers set on it to speed germination and rooting. Most seeds germinate faster and more uniformly when given bottom heat, and cuttings root more quickly when the soil is warm. While flats of seeds or cuttings can be set on a refrigerator or on a board on a radiator, a propagation mat is an efficient, effective, and neater way to provide bottom heat to a large number of pots. Several models of propagation mats are available; most gardeners need one only large enough to accommodate a single flat of seedlings. Lay it on the surface under lights used for germinating seedlings. Place pots of seeds or cuttings in a watertight (no drainage holes) flat. Cover the flat with plastic to provide high humidity. Once seedlings have a set of true leaves or cuttings are well rooted, they can be moved off the heat mat and transplanted.

propagule A structure that falls off a plant and forms a new plant. Propagules can be vegetative—buds, bulblets, plantlets, and other structures that do not involve sexual reproducting are vegetative. Or they can be sexual; in that case they are seeds or spores.

proportion *See* SCALE

propping A technique used to protect long, picturesque branches or reclining trees from breaking. Use a forked wooden post or other support to take the weight off the end of the branch without forcing it upward or out of place. Place padding between the support and the branch or trunk to protect it from rubbing—old carpet or a folded piece of burlap works well.

prostrate This is a general term for a plant that lies flat on the ground.

protandrous This term is used for a flower that sheds pollen before the stigma of the same flower is receptive, thus preventing self-pollination. In incomplete protandry, the flower continues shedding mature pollen after the stigma is receptive, allowing some self-pollination.

prothallus The small, heart-shaped plant produced by the gametophyte generation of ferns and other cryptograms such as mosses. The prothallus bears both male and female structures on the underside (soil side) called antheridia (male) and archegonia (female), which in turn produce sperm and eggs on the same plant. *See also* FERN LIFECYCLE, GAMETOPHYTE

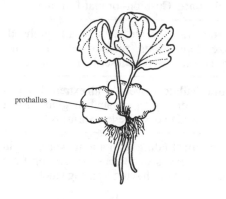

prothallus

protogynous This term is used for a flower that has a stigma that is mature and receptive to pollen before the pollen of the same flower is mature and shedding.

protruding *See* EXSERTED

proximal At or toward the base, where a plant part is attached.

pruning cuts *See* HEADING CUT, THINNING CUT, THREE-STEP CUT

pruning saws Two types of saws commoly are used for pruning: frame saws and pruning saws. A good frame saw has a lightweight tubular frame that holds a narrow, hardened-steel, replaceable blade. A sharp frame saw will easily handle 4- to 5-inch-diameter branches and is useful for maintaining fruits and berries and occasionally pruning trees and shrubs. A conventional pruning saw has a hardened-steel blade that is up to about 2 feet long attached to a wooden or metal handle that's usually curved. The blade can be curved or straight, too, but most experts prefer a curved one. Because there's no frame to get in the way, a prun-

ing saw can get into tight spots, and it's also capable of handling limbs almost as big as those handled by a frame saw. For especially tight spots, such as around the base of a crowded shrub, a pruning saw with a blade under 1 foot long is useful. Pruning saws come in many different models, both with straight blades and curved ones, as well as with different sizes and designs of teeth. Most cut in one direction only, generally on the pull stroke, or draw; some types cut on both the push and pull stroke, a useful feature in tight spots when you can only move the blade a few inches in either direction. Folding saws, which have a blade that folds into the handle, are especially handy. They can be carried with other gardening tools safely and unfolded whenever they're needed.

pruning shears *See* HAND PRUNERS

prunose Having a waxy, white bloom, usually on a black or blue-black background like a prune.

psammophyte Growing in sand.

pseudanthium An inflorescence that looks like a single flower. Daisies and the flowers of most aster-family plants (Asteraceae) are pseudanthiums.

pseudo- A prefix meaning false or not true. For example, zonal and scented geraniums (*Pelargonium* spp.) bear their flowers in pseudoumbels, meaning they resemble umbels, but are not true umbels.

pseudobulb A "false bulb" that is actually a thickened, bulblike stem that stores water. Many species of orchids, especially epiphytic ones, bear pseudobulbs. They arise from the plant's rhizome and usually are above ground. Pseudobulbs generally grow actively for one year, then persist on the plant as backbulbs. Orchids that bear these structures include *Cattleya* spp., *Odontoglossum* spp., and *Miltonia* spp.

pseudocarp *See* ACCESSORY FRUIT

pteridology The study of ferns and fern allies such as club mosses and horsetails. *See* FERN ALLIES

pteridophile A fern enthusiast.

pteridophyte A collective term for ferns and fern allies based on the division Pteriodophyta, recognized by 19th-century botanists. Pteridophytes have roots, stems, leaves, and vascular tissue, unlike more primitive plants such as mosses and liverworts (bryophytes), which have stem and leaf tissue, but lack true roots and vascular tissue. Pteridophytes are a step below higher plants on the evolutionary scale because they reproduce by spores rather than seeds. *See also* DIVISION, FERN ALLIES

ptero-, pterous-, -pterous Prefixes or a suffix meaning winged. The prefixes are combined with a suffix to indicate what organ is winged; pterocarpous indicates winged fruits, for example. When used as a suffix, it is usually accompanied by a prefix indicating a number. Pentapterous means five-winged; tripterous, three-winged, for example.

puberolous, puberulent Covered with soft, minute hairs that are barely visible. Most often used to describe leaf surfaces. Chinese hibiscus (*Hibiscus rosa-sinensis*) has sparsley puberulent to glabrate leaves.

pubescent Downy. Covered with short, soft hairs. This term is commonly used to describe leaves or other plant parts that have any type of hairs. Petunias (*Petunia* spp.) are pubescent, and the undersides of Southern magnolia (*Magnolia grandiflora*) leaves are covered with rusty-colored pubescence.

publication A nomenclatural rule designating that in order to qualify as a validly published name, a new plant name must be distributed in printed media. The rules for valid publication are set forth in the *International Code of Botanical Nomenclature* and *International Code of Nomenclature for Cultivated Plants* and differ for botanical names and those of cultivated plants.

puckered A leaf surface that is heavily textured because of a pattern of wrinkles, puckers, ribs, furrows, and/or folds. *See* CORRUGATED

pulp The fleshy or jucy tissue of a fruit.

pulverulent Dusty or powdery looking.

pulvinate Cushion- or mat-forming.

punctate Covered with small, pinhead-size depressions, pits, or sunken glans. Most often used to describe leaf surfaces.

puncticulate Covered with extremely small depressions, pits, or sunken glans. Most often used to describe leaf surfaces.

pungent Ending with a long, sharp, rigid point. Leaves of yuccas (*Yucca* spp.) are pungent. Also, having a strong smell.

pungent leaf tip

pupa The hardened shell formed by an insect larva undergoing complete metamorphosis, within which the adult develops.

pure color The colors seen in a rainbow or on a color wheel: Violet, blue, green, yellow, orange, and red.

purpurescent Turning purplish.

push hoe *See* HOE

pustulate, pustulose Covered with raised pimples or blisterlike bumps, which often appear at the base of a hair. Most often used to describe leaf surfaces.

pustule A small pimple or blisterlike bump.

PVC Polyvinyl chloride. A material used to make a variety of materials, including flexible water garden liners. For long life and resistance to ultraviolet light, tearing, and puncturing, butyl and EPDM liners are a better, longer-lived option. If you do select a PVC liner, buy the thickest grade available, 32 mils. *See* WATER GARDEN LINERS

pyramid Also called a symmetrical triangle, this is a shape used in flower arranging in which the main flowers, leaves, and other plant materials are positioned so that the tips of the materials in the main part of the arrangement outline an imaginary triangle or pyramid. This is a well-balanced, useful, basic shape for an arrangement that will accommodate many different flower shapes and colors.

pyramid arrangement

pyramidal Pyramid-shaped.

pyrene *See* DRUPE

pyrethrin An organic insecticide derived from the flowers of pyrethrum daisies (*Tanacetum coccineum*). The flowers are dried and ground to make a dust, and the pyrethrins are extracted from the dust to make a sprayable insecticide that attacks the central nervous system of a variety of pest insects. Pyrethrins break down quickly in light and heat, and can be sprayed on food crops up to a day before harvest. They are somewhat toxic to animals and extremely toxic to fish. Pyrethroids are synthetic pyrethrinlike substances and are not organically acceptable.

pyriform Pear-shaped.

quadrangular, quadrangulate Square or four-angled. Members of the mint family (Lamiaceae) have quadrangular, or four-angled, stems.

quadri- Four. A prefix indicating four of a particular organ or characteristic. Quadrifoliate means bearing four leaves or leaflets, for example.

quadrilateral Having four sides. Members of the mint family (Lamiaceae) have four-sided, or quadrilateral, stems.

quartered A flower, usually a rose, with inner petals that are pleated or folded into three, four, or five distinct sections. The outer petals surround the inner, folded ones.

quartered flower

quiescence Dormant. Plants or plant parts that are quiescent will not begin to grow until favorable external conditions exist.

quinate Having five parts.

quinque- A prefix indicating five. Quinquefoliate means bearing five leaves or leaflets, for example.

raceme A type of flower cluster, or inflorescence, with a single stem and flowers that are borne on individual stalks called pedicels. The flowers open from the bottom to the top of a raceme, and racemes are indeterminate, meaning they continue to elongate after the first flowers open. Racemes are usually unbranched. Common snapdragons (*Antirrhinum majus*), hollyhocks (*Alcea rosea*), and hostas (*Hosta* spp.) bear their flowers in racemes.

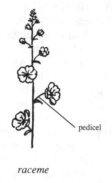

pedicel

raceme

racemiform Bearing flowers that resemble racemes, but do not have the true structure of a raceme.

racemose Racemelike. A flower cluster (inflorescence) that resembles a raceme but may or may not be a true raceme. The term racemose or "racemosa" is sometimes applied to ferns that have fronds that branch along the main stem to give the entire frond a branched appearance.

rachilla A small or secondary rachis, or stem. Primarily used to refer to the stem of a spikelet, which is the basic unit of the flower clusters of members of the grass and sedge families (Poaceae and Cyperaceae).

rachis The main stem, or axis, of a flower cluster (inflorescence) or a compound leaf, including a fern frond. In a branched inflorescence, the rachis is an extension of the peduncle, or flower stalk. In a compound leaf, it is an extension of the petiole, or leaf stalk. So-called walking ferns have an extended rachis that forms a small plantlet where it touches the soil.

radial symmetry The type of symmetry exhibited by a regular (actinomorphic) flower, which has petals and other parts radiating from the center so that a plane or line passed anywhere through the center would yield mirror images. *See also* REGULAR FLOWER

radiate Spreading or sticking out from a common point, like fingers on a hand. Also, bearing ray florets. The daisylike flowers of aster-family (Asteraceae) plants such as oxeye daisies (*Lucanthemum vulgare*) and black-eyed Susans (*Rudbeckia* spp.) are radiate.

radical Attached to, pertaining to, or arising from the roots, rootstock, or rhizomes (rootlike stems). This term is primarily used to refer to leaves that are borne from roots rather than stems.

radicant A root that arises at the node of a rhizome or other prostrate stem.

radicle The rudimentary root contained within a plant embryo. The radicle develops from the hypocotyl and lengthens as the seed germinates, becoming the seedling's primary root. *See* SEED

radius The outermost flowers of a sunflower (*Helianthus* spp.) or other daisylike flower in the aster family (Asteraceae) when the disk florets differ from the ray florets. *See* HEAD

raised beds A garden bed with soil that is higher than the surrounding area.

Raised beds are ideal options for sites with poor soil or for areas that are too wet. They allow excess surface water to drain away more quickly, lift the rooting zone above subsurface waterlogging, and make it easy to build rich soil on top of poor sites. A raised bed can be created by simply mounding up soil to create a planting area. (Because they increase soil volume and organic matter content, double and single digging also create this type of raised bed.) Beds made by mounding up the soil are temporary, and typically, gardeners install sides to create more permanent raised beds: Boards, landscape ties, rocks, and bricks all make suitable sides for a raised bed. Build raised beds directly on top of the ground, or for a deeper root run, till the site first as deeply as possible and incorporate a couple of inches of compost or chopped leaves into the soil at the same time. Then install the sides and fill up the bed as necessary with topsoil mixed with compost. Water it thoroughly to settle it, top it off, then plant. *See also* SOIL BUILDING, INTENSIVE GARDENING

rake Both garden rakes and leaf rakes are useful garden tools. Garden rakes are used to smooth out garden soil and break up clods of dirt, and to remove rocks (either by pushing or pulling) to prepare seedbeds. Two types are available. A standard garden rake, also called a flathead rake, has a flat edge with teeth along one side. It can be flipped over (on the flat side) and used to level out soil, and is best for preparing a level bed just before sowing. A bowhead rake has a row of teeth attached along a metal bow, which gives it a slight springing action when you use it. Bowhead rakes are the tool of choice for areas where you have to rake up stones. In addition to preparing soil, rakes are handy for thinning seedlings. (*See* THINNING for details.) Leaf rakes have a fan of steel or bamboo tines. Both are efficient for raking leaves, but steel-tined models can be used for heavier-duty projects such as aerating lawns.

rameal Branched, relating to branches.

ramentaceous Bearing or covered with small, loose, brown scales called ramenta (*sing.* ramentum).

rami- A prefix that refers to branches. Ramiform means branchlike. Ramispinus means branched spines.

ramification A term used to refer to the arrangement of branches or branching parts.

ramiflorus Bearing flowers directly on the branches and twigs, but not on the trunk.

ramose Having many branches.

ramus Branch.

rank A vertical row or column. This term is usually used to refer to leaves. Hemlocks (*Tsuga* spp.) and coastal redwoods (*Sequoia sempervirens*) both bear leaves arranged in two vertical ranks or rows, that are opposite one another along the stem. In addition, the term rank is also used in plant taxonomy to designate the level or position a particular category occupies in the taxonomic hierarchy. The principal ranks currently in use are Class, Order, Family, Genus, Species. This term is used to describe shoots or growth that was produced very quickly and is unusually succulent or soft as well as out of control or wayward.

ranked Arranged in vertical rows.

rapiformis Turnip-shaped.

ratchet pruners, **ratchet loppers** Pruning tools that use a ratchet mechanism to increase cutting power while minimizing effort from the user. *See* ANVIL PRUNERS, LOPPERS

ratoon A new shoot that grows from the base of a tree or other plant that has been cut down.

ray A single branch of an umbel or umbel-like flower cluster, especially one of the branches of a compound umbel. Also, a ray floret or "petal" of the daisylike inflorescence (head) of a member of the aster

family (Asteraceae). *See also* COMPOUND
UMBEL, RAY FLORET

rayed Bearing rays.

ray floret, ray flower An individual
flower with a flattened, strap-shaped (ligulate) corolla that forms one of the "petals"
of a daisylike inflorescence (head) of a
plant in the aster family (Asteraceae).
While a ring of ray florets makes up the
petals of a daisy, in double-flowered aster-
family plants (such as perennial sunflowers *Helianthus* × *multiflorus* 'Flore-
Plena' and 'Loddon Gold'), ray florets
replace the smaller, less showy disk florets
to create the double blooms. *See also*
HEAD, DISK FLORET

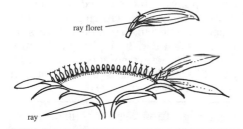

re- A prefix meaning again, anew. Refoli-
ate means to produce foliage again or a
second time, such as after a drought or
attack by disease.

receptacle The top or end of a flower stalk
upon which all the other flower parts are
borne. A receptacle is enlarged or elongated, and can be flat, concave, or convex.
The receptacles on flowers in the aster
family (Asteraceae) are quite enlarged
because they bear many individual florets.
The base of a sunflower, where the individual disk and ray florets are attached, is a
receptacle, as is the swollen portion at the
tip of any flower stem where sepals, petals,

stamens, and ovary are attached. Also
called a thalamous or torus.

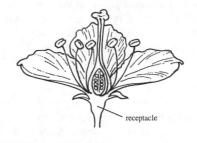

reclining, reclinate Gradually leaning or
bending down from the vertical.

recumbent Prostrate. Lying or reclining
on the ground. This term commonly is used
to describe a plant's habit or to describe the
position of branches. Decumbent plants
also are prostrate but have ascending growing tips.

recurved Curved backward.

reduced An organ that is smaller than normal, generally at least half normal size.

reed sedge peat *See* PEAT MOSS

reflexed Bent downward or backward at
more than a 90-degree angle.

refracted Bent backward from the base.

regular flower A flower that is symmetrical, with its parts radiating from the center,
so that a plane or line passed anywhere
through the center would yield mirror
images. Roses (*Rosa* spp.), tulips (*Tulipa*
spp.), and plants with daisylike flowers
such as cosmos (*Cosmos* spp.) and sunflowers (*Helianthus* spp.) have actinomorphic, also called regular, flowers.

regular flower

rejuvenation *See* RENEWAL PRUNING

---

relict A species from an earlier geologic epoch that has survived despite an environment that has changed considerably. Fossil evidence shows that ginkgo (*Ginkgo biloba*) is a relict tree species from the era when dinosaurs roamed the earth, 175 to 200 million years ago.

---

remontant Blooming repeatedly or a second time during a single season. Many remontant roses, including hybrid teas and grandifloras, flower continuously from late spring through fall, or produce two or more flushes of bloom during a single summer. There also are remontant tall-bearded irises, which bloom in spring and again in late summer or early fall.

---

renewal pruning Sometimes called renovation or rejuvenation, renewal pruning is a pruning process that uses thinning cuts to promote new, vigorous growth on shrubs by removing old wood that is no longer blooming. While some shrubs respond to this process with vigorous new growth, not all shrubs can tolerate such radical pruning. Only use it on plants that sprout readily from old wood. Shrubs that sprout readily from old wood include forsythias, spireas, old-fashioned weigela (*Weigela florida*), and beauty-bush (*Kolkwitzia* spp.) If you aren't sure whether a given plant will withstand rejuvenation, ask at a nursery or look for suckers among the older stems, a good indication that it will resprout. Shrubs can be renewal pruned, or rejuvenated, radically or gradually. For radical rejuvenation, simply cut the entire shrub to within a few inches of the ground in late winter or early spring. Some aged or crowded shrubs may not require or respond well to such drastic treatment and can be cut to 2 feet or more above the ground; cotoneasters, privets (*Ligustrum* spp.), and lilacs can be rejuvenated in this way. Suckering plants can be rejuvenated by removing the old growth and encouraging selected suckers. To rejuvenate a shrub gradually, remove a portion of the oldest stems or canes each year for 2 or 3 years. Remove up to one-third of the oldest stems on vigorous plants; remove only a stem or two on less vigorous specimens.

---

reniform Kidney-shaped. A reniform leaf is roughly crescent-shaped (lunate), with a rounded or nearly rounded tip, but it has an indentation at the base either where the blade is attached to the stem, or petiole. The two outer corners of the leaf (on either side of the petiole), are broadly rounded, rather than acutely angled, as in a lunate leaf. The term reniform also is used to describe a leaf base that has an indentation where the stem is attached and two rounded lobes on the sides.

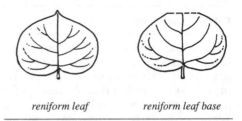

reniform leaf   *reniform leaf base*

---

renovation The process by which old, overgrown trees (especially fruit trees such as apples) are pruned and encouraged to produce vigorous new growth. To renovate a tree, remove dead and diseased wood. Then over the course of several seasons (pruning in the dormant season in late winter or very early spring), remove crowded, congested growth along with crossing or rubbing branches. Select main scaffold branches and prune so that they have plenty of room to develop. The term renovation also is used to refer to a pruning process used primarily on shrubs. *See* RENEWAL PRUNING

---

repair grafting *See* INARCHING, BRIDGE GRAFTING, BRACING

---

repand Slightly sinuate or somewhat wavy or uneven. This term is commonly used to describe the edge, or margin, of a leaf, leaflet, or other organ that goes slightly in and out.

repand leaf margin

repent Prostrate or creeping.

repetition This is a design technique that gives a finished, harmonious look to a yard or garden by repeating similar elements or elements with similar characteristics—be they plants, building materials, colors, or textures—throughout the design. Repetition is a fundamental principle used in flower arranging as well, just on a smaller scale. In the same way that repeating fabrics or colors indoors in a single room or throughout the house creates a stylish, unified-looking interior, repetition can be used in the garden, either within a single planting or throughout the yard as a whole, to create an overall garden style. For example, using a certain color of brick or type of stone in all the walkways, raised beds, or walls throughout a yard will give plantings a harmonious, unified look. Plants can be used to similar effect: Drifts or edgings of annuals such as impatiens in a special color (or combination of colors) or clumps of ornamental grasses repeated throughout the yard will unify the overall design. Repeating elements within a single bed or border is another way to use repetition. Colors or textures repeated at intervals in a planting will unify the design. In this case, repetition can be accomplished with a mix of plants that all feature the same color flowers or foliage texture. Clumps of one primary plant can be repeated in several places and the effect can be augmented with accent plants that have similar characteristics. *See also* RHYTHM, TEXTURE

replicate Folded backward.

repotting To move a container-grown plant from one pot to another, usually from a smaller pot to a larger one. Repotting is beneficial because it means old soil can be scraped away and replaced with new soil. It also can involve cutting a plant apart and moving it into more than one pot or discarding older portions of a clump so they will fit back into the same pot.

resin A viscous (semisolid) translucent yellow or brown to clear substance that is generally sticky. Many plants, especially conifers, have buds that are protected by a coating of resin. Resin hardens when it comes in contact with air and does not dissolve in water.

resinous Producing resin, and thus sticky.

resting bud *See* TURION

resting period Dormant period. A period during which a plant makes little or no growth, usually because of environmental conditions such as cold temperatures or seasonal drought.

resupinate Upside down. Members of the genus *Impatiens*, including impatiens and garden balsam (*I. walleriana* and *I. balsamina*) have resupinate flowers. The flowers are turned 180 degrees on their stems so the petals and sepals that morphologically are at the top of the bloom appear to be at the bottom, and vice versa.

reticulate Netted or netlike. Leaf veins that form a netted or networklike pattern. It can also refer to ribs on a leaf or to a color pattern on a leaf, petal, or bract. Some bulbs and corms also have netted, or reticulate, coverings called tunics. Reticulated irises, including *Iris reticulata*, are an example.

reticulate leaf veins

retrorse, retrorsely Curved, turned, or pointing downward, toward the base. Commonly used to describe the position of small plant parts such as thorns or prickles.

retuse Shallowly notched. A tip or base with a very small notch. A retuse leaf is rounded or blunt and has a notch that reaches less than one-sixteenth of the distance to the midpoint of the leaf blade.

While most commonly used to describe a leaf base or tip, this term can be applied to other plant parts such as bracts (modified petal-like leaves) or the petals or sepals of a flower.

retuse leaf tip

reverted growth Growth on a plant that has returned to normal type, meaning that it no longer exhibits the characteristics for which it was planted, such as variegated foliage, an unusual flower color, or a dwarf habit. On shrubs and trees, remove this growth with thinning cuts. On perennials, dig up reverted sections of the clumps and discard them.

revolute Rolled or curved inward toward the bottom, as in a leaf whose edges curl underneath.

reworking *See* TOP-WORKING

rhizo- A prefix referring to the roots. Rhizogenic means root-producing, for example.

rhizoid A rootlike structure that does not have the water- and nutrient-conducting tissue of a true root.

rhizomatous Spreading by or bearing rhizomes.

rhizome A specialized stem that is horizontal and runs underground or on the surface of the soil. Since it is a stem, a rhizome contains nodes and internodes. It also produces adventitious roots at the nodes. To divide a plant with a rhizome, simply dig it up and sever it into sections with a sharp spade or knife. Plants will root at the nodes. There are two general types of rhizomes. The first features thick, fleshy well-branched rhizomes that are almost tuberlike. Plants with this type of rhizome, called a pachymorph rhizome, produce dense clumps with short individual sections. Pachymorph rhizomes are determinate, meaning each one ends with a flower, and subsequent flowers are produced from side (lateral) branches. Bearded irises (*Iris germanica* and its many cultivars) grow from this type of rhizome. Frequent dividing (bearded irises need dividing every 3 years or so) ensures an ample supply of new lateral branches, which produce the flowers, along with room for them to grow. The other type of rhizome, called a leptomorph rhizome, is thin and has long internodes, most of which have buds that remain dormant. Leptomorph rhizomes are indeterminate, meaning they can continue to grow indefinitely, and plants with this type of rhizome spread widely. Many good garden plants bear these wide-spreading rhizomes, but they tend to bear watching, because they can spread fast and far. Lily of the valley (*Convallaria majalis*), mints (*Mentha* spp.), and many types of grasses bear leptomorph rhizomes, as do notorious weeds such as Canada thistle (*Cirsium arvense*). There are plants (called mesomorphs) that have rhizomes that are intermediate between these two types. Peonies (*Paeonia* spp.) and asparagus (*Asparagus* spp.) produce so-called crown rhizomes, which increase in size annually, but don't spread very far. Some lilies are rhizomatous as well, including lemon lily (*Lilium parryi*); these produce new bulbs at the end of short rhziomes. Fern growers recognize three general types of rhizomes—long-creeping, short-creeping, and ascending. Ferns with long-creeping rhizomes spread rapidly; some are extremely aggressive spreaders. Hay-scented fern (*Dennstaedtia punctilobula*) spreads rapidly on long-creeping rhizomes, and forms large, handsome colonies. Bracken fern (*Pteridium aquilinum*) also has long-creeping rhizomes, but is a very aggressive, invasive spreader. (Gardeners who have battled this plant say that all the bracken fern in the world is really just a single plant.) Ferns with short-creeping rhizomes—including maidenhairs (*Adiantum* spp.)—form more compact clumps. Ferns with ascending rhizomes form crowns (the rhizome is horizontal and upright, or nearly so, at the tip) from which the ferns emerge.

In this case, the rhizome is usually not branched. Wood ferns (*Drypoteris* spp.) and ostrich fern (*Matteuccia* spp.) bear ascending rhizomes. Christmas fern (*Polystichum acrostichoides*) bears rhizomes that branch to form multiple crowns.

Pachymorph rhizome

Leptomorph rhizome

rhizophyllous Bearing roots that emerge from the leaves. Plants that can be propagated from leaf cuttings such as sansevieria (*Sansevieria* spp.) and some begonias (*Begonia* spp.) are rhizophyllous.

rhomboidal, rhombic Diamond-shaped. Rhomboidal leaves are somewhat oval, but with four distinct sides. The tip and the base of the leaf are pointed, forming acute angles (less than 90 degrees). The angles on the sides of the leaf are obtuse (more than 90 degrees).

rhomboidal leaf

rhythm The feeling of movement in a design, either in a garden or in a flower arrangement. In a design, repeating a particular color or texture at regular or irregular intervals carries the eye from one element to another, thus adding movement and appeal. Repeating a particular group of plants, paving pattern, or feature (even fence posts) also creates rhythm in a landscape. Rhythm helps unify the design. In a flower arrangement, rhythm is established when the main lines of the composition are placed.

rib The main vein running lengthwise in a leaf.

ribbed Having raised, or prominent, ribs or veins in the leaves.

rigid Stiff, not flexible.

rimose Cracked or fissured. Many types of trees, including oaks (*Quercus* spp.) have rimose bark.

rind A tough outer covering. This term is most commomly used to refer to the covering of a fruit such as a pumpkin or other squash, but also can refer to the bark of a tree.

ring budding A seldom-used technique similar to patch budding, but the patch of bark removed from the stock reaches all the way around the stem, essentially girdling it. The patch from the budstick is cut to match, reaching all the way around the scion. Otherwise, wrap and treat like a patch bud. *See* PATCH BUD, BUDDING

ringent Gaping; very wide open. Most often used to describe the corollas of bilabiate flowers such as salvias (*Salvia* spp.)

rings *See* TREE RINGS

riparian Growing along or pertaining to streambanks or other natural watercourses such as those caused by springs or seeps.

ripe Mature; developed fully.

ripening The process a fruit undergoes as the seed matures and becomes ready for dispersal. This term also refers to the maturation process of wood as it hardens, especially soft stems that become woodier as they lignify.

ripewood cutting A cutting taken from hardened, ripe wood. Ripewood cuttings usually are taken in late summer or fall from evergreens, and are treated like semi-ripe cuttings.

rivulose Marked with wavy lines or channels.

rockery A bank, mound, or other site that is covered with rocks and planted with a variety of herbaceous perennials and other plants. A rockery differs from a true rock garden in that it is not planted with alpine species and rock (saxatile) plants.

rock garden An area devoted to the growing of alpine plants, which grow naturally in high mountain areas above the treeline, as well as rock plants, also called saxatile plants, which naturally grow among rocks. Saxatile plants grow in either sun or shade at lower elevations than true alpine plants; they thrive on gravelly soil or around rocks, but do not absolutely require them to grow. Both groups include herbaceous perennials, dwarf trees and shrubs, and ferns that require very well-drained, relatively poor soil. Although a simple raised bed can be filled with an appropriate soil mix and used to grow a wide range of typical rock garden plants, in most cases, rock gardens are built over natural rock formations or on rocks brought to the site and positioned to look as natural as possible. Most rock plants are very deep rooted, and their roots seek the cool, moist conditions found deep in the soil among rocks. Since most also require perfect drainage, rock garden soil mixes usually contain a good portion of crushed stone (*See* ROCK GARDEN SOIL MIX), and the garden also is mulched with crushed stone, such as granite, to ensure very well-drained conditions around the crowns of the plants.

rock garden soil mix To provide ideal conditions for alpine and rock (saxatile) plants, use a soil mix based on the following recipe to fill raised beds, in between rocks, between stones in a rock wall, or in other areas where these plants will be grown. Mix 1 part topsoil, 1 part leaf mold, and 1 part chipped stone or gravel. For best results, sift the topsoil through a ½-inch mesh screen to remove weed roots.

rock phosphate An organic fertilizer consisting of finely ground phosphate rock. It contains about 32 percent phosphorus, 33 percent calcium, and also is rich in trace minerals. The nutrient content slowly becomes available as the rock breaks down in the soil, and the phosphorus is more available in acid soil.

rock plants A general term for all plants that are appropriate in a true rock garden—alpines and other plants that grow among rocks, sometimes called saxatile plants.

rogue A plant that does not exhibit characteristics that are desired or expected.

roguing, roguing out Removing and destroying plants that do not exhibit desired characteristics. Culling.

room, outdoor *See* OUTDOOR ROOM

root The portion of a plant that supports it, draws nutrients and water from the soil, and stores excess food. Roots lack nodes and internodes, which are characteristics of rootlike structures such as rhizomes, as well as leaves. (Root branches arise from inside the root itself, rather than a bud on the surface at a node.) Roots also are generally, but not always, underground. (*See* prop root for one example of an above-ground root.) There are two general types of root systems—fibrous roots and taproots. Fibrous roots, such as those borne by grasses, are heavily branched and wide-spreading. Plants with taproots—carrots are the best-known example—send one or more main, sparsely branched roots deep into the soil. Some plants produce both kinds of roots—a main anchoring taproot combined with surface-feeding fibrous roots. Gardeners who practice companion planting often pair plants with different types of root systems—fibrous-rooted lettuce or spinach with taprooted carrots, for example—because they use underground garden space very efficiently. *See also* TAPROOT, FIBROUS ROOTS, TUBEROUS ROOTS

root ball A collective term for the roots and soil of a container-grown or balled-and-burlapped plant.

rootbound *See* POTBOUND

root bud *See* TURION

root cap A cushion of cells at the tip of roots that protects the apical meristem, or growing point. The root cap prevents the meristem from being damaged by hard or sharp soil particles.

root cuttings Pieces of roots that are induced to form new shoots and grow into individual plants. Gather root cuttings from late winter to early spring. To gather them, either dig up an entire plant and wash the soil off the roots to find suitable ones, or dig carefully around the base of the plant. On plants with relatively fine roots, cut off whole roots with garden shears, then snip them into 2-inch sections. Where the roots are thick or fleshy, select pencil-thick roots and cut off 2- to 3-inch-long sections. Like all cuttings, root cuttings exhibit polarity and must be planted right side up. To keep track of which is which, make a straight cut on the end that was closest to the crown of the plant, a sloping cut at the other end. Collect the cuttings in a plastic bag to keep them moist until they are planted. Replant or recover the parent plant once you have collected cuttings; it's best to take no more than about five roots from any plant. Plant root cuttings in pots filled with cutting mix, and set them in a cold frame or a cool, bright room. Cuttings taken from hardy plants such as shrubs or vines can be planted directly in an outdoor nursery bed. Lay thin-rooted cuttings horizontally on the surface of the mix, about 1 inch apart, and cover them with $^1/_2$ inch of mix. Stick thicker cuttings vertically into the mix, with the flat end of the cut-

tings pointing up. Space them about 2 inches apart, with the tops even with or just below the surface. Water thoroughly, and keep the medium evenly moist but not wet. Root cuttings often produce topgrowth before well-established roots are formed; wait until roots come through the pots' drainage holes before transplanting to individual pots or to a nursery bed. Transplant to the garden in fall if plants are large enough, or leave them in a cold frame or nursery bed for an extra growing season. Bear's breech (*Acanthus* spp.), purple coneflower (*Echinacea purpurea*), Oriental poppies (*Papaver orientale*), and a number of other perennials, shrubs, and vines are easy to propagate by root cuttings.

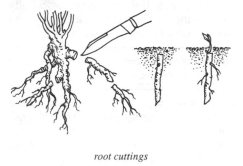

root cuttings

root division A somewhat confusing term that simply means dividing a plant. *See* DIVISION

root grafting A technique used to graft the rootstocks of seedlings, rooted cuttings, or even layered plants to scions. Also called bench grafting, root grafting is used commercially to produce large quantities of grafted plants, especially apples, pears, grapes, wisterias, and rhododendrons. There are two forms: A whole-root graft uses an entire root system, while a piece-root graft uses sections of roots. The rootstocks are dug up for grafting, and the stock and scion normally are joined with a whip-and-tongue graft. The grafted plants are stored in damp sand for callousing for about two months before being planted outdoors. They're grown on for a year before sale. *See also* NURSE-ROOT GRAFTING

root hairs Extensions of the cells near the tips of growing roots that greatly extend the surface area of the root and thus increase its ability to absorb water and nutrients from the soil. Root hairs are found near the tips of roots; they die farther back on the root as it grows.

root pruning A pruning technique used to prepare plants for transplanting by encouraging a dense, well-branched root system. Ideally, start the process in late spring by slicing through the roots at the drip line and undercutting taproots with a sharp spade. This encourages the roots to branch close to the trunk and remain near the surface. Water the plant regularly all summer long to compensate for its reduced root capacity. Then transplant in fall. Root pruning essentially spreads the shock of transplanting over an extended period, reducing its impact.

root run The area of soil in which a plant's roots spread.

root sucker A sucker that arises from the rootstock of a grafted plant, below the graft union. Roses, for example, are commonly grafted onto vigorous multiflora rose (*Rosa multiflora*) rootstocks. One way to recognize root suckers is that they usually have foliage that differs from the rest of the plant; their flowers certainly will differ. Remove root suckers as soon as they appear by digging down into the soil and cutting them off flush with the rootstock. Or cut them off as close as possible to their point of origin.

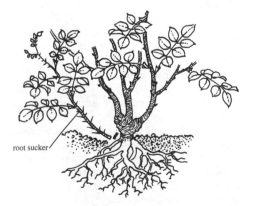
root sucker

root zone The area of soil in which a plant's roots spread. On a tree, the root zone generally extends to the drip line.

rooting cuttings Exposing various types of cuttings to the conditions that promote the formation of roots. *See* CUTTINGS

rooting hormone Plant growth regulators used to treat cuttings to induce the formation of roots. The active ingredient in rooting hormones is usually indolebutyric acid (IBA) and is expressed as a percentage, normally ranging from 0.1 percent to 0.8 percent. For softwood cuttings, 0.1 percent is best; higher concentrations are used for more difficult-to-root species. Both powder and liquid forms are available, but home gardeners most often have access to the powdered forms (Rootone is one brand). These usually also contain a fungicide to prevent fungal diseases. Liquid forms are used commercially to treat difficult-to-root species because they can be diluted to different concentrations. To treat cuttings with rooting hormone, tip a small quantity of powder into a small container such as a bottle cap or onto a small saucer. Dip the base of the cutting in the powder, turning it as necessary to cover, then tap it gently to shake off the excess. Discard excess powder, rather than returning it to its container, to avoid contamination.

rooting mix A medium blended for rooting cuttings. *See* CUTTING MIX

rootlet A small or secondary root.

rootstock A general term for the roots of a plant, especially when they are thick and fleshy. This term also refers to the plant that provides a root system for a grafted or budded plant. *See* STOCK, GRAFTING

rose In addition to being a well-known, well-loved flower, a rose is the attachment at the end of a watering can spout that breaks up the stream of water to create a fine spray. Roses come in oval and round; an inverted rose points upward and creates an extremely fine spray of water ideal for seedlings.

rosette A cluster of leaves that arise from a crown or center and radiate in all directions. In a rosette, leaves are usually held on or very close to the ground.

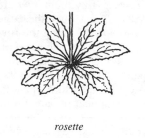

rosette

rosette cutting Rosettes can be detached from some plants and rooted as cuttings to produce separate plants. Hen and chickens (*Sempervivum* spp.) are easy to propagate in this matter; treat the "chicks" as semi-ripe cuttings or simply plant them out individually.

rostellum A small beak. Also, the beak-like structure that separates the anther from the stigma in an orchid flower.

rostrate Bearing a beaklike structure called a rostrum.

rosulate Having leaves arranged in rosettes at the base of the plant. Echiums (*Echium* spp.) have their leaves arranged in this manner.

rotate Wheel- or disc-shaped. A flat, circular flower that has widely spreading lobes and little or no tube at the base. Tomatoes (*Lycopersicon esculentum*) bear rotate flowers.

rotate flower

rotation, crop *See* CROP ROTATION

Rotenone An organic insecticide extracted from the roots of legumes native to South America that belong to the genus *Lonchocarpus*. It is a nerve poison that slowly paralyzes insects that eat it, and is very effective on leaf-eating beetles or other insects with chewing or piercing mouthparts, including flea beetles, Colorado potato beetles, aphids, cucumber beetles, and whiteflies. It also is toxic to fish, birds, and pigs. It is applied as a spray or dust.

rots These are fungal and bacterial diseases that cause wilted, off-color plants and roots that either turn dark and dry or mushy and white. Rots are especially problematic in waterlogged soil. To prevent rots, improve soil drainage, wait until the soil is warm to set out transplants, set plants so the crown is slightly higher than the surrounding soil, and plant in raised beds. Remove and destroy affected plants.

rotund Round or rounded.

round A shape used in flower arranging in which the main flowers, leaves, and other plant materials are positioned so that the tips of the materials in the main part of the arrangement outline an imaginary circle. This shape, also called a circle, can be either formal or informal. A half-round shape often is used for centerpieces.

round arrangement

rounded A tip or base that has even, convex edges, or margins, and is gently curved. While most commonly used to describe leaves, this term can be applied to other plant parts such as bracts (modified petal-like leaves) or the petals or sepals of a flower. Orbicular is the term used to describe a round or nearly round leaf.

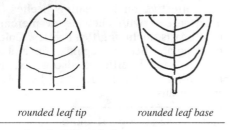

| *rounded leaf tip* | *rounded leaf base* |

round-point shovel *See* SHOVEL

row cover A layer of insulating material used to cover crops, especially vegetables, to protect them from cold temperatures and wind. Row covers usually are used to extend the growing season by providing protection in spring as well as in fall. Plastic sheeting is commonly used as a row cover, and it provides better frost protection than the other main material used for this purpose, spun-bonded floating row cover. However, most commonly used plastics hold in air and moisture, causing heat to build up quickly underneath them in sunny weather and the reduced ventilation also causes perfect conditions for fungal diseases to foster. (Polyethylene is the cheapest and most common plastic used in gardens. Materials such as polypropylene and polyvinyl alcohol are stronger, longer-lasting, and are permeable to air and water.) Remove plastic on sunny days or spread it over hoops or other supports to form a growing tunnel, which will need to be vented on sunny days. Preslit plastic comes with slits in place so that it vents itself. Floating row covers are made of spun-bonded polyester or another synthetic material and look like fabric. They provide crops with 4 to 6°F of frost protection. They can be laid directly over crops, without the need for a supporting framework. In addition, floating row covers have the advantage (over most plastic) of allowing water from rain or irrigation to reach plants. Heat isn't trapped under them either, so plants don't overheat, and the covers can be left in place indefinitely. (In humid climates support them on hoops to keep them above the foliage; moisture doesn't evaporate as quickly under row covers and in very wet weather fungal diseases can become a problem.) Floating row covers also are used to protect plants against insects: Lay them over crops early in the season, and bury the edges of the covers with soil all along the row. Insects will not be able to reach the plants, but keep in mind that if you are growing a crop that depends on insect pollinators—squash is one—you'll need to remove the covers once flowers appear or hand pollinate.

rows Traditionally, vegetable gardens have been arranged with rows of crops separated by paths used to cultivate and harvest, and many gardeners still arrange their plantings this way. It is easy to lay out a garden planted in rows—string a line, make a furrow, sow, and repeat—but there are more space- and time-efficient systems. The reason planting in traditional rows isn't particularly space-efficient lies in the fact that a 1 $\frac{1}{2}$-foot-wide path lies on each side of the row. The paths in a traditional vegetable garden need to be weeded regularly and/or covered with mulch, and paths actually occupy more space than crops do. For a more space-efficient option, try planting in wide rows or bands. To plant this way, create wide rows by sowing several rows of crops close together—space them at the recommended row spacing within the rows and between rows. Separate each wide row by 1 $\frac{1}{2}$-foot-wide paths to provide access to cultivate and harvest. Wide rows should range from about 2 to 4 feet wide. You need to be able to easily reach the center of each row to tend plants. This method cuts down on space wasted on paths as well as space potentially occupied by weeds; mature crops will fill in the row to create a solid band of plants. Keep in mind that a garden planted in wide rows will probably look like it is planted in blocks; because so many more plants fit in each row, you'll probably want to sow small sections at a time. (*See* INTENSIVE GARDENING, INTERPLANTING, AND SUCCESSION PLANTING for options.) Flower gardeners also use row planting. This type of arrangement is traditional for formal gardens and makes caring for cut flowers easy in a cutting garden, where wide-row planting offers the same benefits it does to vegetable gardeners. Keep in mind that there's no reason rows have to be straight; try planting snaking lines of flowers, herbs, or even vegetables such as lettuce along a bed or other planting.

rubber budding strips Long, narrow strips of rubber designed for holding scions in place for budding and some forms of grafting. The rubber holds the stock and scion together, yet expands as the plant grows. When exposed to sun and air, it normally will drop off naturally—usually after the graft union has healed. These strips don't have to be tied in place: Simply hold the end in place when you start to wrap and cover it with a loop or two. Once the strip is in place, either stick the end under an earlier loop and pull it tight or tie the end. Raffia and waxed string can be substituted for rubber budding strips; be sure to remove them after the union has healed.

rubbing alcohol *See* ALCOHOL

rubbing branches Two branches that touch one another so that they rub when the wind moves. The rubbing creates a wound, usually in both branches, through which diseases and insects can enter. To eliminate this condition, use a thinning cut to remove one of the branches—usually the thinnest one or the one that is pointing in the worst direction.

rudimentary Imperfectly developed, fragmentary, or vestigial.

rufescent, **rufus** Red-brown.

ruglose Slightly wrinkled.

rugose Wrinkled. Most often used to describe leaf surfaces.

run This term is used to describe a plant that spreads quickly by runners or creeping stems. Also, run to seed means a plant that has bolted or set seed prematurely.

runicate A pinnatifid arrangement of a leaf, petal, or petal-like structure that has

pairs of coarsely toothed lobes or segments along the midrib. A runicate leaf is generally obovate (reverse egg-shaped) in outline and has a pointed tip. The toothlike lobes point toward the base of the leaf.

runicate leaf

runner An elongated, usually slender, horizontal, aboveground stem that extends along the ground, rooting and forming small plantlets at the nodes and at the tip. Some sources (and many gardeners) use the terms runner and stolon interchangeably; technically, runners root and form plantlets at the the nodes along their length, while stolons root only at the tip. *See* STOLON

running habit A plant that spreads rapidly, generally by rhizomes. *See* RHIZOME

runoff Water, from rainfall or irrigation, that is not absorbed by the soil and instead flows off the land. Runoff can be directed by building earth berms or digging swales. Terracing a slope also is a good management technique: Terraces, which are filled with loose soil, absorb a great deal of water, especially if the soil is prepared deeply and amended with organic matter.

rushlike Resembling a grass or member of the rush family (Juncaceae). Rushlike plants have narrow, grassy leaves and small flowers.

rust A fungal disease that produces whitish or yellowish spots on the tops of leaves and powdery, yellow to orange spots on the undersides. Infected leaves turn yellow, dry up, and drop early. To prevent problems, grow resistant cultivars, mulch plants, and use drip irrigation to keep the leaves dry.

Remove and destroy infected leaves. Dust infected plants with sulfur every 1 to 2 weeks.

Ryania An organic insecticide extracted from the South American shrub *Ryania speciosa*. Ryania is a contact and stomach poison that paralyzes pest insects and prevents them from feeding. It kills caterpillars—including those of butterflies—and some larvae, including codling moths, cabbage worms, Japanese beetles, and Mexican bean beetles. It is applied as a spray or dust.

Sabadilla An organic insecticide extracted from the seeds of *Schoenocaulon officinale*, a lilylike plant from South America. It is toxic to bees and somewhat toxic to mammals, and should be used only as a last resort for difficult-to-control pests. It can be applied as a dust or spray.

sac A bag- or pouch-shaped chamber or cavity. Locule.

saccate Pouched or bag-shaped. The lip of many orchids, including lady's slipper orchids (*Cypripedium* spp.) are saccate.

saccate flower

sachet A mixture of dried flower petals, flower buds, leaves, and other plant parts mixed with spices and other ingredients. Sachets are made just like dried potpourris, except that the ingredients are crumbled and placed inside a decorative fabric bag or small pillowcase. *See* POTPOURRI

sagittate Arrowhead- or spear-shaped. A sagittate leaf has two pointed lobes at the base that point down, rather than out as they do in a hastate leaf. Arrowheads (*Sagittaria* spp.) are aquatic perennials that have sagittate leaves. This term is used to refer to the overall shape of a leaf or just the base.

sagittate leaf

sagittate leaf base

Saikei The Japanese art of creating living miniaturized landscapes of trees, rocks, plants, and sometimes figurines. It is an outgrowth of bonsai. Saikei compositions frequently feature stunning groves of trees that echo nature.

salt hay Also called saltmarsh hay, this is a mulch consisting of various grasses harvested from coastal marshes.

salverform A flower that has a slender tube at the base and an abruptly flaired and flattened face, or limb. Phlox (*Phlox* spp.) and primroses (*Primula* spp.) have salverform flowers.

salverform flower

samara A one-seeded fruit that does not open at maturity (is indehiscent) and has a prominent, membranelike wing. Ashes (*Fraxinus*) and elms (*Ulmus* spp.) produce samaras, as do maples (*Acer* spp.), which bear them in pairs.

samara

samaroid Resembling a samara.

sand, sandy soil One of the three major mineral particles in soil (the other two are silt and clay), sand particles range in size from 2 millimeters down to 0.5 millimeters. Sandy soil is easy to dig whether it is wet or dry. Roots penetrate it easily, but water passes through it quickly (together with dissolved nutrients) so it dries out quickly after a rain, tends to be droughty, and usually is poor in nutrients. For plant propagation, straight sand is a good medium to use for some types of cuttings, especially evergreens. Use washed sharp builder's or plaster sand (not sandbox sand). *See also* SOIL TEXTURE, SOIL STRUCTURE

sanding *See* SCARIFICATION

sanguine Red. Blood-colored.

sap The juice or fluids within a plant.

sapid Tasty. Having an agreeable taste.

sapling A young tree that is at any stage between a seedling and when the heartwood turns hard.

saponaceous Soapy.

sapor The taste or flavor of a plant or other substance.

sappy This term is used to describe very succulent or soft and juicy stems. Also called rank growth.

saprophyte A plant that grows on and gleans nutrients from dead organic matter. Saprophytes usually lack chlorophyll. Indian pipes (*Monotropha* spp.) are native woodland wildflowers that are saprophytic. *See also* EPIPHYTE, PARASITE

sapwood The light-colored, secondary xylem tissue toward the outer portion of a tree trunk that still conducts water. *See* XYLEM

sarco- A prefix meaning fleshy. Sarcocaulous means fleshy-stemmed, for example.

sarcous Fleshy.

sarment A long, slender runner or stolon.

sarmentose Bearing long, slender runners. Flagellate.

saturated colors *See* PURE COLORS

sausage-shaped *See* ALLANTOID, BOTULIFORM

saving seed Collecting seed from garden or wild plants is a time-honored gardening tradition, whether the seeds are used to grow next year's garden or to donate to a seed exchange. When collecting seeds, always collect from open pollinated plants; hybrids do not come true from seeds. (*See* OPEN-POLLINATION, HYBRID) Also save seeds from the most vigorous plant and the best fruit. It is important to wait until seeds are fully ripe for harvesting; most turn slightly darker in color as they mature, so watch for seeds that turn from cream or green to tan, brown, or black to determine when to collect. Seeds borne in fruits (such as tomatoes) are ready when the fruit is just overripe. Harvest edible seeds such as beans, corn, and peas when they are dry. As you collect, keep uncleaned seeds in paper bags and be sure to label them with the name of the plant and the date collected. *See* SHATTER for tips on catching seeds of plants that are dispersed quickly. *See also* CLEANING SEED and STORING SEED

saw-kerf grafting A grafting technique used to unite scions with the trunk of a small tree or the main scaffold branches of a larger tree. Also called notch or wedge grafting, saw-kerf grafting is similar to cleft grafting, and can be used for top-working. It is best used for branches (the stock) that are from 2 to 4 inches or more in diameter. One advantage to this method is that the stock branches don't need to be split deeply to accommodate the scions (they're cut instead), which reduces the chance that disease-causing organisms can enter the wounds. Also, unlike cleft grafts, saw-kerf grafts can be made on wood that doesn't split cleanly and/or has knots. They also can be made 2 to 3 months earlier than most grafts, well before the stock has begun growing in spring. To prepare the stock (branch), saw it off cleanly at a right angle to the branch. Use a narrow-bladed saw to make three cuts down from the top of the branch stub. Extend the cuts nearly to the center of the branch, then widen them with a sharp, round-bladed knife. The cuts should be about 2 to 3 inches long. Prepare three 3- to 4-inch-long scions, each with two to three buds, for each stock branch. To prepare them, make smooth, gently tapering 2-inch-long cuts on the bottom to create a wedge. For best results, make a slightly lopsided wedge, leaving one edge along the length of the cut slightly wider than the other. Fit the widest edge of the scion next to the cambium layer of the stock. The scions need to match the cuts in the stock and fit tightly into place with a light tap from a hammer. The cambium layers need to match as well; adjust either stock or scion if they don't. Wax the entire cut end of the stock, along the length of the cuts and scions, and dab a bit of wax on the cut end of the scions as well. *See* GRAFTING

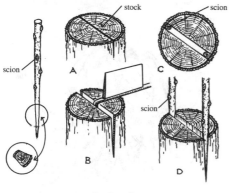

saw-kerf grafting

saws *See* PRUNING SAWS

saxatile plant A plant that grows among rocks. Saxatile plants are found in either sun or shade and occur at lower elevations than true alpine plants.

saxicolous Growing on or near rocky soil or rocky places. Growing on rocks.

scaberulose Slightly rough or harsh-textured.

scabrous Rough or harsh-textured due to scales, bristles, tiny teeth, or other projec-

tions. Most often used to describe leaf surfaces or stems. The leaves of many squashes (*Cucurbita* spp.) are scabrous.

scaffold, scaffold branch A main, permanent branch of a tree. Ideally, scaffold branches should form a spoke pattern out from the trunk, with about five branches to each wheel or tier of branches. For a large shade or ornamental tree, the optimum vertical distance between tiers of branches is 3 to 4 feet. To train a tree that has a strong structure of scaffold branches, remove weak lateral branches or side shoots annually on young trees to encourage growth of the main scaffold branches. Also thin out branches that stick out from the trunk at odd angles, point into the center of the canopy, and that rub or cross. If two branches are growing too close together, thin out the weaker branch, especially if one is growing directly over the other.

scale (botanical) A scale is a thin, flat, dry leaf or bract that is brown and is usually pressed against a stem or other strucutre.

scale, in scale (design) This term is used in reference to the size relationship of the various elements in a composition, whether it be a flower arrangement or a garden design. A design is said to be in scale or in proportion when the size of the plants and other elements in it fit well together and also look natural together on their site. A postage-stamp-size garden bed isn't in scale with a large yard and house, for example, just as an enormous hedge or shrub can overwhelm a tiny yard. In flower arranging, a tiny bouquet is not in scale if it is set in an enormous entry hall. An arrangement is not in scale if giant blooms are combined with tiny flowers and delicate foliage.

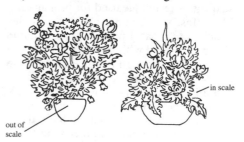

scale insects Pests that suck plant juices from shoots and leaves, causing stunted, off-color growth. The adult females are small, waxy, soft- or hard-bodied insects that are stationary and may be red, white, brown, black, or gray in color. The males are tiny and winged. The tiny nymphs have legs and can move around before molting to the adult form. Scale insects exude a sticky honeydew that fosters the growth of sooty mold. These pests attack many plants, attacking outdoor plants through most of the season, and indoor plants year-round. To control them, prune off and destroy scale-infested growth. Use a soft brush and soapy water (rinse plants afterward) to remove scale insects from stems. Spray with horticultural oil. Treat serious infestations with pyrethrins or rotenone as a last resort.

scalelike This term is used to describe small, thin, flat leaves that generally are densely packed and hug the stems. Scalelike leaves are characteristic of many conifers, including cedars and arborvitae (*Thuja* spp.) as well as some junipers such as eastern red cedar (*Juniperus virginiana*) and Rocky Mountain juniper (*J. scopulorum*).

scalelike leaves

scaling A technique used for propagating lily bulbs, which consist of loose scales attached to a basal plate. This technique also can be used with fritillary (*Fritillaria* spp.) bulbs, although in some cases these bulbs have extremely small scales. Scaling is slower than propagating by bulbils or bulblets, but produces large quantities of bulbs. To scale a bulb, dig it after flowering in late summer or fall, and pull off the outer two rows or layers of scales. Replant the mother bulb. Discard scales that show signs of disease, treat the base with a fungicide, then stick the scales into a container filled with moist cutting mix. (*See* CUTTING MIX) The tops of the scales should just emerge from the medium. Cover the container loosely with plastics; some air circulation is beneficial, but it is important that the scales do not dry out. Set the container in a warm (68 to 70°F) spot out of direct sunlight. Bulblets will appear in 1 to 2 months. Individual scales also can simply be mixed with barely moist vermiculite in a plastic bag and stored as above. The bulblets that form are usually dormant. To overcome dormancy, place the containers or bags of bulblets in the refrigerator for 2 months. Harden off the bulblets gradually and pot them up or plant them out in a nursery bed.

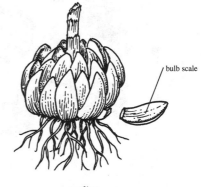

bulb scale

scaling

scalloped *See* CRENATE

scaly bulb *See* BULB

scandent Scrambling or climbing loosely.

scape A flower stalk (peduncle) that rises from the ground and lacks leaves, although it may bear bracts (small modified leaves). Daffodils (*Narcissus* spp.), dogtooth violets (*Erythronium* spp.), and daylilies (*Hemerocallis*) bear their flowers on scapes, as do florist's amaryllis (*Hippeastrum* hybrids). Hostas (*Hosta* spp.) bear their flowers on scapes that have either large, leafy bracts or smaller ones borne under the flowers.

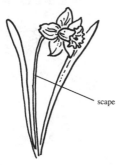

scape

scapiform Resembling a scape, but bearing some leaves.

scapose Bearing flowers on scapes. Scapelike.

scar *See* LEAF SCAR

scarabaeiform Beetle-shaped.

scarification The process of nicking, sanding, or otherwise wearing down hard seed coats to hasten the uptake of water and thus speed seed germination. To scarify, rub hard-coated seeds on sandpaper or nick the seed coat with a utility knife or razor blade. In this case, hold the seed with pliers and take care to cut only into the seed coat and not damage the embryo itself. Also avoid knicking into the hilium, or seed scar. Scarification is recommended for morning glories (*Ipomoea* spp.), lupines (*Lupinus* spp.), and baptisias (*Baptisia* spp.). Soaking seeds in warm, but not boiling, water overnight (from 12 to 24 hours) is an alternative to scarification.

scarious, scariose Dry, brown, thin, and membranelike.

scattered Arranged sparsely and irregularly.

scheduling sowing dates *See* FROST DATES

scherophyllous Bearing leaves, called scherophylls, that are stiff, firm, and often leathery because of thick cell walls that retain water. Scherophyllous leaves are characteristic of many plants native to desert regions as an adaption for drought.

schizo- A prefix meaning split or splitting. Schizopetalous means split or deeply cut petals, for example.

schizocarp A dry fruit that does not open at maturity (is indehiscent) and splits into two separate, closed, one-seeded segments at maturity. The halves are called mericarps. Most members of the carrot family (Apiaceae, formerly Umbelliferae), such as parsley, carrots, dill, and coriander, bear schizocarps. The fruits of maples (*Acer* spp.) also are schizocarps that break into two samaras, which are winged, one-seeded fruits.

scion The upper portion of a grafted plant. Wood collected for use as scions should be from the current season's growth (one year old or less). It should be vigorous, but not too succulent, from $1/4$ to $1/2$ inch in diameter, and not show any evidence of viral diseases. (Scions are available from some mail-order companies specializing in fruit and nut trees.) Select scions with healthy, plump leaf buds that are fairly closely spaced: Ones that do not have flower buds are best. Collect scions for deciduous plants, such as apples, in winter while they are dormant; trying to graft after buds are growing is an exercise in failure. (You can collect dormant scions and use them immediately, without storage.) Wrap bundles of collected scions in plastic or place them in plastic bags (be sure to label them with the name of the plant). Store them in the refrigerator for up to 3 weeks at temperatures between 40 and 50°F; for longer storage, up to 3 months, store them at 32°F. (A freezer is considerably colder than this—to about 0°F—and freezer storage will damage the buds.) In the North, bundles of scions can be buried in a protected location for storage. Select a site with very well-drained soil and bury them at a depth of 1 to $1^1/_2$ feet on the north side of the house. Collect scions for broad-leaved evergreens in spring, before they are growing actively, and remove the leaves; use them immediately without storing them. Collect and use scions of herbaceous plants immediately as well. The best scion wood is from the bottom two-thirds of the shoot. In most cases, before grafting, scions are cut into short lengths, from 3 to 5 inches, each usually with two to three buds.

scion wood *See* SCION

sciophilous This term is applied to plants that prefer shady sites.

sclerenchyma These are cells with lignified, or woody, cell walls and are nonliving once mature. There are two types of sclerenchyma cells: sclereids and fibers. Sclereids, sometimes called stone cells, are variable in size and are scattered in various locations through the plant. They sometimes form layers. For example, sclereids form the pits in stone fruits such as cherries and peaches. Stone cells also give pears their gritty quality. Fibers are long and thin, with thick, lignified cell walls. Linen fabric is made from the sclerenchyma cells of flax (*Linum usitatissimum*).

sclerophyll A plant or tissue that contains sclerenchyma tissue.

scooping *See* BASAL CUTTAGE

scorch *See* LEAF SCORCH

scoring Making shallow cuts down the sides of a root ball with a knife or other sharp tool, such as a trowel. Scoring at planting time cuts through roots of container-grown plants and encourages them to spread out into the soil rather than to continue winding around the pot. Scoring is also a bulb propagation technique. *See* BASAL CUTTAGE

scorpioid Coiled or curved like a scorpion's tail.

scorpioid cyme This type of cyme has branches that appear on alternate sides, giving the main stem, or axis, a zigzag look. The main stem is also commonly coiled. Chinese forget-me-nots or hound's tongues (*Cynoglossum* spp.) bear their flowers in scorpioid cymes. *See also* CYME

scorpioid cyme

scrambler This is a general term for a plant with long, thin stems that climbs over and up shrubs, trees, rocks, or other obstacles without the aid of holdfasts such as tendrils. Scramblers often use prickles or thorns to help them climb. Some tall, long-caned roses can perform as scramblers.

scree In a rock garden, a scree is an area covered with rock fragments and particles and mixed with a small amount of organic matter or rock garden soil mix. A scree retains very little water and provides extremely well-drained growing conditions required by some species of alpine plants.

scuffle hoe *See* HOE

scurfy Covered with tiny, loose scales. Most often used to describe leaf surfaces. Several species of saltbush (*Atriplex* spp.) bear stems and leaves that are scurfy and thus have a farinose, or mealy, texture.

scutellate, scutelliform Saucer- or shield-shaped.

scythe A tool used to cut tall grass that has a curved blade attached to a handle that can be either straight or curved. Grips are attached to the handle for both hands—one near the top and the other near the middle. To cut with a scythe, hold the blade level to the ground and swing the blade back and forth by twisting from the waist.

sebaceous Fatty or tallowlike.

secauters *See* HAND PRUNERS

secondary Below the first, or primary. The leaflets below the primary leaflet, which is at the tip of a compound leaf, are secondary, for example.

secondary colors Green, orange, and violet. These are mixed by combining the primary colors in equal amounts: Red and blue make violet; blue and yellow make green; and yellow and red make orange. *See* COLOR WHEEL for more on colors.

secondary phloem *See* PHLOEM

secondary xylem *See* XYLEM

section A rank used to organize species in especially large genera. *See* SUBGENUS

seculate Sickle-shaped.

secund Arranged on only one side of a stem or axis.

sedge peat *See* PEAT MOSS

seed A reproductive structure containing a fertilized, ripened ovule that contains a dormant embryonic plant and stored food (endosperm) to fuel it. Seeds contain very little water (as little as 2 percent; a normal plant consists of 95 percent water), a factor that protects them in freezing temperatures because water would expand and damage the embryo or crack the seed coat prematurely. Seeds vary greatly in size, from dustlike petunia seeds to coconuts. *See also* GERMINATION

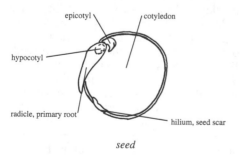

seed

seed bed An area of soil that has been cultivated and raked to provide a smooth area for sowing seeds.

seed coat The outer covering on a seed, also called the testa.

seeder These devices are handy because they space seeds sown outdoors automatically, thus reducing the need to thin. Various hand-held models are available. Mechanical seeders may be practical for very large gardens.

seed exchange Many plant societies organize exchanges of seeds between members, and these present an excellent way to obtain seeds of unusual and heirloom plants collected and donated by other members—in many cases from all over the world. You need to be a member and pay a small fee to participate; individuals who donate seeds usually get first choice of the offerings. To find organizations that offer seed exchanges (as well as plant and cutting exchanges) look through the Horticultural Societies list in *Gardening by Mail* by Barbara Barton (Houghton Mifflin, 1997) for organizations specializing in plants that interest you. *See* PLANT EXCHANGE

seed germination *See* GERMINATION

seeding The process of planting seeds. This term is most often used to refer to sowing grass seeds (for other types of seeding, *See* SEED SOWING). To sow a lawn, start by preparing the soil and amending it with organic matter. Rake it smooth, and then broadcast the seeds evenly over the surface according to the rate recommended on the pacakge. Either use a spreader or broadcast by hand; in the latter case, to ensure even coverage, divide the seed into two batches and walk the site in rows from end to end tossing seeds in the first batch. Then spread the second half of the seeds while walking in rows at right angles to the first. Lightly rake the site to cover the seeds, then roll the site with a lightweight lawn roller or tamp it down gently with a rake to ensure good seed-to-soil contact. Mulch lightly with weed-free straw to help hold in moisture. Keep the soil evenly moist until grass seedlings are well established. The optimum time for the first mowing will depend on the type of grass planted.

seed leaf Cotyledon. This term refers to the primary leaf or leaves of a plant embryo, or seed. In some plants, they stay inside the seed upon germination; in others, they emerge above ground. Monocots bear seeds that have one cotyledon; dicots have two seeds.

seedling A young plant that has grown from a seed.

seedling rootstock A rootstock grown from seed for the purpose of grafting. Seedling rootstocks usually are virus-free and often more vigorous than the scions to which they are grafted.

seed potato A section of a tuber, specifically a potato, with one or more buds, or "eyes." *See* TUBER

seed saving *See* saving SEED

seed scar *See* HILIUM

seed sowing Planting seeds, from scattering them over the ground outdoors in the garden to carefully placing them in containers to be coddled indoors. For specifics on sowing methods, *see* SEED SOWING IN-DOORS, DIRECT SOWING, BROADCASTING, CONTAINER SOWING OUTDOORS, SEEDING ROWS, HILLING. For sowing techniques, *see* STRATIFICATION, SCARIFICATION, PREGERMINATING, FROST DATES, GERMINATION TESTING, SEED-STARTING MIXES, BOTTOM HEAT, TRANSPLANTING, DIFFICULT TO TRANSPLANT, THINNING, HARDENING OFF.

seed sowing indoors Gardeners start seeds indoors for any number of reasons. Indoor sowing makes it possible to start plants (especially tender annuals, vegetables, and herbs) weeks before warm spring weather arrives. (With an extra-early start, some perennials will bloom the first year from seed, too.) It makes it easy to give germinating seeds and young seedlings the perfect conditions they need to grow—warmth, humidity, even moisture, and light. Indoor sowing also makes sense for extremely tiny seeds and expensive or rare seeds. To sow indoors, fill containers with premoistened germinating mix and gently press it down so the mix is about $1/_2$ inch below the rim of the container. Spread the seeds evenly over the soil surface, or sow in tiny rows. Don't sow too thickly, or the seedlings will be crowded and hard to untangle for transplanting. Cover the seeds with additional mix according to the directions on the seed packet or simply with a layer of mix that is about two to three times the width of the seeds. Sowing too shallow is better than too deep. Just press tiny seeds—begonias and petunias, for example—as well as seeds of species that require light to germinate, into the surface of the medium. Label each pot with the name of the plant and the date sown. Place sown pots in flats. To provide high humidity, set the flats in plastic cleaners' bags draped over wire hoops to keep the plastic off the surface of the mix and the germinating seedlings. Loosely close the bags with a twist tie. (A hoop framework is easy to make from wire clothes hangers.) Providing bottom heat by setting the flats on a heat mat speeds germination and growth. Keep the medium evenly moist but not wet; watering from below is best because it avoids washing small seeds out of the pots and helps prevent damping off, a fungal disease that rots seedlings at the soil surface. Most seeds don't need light until they germinate (except those that require light for germination). Once sprouts appear, set the flats under a shop light with fluorescent bulbs suspended 4 to 6 inches over the pots. Or set them in a bright window, but out of direct sun (plants will heat up quickly under plastic). Once seedlings have at least one set of true leaves, begin opening the plastic bag for a few hours each day, increasing the time daily, until seedlings are accustomed to normal humidity. Transplant seedlings to individual pots when they have at least one set of true leaves. *See* SEED-STARTING MIXES, SEED SOWING

seed-starting mix A medium blended specifically for starting seeds. Ideally, they hold plenty of moisture but are light in texture so roots receive adequate air as well. A good seed-starting mix doesn't contain soil and is relatively free of organisms such as fungi that cause diseases. Commercial seed-starting mixes are available, but you can mix your own by blending 2 parts peat moss with 1 part perlite or vermiculite, measured by volume not weight. Premoisten the medium and use it to fill clean containers. *See* PREMOISTEN, CLEANING CONTAINERS, GROWING MIX, CUTTING MIX

seed storing *See* SAVING SEED, CLEANING SEED

segment A section or division, such as the sections of a grapefruit or orange. This term also is used to refer to individual leaflets on a compound leaf.

selection A particular, distinct form of a plant that has been identified and propagated either sexually or asexually.

self, self-colored A flower that is a single, solid, uniform color.

self-clinging A vine that uses tendrils or aerial roots to climb and thus does not need tying or other support.

self-fertilization Fertilization (the union of a male and female gamete) that results from self-pollination.

self-fruitful A tree that produces pollen that can pollinate its own flowers.

self-pollination The transfer of pollen from the anther(s) of a flower on one plant to the stigma of a flower on the same plant. Self-pollinated plants usually are easy to maintain by seed and are normally uniform genetically (homozygous). *See* CROSS-POLLINATION

self sow, self seed To grow from seed that is distributed in the garden naturally, without the intervention of the gardener. This term usually is used to describe annuals that reappear year after year without being replanted—larkspur (*Consolida ajacis*) and cosmos (*Cosmos* spp.), for example—but biennials, perennials, and all manner of woody plants also self sow.

self-sterile A tree that produces pollen that cannot pollinate its own flowers.

semi- A prefix meaning half or nearly half.

semi-deciduous *See* SEMI-EVERGREEN

semidouble A flower that has either two or three times the normal number of petals for the species. The flowers usually are arranged in two or three whorls.

semidouble flower

semi-evergreen Retaining some green leaves through the winter. Whether a plant is semi-evergreen, evergreen, or deciduous often depends on where it is grown, especially when it comes to perennials. For example, there are species of barrenworts (*Epimedium* spp.), hardy geraniums (*Geranium* spp.), and shield ferns (*Polystichum* spp.) that are evergreen in warm climates and deciduous in cold ones. In between, they are semi-evergreen, especially in mild winters. Unfortunately, they're often described simply as evergreen. *See also* EVERGREEN, DECIDUOUS

semi-hardwood cutting *See* SEMI-RIPE CUTTING

semi-ripe cutting A cutting taken from new growth on a woody plant that has partially matured; the base of a semi-ripe cutting is woody, while the tip is still soft. Sometimes called semi-hardwood cuttings, semi-ripe cuttings are used to propagate a wide range of shrubs, vines, and trees. For deciduous plants, softwood cuttings generally root best, although they also root from semi-ripe cuttings—forsythia (*Forsythia* spp.), wigelia (*Wigelia* spp.), and Japanese barberry (*Berberis thunbergii*) all can be rooted in this manner. Semi-ripe cuttings are especially effective for rooting evergreens, both needle and broad-leaved, including rhododendrons and azaleas (*Rhododendron* spp.), camellias (*Camellia* spp.), and hollies (*Ilex* spp.). Collect and treat semi-ripe cuttings just as you would softwood ones (*See* SOFTWOOD CUTTING). Many propagators remove the shoot tip, cutting it off just above a node. To reduce transpiration, on large-leaved or evergreen plants, cut the leaves in half before sticking the cuttings. Wound the stem tips and treat them with rooting hormone (*See* WOUNDING, ROOTING HORMONE). Set cuttings to be rooted indoors on a heated propagation mat to encourage root formation. For other types of cuttings normally treated as semi-ripe cuttings, *See* LEAF-BUD CUTTING, INTERNODAL CUTTING, HEEL CUTTING, MALLET CUTTING

semi-ripe cutting

senescence The changes in a plant or plant part that occur after maturity that ultimately result in the death of tissue.

sepal One segment of the calyx, located just outside the petals of a flower. Sepals generally are green and leaflike.

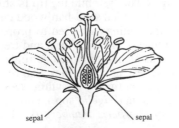

sepaloid Resembling a sepal in both color and texture.

-sepalous A suffix referring to sepals, usually combined with a prefix indicating a number. Octosepalous means bearing eight sepals.

septate Divided by a partition or partitions. An ovary or seed pod (fruit) that is divided into sections is septate.

septentate Bearing parts in sevens.

septicidal dehiscence *See* DEHISCENT

septum, *pl.* **septae** A partition, especially within an ovary or seed pod (fruit).

seriate Borne in rows or in a series.

sericeous Silky. Covered with long, fine, soft hairs that are somewhat pressed down onto the surface. Most often used to describe leaf surfaces.

series *See* SUBGENUS

serpentine layering This is a variation of simple layering (*See* LAYERING) used to produce several plants from long, flexible stems, which are "snaked" above and below the soil to induce production of roots at selected leaf nodes. Vines such as clematis (*Clematis* spp.) are ideal candidates for propagating in this manner. To make a serpentine layer, in late winter or early spring select a stem, then loosen and improve the soil along the area where it will touch the ground as for a simple layer. Roots form at buried leaf nodes and shoots at the ones left above ground, so you need to have at least one bud above ground for each one that is buried (more aboveground buds usually makes "snaking" the stem easier). Identify which buds will be buried, then either pick all the leaves off except those at the tip or remove all but a leaf or two from the sections that will remain above ground. Then use a sharp knife to wound the stem at each leaf node that will be buried by slicing into it to form a thin 1- to 2-inch-long flap or tongue of bark on the bottom of the section that will be buried. Take care not to cut too deep. Place a toothpick or thin sliver of wood in each wound to keep it open. Bury the first wounded section about 3 inches deep, pinning down the stem with a U-shaped wire pin, then use a small stake to keep the aboveground portion more or less erect. Repeat the process along the length of the stem, staking the tip. Keep the soil moist all summer. The following spring, check for roots at each buried section, then cut apart and pot up the new plants.

serpentine layering

serra A tooth on the margin of a serrate leaf.

serrate Saw-toothed. Edged with sharp teeth that point toward the tip of the leaf. This term is commonly used to describe the edge, or margin, of a leaf or leaflet. On a biserrate leaf, the individual teeth are further divided into smaller teeth. Hellebores (*Helleborus* spp.) typically have serrate leaf margins. *See also* DENTATE

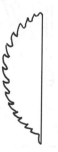

serrate leaf margin

serrulate Finely serrate or finely saw-toothed. Edged with very small sharp teeth that point toward the tip of the leaf. This term is commonly used to describe the edge, or margin, of a leaf or leaflet.

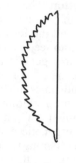

serrulate leaf margin

sessile Without a stalk. This term is commonly used to describe leaves or flowers that are attached directly to a stem. Redbud flowers (*Cercis* spp.) are sessile; since they are borne directly on stems or branches on old wood, they also are cauliflorus.

sessile leaf

set This term once was used to refer to bedding plants being planted, or set out, in the garden. Today it is used to refer to potatoes or other tubers that are being planted as well as small onions or scallons that are to be set out.

seta A bristle.

setaceous Bristlelike.

setiferous Bearing bristles.

setose Covered with sharp, stiff bristles. Can be used to describe leaf surfaces as well as stems, flower buds, pods, or other organs. The stems of winter squash (*Cucurbita maxima*) range from setose to hirsute.

setulose Bearing very small seta, or bristles.

sexual reproduction The cycle of reproduction in which male and female sex cells (gametes) unite, and the fertilized female gametes develop into seeds, and ultimately, seedlings, that carry genetic matter from both parents. Gametes contain half the number of chromosomes in a normal cell; once they unite, the resulting zygote has the correct number of chromosomes. Depending on the genetic makeup of the parent plants, the offspring of sexual reproduction can resemble either parent, both parents, or neither parent. *See* ASEXUAL REPRODUCTION, HOMOZYGOUS, HETEROZYGOUS

shade This term has meanings that relate to selecting sites for plants—a shaded spot is one where the rays of the sun are intercepted by trees, buildings, or other obstacles. (*See* PARTIAL SHADE, FULL SHADE) In terms of color, a shade is a color that has been darkened by adding black. Maroon is a shade of red, for example.

sharp drainage A general term for soil that drains very rapidly. Also called free-draining, such soils usually have high content of sand and/or stones.

shatter This term is used to describe seed pods that open, or dehisce, easily to spread or spill their seeds. To collect seeds from plants bearing pods that shatter, harvest them just before the pods are completely ripe and place small bunches of stems in paper bags hung or set in a warm, dry place. The seeds will shatter into the bag. Dill (*Anethum graveolens*) and many mustard-family (Brassicaceae) plants shatter, as do many wildflowers. Some plants, including hardy geraniums (*Geranium* spp.), bear pods that dehisce in such a manner that the seeds are thrown in all directions. To collect seeds from these plants, wrap a piece of cheesecloth around a seedhead or enclose it in a small paper bag while it is still on the plant. When ripe, the seeds will fall into the cheesecloth or bag. This technique also works for wildflowers, where cutting stems may not be appropriate.

shearing Pruning a shrub or hedge by cutting its stems back uniformly with hedge clippers or an electric hedge trimmer to conform with a particular, desired shape. Hedges and specimen shrubs are sheared, as are topiary and knot gardens. Shearing also is used to deadhead some perennials: In this case, cut them back by one-third to one-half with hand pruners or hedge clippers after the main flush of bloom has finished. Shearing many perennials induces a second flush of bloom. It also is used simply to cause plants to produce a more compact, attractive mound of foliage after they have finished blooming. *See* DEADHEADING, HEADING CUT

shears, bonsai *See* SHEARS, GARDEN

shears, garden A pruning tool much like a pair of scissors but with sharp, heavier-duty blades designed for cutting small woody twigs, flower stems, and the like. Japanese pruning shears or bonsai shears both have short blades that are exceptionally sharp. They are especially useful for cleanly nipping out small twigs in tight spaces. *See also* HEDGE SHEARS, GRASS SHEARS

sheath A tubular or tubelike structure that surrounds another plant part. The bases of palm fronds and grass leaves, including those of corn (*Zea mays*), form sheaths around the stem.

sheath

sheathing Forming a sheath. Many grasses bear leaves that enlarge at the base and surround the stem to form a sheath.

sheet composting A composting technique that involves spreading materials to be composted over the soil surface or in shallow trenches and then digging them into the soil to decompose.

shelterbelt A planting of trees and shrubs arranged, designed, and located to provide protection from winds. Shelterbelts are normally planted along the edge(s) of a property and are designed to block prevailing winds. They can be as simple as a hedge, or can consist of a mixture of deciduous trees and evergreens, as well as deciduous and evergreen shrubs arranged in layers by height.

shield budding *See* T-BUDDING

shield The shield-shaped staminode, or stamenlike structure, that is just above the pouched lip of a lady's slipper orchid (*Cypripedium* spp.). Also, the tip of a scale on a pinecone.

shoot A young stem or a new branch or twig.

short-day plant A plant that flowers when nights are getting longer and days shorter. *See* PHOTOPERIODISM

short-lived perennial A perennial that lives for only 2 or 3 years; many of these are grown as biennials. *See* PERENNIAL

shovel Also called a round-point shovel because the tip of the blade is rounded to a point, this implement is a multipurpose digging tool in nearly every gardener's shed. The pointed tip makes it easy to penetrate soil, and a long handle allows you to stand up and use leverage when loosening it. Most models have a straight shaft without a handle and have folded treads at the top of the blade to make it easy to step on the blade to exert force. The blade is slightly curved, which adds strength and also makes it an ideal implement for moving everything from soil and compost to gravel. A floral or border shovel is a lightweight tool designed for working closely among plants. It has a short handle and a blade that is from one-half to two-thirds the size of a standard shovel.

shrub A woody plant that produces multiple stems, shoots, or branches from the base of the plant. This is a somewhat loose term, as training can affect whether a plant is a shrub or a small tree. Turning a large shrub into a small tree takes some pruning, but isn't difficult. Restrict it to a single main trunk or stem, or only two or three stems, then gradually remove the lower limbs to create a treelike profile. Some shrubs perform more like perennials, depending on where they are grown. *See* CUTBACK SHRUB

shrubby Shrublike, somewhat shrubby. A plant that has a shrublike habit, but does not necessarily have woody stems. This is a general term often used to describe large, shrub-size annuals or perennials such as baptisias (*Baptisia* spp.).

shrublet A small shrub or any low-growing, woody-based, densely branched plant.

sickle A tool used to cut tall grass, especially in rough places where a scythe might hit rocks or other obstacles. A sickle has a very sharp, curved blade attached to a straight handle. To cut with a sickle, hold the blade level to the ground and swing it back and forth by twisting from the waist.

sickle-shaped *See* FALCATE

side-dressing A technique for spreading fertililizer in which the material is spread in a band along the rows of crops. Side-dressing is used to feed annual crops during the growing season. Keep the fertilizer away from the stems of the plants, and then work it into the top few inches of soil with a rake, spade, or fork.

side grafting This is a general term for various types of grafts that allow a scion to be inserted into a stock that is larger in diameter. *See* STUB GRAFT, SIDE-TONGUE GRAFT, SIDE-VENEER GRAFT

side-tongue graft A type of side graft in which a tongue is cut in both stock and scion to create interlocking wood, as in a whip-and-tongue graft. This type of graft primarily is used for small plants, especially broad- and narrow-leaved evergreens. Select a stock that has a smooth section of stem just above the crown of the plant. Prepare the scion as you would for a whip-and-tongue graft. To prepare the stock, make a shallow cut (remove bark and a small sliver of wood) the same length as the cut on the base of the scion. Then make a second cut on the stock, parallel to the first, starting about one-third down from the top of the first cut. Gently insert the scion into the stock, interlocking the tongues and matching the cambium layers along one side. Wrap and wax as you would a whip-and-tongue graft. Remove the top of the stock after the graft has healed, either by cutting it off all at once or cutting it back gradually. This will induce the scion to begin growing. *See* WHIP-AND-TONGUE GRAFT, GRAFTING

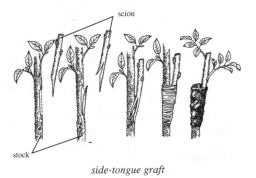

side-tongue graft

side-veneer graft Also called a spliced side graft, this type of side graft is especially useful for grafting small plants such as container-grown evergreen seedlings. Select a stock that has a smooth section of stem just above the crown of the plant. To prepare the stock, make a shallow cut (remove bark and a small sliver of wood) from 1 to 1 $^1/_2$ inches long down the side of the scion, but do not remove a sliver of wood. Instead, make a second, short cut slightly above the bottom of the first that intersects with the base of the first cut and removes the sliver of wood. To prepare the scion, make a smooth, long, slanting cut on one side and a short cut on the other: The cuts on the scion need to mirror those on

the stock both in length and angle so the cambium layers can be lined up properly. Place the stock and scion together, then wrap tightly and wax as you would a whip-and-tongue graft. Remove the top of the stock after the graft has healed, either by cutting it off all at once or cutting it back gradually. *See* WHIP-AND-TONGUE GRAFT, GRAFTING

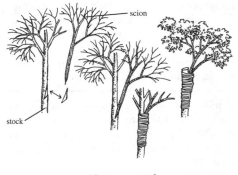

side-veneer graft

sigmoid S-shaped.

silica gel *See* DRYING FLOWERS

siliceous Containing very small fragments of silica.

silicle A type of dry fruit characteristic of some plants in the mustard family (Brassicaceae) that is long and thin—less than twice as long as it is wide. Siliques are formed from two carpels and are dehiscent, meaning they open at maturity to release their seeds. When they open they split along their length, and the two walls, or valves, fall off, revealing a papery partition, called the replum, that remains on the plant. Money plant (*Lunaria annuua*) bears silicles and the silvery, nearly round, central partitions, revealed when the outer valves are removed, are attractive in dried arrangements.

silicle

silique, siliqua A type of dry fruit characteristic of plants in the mustard family (Brassicaceae) that is long and thin—twice to three or more times as long as it is wide. Siliques are formed from two carpels and are dehiscent, meaning they open at maturity to release their seeds. When they open they split along their length, and the two walls, or valves, fall off, revealing a papery partition, called the replum, that remains on the plant. Cabbage (*Brassica oleracea*) and related plants, including broccoli and cauliflower, produce siliques when they go to seed.

silique

silk The tuft of "hair" that comes out of the tip of an ear of corn. The silk is actually composed of the style of the individual flowers on the ear, which is the stalk that joins the stigma and ovary.

silky Having a silklike texture, such as the petals of some poppies (*Papaver* spp.). Bearing leaves covered with fine, soft hairs; sericeous.

silt One of the three major mineral particles in soil (the other two are sand and clay), silt particles are smaller than sand, between 0.5 and 0.002 mm, and can only be seen with the aid of a microscope. Moist silty soil absorbs and retains more water and nutrients than sandy soil. *See also* SOIL TEXTURE

simple Undivided. Not compound.

simple corymb *See* CORYMB

simple layering *See* LAYERING

simple leaf A leaf that is not divided into separate leaflets, as a compound leaf is, although it may be deeply cut.

simple leaf

single A flower that has the normal number of petals or tepals for the species. The number of petals will vary according to the species. A single rose such as 'Dainty Bess' or eglantine rose (*Rosa eglanteria*) usually has five petals arranged in a single row, while a single peony such as 'America' has from five to ten arranged in one or more rows. The term single also is used to refer to plants in the aster family (Asteraceae) that have a single row of petals (ray florets) surrounding an eye or center made up of densely packed disk florets.

single flower

single cordon *See* CORDON

single digging A soil preparation system that involves digging and amending the soil to a shovel's depth. Before single digging, make sure the soil is ready to work. (*See* SOIL BUILDING for a simple test to see if it is.) To single dig, remove grass and weeds from the site and spread a layer of compost or other organic matter over it. Then use a spade or a fork to turn the soil over to a shovel's depth, working in the compost as you go. Ideally, prepare the soil the season before you plant—this gives it plenty of time to settle. If you can't wait, water the site thoroughly to help it settle, then wait a day or so before planting.

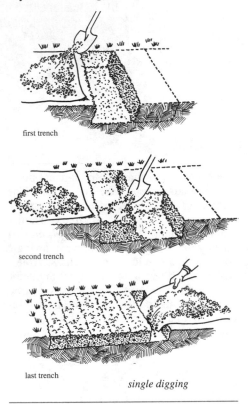

first trench

second trench

last trench

single digging

sinuate Strongly wavy, with the margin going in and out. This term is commonly used to describe the edge, or margin, of a leaf, leaflet, or other organ. A margin that is wavy up and down is undulate, while one that is slightly sinuate or slightly wavy is repand.

sinuate leaf margin

sinuous Having a serpentine or wavy form.

sinus The division or indentation between two lobes or other segments of a leaf or other organ. For example, the indentation between the lobes of a leaf.

site inventory A map that is drawn to scale and indicates the boundary lines of a particular lot or site, along with the location of the house and other buildings. In addition to the basic information on a base plan, a site inventory also indicates other features of the property, both positive and negative, that need to be taken into account when designing the landscape, including soil types, slopes, views (both good and bad), wind direction, surface water drainage patterns, existing plantings, and so forth. *See also* BASE PLAN

site plan This term has several different meanings. Contractors and builders use it to map out an individual lot to scale, and indicate setback requirements and the major building(s) on the property. Landscape architects use a site plan to illustrate proposed designs in detail, including the location of proposed terraces, walls, plantings, or other features. In this latter sense, a site plan is the same as a preliminary design or a master plan. *See also* BASE PLAN, SITE INVENTORY

six-pack *See* MARKET PACK

skeletonized leaves Leaves from which the tissue has decomposed or been eaten away, leaving only the network of veins. Pressed flower designs often feature skeletonized leaves. One method for making them involves soaking leaves for a month in rainwater, then rinsing the leaves under running water to remove the softened leaf tissue. For faster results boil leaves for an hour in a solution of 1 teaspoon baking soda to 1 quart of water. Let the leaves cool, then gently spread them out on newspaper and carefully scrape or brush off the softened leaf tissue. (A palate knife or a dull table knife works well for this.) Dry and use the leaves as is or bleach them in a solution of 2 tablespoons per quart of water for about an hour. Rinse bleached leaves and blot them dry. Spread them out on newspaper overnight to dry completely. You can iron them if you need perfectly flat leaves. Leathery leaves with heavy veins work best for this process (some disintegrate completely). Try leaves from oaks (*Quercus* spp.), magnolias (*Magnolia* spp.), and ivy (*Hedera* spp.).

slice seeder A power tool used in overseeding a lawn that slices through thatch and into soil and sows seeds at the same time. *See* OVERSEEDING

slip A general term for a cutting or a shoot that already has some roots attached and can easily be detached from the plant and grown on. Sweet potatoes are typically started from rooted slips that appear on the tubers.

slip stage A growth stage that indicates whether some types of melons are ripe. Melons that slip develop a scar across the area where the stem attaches to the fruit when they are ripe. The half-slip stage means the stem partially detaches from the fruit. Full-slip stage means the scar covers the area where the stem attaches to the fruit, and the fruit is easy to pick with a gentle tug.

slipping, slips This term is used to indicate that a woody plant's bark can be easily separated from the wood, and is primarily used in relation to budding and bark grafting. Bark slips, or comes away, from the wood easily, when the plant is actively growing and the cambium cells—essential to forming a healthy graft union—are dividing. While early spring is the best time for most grafting techniques, bark usually slips any time the plant is in active growth unless drought or cold temperatures cause it to tighten up. Slipping makes it easy to insert buds or scions under the bark to ensure good contact between the cambiums of stock and scion. Plants with bark that has to be forcibly pried away from the wood are not good candidates for budding or grafting.

slugs Slimy, soft-bodied mollusks that usually are gray, tan, or black in color and leave slime trails on leaves. Slugs lack shells and range from $1/8$ inch to 6 inches or more in length. They usually are most active at night and in damp places. When they feed, they rasp large holes in leaves, stems, and fruit and may completely devour seedlings. To control them, trap slugs and snails under fruit rinds, cabbage leaves, or boards set on the soil, or in shallow pans of beer set into the soil surface; check traps daily and destroy pests. Eliminate mulches and garden debris; these materials provide ideal hiding places. Use barriers of copper screen or sheeting to repel slugs and snails. Plant groundcovers to attract ground beetles and other predators.

small fruits A general term referring to fruits produced primarily on bushes and cane-bearing plants; strawberries, borne on herbaceous plants, also are included in this category. Small fruits include blueberries, currants, gooseberries, and brambles. Brambles are *Rubus* species plants such as raspberries, blackberries, loganberries, wineberries, and dewberries. Small fruits also sometimes are called soft fruits.

snails Slimy, soft-bodied, mollusks that usually are gray, tan, or black in color and have a hard outer shell. Snails may be up to $1 1/2$ inches long and leave slime trails on leaves. When they feed, they rasp large holes in leaves, stems, and fruit and may completely devour seedlings. Snails are less dependent on moisture than slugs, which are most active at night and in damp places. *See* SLUGS for controls.

snakes While many people are alarmed at the sight of snakes, these are beneficial animals that eat a wide variety of garden pests, including insects and rodents. Garter snakes, ribbon snakes, and grass snakes all eat slugs, snails, and insects, while corn snakes, milk snakes, and black rat snakes eat mice and other rodents.

soaker hose A hose designed to slowly leak or sweat water all along its length. Soaker hoses have several advantages: They direct water directly to the soil so little of it evaporates, operate well under low water pressure, and minimize runoff. Soaker hoses made largely from recycled rubber are long-lasting and durable: They can be installed permanently in a garden and covered up with mulch or moved about the garden as necessary.

soaker hose

soaking, soaking seeds *See* SCARIFICATION

soap sprays *See* INSECTICIDAL SOAP

soboliferous Producing branches, called sobols, that arise below ground from the base of a stem or rhizome. Clump-forming or producing suckers from such below-ground stems. Bottlebrush buckeye (*Aesculus parviflora*) is soboliferous.

sod A rectangular strip of living lawn-grass, complete with a dense layer of matted roots.

sodding The process of planting, or laying, sod. Start by preparing the soil and amending it with organic matter. Have the sod delivered *after* the soil is prepared, because it is important that the sod doesn't dry out or heat up before it is laid. To lay sod, start against a straight edge—the edge of a terrace or a 2-by-4 placed in the area to be sodded. Roll out rectangles of sod, and position them as you would bricks, so they fit together as tightly as possible without overlapping, and stagger the ends of pieces so they do not line up in adjacent rows. Use pegs or U-shaped pieces of wire to hold sod on slopes. Kneel on a board as you work to keep from recompacting prepared soil. Firm the soil in place with a light-

weight roller (available at rental stores), then topdress lightly with soil to fill in any cracks between pieces. Keep the sod evenly moist until it begins growing again.

soft fruits *See* SMALL FRUITS

soft-stemmed cutting *See* SOFTWOOD CUTTING, HERBACEOUS CUTTING

softwood New growth on woody plants such as shrubs that has not yet formed any harder, woody tissue. Also, pines (*Pinus* spp.), spruces (*Picea* spp.), and other trees that are gymnosperms are called softwoods. Softwoods transport water in xylem tissue composed of tracheids, while hardwoods transport it in vessels. *See* HARDWOOD, XYLEM

softwood cutting A stem cutting taken from the new nonwoody growth at the tip of a leafy stem. Because softwood cuttings can lose moisture and wilt rapidly (they have leaves, are actively growing, and continue to transpire water), minimizing moisture loss before new roots form is essential to success in rooting them. For this reason, before you collect them it's best to fill pots with premoistened rooting medium and set up a system for maintaining high humidity around the cuttings. (*See* HUMIDITY) Collect softwood cuttings from early to late summer; many gardeners gather cuttings of tender perennials in late summer for overwintering indoors. Gather them early in the day while the stems are full of moisture. Cuttings from wilted or water-stressed plants are not likely to recover and root well; watering the day before gathering cuttings is a good idea if the weather has been dry. Take cuttings from healthy, vigorous growth that has hardened a bit and has fully expanded leaves. Spindly shoots or very fast-growing ones are not good candidates for taking cuttings. To determine if a shoot is at the best stage for cutting, try bending one of the plant's stems firmly. Growth that snaps off cleanly is ideal, while stems that simply bend over are too soft and ones that crush or break partially are old and may be slow to root. Cut off 2- to 6-

inch shoots with pruning shears, making sure each shoot has at least two leaf nodes. Gather cuttings in a plastic bag to keep them from drying out, and keep them out of direct sun. If you can't plant cuttings immediately, wrap them in a moist paper towel and keep them in the plastic bag in a cool, shady spot. To prepare cuttings for sticking, use shears or a sharp knife to trim each stem to a length of 2 to 4 inches. Try to leave at least two nodes on each cutting, and make the bottom cut just below a node. Remove the leaves from the bottom half of the cutting as well as any flowers or flower buds. While many plants root quickly without special treatment, treating the stem bases with rooting hormone can speed root formation. (*See* ROOTING HORMONE) Some plants root so readily from softwood cuttings—including coleus (*Solenostemon* spp., formerly *Coleus* spp.), impatiens (*Impatiens* spp.), and begonias (*Begonia* spp.)—they can simply be set in a jar of water for rooting. To stick cuttings in pots, use a finger or a pencil to poke a hole in the growing medium, then stick the cutting about halfway in, to just below the lowest leaves. Press the medium down to support the cutting. Stick the remaining cuttings (several will fit in a single pot), spacing them 1 to 4 inches apart. The cuttings shouldn't touch, so if the leaves are large, either space the cuttings farther apart or trim the leaves slightly (by no more than one-half). Use a separate pot for each type of plant, since roots form at different rates. Label each pot with the name of the plant and the date and water thoroughly. Set the cuttings in a warm (65 to 75°F) spot in a humid enclosure you prepared. For best rooting, the growing medium should remain at a constant 70 to 75°F; a heated propagating mat provides ideal conditions. Give cuttings good light, but not direct sun. Indoors, set them under fluorescent lights such as those used to start seeds; outdoors, set them at the base of a north-facing wall or in a spot that's lightly shaded all day. Keep the medium evenly moist, but never wet, and immediately remove any dead leaves or cuttings to prevent disease. Open the plastic or other enclosure for an hour or so about three times a week to allow some air circulation. Most softwood cuttings start rooting in 2 to 5 weeks. When you see new growth, tug lightly on a stem; cuttings that feel firmly anchored are ready for transplanting to individual pots. Gradually remove or open the enclosure over a period of a few days to increase ventilation and to decrease humidity. This will help the new growth harden off and reduce the chance of wilting. Then transplant. *See* TRANSPLANTING

softwood cutting

soil A complex mixture of rock particles, organic matter, air, water, and various organisms that supports plants as well as provides them with essential nutrients and water. Surprisingly, good soil isn't solid: While the exact proportions vary, soil consists of only about 45 percent rock and mineral particles (sand, silt, and clay). About half of the soil volume is pore spaces filled with air and water—25 percent air and 25 percent water. The remaining 5 percent consists of organic matter, which consists of everything from roots and living organisms to decomposing plant and animal residues. Microorganisms abound in healthy soil: Nematodes, protozoa, fungi, bacteria, and actinomycetes all play an important role in the decay cycle. They are constantly breaking down leaves, stems, roots, and other plant debris as well as microorganisms that have died. In the process, they release essential nutrients such as nitrogen, phosphorus, and sulfur, converting them to a form that plants can absorb through their roots. Various acids are released as well and these help dissolve rocks and release the minerals that plants need. Eventually, the organic matter is broken down into humus, a relatively stable material that holds large amounts of water and nutrients in soil. Organic matter and humus also are vitally important in improving and maintaining soil structure because they cause soil particles to lump together to create pore space for air and water, which is essential for plant roots as well as soil organisms. Soil that has ample pore space also is easier to dig, easier for plant roots to penetrate, and easier for water to penetrate deeply. *See* PORE SPACE, SOIL TEXTURE, SOIL STRUCTURE, pH, MACROFAUNA, MICROORGANISMS, ORGANIC MATTER, DOUBLE DIGGING, SINGLE DIGGING, SOIL BUILDING

soil amendment A material added to the soil to improve soil structure. The terms soil amendment and soil conditioner are used interchangeably. They either add organic matter and feed soil organisms or improve growing conditions by adding materials such as lime, gypsum, or coarse sand. Some materials are found both on lists of fertilizers and of amendments. This is especially true of bulky materials like manure, compost, and other plant and animal residues as amendments. While these materials provide nutrients to plants, gardeners value them more for the fact that they also feed the soil and improve its physical structure.

soil animals *See* MACROFAUNA, MICROFAUNA

soil blocks These are "containers" for seedlings that consist of cubes of compressed growing medium without an actual pot. They are great for growing transplants for the vegetable garden or seedlings of hard-to-transplant species, because each plant is self-contained. Since roots are air-pruned as they emerge from the sides, they do not circle around the inside of the container and plants do not become rootbound. Seedling roots easily penetrate the sides to spread into the soil, and plants are transplanted to the garden block and all. To make them, you need a tool called a soil blocker, which is a metal mold with a han-

dle and a spring ejection device. Soil blockers are available in several sizes; a 2-inch model is suitable for most uses. To make blocks, buy a special blocking mix or make your own (*See* BLOCKING MIX for recipes). Place the mix in a large container such as a 5-gallon bucket or wheelbarrow and wet it thoroughly; wet blocking mix has the consistency of mud. Jam the mold into the mix and eject the cubes into a flat that has holes in the bottom. When sowing soil blocks, just press the seeds into the soil surface.

soil blocks

soil building The continuing process of improving soil, accomplished by techniques such as adding organic matter, mulching, not working the soil when it is too wet or too dry, and not walking on prepared soil. Adding organic matter regularly is the best thing gardeners can do to keep soil fertile. Spreading a layer of compost over the garden (or at least around the plants) is an excellent way to add organic matter. Organic mulches such as shredded bark and chopped leaves also add vital organic matter, albeit more slowly than compost does. Mulch also protects the soil from erosion by wind or water and compaction by raindrops, which exert considerable force when they pound down on bare soil. Although most ornamentals don't need to be fertilized regularly throughout the growing season as vegetables do, most benefit from an annual feeding. In spring, feed them with very well-rotted manure or a balanced organic fertilizer. Or use fresh manure in late fall so there is plenty of time for it to rot over winter. Also, avoid working soil when it is either too wet or too dry, because this can destroy soil structure. Before digging or cultivating, squeeze a handful of soil to test its moisture content. If it stays in a lump when you open your hand but breaks apart when you tap it lightly, it's at the ideal stage for digging. If it stays in a claylike lump, wait a few days to let it dry out then test it again. If it is dusty dry, water thoroughly, then wait a day and test again. After digging, stay off prepared soil as much as possible, because walking, sitting, kneeling, or standing on soil compresses soil pores, thus reducing the amount of large pores that hold air, which plant roots need to grow, and impeding soil drainage. Compacting the soil also simply makes it more difficult for roots to penetrate. Walk around garden beds or lay down stepping stones if you are inclined to cut through them. *See* SOIL

soil conditioner *See* SOIL AMENDMENT

soil fertility *See* FERTILITY, SOIL BUILDING

soilless mix, **soilless medium** A medium blended for growing seedlings, rooted cuttings, or plants that does not contain any real soil. *See* POTTING MIX

soil microorganisms These include bacteria, fungi, and actinomycetes as well as nematodes, protozoa, and rotifers, sometimes referred to as microfauna. Like many soil microorganisms, bacteria, the most numerous, can be harmful or beneficial. While some bacteria cause plant diseases, others break down organic matter into humus, both in the soil and in the compost pile. A few perform chemical conversions that are useful to plants: Some bacteria, called nitrogen-fixing bacteria and generally found in nodules in the roots of legumes, can transform atmospheric nitrogen (a gas most plants can't use) into nitrates (a nutrient plants need for growth and can readily absorb). Gardeners commonly innoculate beans, peas, and other legumes with these bacteria at planting time to encourage this process. (*See* INOCULANT) Fungi, whose tangled masses of threadlike filaments (called mycelia) weave

through the soil, also can be harmful or beneficial. While some cause diseases, others decompose plant residues and other debris in soil as well as the compost pile. Mycorrhizal fungi are important beneficial fungi. (*See* MYCORRHIZAE) "Feeding" microorganisms in the soil by regularly adding organic matter in the form of compost, chopped leaves, grass clippings, or other garden debris, is the best way to build healthy populations of beneficial bacteria and fungi in soil. In both soil and compost, microorganisms also require well-aerated conditions. *See* AERATION, SOIL STRUCTURE

soil mix *See* POTTING MIX

soil, potting *See* POTTING MIX

soil sample A representative sample of soil collected for purposes of testing for pH, nutrient content, and other factors. To collect a soil sample, scrape away plants and surface litter from a small area and dig a small hole. Use a stainless steel trowel or large spoon to collect a slice of soil from the hole. Repeat the process at about ten locations throughout the area you want to sample (a single garden bed or throughout your landscape). Mix the samples together in a clean plastic, stainless steel, or glass container. Collect a portion of the mixed sample and submit it to the Cooperative Extension Service or a soil-testing laboratory for testing.

soil solution The water found in the pore spaces of soil and all the minerals and other substances dissolved in it.

soil staples U-shaped pieces of wire designed to hold stems down to layer them or cause them to root along their length. Soil staples also can be used to hold fabric mulch, such as burlap, on a sloping site.

soil structure The manner in which individual soil particles clump together, or aggregate, is referred to as soil structure. The sizes and shapes of these aggregates determines pore space, and thus how water and air move through the soil. Aggregates are formed by various influences: Cycles of freezing and thawing or wetting and drying cause particles to clump together. Humus compounds, which are released from organic residues, stabilize aggregates. Fine, fibrous roots, such as those of grasses, also bind soil into clumps. Ideal garden soil has plenty of aggregates that form a loose, granular or crumblike structure. Granular or crumblike structure is common in soils that are high in organic matter, because as soil organisms decompose organic debris they release sticky materials that help form soil aggregates and hold them together. Not all soils have structure. Compacted clay soils can be so tightly packed they are all but impossible to dig. Soils with a high sand content may not hold together at all. To determine soil structure, take a handful of moist soil and crumble it lightly in your hand. If the sample easily falls apart into rounded crumbs, it has a granular structure. If it takes a little pressure to break it apart into cubes with sharp or somewhat rounded edges, it is probably blocky. (Blocky soil is characteristic of subsoil layers.) Keep in mind that soil structure isn't a static characteristic: You can improve or destroy it. Walking on soil, driving or parking cars on it, digging or disturbing it when it is too wet (*See* SOIL BUILDING for description of test for soil moisture to determine if soil is too wet before digging), or even leaving it exposed to heavy rain can all break down aggregates. When the aggregates break down, the soil gets compacted, meaning that air, water, as well as roots won't be able to penetrate it easily. It is especially easy to break down the aggregates in clay soils: Never till or cultivate clay soil when it is wet. To improve soil structure, promote the formation of aggregates by adding plenty of leaf mold, compost, or other organic matter. (Organic matter improves structure in both clayey and sandy soils; it loosens and aerates clay soils by helping to form aggregates, while it increases moisture-holding capacity of sandy soils by adding humus and promoting aggregate formation as well.) To maintain good structure, avoid walking on prepared soil and protect the soil surface with mulch or ground covers. *See* SOIL, SOIL BUILDING, AGGREGATES, PORE SPACE

soil texture The relative proportions of sand, silt, and clay particles in soil, which determine how coarse or fine it is. (Particles larger than sand, such as rocks, are not considered part of the soil.) A soil never has just one type of particle—all clay or all sand, for example—even though they may seem as if they do. Soils are classified and given names, called textural classes, according to the percentage of each particle they contain. For example, soils that have moderate amounts of all three particles are called loams, which are ideal gardening soils. (*See* TEXTURE TRIANGLE for more on these classifications.) Texture plays a large role in determining how well soil holds water and nutrients. An easy way to get at least a rough idea of your soil's texture is to dig up a small sample of moist soil and rub a bit of it between your thumb and forefinger. Sandy soil feels coarse, grainy, and/or gritty, while silty soil feels slippery like talcum powder. Clay feels sticky. Next, take a handful of the soil, squeeze it, then open your hand. Sandy soil crumbles apart immediately, while soil with more silt and clay will stay in a lump. If the lump falls apart with a light tap, your soil is in the loam range. If you can mold the soil lump or roll out a "worm" with your fingers, it's high in clay. Attempting to change the texture of your soil is not the best way to improve your garden; in fact, it is extremely difficult. For example, to improve a clay soil in a 20 × 50 foot garden bed you would have to add 3 to 5 tons of sand to the top 6 inches of soil. Fortunately that isn't necessary, because improving soil structure will create conditions that will keep most plants happy. *See* SAND, SILT, CLAY, PERCOLATION, SOIL STRUCTURE, SOIL

solarization An organic method for eliminating disease-causing fungi and other pathogens, as well as nematodes, weed seeds, and other organisms by using the heat of the sun. To solarize a garden bed, start in midsummer by removing plant residue and cultivating the soil surface. Rake the soil surface and water, then dig a trench around the outside of the bed. Spread a layer of clear plastic (1 to 4 mils thick) over the bed, press it onto the soil surface, and bury the edges all around with soil.

Leave the plastic in place for 1 to 2 months, during which time heat will build up underneath it and kill organisms in the top few inches of soil. After removing the plastic, do not retill the soil before planting.

solid socket construction A method for attaching the metal head of a tool to its handle by means of a steel cylinder, or collar, that is at the top of the tool head; head and collar are forged all in one piece. The handle is inserted into this collar and fastened with a rivet or pin. This type of construction is a mark of a top-quality shovel, spade, fork, or other digging tool.

solid strap construction A method for attaching the metal head of a tool to its handle by means of two flat, steel straps at the top of the head that are forged in one piece with the head. The handle fits between the two straps, which run partway up its length, and is fastened with rivets or pins. This type of construction is a mark of a top-quality shovel, spade, fork, or other digging tool.

solitary Borne one per stem, rather than in a cluster. Most often used to describe flowers that are carried one per stem.

solitary

sorus, *pl.* **sori** A cluster of sporangia, usually protected by a specialized flap called an indusium, that is most often borne on the underside of a leaf. Since sori are arranged in a consistent manner for each genus, they provide one clue botanists use to identify fern species. Sori can look like rows of green or brown dots on the underside of a leaf, as they do for wood ferns (*Dryopteris* spp.), shield ferns (*Polystichum* spp.), and

polypody ferns (*Polypodium* spp.). They can also be arranged in a continuous line along the edge of the leaflets, as they are in maidenhair ferns (*Adiantum* spp.) or along the veins of the leaflets, as in chain ferns (*Woodwardia* spp.). Sori usually are pale green when they first emerge and turn brown, cinnamon, tan, or nearly black; some ferns have sori that are golden or green when ripe. To collect spores for propagation, examine the back of a fern frond with a small hand lens. Look for shiny, dark sporangia inside the sori; sori that lack them have already shed their spores. (Each frond usually has sori at different levels of maturity.) Pick a frond that seems to have a large percentage of ripe sori (late spring or early summer is usually the best time to collect them), and place the frond in a white envelope. After a few hours or overnight, take out the frond and look for spores inside the envelope; they will look like very fine dust. (If you don't see dust, try another frond.) Discard the frond and store the spores in a paper envelope or a glass vial; avoid plastic as they stick to it. Before sowing, separate the spores from other parts of the sori by tapping the contents of the envelope onto a piece of white paper. Then tap the spores and chaff to the edge of the paper (have another underneath for insurance if you tap too hard): The chaff will fall off first, leaving the spores. *See* FERN SPORES for details on germinating the spores.

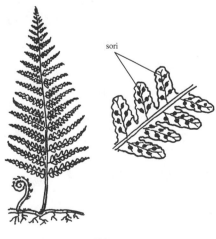

sorus

sour soil A general term for soil that is not in good condition for gardening because it has an acid pH or because it is waterlogged or has poor structure. *See* ACID SOIL

sowing seeds *See* SEED SOWING

spade A digging tool with a nearly flat, rectangular blade that is sharpened all the way across the bottom edge. Most models have a handle rather than a straight shaft (*See* TOOL HANDLES for details on handle types) as well as folded treads at the top of the blade to make it easy to step on the blade to exert force. They have a shorter handle than a shovel: While standard spades range from about 35 to 40 or more inches long, shovels range from about 52 to 60 inches long. A spade is the tool of choice for double or single digging a garden bed, and it also is perfect for tasks such as edging a bed or border, slicing grass off a site to create a new garden, cutting through roots, transplanting, and planting. An Irish spade has a longer, narrower blade than a conventional spade and a longer shaft, usually without a handle. A border spade, sometimes called a ladies' spade, is lighter in weight than a standard spade and has a somewhat smaller blade. A nursery spade is a heavy-duty spade designed to dig up trees and shrubs that are to be balled-and-burlapped, and to cut roots and pry plants out of the soil as necessary.

spade

spadiceous Bearing a spadix. Spadixlike

spading fork *See* FORK

spadix This is a type of spike with a thickened central stem, or axis, covered with small, densely packed flowers. Members of the arum family, Araceae, including Jack-in-the-pulpit (*Arisaema triphyllum*), calla lilies (*Zantedeschia* spp.), and anthuriums (*Anthurium* spp.), which are popular tropical cut flowers, bear their flowers on a spadix. A spadix is commonly surrounded by a leaf- or petal-like bract called a spathe. *See* SPATHE

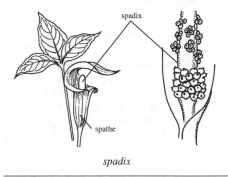

spadix

spathe

spadix

spathaceous Bearing a spathe. Spathelike

spathe A large bract borne directly below a spadix or other type of inflorescence and often enclosing or surrounding it. On a Jack-in-the-pulpit (*Arisaema triphyllum*), the "pulpit," which wraps around the base of the Jack, or spadix, and forms a lip over the top of it, is a spathe. In calla lilies (*Zantedeschia* spp.), the spathe looks like a petal and is generally cup- or trumpet-shaped. Ears of corn, which are the ripened female flowers, also are covered by spathes, commonly called husks.

spathulate, spatulate Spatula- or spoon-shaped. An oblong leaf, which is from two to four times longer than it is wide, that is rounded at the tip and narrows at the base.

spathulate leaf

spear-shaped *See* HASTATE

species A group of plants with similar characteristics within a genus. A species contains closely related individuals that are morphologically similar. A species may be further divided into subspecies, varieties, or forms and also may contain cultivars. The species name, or specific epithet, is a basic unit of a plant name. The botanical name of a species consists of the genus name and a specific epithet. Both are set in italics or underlined in type. Previously, the specific epithet was capitalized if it had been derived from a proper name, but today it always begins with a lowercase letter. *See* BINOMIAL NOMENCLATURE

specific epithet Species name. *See* EPITHET, SPECIES

specimen plant An ornamental plant that is set apart from other plantings in a prominent spot so that it can be seen from several angles and shown to best advantage. Trees, shrubs, large ornamental grasses, and large herbaceous perennials are all used as specimen plants.

sperm A male gamete. *See* GAMETE, FERTILIZATION

spermatophyte A plant that reproduces by seeds. This term is based on Spermatophyta, one of the four divisions of the plant kingdom used by 19th-century botanists. Most commonly cultivated plants (with the exception of ferns) are spermatophytes. In addition to reproducing by seeds, all have roots, stems, leaves, and vascular tissue. *See also* GYMNOSPERM, ANGIOSPERM.

-spermous A suffix referring to seeds, usually combined with a prefix indicating a particular characteristic. Pterospermous means winged seeds, for example.

sphagnum moss Not to be confused with sphagnum peat, more properly called peat moss, sphagnum moss consists of the dried remains of living plants—bog-dwelling mosses in the genus *Sphagnum*. (Peat moss/ sphagnum peat is the decomposed remains of dead plants.) Sphagnum moss is light tan in color, relatively sterile, and boasts extremely high water-holding capacity; it can hold from 10 to 20 times its weight in water. It contains very few nutrients and has a pH of about 3.5. Sphagnum moss is used to line baskets and can be incorporated in growing mixes for epiphytic plants such as staghorn ferns (*Platycerium* spp.). Milled sphagnum is finely ground sphagnum moss and has the same characteristics. It is sometimes used to cover seeds because of its moisture-holding capacity as well as its acid pH, which discourages fungal diseases such as damping off.

sphagnum peat This is another name for peat moss, which consists of decomposed sphagnum moss and/or other species of moss found in bogs. It is not the same as sphagnum moss, which is undecomposed sphagnum. *See* SPHAGNUM MOSS

spherical Globose. Round.

spicate Spikelike; a flower cluster, or inflorescence, that resembles a spike but may or may not be a true spike.

spice An aromatic and usually pungently flavored plant or plant part used to flavor food. There is no clear distinction between which plants are considered herbs and spices, but in general, the term spice is used to refer to plants that come from the tropics. Herbs usually have subtle flavor and are green in color, while spices are pungent and come in shades of brown, black, or red. Finally, plants grown for their fresh or dried leaves usually are called herbs, while those grown for seeds, roots, bark, fruits, or flowers are normally called spices.

spiciform Spikelike. A flower cluster, or inflorescence, that resembles a spike but does not necessarily have the structure of a true spike.

spiculate Covered with short, pointed, needlelike projections.

spider mites *See* MITES

spiders Beneficial, eight-legged animals that are arachnids, not insects. Spiders catch and consume a wide variety of insect pests.

spider

spike A type of flower cluster, or inflorescence, with a single stem and flowers that are attached directly to the stem without a stalk (sessile) or nearly so (subsessile). The flowers open from the bottom to the top of a spike, and spikes are indeterminate, meaning the main stem continues to elongate after the first flowers open. Spikes are usually unbranched. Gladiolus (*Gladiolus* spp.) bear their flowers in long spikes, and lavenders (*Lavandula* spp.) produce short, dense spikes. Wheat (*Triticum aestivum*) also bears spikes. The term spike also commonly is used for plants with similar-looking inflorescences: Blazing star (*Liatris spicata*) is one example. It produces spikelike blooms that consist of small buttonlike flowerheads along a central stem. In another departure from true spikes, blazing stars open from the top down. A spadix—the "Jack" in a Jack-in-the-pulpit (*Arisaema triphyllum*) flower—is a type of spike. *See* SPADIX

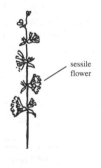

sessile flower

spike

spikelet A small or secondary spike consisting of reduced (small) flowers and bracts (small leaves) along an unbranched stem, called a rachilla. Spikelets are the basic unit of the flower clusters of members of the grass family (Poaceae), including corn (*Zea mays*) and popular ornamental grasses such as fountain grass (*Pennisetum* spp.) and pampas grass (*Cortaderia* spp.), as well as members of the sedge family (Cyperaceae), including sedges (*Carex* spp.). *See* GLUME for a diagram of a grass spikelet and more information on its parts.

spill stone A flat stone set at the top of a waterfall over which water passes from one level of a water garden to another.

spindle-shaped Widest at the middle and tapered at both ends.

spine A stiff, thin structure with a sharp point on a leaf, stem, or other organ. A spine actually is a modified leaf that has a sharp, rigid leaf stem, midrib, vein, or stipule. (A stipule is a leaflike appendage at the base of the leaf stem, or petiole.) Barberries (*Berberis* spp.) and some hollies (*Ilex* spp.) bear true spines. Spines, thorns, and prickles are technically different, but the term spine also is used to refer to any sharp, spinelike structure. *See also* THORN, PRICKLE

spinose Spiny, or bearing spines. English holly leaves (*Ilex aquifolium*) are spinose.

spinose leaf

spinule A small spine.

spinulose Bearing small spines, called spinules.

spiny Bearing spines.

spiral A shape used in flower arranging in which the flowers, leaves, and other plant materials are positioned to form a gentle spiral that runs over the top of the container and usually extends to its base.

spiral arrangement

spit A digging term used to designate the approximate depth of a spade, about 10 to 12 inches.

splice graft A graft that is similar to a whip-and-tongue graft used for uniting relatively small stocks and scions (from $^1/_4$ to $^1/_2$ inch in diameter is best). Make the first cut on the stock and the scion as you would for a whip-and-tongue graft, but omit the second cut on each piece that creates the interlocking tongues. Wrap and wax as you would a whip-and-tongue graft. *See* WHIP-AND-TONGUE GRAFT, GRAFTING

spliced approach graft *See* APPROACH GRAFTING

spliced side graft *See* SIDE-VENEER GRAFT

split *See* CLEFT, DIVIDED, PARTED

spoon A flower, usually a chrysanthemum, that is semidouble and has petals or ray florets that have broad, spoon-shaped tips. Also, spoon-shaped. *See* SPATULATE

sporadic Dispersed widely or scattered, rather than occurring in a clearly defined, continuous range. Occurring or appearing occasionally. This term is used to describe a species that is found growing on scattered sites rather than in a continuous range, or to specify that some function, such as flowering, only occurs at irregular intervals.

sporangiophore A stalk that bears sporangia.

sporangium, *pl.* **sporangia** A spore-producing case or body. Cryptograms—ferns, mosses, and fungi—all bear sporangia and reproduce by spores rather than seeds. Sporangia, sometimes called spore cases, usually are arranged in clusters, called sori, but some ancient ferns do not bear sporangia arranged in sori. Flowering ferns (*Osmunda* spp.) bear sporangia arranged in large patches, while climbing ferns (*Lygodium* spp.) bear them singly. In all but the most primitive ferns, each sporangium produces 64 spores. *See also* SORUS, SPORE, FERN LIFECYCLE

spore The basic unit of reproduction consisting of a single cell that is capable of developing into a new plant, a gametophyte. This term is most often used to refer to ferns and fern allies such as mosses. Spores are borne in sporangia (*See* SPORANGIUM), which are usually clustered in sori. They are released at maturity and can either drop to the ground or be blown by the wind for up to a mile or more. A single fern can produce several million spores each year. *See* SORUS for details on collecting spores; FERN LIFECYCLE and FERN SPORES for germination information.

spore case *See* SPORANGIA

sporeling A small fern that grows from a prothallus. *See* FERN LIFECYCLE

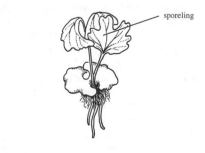

sporeling

sporiferous Spore bearing.

sporocarp A body that produces spores. Or, a nutlike sac or capsule that contains sporangia. Ferns that produce two kinds of spores (are heterosporus) bear sporocarps.

sporophyll A leaf that bears sporangia.

sporophyte The spore-bearing generation in the lifecycle of a plant, as opposed to the gametophyte generation. In both flowering plants (angiosperms) and ferns, this is the leafy, vegetative plant itself. *See also* GAMETOPHYTE

sport A plant, plant part, or other organism that exhibits a marked change from the parent stock. A mutation. *See* MUTATION, BUD SPORT

spotted A variegation pattern in which color is distributed in small round spots or dots. *See also* DOTTED

sprawling Spreading out and down. Sprawling plants curve or bend toward the ground or can support themselves on neighboring plants.

spray A slender shoot or branch with foliage, flowers, and/or fruit attached.

spreading A plant habit in which the branches extend out nearly horizontally and the plant is nearly prostrate.

sprigging Planting individual plants, runners, cuttings, or stolons. When this process is used to plant a lawn, the sprigs are created by shredding pieces of sod. Sprigging is used to plant warm-season grasses such as St. Augustine, Bermudagrass, centipede grass, and zoysiagrass. Sprigging also is an erosion-control technique whereby cuttings of fast-growing, vigorous plants are stuck directly in the ground in winter or early spring. From 8- to 10-inch-long cuttings of 1- to 2-year-old wood are arranged in a grid pattern covering a slope.

spring cutting A cutting taken of partially ripened growth just at the end of the period of most active growth. *See* SEMI-RIPE CUTTING

spring ephemeral *See* EPHEMERAL

spring frost date *See* FROST DATES

sprout A new shoot or a newly germinated seedling.

spumose Foamy, frothy.

spur A slender, hollow, or sacklike projection from a flower that is formed by a petal or a sepal. It usually points backward and has a gland that secretes nectar. Columbine (*Aquilegia* spp.), delphinium (*Delphinium* spp.), and violet (*Viola* spp.) flowers all have spurs. Spur also refers to short branches or branchlets that are produced on some trees, especially fruit trees such as apples. These have very closely spaced nodes (the point on the branch where leaves are attached) and bear whorls of leaves, clusters of flowers, and fruit. When picking apples or other fruit borne on spurs, it is important to avoid damaging (or pulling off) the spurs in the process, because they bear fruit for years.

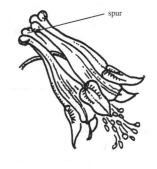

spur

spur pruning Pruning lateral branches to encourage the formation of flower buds near the bases of the shoots, primarily on apples or other fruit trees that bear fruit on spurs. This encourages flowers, and thus fruit, to develop close to the main branches of the tree. Spur pruning also is a pruning and training system specifically for grapes designed to keep the plants in check so that they produce large clusters of fruit. First train the vine to establish a trunk against a stake the same way you would for cane pruning and prune it the same way until the third winter. (*See* CANE PRUN-ING) The third winter, shorten all of the shoots on the two cordons that are stretched along the wires back to two buds; these become the spurs, which will produce the fruit. Leave a two-bud spur every 4 to 5 inches along the cordons. The fourth winter and every year thereafter, select a new pencil-size shoot that arises near the base of each spur and cut it back to two buds to make new spurs for that year's fruit.

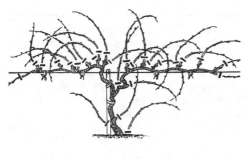

spur pruning

spurred Producing or having spurs. This term is commonly used to describe a flower that has one or more spurs. Columbines (*Aquilegia* spp.) have spurred petals. *See* SPUR

squama, *pl.* **squamae** A scale.

squamella, *pl.* **squamellae** A small scale.

squamose, **squamate** Scaly. Covered with scales.

squamulose Covered with very small scales.

squarrose Rough-textured because of bracts (modified scalelike leaves) that have outward-curving (recurved) tips. This term is also used to designate plant parts that stick out at right angles to a common axis.

stachy-, -stachys, -stachyous A prefix or suffixes relating to a spike. Polystachyous means bearing many spikes, for example.

stakes and string A traditional staking method for supporting clump-forming plants such as peonies. Start with stakes (wooden ones or metal covered with green plastic are fine) that are about 1 foot taller than the plants will be at maturity and pound four of them into the ground around the clump. Then wind string around the outside of the stakes and through the center of the clump to form a spiderweb-type pattern. Add another tier of string, if necessary, as the plant grows. As the plant's stems grow up through the string, the string that crosses the center will provide even support; if you'd simply supported the clump around the perimeter, all the stems would tend to flop to one side or the other, giving a lopsided look. For best results, install stakes and string early in the season when the plants are only 6 to 8 inches tall.

staking This is a general term for a variety of plant support techniques, but also refers specifically to tying plants to poles or other supports to keep them upright. For plants with tall stems, such as delphiniums and dahlias, staking each stem individually with a bamboo stake or wooden pole often is the best approach. Metal stakes covered with green plastic work well, too. Use wooden poles for tall, heavy ornamentals such as dahlias as well as for tomatoes. Stakes need to be at least a foot longer than the height of the plants at maturity so they can be pushed or driven solidly into the ground. Install stakes before flower stalks are much more than a foot high, taking care not to drive them into the crowns of the plants. Tie stems to stakes with yarn, old shoelaces, strips of nylon stockings, or soft string. Be careful not to tie them too tightly, or you'll constrict the stems. Figure-eight ties—around the stake, crossing over in the center, and around the stem—work best. Several commercial staking systems are available, including hoops that fit over clumps of plants, individual supports for flower stems, and stakes that link together to form circles or triangles around clumps or simply lines in beds that hold plants up and back from pathways or shorter plants toward the front.

See also STAKES AND STRING, PEA STAKES, CAGING, TRELLISING, STRINGING

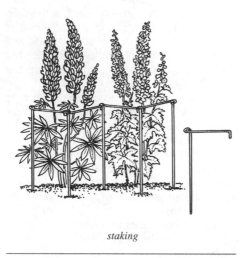

staking

stalham hoe *See* HOE

stalk A general term for the main, supporting stem of an organ. A petiole also is called a leaf stalk, and a peduncle is commonly referred to as a flower stalk, for example.

stamen The male reproductive organ of a flower, consisting of an anther and a filament.

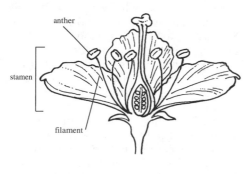

staminate flower A male flower, which has stamens (male reproductive organs) but no pistil or pistils (female reproductive organs).

staminode A stamenlike structure that is sterile and may or may not be petal-like. Some peonies bear clusters of curled, ornamental staminodes at the center of the blooms. Plants in the ginger family (Zin-giberaceae) bear flowers with showy staminodes that form the petal-like lip of the flowers.

stamped A construction technique used to make medium- and low-quality tools in which a machine cuts a piece from a flat sheet of metal, then bends it into the shape of a shovel or other implement. Stamped tools are cheaper and lighter in weight than higher-quality forged ones, but they also bend much more easily because the metal is of uniform thickness.

standard The large, uppermost petal in a papilionaceous flower such as a sweet pea (*Lathyrus odoratus*). The word standard also refers to one of the inner petals of an iris (*Iris* spp.) or other related plant, which normally point up or out. A tree or shrub grown with a single, bare stem and trained to produce a round, dense head on top also is called a standard. To train a standard, start with a single-stemmed plant. Plants suitable for training as standards include scented geraniums (*Geranium* spp.), sweet bay (*Laurus nobilis*), rosemary (*Rosmarinus officinalis*), and common myrtle (*Myrtus communis*). Roses sold as standards are grafted plants consisting of a cultivated rose grafted to the top of a stem trained as described here. To train a standard, stake the main stem and gradually remove side branches that appear, starting at the base of the plant. Once the main stem has reached the desired height, pinch out the tip to encourage branching. Continue pinching out the tips of branches that appear at the top of the plant to encourage a full, rounded ball of foliage at the top. Also continue removing branches that appear on the bottom part of the trunk.

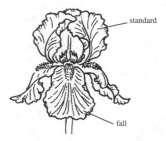

standard

steel-strapped head *See* SOLID STRAP CONSTRUCTION

stele The central or main vascular tissue in stems and roots of vasular plants.

stellate Star-shaped. Most often used to describe hairs that have branches that radiate out in a star-shaped pattern. Staghorn ferns (*Platycerium* spp.) and felt ferns (*Pyrrosa* spp.) have stellate hairs on the undersides of the leaves, which are visible with a hand lens. Several *Hibiscus* species, including rose mallow (*H. moscheutos*), have shoots covered with stellate hairs, or pubescence, as does night-scented stock (*Matthiola incana*).

stem The main axis of a plant that has nodes and internodes and bears and supports its organs, such as leaves, flowers, and fruit. A typical stem consists of an epidermis, cortex, pith, and vascular bundles that contain phloem and xylem. Vascular cambium separates the phloem and xylem as well as the cortex and pith.

stem cutting A general term that refers to the various types of cuttings taken from stems. *See* CUTTING, SEMI-RIPE CUTTING, SOFTWOOD CUTTING, HARDWOOD CUTTING

-stemonous A suffix referring to stamens, usually combined with a prefix indicating a number. Octostemonous means bearing eight stamens, for example.

stem tip cutting A general term for any cutting that is taken from the tip of a shoot or stem.

stem tuber Also called tuberous stems, the "tubers" of tuberous begonias (*Begonia* × Tuberhybrida hybrids) are actually formed from swollen stem tissue. They are perennial, and increase in size each year. Unlike true tubers, they have an upright orientation in the soil: Leaf and flower buds arise from the top; roots from the sides or bottom. Poppy anemone (*Anemone coronaria*) and cyclamen (*Cyclamen* spp.) also grow from stem tubers. For propagation, stem tubers can be cut into individual pieces that each have at least two or more buds, or "eyes." Large pieces work best; only attempt this with good-size tubers. Let the pieces dry for a day or so and dust the cuts with sulfur or another fungicide. *See also* TUBER

steno- A prefix meaning narrow. Stenopetalous means bearing narrow petals, and stenophyllous means bearing narrow leaves, for example.

stepover A cordon that is trained with a horizontal trunk that is quite low to the ground, generally low enough to be stepped over.

stereomorphic Actinomorphic. A flower that is symmetrical, with its parts radiating from the center, so that a plane or line passed anywhere through the center would yield mirror images.

sterile Not fertile. A stamen that does not bear pollen and a flower that does not bear seeds are both sterile. A sterile shoot, sometimes called vegetative, bears leaves but no reproductive parts. A sterile plant does not produce functional reproductive parts and/or does not produce fruit.

sterile frond A frond that does not produce sporangia, and thus does not produce spores. Also called a vegetative frond. Some ferns, including staghorn ferns (*Platycerium* spp.) and flowering ferns (*Osmunda* spp.), bear separate sterile and fertile fronds on the same plant.

sterilizing A general term for the process of treating pots or soil to remove unwanted disease-causing organisms as well as pests. For information on removing pathogens and other unwanted organisms from potting soil, *See* PASTEURIZATION; from garden soil, SOLARIZATION; and from containers, CLEANING CONTAINERS

-stichous A suffix referring to arrangement in a row or line, usually combined with a prefix indicating a number. Octostichous means arranged in eight rows, for example.

stick cuttings To plant or place stem, root, or other types of cuttings in a rooting media to begin the rooting process.

sticktight A plant that has barbed or clinging seeds or fruits. This term also is used to refer to the clinging seeds or fruits themselves.

stigma The surface where the flower receives pollen. The stigma is generally located at the top of the pistil, which is the female reproductive organ of a flower.

stigmatic Attached to or belonging to the stigma.

stilt root Adventitious roots borne by woody plants that have a supporting function. They are most often found on plants growing in shallow soils in warm climates or on sites that are frequently flooded. Mangroves (*Rhizophora* spp. and *Conocarpus* spp.) as well as screw pines (*Pandanus* spp.) bear stilt roots. *See also* BUTTRESS ROOTS

stinging hairs Stinging nettle (*Urtica dioica*) bears an abundance of stinging hairs.

stipe The stalk supporting a single, small organ, especially the short stalk that attaches an ovary to the receptacle of a flower. A stipe is also the leaf stalk of a fern or palm frond.

stipe bundle The vascular bundles in the leaf stalk, or stipe, of a fern.

stipel A small stipulelike structure borne at the base of a leaflet.

stipellate Bearing stipels.

stipulate, **stipular** Bearing or having stipules. Relating to stipules.

stipule Small, leaflike appendages at the base of a petiole, or leaf stalk. Stipules are generally borne in pairs and are shed soon after the leaf opens.

stirrup hoe *See* HOE

stock Rootstock. The plant that provides a root system for a grafted or budded plant. Plants grown specifically to produce root systems for grafting. Also, plants grown for a particular attribute, such as virus-free or certified stock. *See* CERTIFIED SEED

stock plant A plant that is specifically grown and managed to provide cuttings, divisions, seeds, or other plant material for propagation.

stolon A horizontal or arching, usually enlongated, stem that exends along the ground and roots at the tip, forming a small plantlet. Stolons are usually, but not always, above ground. Some sources (and many gardeners) use the terms stolon and runner interchangeably; technically, runners root and form plantlets at the nodes along their length, while stolons root only at the tip. Strawberries (*Fragaria* spp.) bear stolons, as does strawberry geranium (*Saxifraga stolonifera*, formerly *S. sarmentosa*). Bugleweed (*Ajuga reptans*) spreads quickly by both rhizomes and stolons. To propagate a stoloniferous plant, simply sever the individual plantlets and either pot them up or move them to a new spot in the garden.

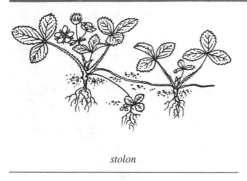

stolon

stoloniferous Bearing or spreading by stolons.

stoma, *pl.* **stomata, stomate** A pore or opening that allows for the exchange of gases in the outermost layer of cells (the epidermis) of a leaf or stem. Stomata release water and take in carbon dioxide, for example.

stone cell *See* SCLERENCHYMA

stone fruit A drupe. This term is commonly used to refer to fruit crops such as peaches, nectarines, apricots, and almonds that bear drupes, which are fleshy fruits that do not open at maturity and bear a single seed inside a stony casing, called an endocarp. The seed-bearing endocarp is surrounded by a fleshy or fibrous outer layer.

stool The base of a plant that gives rise to new stems each year. Several stems that arise from the same root.

stooling, **stool layering** *See* MOUND LAYERING

storing seed Clean, dry seed retains viability best when stored in an airtight container such as a jar that has been placed in a cold (32 to 40°F) location. Seeds also can be frozen for storage. To keep the moisture level as low as possible, place a tablespoon of dry milk in the middle of a facial tissue and fold it up to make a packet. Place one packet in each jar. Be sure to label stored seeds with the plant name and date collected. Even with ideal storage conditions, seed viability varies.

Some species germinate readily after years of storage; others last only a year or less. Test viability before depending on stored seeds for a crop. *See* GERMINATION TESTING

storm-proofing A general term for a variety of techniques an arborist can use to remove weak growth and thin out a tree's branches to reduce wind resistance, as well as to reduce the weight and shape of the crown so that if the tree falls, it will fall away from your house or other buildings. Storm-proofing combines techniques such as crown thinning and reduction as well as cabling and bracing, in order to make a tree safer in a windstorm. For valuable specimens or trees on high spots, arborists also can install cables that ground a tree and minimize lightning damage. *See* CROWN REDUCTION, CROWN THINNING

stramineous Strawlike in texture, color, or shape.

strap-shaped *See* LORATE, LIGULATE

stratification Exposing seeds to cool-moist and/or warm-moist storage to overcome seed-dormancy factors or to aid germination. Some seeds germinate faster if stratified, but do not absolutely require it. Seeds requiring cool-moist stratification are most common, and need to be exposed to temperatures of 32 to 45°F for a specified period, which varies from species to species—from 1 to 3 months is most common. Some perennial and many woody plant seeds also require a period of warm-moist storage—at temperatures between 68 and 86°F—followed by cool-moist stratification. (In this case, the seed coat decomposes during the period of warm temperature storage.) An easy way to stratify seeds is to sow them in pots and either place the pots in the refrigerator for the recommended period or set them outside over winter. (*See* SEED SOWING) Another option is to mix seeds with moistened vermiculite or peat moss, place the mix in a plastic bag, add a label with the plant name and date stratification started, and set the bag in the refrigerator. After the recommended period, either pick out the seeds for sowing or

sow the entire mix. Seeds also can be stratified on moist paper towels. Simply place
the seeds on the towel and fold, then place
it in a loosely closed plastic bag set in the
refrigerator. Either use a separate bag for
each type of seed and enclose a label with
the name of the plant and the date "sown"
or place several towels in a single bag and
fold a label into each towel so you don't
lose track of which plant is where. With
any of these methods, a note on the label or
on a calendar as to when the stratification
period is up is helpful. At the end of the
recommended period, sow the seeds. Seeds
may germinate while still in the refrigerator; if they do, pot them up and give them
light, humidity, and moisture as you would
any seedlings. All of these methods also
can be used to satisfy dormancy requirements of seeds that need warm-moist
followed by cool-moist conditions; simply
pot up or bag the seeds and expose them to
warm conditions for the specified period,
then move them to the refrigerator. Seeds
that need a period of warm-moist stratification followed by cool-moist also can be
sown in summer in pots set outdoors and
left there over winter; germination will
occur the following spring.

strawberry jar Containers, usually ceramic or terra-cotta, with six to nine openings
in their sides as well as in the top. As the
name suggests, they were designed for
growing strawberries, but also are ideal for
growing hen and chickens (*Sempervivum*
spp.), small sedums (*Sedum* spp.), and other
plants that thrive in well-drained soil.

streptocarpous Having twisted fruits.

striate Marked with fine grooves or lines
that usually are parallel.

strict Straight and very upright. Not
spreading.

striga A bristle that is pressed against or
borne flat on another plant part.

strigose Covered with stiff, sharp hairs
that lie flat against the surface. Most often
used to describe leaf surfaces.

strike, striking To cause a cutting to form
roots or to propagate a plant by taking and
rooting cuttings. A struck cutting is one
that has formed roots.

stringing A technique for supporting vines
by suspending strings over a framework
and training the vines onto the strings.
Stringing is a useful technique for the
vegetable garden, but also can be used
ornamentally: Annual vines can be trained
to strings that are suspended from a frame
hung out a window and attached to stakes
in the ground. Use strings to train vines up
to deck railings or other structures. At the
end of the season, cut the vines down,
strings and all, and add them to the compost pile.

striped A variegation pattern in which a
background color is crossed by stripes of
another color that run lengthwise on the
leaf or other surface. *See also* BANDED

strobiloid, strobilaceous, strobiliform
Conelike (strobilus) or pertaining to a cone.

strobilus, strobile A cone or conelike
fruit, with seeds borne along a common
stalk or axis, interspersed with overlapping scales. The cones of conifers such as
pines (*Pinus* spp.) and spruces (*Picea*
spp.) are strobiles. Hops (*Humulus lupu-
lus*) also bear their seeds in a conelike
arrangement.

strobilus

strombus Sprially coiled. This term is primarily used to describe legumes, which are
a type of dry fruit that opens at maturity
along two lines. Alfalfa (*Medicago sativa*)
and other medics (*Medicago* spp.) bear
strombus-shaped legumes.

structure *See* BONES

strumose *See* BULLATE

stub graft A type of side graft used to unite a scion with a branch (the stock) that is too thick for a whip-and-tongue graft yet too thin for methods such as cleft grafting. Use pencil-thick scions that have two or three buds and are about 3 inches long; 1-inch-thick stock is best. Use a chisel or heavy, sharp knife to make a cut into the stock at a 20- to 30-degree angle. Cut about 1 inch deep (one-third to one-half of the way into the stock). To prepare the scion, make smooth, gently tapering, 1-inch-long cuts on the bottom to create a wedge. Gently bend the stock (branch) back to open the cut, then insert the scion at an angle to line up the cambium layers. When the branch bends back into place it should hold the scion in place, although you can secure it with one or two very small wire nails. Wrap with nurseryman's adhesive tape. Once the graft union has formed, very carefully clip off the top of the stock. *See* SIDE GRAFT, GRAFTING

style The long, narrow stalk that joins the stigma and ovary of a pistil, which is the female reproductive organ of a flower. A flower with a sessile stigma, meaning it is attached directly to the ovary, lacks a style. The silk on the tip of an ear of corn is composed of the styles of the individual flowers on the ear.

suaveolent Sweetly fragrant.

sub- A prefix that means somewhat, nearly, or slightly. Thus the word subglobose means nearly globose, or nearly spherical. Subcordate means nearly cordate. Subopposite means nearly opposite, but with one leaf slightly above or below the other. The prefix sub- also is used in plant taxonomy to designate a subordinate division of a higher taxa. A subclass is a subdivision of a class used to further categorize or organize the orders in that class. Some experts use subfamilies to organize the genera in very large families. The names of subfamilies end with the suffix -oideae.

suber Cork.

suberose Corky.

subgenus A rank used to organize species in especially large genera such as *Rhododendron* and *Primula*. Typically, species in these large genera are organized by similar characteristics into subgenera, which are then further divided into sections. Sections are sometimes further divided into subsections or series to clarify their relationships.

sublateral vein A small leaf vein that branches off a lateral vein. Lateral, or secondary, veins branch off the main vein, or midrib, of the leaf. Also called tertiary veins.

submerged plants Plants with leaves that are partially or completely submerged in the water. Most root at the bottom of a pond or water garden. They are grown in water gardens to add oxygen to the water during the daytime (they release carbon dioxide at night). Submerged plants also help shade the water and give baby fish places to hide. They absorb nutrients such as fish waste through both their roots and leaves, thus helping to keep the water clean. Submerged plants include eelgrass (*Vallisneria spiralis*), anacharis (*Egeria densa*), and water milfoil (*Myriophyllum* spp.).

subsessile Somewhat or nearly sessile, or stalkless.

subshrub A small, low-growing, woody-stemmed plant. Or a plant that has a persistent woody base and soft-stems. Many thymes (*Thymus* spp.) are subshrubs, for example, as is perennial candytuft (*Iberis sempervirens*). Also called a suffrutex.

subshrubby Resembling a subshrub. This is a general term applied to shrublike plants that have somewhat woody bases and usually have longer or larger herbaceous shoots than subshrubs, which tend to be low-growing. Coleus (*Solenostemon scutellarioides*, formerly *Coleus* spp.) are subshrubby in habit, especially by the end of the growing season when they have developed woody growth at the base of the plants.

subsoil A general term for the layers of soil below the topsoil. Subsoil usually has a low organic matter content and has poor structure and fertility. Because of these characteristics, when double digging or otherwise cultivating a bed, it is best not to mix subsoil with topsoil.

subspecies A taxonomic category that distinguishes a group of naturally occurring plants sharing characteristics that set them apart from other individuals in the species. A subspecies is the highest division of a species, higher than a botanical variety, and subspecies names are set in italics, preceded by the abbreviation "ssp." or "subsp." For example, Spanish lavender (*Lavandula stoechas* subsp. *pedunculata*) is a subspecies of French lavender (*Lavandula stoechas*).

subtend Borne beneath but close to another organ. This term is commonly used to describe bracts borne beneath flowers, especially when the bract is showy or persistant.

subterranean Below the soil surface.

subulate Awl-shaped. Subulate leaves, which are generally small and scalelike, have a narrow base and taper to a very sharp point.

subulate leaf

succession planting A vegetable gardening technique used to make optimum use of the garden space available by replacing a crop as soon as it is harvested with another crop. This technique works be-

cause many crops need only part of the season to mature. An early season cool-weather crop like spinach or lettuce can be followed in the same spot by a summer crop of peppers and another quick cool-season crop in fall. Another succession planting technique that can be used with fast-growing, cool-weather annuals such as China asters (*Callistephus chinensis*) and love-in-a-mist (*Nigella damascena*) is to sow seed at 2-week intervals where the plants are to grow. Or start an early crop indoors and follow it with outdoor sowings.

succulent Firm and generally thick, but soft and jucy. This term commonly is used to refer to a wide variety of plants that have thick, succulent, fleshy leaves or stems that are filled with sap. Most succulents are found in arid regions, and store moisture in their fleshy leaves to combat drought. There are succulent plants in a wide range of families, and they come in a fascinating array of shapes, sizes, and colors. Collectors are especially attracted to succulents that exhibit unique, sometimes grotesque, forms. The most common succulents include aloes (*Aloe* spp.), jade plants (*Crassula* spp.), succulent-leaved spurges (*Euphorbia* spp. native to Africa), sedums (*Sedum* spp.), and hen and chickens (*Sempervivum* spp.). In general, succulents are easy to grow. Most require full sun and well-drained, gritty soil.

succulents, potting mix for See POTTING MIX

sucker A shoot that arises from the roots of a plant or from the crown or an underground stem. Suckers can be used for propagation: Gently dig down to their base to check for roots, and if they are present, sever the connection to the parent plant and pot up or move the sucker. On grafted plants, suckers can arise from the rootstock, below the graft union, in which case they are called root suckers and should be removed. (*See* ROOT SUCKER) Sucker also is a general term for a fast-growing, upright shoot. The shoots that emerge from the leaf axils of tomatoes are called suckers.

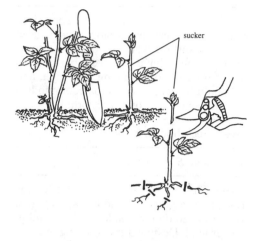

sucker

suckering Producing suckers. This term is especially used to refer to plants that are producing excessive numbers of suckers.

suffrutex *See* SUBSHRUB

suffruticose, suffrutescent Shrubby or somewhat woody. Having the habit of a subshrub, with a persistent woody base and soft stems.

suffused Washed or tinged, generally with a color.

sulcate, -sulcate Marked with deep groves or furrows that run lengthwise along the axis of an organ. Also used as a suffix, in which case it is usually linked to a prefix indicating number. Trisulcate means having three furrows or grooves.

sulfur A macronutrient required by plants that also is used to reduce the pH of alkaline soils. (*See* ALKALINE SOIL) Sulfur also is an organic fungicide and insecticide that can be used as a spray or dust. As an insecticide, it kills mites, but also beneficial insects, soil organisms, and fish. It also controls fungal diseases such as blackspot, powdery mildew, and various rots. Dust sulfur on the roots of flowers that are being stored over winter such as dahlias.

Do not apply to plants within a month of using a horticultural oil spray, and do not spray it on plants when temperatures exceed 80°F.

summer annual An annual that germinates in spring and dies in fall. Usually called a warm-weather annual. *See* WARM-WEATHER ANNUAL

summer bulbs A general term for summer-blooming plants that grow from bulbs, corms, fleshy rhizomes, and other similar structures that bloom from summer to early fall. This includes some plants that can be grown as hardy plants as well as annuals or tender perennials. (For information on keeping the the bulbous structures from year to year, *see* OVERWINTERING.) Summer bulbs include achimenes (*Achimenes* spp.), lilies-of-the-Nile (*Agapanthus* spp.), Peruvian lilies (*Alstroemeria* spp.), tuberous begonias (*Begonia* × Tuberhybrida hybrids), caladiums (*Caladium*, spp.), cannas (*Canna* spp.), taro (*Colocasia* spp.), dahlias (*Dahlia* spp.), summer hyacinths (*Galtonia* spp.), glads (*Gladiolus* spp.), spider lilies (*Hymenocallis* spp.), magic lilies (*Lycoris* spp.), tuberoses (*Polianthes* spp.), callas (*Zantedeschia* spp.), and rain lilies (*Zephyranthes* spp.).

summer cutting A cutting taken of soft, succulent growth early in the season while plants are growing actively. *See* SOFTWOOD CUTTING

summer oil *See* HORTICULTURAL OIL

sun, full *See* FULL SUN

sunscald A general term for damage caused by excessive exposure to sunlight. Trees growing along a street or parking lot, for example, are exposed to a great deal of reflected heat from the sun, which can cause leaf edges to burn.

super-, supra- Prefixes meaning attached or borne above, superior to, or greater than.

superficial On the surface.

superior Attached or borne above; uppermost. A flower with a superior ovary features petals, sepals, and stamens that are attached to the receptacle, which is below the ovary. Poppies (*Papaver* spp.) have superior ovaries.

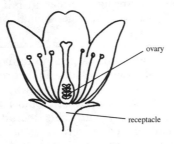

superior ovary

superior oil An organic insecticide. *See* HORTICULTURAL OIL

supports, plants *See* STAKING

supreme oil *See* HORTICULTURAL OIL

surculose Developing runners or suckers that arise from the base of the plant or from the rhizome or rootstock.

surculum The rhizome of a fern.

surcurrent A base of a leaf, leaflet, or other plant part that extends up from the point where it is attached to the stem. The base is adnate, meaning it is fused or nearly fused to the petiole (if there is one) and the stem.

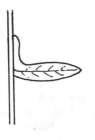

surcurrent leaf base

surficial Prostrate. Growing near or spreading over the ground.

suture A groove, seam, line, or other marking between organs. The line or seam between parts of a seed capsule is a suture.

swale An elongated ditch or depression, usually with very gently sloped sides, used to direct surface water on or off a site. A swale should have an even bottom, so water doesn't collect along its length, and it should be deep enough to accommodate water at the height of a rainstorm.

swan-neck hoe *See* HOE

sweet soil *See* ALKALINE SOIL

swoe This variation on the scuffle hoe resembles a golf club and has a blade that is sharpened on three sides and parallel to the ground. Designed for weeding, but not for cultivating the soil, it is used by pushing and pulling the blade across the soil. The blade cuts off weeds at or just under the soil surface.

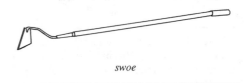

swoe

sword-shaped *See* ENSIFORM

syconium The fruit of a fig (*Ficus* spp.), an entire ripened inflorescence that is hollow and contains the flowers inside the fruit.

symmetric, symmetrical *See* ACTINOMORPHIC

symmetrical balance A design that creates the impression of stability by making both sides of the design virtually identical. Two garden beds filled with mirror-image plantings are symmetrically balanced; this type of planting is characteristic of a formal garden. In a flower arrangement, a symmetrically balanced design is one in which the flowers and foliage on either side of the composition are basically the same. *See* ASYMMETRICAL BALANCE

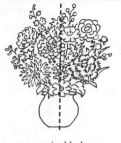

symmetrical balance

symmetrical triangle *See* PYRAMID

sympetalous A flower with petals that are at least partially united by their edges, or margins, to form a tubular base. *See also* GAMOPETALOUS

sympodial A type of growth that is periodically terminated by branching. In this case, the terminal bud dies or terminates in a flower, and the stem or rhizome continues growing from a lateral branch. Cattleya orchids (*Cattleya* spp.) exhibit this type of growth. *See* MONOPODIAL

syn-, sym- A prefix meaning united.

synanthous This term is used to describe leaves that appear with the flowers.

syncarp A compound "fruit" that actually consists of individual fruits massed together.

These can result from one flower bearing many fruits or many flowers that produce fruits that are tightly massed together at maturity. A syncarpous fruit that grows from a single flower with multiple carpels is called an aggregate fruit; the "berries" of raspberries and blackberries (*Rubus* spp.) are an example. Magnolias (*Magnolia* spp.) bear conelike aggregate fruits. A "fruit" that grows from several individual flowers is called a multiple fruit; mulberries (*Morus* spp.) and pineapples (*Ananas comosus*) are examples of multiple fruits.

syncarpous Bearing a compound "fruit" called a syncarp, or having fused or united carpels.

synonym One of two or more names used for the same taxon. *See also* COMMERCIAL SYNONYM

synthetic fertilizer A fertilizer processed or produced in a chemical plant. Also called a chemical fertilizer, and not used by organic gardeners. *See* CHEMICAL FERTILIZER

syrup *See* HERBAL SYRUP

systematic botany The study and practice of classifying and naming plants. Also called taxonomic botany or taxonomy.

tachinid fly *See* BENEFICIAL INSECTS

take A cutting that has formed roots is said to have taken.

take cuttings To sever stems, leaves, roots, or other plant parts with the purpose of rooting them. *See* CUTTING

tamping Packing down by pressing or pounding. Tamping should be a gentle operation when filling containers with growing-, potting-, or seed-starting mix; lightly press down on the surface of the mix with your fingers to firm it and eliminate excess air pockets, but don't press so hard you compress the soil. When installing a base layer of sand or screenings for a walkway, tamping means pounding it in place to create a firm, flat foundation upon which to work.

tang-and-ferrule A method for attaching the metal head of a tool to its handle by means of a prong, or tang, at the top of the tool's head. The tang is stuck into the handle and held in place with a separate collar, or ferrule. This creates a lighter-weight, but weaker, connection and is not used in top-quality tools. *See* TOOLS

taping A technique for covering wires used to support or replace the stems of flowers or leaves in arrangements. Florist's tape is the preferred tape to use for this process: It is a somewhat rubbery-textured tape that stretches slightly when pulled and sticks to itself once it has been stretched. Florist's tape comes in colors such as green, white, and brown. To tape a wired flower, start where the two ends of the wire emerge from the flower and twirl the tape around the stem so it extends from the base of the flower down the stem/wire. To get the tape started, be sure to overlap the end of the tape by covering it with the first and/or second layer. Pull gently on the tape as you twirl to make sure subsequent layers stick to one another. Also called guttaring.

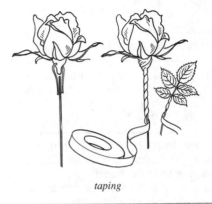

taping

taproot A root system featuring one or more thick, main, relatively unbranched root and smaller roots branching off to the sides. A carrot has a taproot, for example. Taproots are a feature of drought-adapted plants—columbines (*Aquilegia* spp.), baptisias (*Baptisia* spp.), and purple coneflowers (*Echinacea* spp.) all have taproots. Taprooted plants are more difficult to dig for transplanting or division, because it is easy to disturb or sever the deep roots. Trees with taproots, including many oaks (*Quercus* spp.) and hickories (*Carya* spp.), are especially difficult to transplant, but are great to garden under because their deep-diving roots don't interfere with shallower-rooted trees whose roots stay nearer the soil surface.

taproot

tassel The male inflorescence (staminate) of a corn plant (*Zea mays*).

taxon, *pl.* **taxa** A group of plants of any rank. Asteraceae is a taxon at the family level, *Catalpa* and *Catharanthus* are taxa at the genus level. *Catharanthus roseus* is a taxon at the species level.

taxonomic botany, taxonomy The study and practice of describing, naming, and classifying plants. Also called systematic botany.

T-budding A commonly used budding technique also called shield budding because it involves inserting a shield-shaped bud into a T-shaped cut. T-budding is usually performed on stock that ranges from $1/4$ to 1 inch in diameter. It is best used on thin-barked species, and the bark must be slipping in order for this operation to be successful. To prepare the stock, make a vertical cut from 2 to 10 inches above the soil surface, then make a horizontal cut across the top of the first cut. To prepare a bud for inserting, make a shallow cut beginning $1/2$ inch below a bud on the budstick that extends about 1 inch above the bud. Then cut across the top about $1/2$ to $3/4$ inch above the bud to make a shallow shield of bark that has a sliver of wood beneath the bud (some budders remove the sliver of wood). Insert the bud under the flaps of wood in the stock until the top cuts on both line up. The bud should be exposed and the flaps of bark should cover most of the shield. Fasten the bud and bark flaps down with a rubber budding strip or a piece of raffia. Do not cover the bud. Rubber budding strips will drop off soon after the graft union has formed; gently cut away raffia or other materials used to tie the bud in place before they constrict the stem. *See* BUDDING, RUBBER BUDDING STRIP

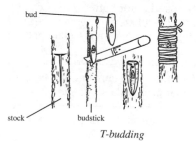

bud

stock   budstick

T-budding

tea An herbal preparation made by brewing herbs—usually leaves, flowers, and stems—in water. In addition to the common beverage, herbalists recognize two types of teas: infusions and tisanes. These are distinguished by the length of time the herbs are steeped.

teeth Relatively small, sharply pointed marginal lobes. *See* TOOTHED

tempered *See* FORGED

tender This term is used to describe plants that are unable to withstand some degree of cold or freezing temperature.

tender annual Annuals that will be killed outright or severely damaged by frost. Tender annuals, also called warm-weather annuals, languish if moved to the garden too early in the season, when the soil is still cool and air temperatures routinely dip below 40 or 45°F at night. *See* WARM-WEATHER ANNUAL

tender perennial A plant that is killed by cold temperatures at the end of the season in northern areas but grows as an herbaceous perennial or even a woody plant in warmer climates. Where they are not hardy, tender perennials are either grown as annuals—they are replaced each year—or brought indoors for overwintering. Coleus, impatiens, and rosemary are three plants often described as tender perennials. Which plants are tender perennials depends on where you live. Rosemary, for example, survives temperatures as low as 10°F and can be grown as a shrub in Zone 8 and south. North of Zone 8 it is considered a tender perennial. Coleus, which cannot survive any frost at all, is a tender perennial everywhere that winter temperatures dip below 32°F. Tender perennials can be grown as annuals, in which case they are simply pulled up and discarded after frost, and then replaced in spring. Or they can be brought indoors in later summer or fall, kept indoors over winter, and set out again the following spring or early summer. *See* OVERWINTERING

tendril A twining, threadlike organ by which a plant grasps and clings to a support. It is a modified branch or portion of a leaf. Also called a pampinus.

tendril-pinnate A compound leaf divided in a featherlike fashion (pinnate), with pairs of leaflets attached along a main stem, or rachis, and ending with a tendril at the tip. Perennial peas (*Lathyrus latifolius*) and cup-and-saucer vines (*Cobaea scandens*) are tendril-pinnate.

tentacle A threadlike, glandular hair or filament that is sensitive to touch. The leaves of sundew (*Drosera* spp.) bear tentacles that entrap insects, for example.

tenuous Thin or slender.

tepal A petal-like segment of a perianth, which is the collective term for the calyx (sepals) and the corolla (petals) of a flower, that cannot be distinguished as either a sepal or a petal. Lilies (*Lilium* spp.), tulips (*Tulipa* spp.), and begonias (*Begonia* spp.) all bear flowers with showy tepals rather than distinct sepals and petals.

terete Cylindrical or round in cross section. Most often used to describe stems.

terminal Borne at the tip, or apex, of a stem.

terminal flowers

ternate Borne in threes. A leaf that is divided into three leaflets, such as those of clover (*Trifolium* spp.) is ternate.

terrace A flat, paved area that is separated from the rest of the garden. Terrace also refers to a flat area carved out of a slope to create a level garden bed. Typically, terraces have retaining walls constructed of brick, stone, landscape ties, or other materials. A terraced slope contains a series of these level beds, and terracing is an excellent way to prevent erosion, decrease runoff, and simply find more space for growing plants.

terrarium An enclosed glass or plastic container used to grow plants.

terrestrial Growing in soil. All plants that grow on land are terrestrial.

tertiary veins A small leaf vein that branches off a lateral vein. Lateral, or secondary, veins branch off the main vein, or midrib, of the leaf. Also called sublateral veins.

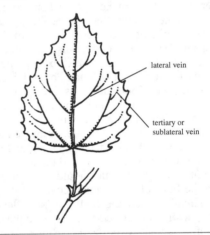

lateral vein

tertiary or sublateral vein

tesselate, tessellated Checkered pattern. This term is commonly used to describe the venation pattern in which the main veins run the length of the leaf, and secondary veins cross them at right angles. Variegation and color patterns also can be tessellate. Checkered lily (*Fritillaria meleagris*) blooms have a tesselate pattern on the petals.

testa, *pl.* **testae** Seed coat or outer layer or covering that protects a seed. *See* SEED

testing germination *See* GERMINATION TESTING

tetra- A prefix indicating four. Tetrandrous means bearing four stamens, for example, and tetramerous means arranged in sets of four.

tetragonal Four-sided. Most members of the mint family (Lamiaceae) have tetragonal stems, including mints (*Mentha* spp.) and salvias or sages (*Salvia* spp.).

tetraploid Having four sets of chromosomes. While most plants and other organisms are diploid, hybridizers have developed plants that have extra chromosomes. Tetraploid daylilies (*Hemerocallis* spp.), for example, have larger flowers with heavier substance than typical diploid ones.

texture A key characteristic of soil (*See* SOIL TEXTURE), the word texture also has significance in a garden design sense, where it is used two slightly different ways. Texture can refer to the visual appearance or feel of the surfaces of leaves, bark, or other plant parts as well as to design elements such as brick and cut or uncut stone. Sedums tend to be glossy and hard; lamb's ears (*Stachys byzantina*) is woolly; hosta leaves can be ribbed or corrugated. Texture also refers to the overall visual appearance of leaves and flowers as determined by their size and shape. Ferns and grasses, for example, are fine-textured, while large-leaved hostas are bold-textured. A large drift of fine-textured ferns will look bold in most gardens, however. Combining plants with different foliage and flower textures adds a rich dimension to plantings. To the eye, bold textures will look closer than fine textures, an illusion you can use to add depth to a planting.

textural class *See* SOIL TEXTURE, TEXTURE TRIANGLE

Texture Triangle A triangular diagram, developed by the USDA, indicating percentages of sand, silt, and clay on its three sides and used to determine the textural class of a soil. To determine soil texture, first gather a sample of soil and remove any rocks or organic debris. Put 1 cup of soil and 2 cups of water in a clear glass mason jar, close it tightly, then shake the jar vigorously until all the soil is suspended in the water. Set the jar in an out-of-the way spot where you can leave it undisturbed for 24 hours. Sand particles will settle to the bottom in about 1 minute. Measure the depth of the sand layer with a ruler. Silt particles will take an hour to settle out. Measure the depth of both layers, then, to determine the width of the silt layer, subtract the width of the sand layer. Clay takes 24 hours to settle out. To determine the width of the clay layer, measure the layers again and subtract sand and silt layers. To calculate the percentages of sand, silt, and clay, divide the depth of each layer by the total depth of settled soil, then multiply by 100. For example, if the sand layer is $^3/_4$-inch deep and the soil totals 3 inches deep, you'd divide $^3/_4$ by 3 (result 0.25) then multiply by 100 to get the percentage: 25 percent. Repeat the process to get the percentages of silt and clay. Next, locate the percentage of sand, silt, and clay in your soil sample on the sides of the USDA Texture Triangle. To determine textural class, find the point where the three lines meet at the center. *See* APPENDIX, page 312

thalamus *See* RECEPTACLE

thallus, *pl.* **thalli** A plant growth or body that is undifferentiated, meaning it does not have separate stems, roots, or leaves.

thatch A layer of matted grass clippings, roots, stems, and stolons that builds up on the soil surface, at the base of grass plants in a lawn. A thin layer of thatch—under about $^1/_2$ inch—is actually beneficial, because the decomposing organic matter enriches the soil by releasing nitrogen and breaking down into humus. A thick layer of thatch, on the other hand, keeps out water and air, and also can harbor insects and disease organisms. Thatch buildup is usually caused by excessive use of chemical fertilizers and other products such as fungicides and insecticides. Letting grass grow long and then cutting it short also can contribute to thatch buildup. Fertilizing heavily encourages grass plants to grow rapidly, and other chemical products affect the populations of organisms such as earthworms, insects, and microorganisms that decompose thatch. Soil compaction also contributes to thatch build-up. Several treatments help eliminate thatch problems. Top-dressing with a thin ($^3/_8$-inch thick or less) layer of rich topsoil or compost adds essential organic matter and speeds up the natural decomposition process. Commercial treatments that contain thatch-destroying microorganisms also are available. Raking off excess thatch using a tool called a thatch, or cavex, rake is another option. On sites where the soil is very compacted, rent an aerating machine or hire someone to aerate your lawn. Leave the plugs of soil it pulls up on top of the soil and, if possible, topdress with compost or topsoil; plugs and topdressing will disappear quickly as the grass grows. To keep thatch from building up again, begin using only organic fertilizers, insecticides, herbicides, and fungicides. Feed sparingly, no more that twice a year, and mow the grass high and more frequently; ideally, you should remove no more than one-third of the blades each time you mow.

theme garden A garden that is designed and planted with a particular theme in mind. A pizza garden might include all the ingredients of pizza, including tomatoes, basil, oregano, peppers, and so forth. A Shakespearian garden might feature plants mentioned in Shakespeare's plays, while an edible flowers garden would feature only flowers that can be used as garnishes, fresh in salads, or in cooking. Color theme gardens also are popular and feature flowers or foliage that are variations on a particular hue.

thickening meristem *See* MERISTEM, MONO-COT

thinning This is a term used by pruners, planters, and fruit growers. For information on thinning as a pruning technique, *see* THIN-NING CUT; in reference to fruit growing, *see* THINNING FRUIT. As a planting technique, thinning is the act of reducing the number of seedlings planted in a given area to allow enough room for the remaining plants to thrive. Thinning is beneficial because over-crowded seedlings can become stunted or grow more slowly, and are more subject to pest and disease problems because of reduced air circulation. Seeds sown both indoors and out commonly need thinning. Indoors, if you have sown only a few seeds per pot, use scissors to clip off excess seedlings right at the soil line. Clip off all but the strongest seedling, or leave two widely spaced seedlings if you plan on transplanting them into separate pots when they get a little larger. Some gardeners thin to a small clump of two or three seedlings, which they then treat as a single plant. Clipping off extra seedlings works better than pulling them up, because it prevents damage to the roots of the remaining plants. Outdoors, thin seedlings to the spacing recommended on the seed packet by cutting them off with scissors or pulling them up. (Or, dig up excess seedlings with a thin-bladed trowel and move them elsewhere.) With outdoor-sown plants it is sometimes best to thin in two stages, once when the plants are 2 to 3 inches tall and again when they are 4 to 5 inches tall. This ensures a well-spaced planting of healthy plants. Some gardeners actually thin by gently raking over rows of plants in the vegetable garden. Plantings treated in this manner are quite disheveled looking for a day or so, but recover in a few days. Keep in mind that thinnings of edibles such as lettuce, spinach, and other leafy crops are great for adding to salads.

thinning cut A pruning cut that removes a branch or shoot at its base, where it arose from a larger branch or the trunk of the tree. To make a proper thinning cut, cut just outside the branch collar. (Leaving the branch collar intact promotes healing of the wound. *See* BRANCH COLLAR.) Depending on the size of the branch or shoot you are removing, thinning cuts can be made with pruning shears, loppers, or a saw. For large branches that require a saw, always make a three-step cut to remove the branch with a minimum of damage to the plant. *See* THREE-STEP CUT Use thinning cuts to remove dead and damaged growth, open up the center of a plant to let in light and air, and eliminate rubbing or crossing branches. Also use them to remove stems from overcrowded shrubs by cutting them off at the base of the plant or as close to ground as possible to remove old, nonblooming wood or as a function of renewal pruning (*See* RENEWAL PRUNING). To use thinning cuts to reduce the size of a shrub without stimulating the rampant growth repeated shearing does, simply remove large branches and leave smaller ones behind. Thinning cuts do not cause a flush of new growth the way heading cuts do, but they do tend to invigorate plants because they change the amount of topgrowth the roots are supporting.

thinning cuts

thinning fruit Fruit growers use thinning to prevent trees such as apples and peaches from bearing a crop that is too large. This may not seem like a problem, but a large crop of fruit actually can break branches, and crowded fruits are more subject to diseases such as brown rot. A tree that bears too large a crop one year may also bear a small crop—or not bear at all—the following one. Thinning also directs the tree's energy into fewer, larger fruit. To thin fruit, remove it by clipping off or twisting off small fruit (the earlier in the season you thin, the better). Remove all fruit that shows signs of insects or deformities, and then remove additional fruit on apples, peaches, and nectarines so the remaining ones are 6 to 8 inches apart. Thin smaller fruit, such as apricots and plums, to 3 to 5 inches. If you can't reach upper branches, use a pole with an old towel wrapped around it to gently beat the branches and dislodge some of the fruit.

thong root A thick root that descends from the crown of a plant.

thorn A thin, stiff, sharp-pointed structure that is actually a modified branch or stem, or an outgrowth of the wood of a stem. Honeylocusts (*Gleditisa* spp.) bear true thorns. Thorns, spines, and prickles are technically different, but the term thorn commonly is used to refer to any sharp thorny structure borne on a branch. *See also* PRICKLE, SPINE

threadlike *See* FILLIFORM

threadworms *See* NEMATODES

three-pinnate *See* TRIPINNATE

three-ranked Arranged in three vertical rows, or ranks.

three-step cut The correct technique for pruning off large branches, by using three separate pruning cuts. Make the first cut 6 inches or more out from the trunk, cutting halfway up through the branch. Second, just outside the first cut, saw down from the top to sever the limb. Third, make a clean, straight cut just outside the branch collar, which is a bulging or ridged area at the base of the branch. A three-step cut is much better than simply sawing off the branch outside the branch collar because it reduces the weight of the branch first, eliminating the danger that the partially severed branch will fall off, splintering wood and tearing bark off as it goes. A three-step cut leaves a clean, smooth wound that heals much more quickly than a rough one.

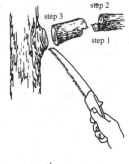

three-step cut

thresh, threshing To beat or pound seed stalks and seeds in order to separate the seeds from husks, stems, and other plant matter. On a commercial basis, threshing is accomplished by machine, but to thresh small batches beat seedheads from side to side in a bucket. Or spread on newspaper and gently crush them with a rolling pin or wood mallet. A mortar and pestle also works.

thrice-cut Tripinnate or three times pinnate. Divided into three ranks of leaflets, all arranged in a featherlike (pinnate) fashion.

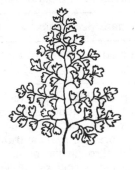

thrice-cut

thrips These are tiny, slender insects with narrow fringed wings that feed on leaves, flowers, buds, and stems. Their feeding causes browning, white flecking, and ultimately deformed plant parts. To control them, remove and destroy infested flowers and buds. Spray with insecticidal soap or superior oil, or dust with diatomaceous earth in the evening; treat serious infestations with pyrethrins.

throat The opening of a flower that has united petals (gamopetalous) or sepals (gamosepalous).

thyrse This type of flower cluster, or inflorescence, can be described as a dense, rounded, or oval panicle of cymes. Like other panicles, a thyrse has a single stem (axis) that is indeterminate, meaning it continues to elongate after the first flowers open. Flowers also are borne on branched side stems, but they are carried in determi-

nate, cymelike clusters. Butterfly bush (*Buddleja davidii*) bears its flowers in this arrangement.

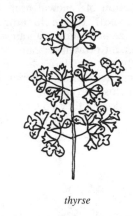

thyrse

thyrsoid Thyrselike. A flower cluster, or inflorescence, that resembles a thyrse but may or may not be a true thyrse. Also used to describe flowers that are borne in a thyrse, as in thyrsoid flowers.

tiller A shoot that sprouts from the base or the roots of a plant. This term is most often used to refer to the side shoots produced by grasses.

tilth Soil with a crumbly structure that holds together if compressed but crumbles easily is said to have good tilth or is described as being friable. Soil that has good tilth is ideal for gardening. In fact, it often is the end product of good cultivation and soil-care practices such as adding plenty of organic matter at regular intervals and avoiding walking on prepared beds. *See* SOIL STRUCTURE

tincture An herbal preparation made by combining herbs in a mix of alcohol and water and steeping them for about 2 weeks in a container with a tight-fitting lid. Shake the mix several times a day before straining or pressing out the liquid to separate out the plant parts. The alcohol in a tincture helps extract and preserve the properties of the herb. A standard proportion for a tincture is 1 part powdered or finely chopped herb to 4 parts alcohol such as diluted vodka.

tine An individual prong, tooth, or spike on a garden fork, rake, or other cultivation tool.

tined hoe *See* HOE

tint A color that has been lightened by adding white. Pink is a tint of red, for example. Pastel colors are very light tints that contain a large amount of white.

tip cutting A general term for any cutting that is taken from the tip of a shoot or stem.

tip layering A type of layering in which a shoot tip is bent to the ground and buried to induce the production of a new plant. Brambles (*Rubus* spp.) such as blackberries and raspberries are commonly propagated in this manner, and will naturally tip layer when their canes arch to the ground. To tip layer, in summer simply bend a vigorous, first-year shoot (not one that is of fruiting age) to the ground and bury it to a depth of 3 to 4 inches. A new plant will emerge at the tip in a matter of weeks. It can be grown in place or severed and moved elsewhere the following spring. *See* LAYERING

tip layering

tisane A type of herbal tea made by brewing herbs in water for 5 or 10 minutes, the length of time it takes to brew a normal cup of tea. Tisanes normally are brewed a cup at a time for immediate use. To make a tisane, combine about 1 ounce of dried herb per pint of water; use 2 ounces of fresh herbs per pint, although dried herbs are normally preferred for this use. Pour near-boiling water over the herbs, and steep, covered.

tissue culture Growing plant or animal tissues or cells in an artificial, sterile nutrient solution, usually in a laboratory. Once called meristem propagation because the tissues or cells used are taken from fast-growing, undifferentiated meristematic tissue (*See* MERISTEM) at the tips of a plant's shoots and roots, tissue culture is an important technique for asexually propagating plants such as orchids and variegated sponts. Also called micropropagation.

toads Beneficial animals that eat a wide variety of garden pests, including slugs, flies, grubs, cutworms, and grasshoppers. A single toad can eat up to 3,000 pests a month. To attract toads and make them feel at home, do not use pesticides. Toads appreciate a shallow saucer of water or a ground-level bird bath, and prefer humid spots that are protected from the wind. Try making a shallow depression in the garden and covering it with a board. Or buy a toad house or make one out of an old clay pot— just crack a "door" out of the rim and place it in a moist, sheltered spot upside down.

tolerant Able to withstand or endure. This term is commonly used to describe plants that are best in one set of conditions but will grow fairly well in another. Describing a plant as shade tolerant can have a range of meanings: It can mean it thrives in shade or merely survives there. Flowers or plants that are described as sun tolerant usually resist fading or simply withstand full sun better than other selections.

tomentose Woolly. Covered with short, soft, woolly hairs that are matted down and tangled together. Most often used to describe leaf surfaces. Beach wormwood or dusty miller (*Artemisia stellarana*) and licorice plant (*Helichrysum petiolare*) have tomentose foliage.

tomentulose Slightly tomentose.

tone A color that has been made duller by adding gray or has been modified by adding some other color.

tongue graft *See* WHIP-AND-TONGUE GRAFT

tongued approach graft A type of approach graft in which two separate plants are united with interlocking tongues of wood, similar to those used in whip-and-tongue grafting. To make a tongued approach graft, select the stock and scion as you would for a spliced approach graft (*See* APPROACH GRAFTING), then make tongued cuts as for a whip-and-tongue graft. *See* WHIP-AND-TONGUE GRAFT

tongued approach graft

tongue-shaped *See* LIGULATE

tools Well-made tools are a pleasure to use, make gardening chores easier, and last for years with good care. Always buy the best-quality tools you can afford: For digging and cultivating tools such as shovels, spades, forks, hoes, picks, and mattocks, that means ones with forged heads made of a single piece of high-quality steel rather than a cheaper model with a stamped head. (*See* FORGED, STAMPED) Handles should be made of hardwood—ash for most digging tools, hickory for picks and mattocks. Avoid tools with painted handles; paint often conceals imperfections such as knots or grain that doesn't run straight along the handle shaft. Good-quality tools with fiberglass and metal handles are available. Spades and forks commonly come with a grip at the top of the handle to make it easier to handle. When looking at a tool, pay special attention to the manner in which the metal head is attached to the wooden handle. The strongest connections are solid socket and solid strap: A tool with a solid socket construction has a steel cylinder, or collar, at the top of the head that is forged in one piece with the head. The handle is inserted into this collar and fastened with a rivet or pin. A tool with solid-strap construction has two flat, steel straps at the top of the head that are forged in one piece with the head. The handle fits between the two straps, which run partway up its length, and is fastened with rivets or pins. Tools with two other types of connections—tang-and-ferrule and open socket— are lighter in weight than tools that employ solid-socket or solid-strap construction, but they are also quite weak. (*See* TANG-AND-FERRULE, OPEN SOCKET) Heads of picks and mattocks are normally attached with an eye socket, which is a strong, heavy construction. (*See* EYE SOCKET CONSTRUCTION) To maintain tools, before you put them away, clean mud off the blades with a stiff brush. To keep the metals clean and rust-free, plunge them into a 5-gallon bucket of sharp sand to which you have added some vegetable oil. This cleans the metal and protects it with a light coat of oil in one step. Sharpen tools at least annually—before you put them away for the winter is a good time—because a tool is only as good as its blade. Before storing them for winter, wipe blades with penetrating oil and wipe them clean. Wipe handles with boiled linseed oil.

tooth A small, sharp lobe on a leaf margin.

toothed *See* DENTATE, SERRATE, SERRULATE, CRENATE, INCISED

top-budding A budding technique that essentially is the same as top-working and is used for the same reasons, except that the trees are budded (usually T-budded) rather than grafted. Top-budding usually is done in midsummer. *See* TOP-WORKING, BUDDING

top-dressing Spreading or sprinkling a material evenly over the soil surface, either by hand or with a spreader, to feed plants or improve fertility. Fertilizers can be applied by top-dressing, while compost and topsoil are common top-dressing materials used to improve a lawn. When top-dressing to feed plants in the vegetable garden, work the fertilizer into the top few inches with a rake, spade, or fork. Remove any mulch layer when applying amendments in this manner, and replace them after you are done.

top-grafting *See* TOP-WORKING

topiary The art of pruning and training trees, shrubs, and other plants to create various shapes, from geometric cones and spirals to whimsical animals. While geometric topiaries can be formed by clipping alone, plants trained in more complex forms usually have a permanent (or nearly so), underlying frame that serves as a guide for clipping and as a support.

topping A mutilating, so-called pruning technique that involves cutting off most of the crown of the tree by sawing off branches without regard to the tree's natural shape. The result is a disfigured tree with a canopy of stumps (somewhat umbrella-shaped) that sprout dense clumps of weak shoots. These shoots need constant pruning to keep them in bounds. The process is extremely stressful for the tree and leaves it open to disease and insect infestations. Topping, sometimes called dehorning, is often the method used to cope with too-large trees that are growing under power lines, but topped trees are seldom worth having and replacement is generally the best option. Avoid this technique at all costs, along with any tree services that recommend it.

topped tree

topsoil A general term that refers to the uppermost layer of soil.

top-working A grafting technique used to change the cultivar(s) of an established tree. A tree or an entire orchard can be changed from an unpopular apple cultivar to a new, more popular one, for example. Top-working also can be used to add a branch or two of an appropriate pollinator to an established tree, thus increasing fruit set. Trees scheduled for top-working are cut back hard and new scions are grafted to the tips of the branches, usually using bark or cleft grafts. If more than one scion "takes" from each grafted branch, one is selected to remain and the others are gradually cut back. *See* GRAFTING, CLEFT GRAFT, BARK GRAFT

tortuous Irregularly bent or twisted and turned in many directions. This term is most often used to describe branching habits.

torus, *pl.* **tori** *See* RECEPTACLE

trace elements *See* MICRONUTRIENTS

tracheid *See* XYLEM

trademark name A plant name that is a legally registered trademark. A trademark name is different from the registered cultivar name for a plant. Since anyone using the trademarked name must pay a royalty to its owner, hybridizers often give unusable cultivar names (combinations of letters and numbers, for example) to plants that will have trademarked ones. This ensures the plant will not be made available under the cultivar name because it will not be a name the public recognizes.

trailing Prostrate or creeping, but not putting down roots along the stems.

training The process of shaping a young tree or other plant to a desired form. Trees normally are trained by limiting the number of branches that form, making sure they are strong and well-spaced, and also directing their growth. Training is especially important for fruit trees, because the tree needs to be strong enough to support a good crop of fruit, with a center open to light and air, and branches within reach for easy picking.

translucent Nearly transparent. Money plant (*Lunaria annuua*) bears seedheads with silvery, nearly round, central partitions that are translucent.

transpiration The movement of water vapor through the leaves, usually through the pores or openings in the leaves called stomata.

transplant, difficult to *See* DIFFICULT TO TRANSPLANT

transplanting Moving seedlings or plants from one location to another. *See* TRANSPLANTING SEEDLINGS AND CUTTINGS for information on moving young plants; *See* PLANTING for information on moving hardened-off seedlings along with container-grown, balled-and-burlapped, and bare-root plants to the garden. Spring to early summer or fall, up to about 6 weeks before the first fall frost date, are the best times to transplant perennials, shrubs, or other woody plants from one part of the garden to another; the recommended time varies from plant to plant. Water deeply a day before digging, then dig a hole large enough to accommodate it in the new site (this minimizes the time spent out of the soil and lessens transplant stress). Then dig all around the plant with a sharp spade, lift the plant, and move it to its new location. If the soil is especially crumbly, wrap the roots in a piece of burlap or set the soil ball in a container for the trip. With established trees and shrubs consider root pruning a season or a year before moving them. (*See* ROOT PRUNING) Try to pick a cloudy day when transplanting; moving plants while it's sprinkling is ideal. To replant, set the root ball in place, fill in around it with soil, and firm the soil over the roots. Form a broad saucer of soil around the plant that will collect and direct water. Then water deeply, flooding the soil around the plant to settle it and eliminate air pockets. Mulch, keeping the mulch an inch

or two away from the stems of the plant. Keep the soil evenly moist until the plant resumes growing—ideally, water regularly for the entire first growing season. If the weather promises to be sunny, shade the plant(s) with burlap or bushel baskets propped over them for a few days. Keep in mind that some plants are difficult to transplant because of deep taproots—baptisia (*Baptisia* spp.) and peonies (*Paeonia* spp.) are examples. Move these plants only if necessary, and take extra care to dig up as much of the root system as possible.

transplanting seedlings and cuttings When grown indoors, both seedlings and cuttings need special care before they are moved from the containers in which they were rooted or sown into individual pots. Seedlings generally are ready for transplanting into individual pots once the first pair of true leaves have developed. Once cuttings begin to grow, tug gently on some leaves; if they feel firmly anchored, they're ready for moving to a new pot. To move seedlings or cuttings, first water them several hours in advance. Fill pots with premoistened growing mix and gently press it into the containers. Turn the pot of seedlings or cuttings on its side and tip them out into your hand. Use a pencil or plant label to gently tease the roots apart and separate individual plants. With the pencil or label, make a hole in the medium that's deep enough to accommodate the roots, then lower the plant in place so that the point where the roots join the stem is even with the top of the growing mix. Always hold seedlings by a leaf rather than the stem, because a crushed stem is fatal. Push the medium back around the roots, but don't press it down; just gently tap the bottom of the pot once or twice to settle the mix around the roots. Add extra mix if needed to support the seedling or cutting, label the pot, and water. Keep transplants out of direct light for a day or so, then return them to bright light. Before moving plants started indoors out to the garden, harden them off to lessen the shock of transplanting. (*See* HARDENING OFF) Most annuals and summer vegetables can be transplanted to the garden on or just after the last frost date. Some cool-weather annuals, such as pansies and Johnny-jump-ups, along with cabbage, broccoli, and related crops go out earlier. With warm-weather annuals and cold-sensitive plants like tomatoes, peppers, and egg-plants, earlier transplanting isn't beneficial, because the plants just sit and do nothing until the soil warms up, and cold weather will check their growth, while a late frost can damage or even kill them. Annuals that are kept indoors until the weather has really warmed up will quickly catch up to those that have been stressed by cold weather. *See* PLANTING for details on moving hardened-off seedlings to the garden.

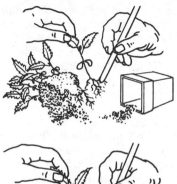

transplanting seedlings and cuttings

transplants Plants grown in containers and moved to the garden. The term trans-plants is most often used to designate the annuals sold at garden centers, grocery stores, and home centers in spring. When buying them, always inspect before you buy. Well-grown transplants will be com-pact and well-branched with healthy-colored leaves. Brown leaf edges indicate sunscorch or exposure to too much heat. Look for indicators of disease such as

black or brown spots or moldy or powdery patches. Also avoid plants with yellowed lower leaves or yellow patches between veins, both indicators of nutrient stress. Look under leaves for signs of pests such as aphids, spider mites, or whiteflies. Plants that are not yet blooming are gen-erally a better buy. They recover from transplanting more quickly, because they can direct energy to growing roots rather than supporting flowers. If you do buy transplants with flowers on them, pinch off all the flowers and flower buds at planting time.

transverse Across the axis of an organ such as a leaf or petiole, at right angles to the longitudinal (lengthwise) axis. Cutting a stem off a plant at a right angle to the stem is a transverse cut.

tray *See* FLAT

tree A tall woody plant that usually has a single main stem, or trunk. The term often is used loosely to refer to any plant with a treelike habit. Woody plants with multiple trunks also are called trees—birch trees such as river birch (*Betula nigra*) are often sold in this manner, for example. Shrubs that have been limbed up and limited to one or only a few main stems also are called small trees. *See also* SHRUB

tree fruits A general term referring to fruits produced on trees, including ap-ples, peaches, pears, nectarines, and most cherries.

tree gator *See* GATOR

tree rings Tree rings are formed from water-conducting tissue called xylem. The xylem cells laid down in the spring are large and have thin cell walls, making them appear lighter and less dense than those produced in summer, which are smaller and thicker.

treillage The French word for trellis, com-monly used to refer to various garden structures such as arbors, galleries or tun-nels, and elaborate trellises.

trellis A support for climbing vines, including annuals, woody perennials, and vegetables, usually constructed of open, wooden latticework. Trellises can be erected against a wall, used as screens or to divide one section of the · garden from another, or erected in the vegetable garden for climbing crops such as pole beans. (In the vegetable garden they commonly are built with a wooden frame and wire or plastic mesh.) An arbor or archway that is made from a latticework trellis also is sometimes called a trellis.

trench layering Sometimes called etiolation layering, this technique is primarily used to propagate rootstocks for fruit trees. To trench layer, start with a young plant and plant it at a sharp angle—30 to 40 degrees—to make it easier to bend to the ground. Grow it for a year, then in late winter to early spring remove weak branches and cut out the tips of the remaining shoots. Bend the plant to the ground so it lies flat in a trench at its base, and fasten down the branches with U-shaped wire pins. Gradually fill in the trench with soil as shoots grow; they will emerge at the bases of the existing branches. Remove the soil from the trench in late summer or early fall to see if the individual shoots have rooted. If they have, sever the stems, taking as many roots as possible with each piece. Pot up the individual plants or move them to a nursery bed or another spot in the garden. If roots haven't formed, recover and check again the following spring or early summer.

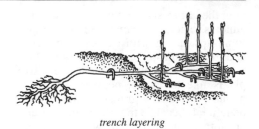

trench layering

tri- Three. A prefix indicating three of a particular organ or characteristic. Triandrous means bearing three stamens, for example, and triangulate means three-angled.

triangular *See* DELTOID

triangulation A mathematical technique that can be used to accurately locate features in a landscape, including property corners, trees set in the lawn away from the house, or buildings. When drawing a map of your property, start from a known line, such as a side of your house, a sidewalk, or lot line, and draw it on a base plan. (Most homeowners have a plot plan or survey that positions the house on the lot they purchased.) To triangulate the position of a tree or other object in the yard, you'll need to measure the distance from two different points on your starting line to the tree or other object. Measure the distance from one corner of your house to the tree and then from the other. Record both distances. To determine the position of the tree and locate it on your base map, you'll need a drafting compass: Using the scale determined for your map, set the compass to the distance from the first point to the tree, then put the point of the compass on one corner of your house and draw an arc on the map. Set the compass to reflect the other distance and draw another arc. The point where the two arcs meet is the location of the tree.

tribe A taxonomic rank between a subfamily and a genus.

trichocarpous Bearing hairy fruit.

trichogramma wasps *See* BENEFICIAL INSECTS

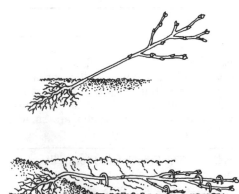

trickle irrigation *See* DRIP IRRIGATION

trifid Divided into three segments that are cut about halfway to the middle of the leaf, petal, or other organ.

trifoliate A plant with three leaves, such as trilliums (*Trillium* spp.). Also used to designate leaves with three leaflets (trifoliolate).

trifoliolate Having three leaflets. Clovers (*Trifolium* spp.) and strawberries (*Fragaria* spp.) are trifoliolate. Poison ivy (*Toxicodendron radicans*) is usually, but not always, trifoliate.

trimonoecious Bearing three kinds of flowers on the same plant: male, female, and bisexual.

trioecious Bearing three kinds of flowers on separate plants: male, female, and bisexual.

tripartate Having three parts, such as lobes.

tripetalous Having three petals. Spiderworts (*Tradescantia* spp.) and trilliums (*Trillium* spp.) are tripetalous.

tripinnate Thrice-cut or three times pinnate. Divided into three ranks of leaflets, all arranged in a featherlike (pinnate) fashion.

tripinnate

tripinnatifid Three times pinnatifid. Divided into three ranks of lobes or segments, all arranged in a featherlike (pinnate) fashion, with indentations (sinuses) cut halfway to the midrib of the leaf but not all the way to the midrib. The individual segments are not separated into individual leaflets. *See* PINNATIFID

tripinnatisect Three times pinnatisect. Divided into three ranks of lobes or segments, all arranged in a featherlike (pinnate) fashion, with indentations (sinuses) cut all the way to the midrib of the leaf. The individual segments are not separated into individual leaflets. *See* PINNATISECT

trompe-l'oeil Translated, this term means "deceive the eye," and it is a technique used in garden and landscape design to manipulate or deceive a visitor's perception of a space, usually by using false perspective to create the illusion that the space is larger than it actually is. A mirror or painting at the end of a garden walk can create this impression, as can a trellis constructed in such a way that it seems to have depth (with the cross pieces slanted and vertical supports shortened toward a vanishing point to create perspective). A path that narrows as it leads away from the house will seem longer than one that does not. Bold plants or large plants or plantings set in the foreground, with finer-textured and smaller plants and plantings in the background create the illusion of depth. Cool colors seem farther away than warm colors, a fact that also can be used to manipulate the perceived size of an area.

trophism The movement of a plant or other organism in a direction related to an environmental stimulus such as light.

trough, trough garden A garden in a shallow container—historically a livestock watering trough carved out of a block of rock—that is planted with rock plants. A trough provides ideal conditions for many rock garden plants, most notably perfectly drained soil that stays on the dry side. Troughs make it easier to grow tiny plants, which may become overwhelmed in the garden, and they also make it easy to grow plants that require different soil mixes. Today, troughs are made of a material called hypertufa (*See* HYPERTUFA), which is considerably lighter than expensive, hard-to-find rock troughs. Troughs can be purchased at specialist nurseries, but many rock gardeners build their own.

trowel An essential hand tool with a curved blade and usually a wooden handle that is used to dig holes for planting and transplanting all manner of plants. Trowels also are useful weeding tools, because they can uproot even perennials with deep taproots. Long-handled trowels are useful for extending your reach and eliminate the need to kneel—a handy feature when planting among closely spaced, taller plants. Narrow-bladed trowels make excellent weeders, especially in rock gardens and other difficult spots.

true leaf The first leaf or leaves a seedling produces after the seed leaves, or cotyledons. The first true leaves resemble, or somewhat resemble, the leaves of the mature plant. As the seedlings use up the food stored in the cotyledons, the true leaves take over the process of photosynthesis and begin producing food for the young plant. *See* COTYLEDON

true-to-type This phrase is used to describe plants that display the characteristics of a specific cultivar or hybrid, such as a specific flower color, habit, leaf color, or fruit shape or flavor. In a breeding or production program, plants that are not true-to-type are rogued out or eliminated.

trumpet The round, projecting corona (called a trumpet or cup) of a daffodil (*Narcissus* spp.). The term trumpet is used when the corona is as long as or longer than the individual petals that surround its base, which are more properly termed perianth segments. When the corona is smaller than the perianth segments, it is commonly called a cup.

trumpet-shaped Flowers shaped like a trumpet. Several species of lilies bear trumpet-shaped blooms, including Easter lily (*Lilium longiflorum*) and regal lily (*L. regale*).

trumpet-shaped flower

truncate Blunt. A tip or base that is flat or nearly so. A truncate leaf has straight edges, or margins, and the margins approach the tip or base of the leaf at right angles to one another. While most commonly used to describe leaves, this term can be applied to other plant parts such as bracts (modified petal-like leaves) or the petals or sepals of a flower.

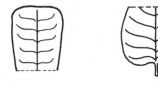

truncate leaf tip   *truncate leaf base*

truncheon A section of 2- or 3-year-old wood used as a cutting or for grafting. A truncheon is collected and treated as a type of hardwood cutting, but is laid horizontally in the soil and buried to a depth of several inches for rooting. Shoots develop along its length from latent buds and adventitious roots appear either at the base of the new shoot(s) or from the original cutting.

truncheon

trunk The main stem of a tree.

truss A compact flower cluster that arises from a central point or stem. This term is most often used to refer to the flowers of rhododendrons (*Rhododendron* spp.).

tryma *See* DRUPE

tuber A fleshy, swollen, modified underground stem that stores food for the plant and serves as a reproductive organ. The common potato (*Solanum tuberosum*) is the best-known example of a true tuber, but caladiums (*Caladium* spp.), waterlilies (*Nymphaea* spp.), Jerusalem artichokes (*Helianthus tuberosus*), and tuberous nasturtium (*Tropaeolum tuberosum*) also form these structures. Tubers have all the parts of a typical stem, including buds, usually called "eyes," that mark the nodes as well as pith, cortex, and a vascular system. (Tuberous roots lack these parts.) Tubers form at the tips of underground stolons or rhizomes. For propagation, tubers can be planted whole, or they can be cut into pieces that each have at least one bud, or "eye." (When made from a potato, these pieces are commonly known as seed potatoes.) To make them, cut a tuber with a sharp knife and store the pieces for a day or two in a warm, humid spot to let the cut ends dry before setting them in the soil. Gardeners also use the word tuber as a general term for any tuberlike structure. *See* TUBEROUS ROOT, STEM TUBERS, OVERWINTERING

tubercle A small aerial tuber that is borne in the leaf axils along a stem. Hardy begonias (*Begonia grandis* subsp. *evansiana*) bears tubercles. Tubercles will grow into separate plants once they drop to the ground, but they also can be detached in fall, stored over winter, and planted out the following spring. Also, a small swelling or projection that looks like a tuber.

tubercule A small swelling or nodule, usually on a root. Legumes such as peas and beans bear tubercules on their roots.

tubercular, tuberculate Pertaining to or bearing tubercles.

tuberiferous Bearing tubers.

tuberoid A tuberlike root that resembles a tuber.

tuberous Bearing tubers or resembling a tuber. Dahlias have tuberous roots, for example.

tuberous root A fleshy, swollen section of a root that stores food for the plant and serves as an overwintering device during the dormant season. True tuberous roots—sweet potatoes (*Ipomoea batatas*) and dahlias (*Dahlia* spp.) are examples—have the internal and external structure of a root. They do not have nodes or internodes and only have buds on the end near the crown or stem of the plant. (Sweet potatoes will produce adventitious shoots on the swollen root itself. (*See* SLIPS for details.) That's why, when dividing dahlias, it is essential to include part of the main stem or crown with each piece; the individual fleshy roots cannot sprout because they don't have buds. Dahlias usually produce fibrous roots at the end away from the stem or crown. Tuberous roots usually are biennial; they form one year, overwinter, and sprout the following spring. During the second season, they shrivel once the food stored in them is used up, and they are replaced by new roots. The tuberous roots of dahlias and sweet potatoes are commonly used to propagate and/or overwinter these plants. (*See* OVERWINTERING) Divide overwintered clumps in spring with a sharp knife.

tuberous roots

tuberous stem *See* STEM TUBER

tubular Tube- or cylinder-shaped. Torch lilies (*Kniphofia* spp.) bear tubular flowers.

tubular flower

tufted Borne in dense clusters.

tumescent Somewhat swollen.

tumid Swollen.

tunic A dry, loose covering or skin on a bulb or corm that can be membranous, papery, fibrous, or reticulate. Also, the outer coating of a seed.

tunicate Enclosed in a tunic. This term is used to refer to bulbs that have concentric layers, with the outermost layer being a tunic. Tulips (*Tulipa* spp.), onions (*Allium* spp.), and daffodils (*Narcissus* spp.) all arise from tunicate bulbs. When planting this type of bulb, leave the papery covering intact, as it is thought to help guard against disease. (Avoid buying tulip bulbs that lack a tunic, and if the tunic breaks off, try to slip it back over the bulb as you plant.) Most species that grow from tunicate bulbs produce new roots each year; grape hyacinths (*Muscari* spp.) are an exception, as they bear prerennial roots. Tunicate bulbs exhibit three kinds of growth habits. Tulip bulbs die each year and are replaced by one or more daughter bulbs, also called offsets. Daffodil bulbs, along with many other hardy bulbs, divide annually, and thus provide a continuous supply of new bulbs that duplicate the original bulb, which survives for several years. Amaryllis (*Hippeastrum* spp.) bulbs do not divide annually, although they produce offsets. Instead they produce a new primordial bulb at the center each year, and scales are gradually pushed to the outside of the bulb, eventually becoming the papery tunic.

tunnel A season-extending device designed to protect crops from cold weather and made from a sheet of plastic (usually polyethylene) suspended over a garden row on half-hoops of metal or PVC. (*See* ROW COVER) Also, a garden design structure. *See* GALLERY

turbinate Top-shaped.

turf An area covered densely with lawngrass and/or low meadow plants. This term also is used to refer to pieces of lawngrass, more commonly called sod.

turgid Swollen and firm due to water pressure. Inflated.

turgor The normal distention of plant cells caused by internal pressure of water taken in by osmosis. A plant that is wilting is losing turgor.

turion A pebblelike bud, usually fleshy and thick, that is detatched from the parent plant. Some aquatic plants, including frogbit (*Hydrocharis morsus-ranae*) and water violet (*Hottonia palustris*) overwinter by turions, which are borne on the roots and detach in fall. They sink to the bottom of the pool or pond and resprout in spring. Turions, also called winter buds, resting buds, or root buds, can be collected and potted up to propagate the plants in much the same way as cuttings. The term turion also refers to a young shoot or sucker such as the emerging stems of asparagus or the new shoots that arise from a clump of brambles (*Rubus* spp.).

tussie-mussie Made popular by the Victorians but used in England for centuries, these are small bouquets or nosegays made from herbs, flowers, and foliage that generally are backed by a small doily and decorated with a ribbon. Traditionally used to communicate between lovers, the plants in the bouquets were selected carefully using the language of flowers. A tussie-mussie with rosemary in it symbolized remembrance; marjoram, joy; violets, modesty and devotion. A bouquet containing tansy, for hostility, or yellow roses, for infidelity, communicated an entirely different message. Today, tussie-mussies are more likely to be used to give pretty, fragrant, and meaningful bouquets as gifts to friends. To make a tussie-mussie, gather two or more types of herbs, flowers, and foliage into an attractive bunch—6 to 8 inches across is a good-size bouquet. (Originally, one sprig of each plant was used to communicate meanings, but small clusters of several flowers make a more attractive bouquet.) Place a moistened cotton ball in the center of a square of plastic, place the stem-tips in the cotton ball, wrap the plastic around the stems, then secure the plastic with florist's tape. (To put the bouquet in water, cut off the tip of the plastic.) To finish, cut an "X" in the center of a paper doily, stick the plastic-wrapped stems through it, secure the doily with a florist's or corsage pin, and tie on a ribbon. *See also* TAPING, LANGUAGE OF FLOWERS

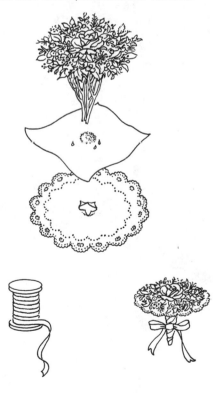

tussie-mussie

tussock A tuft or small clump of a grass or sedge.

tuteur French for trainer, or obelisk. *See* OBELISK

twice-cut Bipinnate. Divided into pairs of segments (leaflets) arranged in a featherlike (pinnate) fashion. The individual segments are further divided into pairs of leaflets

twice-cut

twig A small, very thin branch, portion of a branch, or shoot of a woody plant such as a tree or shrub.

twiggy brush *See* PEA STAKES

twining, twiner Spiraling around. A plant that climbs by twining or spiraling around another plant or other support. Runner beans (*Phaseolus* spp.) and wisterias (*Wisteria* spp.) are twining climbers.

twin-scaling A propagation technique similar to chipping in which the individual chips are subdivided. Because the individual pieces are so small, aseptic conditions are required for success; a sheet of glass makes a good work surface. Daffodils (*Narcissus* spp.), amaryllis (*Hippeastrum* spp.), nerines (*Nerine* spp.), and hyacinths (*Hyacinthus orientalis*) can be propagated in this manner. Collect bulbs for twin-scaling from midsummer to fall and dry them. Discard any that show signs of disease. Cut off the bottom of the basal plate to reveal clean tissue and cut off the nose end of the bulb to make the top flat. Strip away the dry, papery layers on the outside of the bulb. Then wash the bulb with denatured alcohol. Use a scalpel or razor blade to cut the bulb from the top down through the basal plate, to make 6 to 16 pieces, as you would for chipping.

Sterilize the blade after each cut. Then carefully cut the chips into smaller segments that each contain a fragment of basal plate and two scales. Again, sterilize after each cut. It is possible to obtain from 30 to 40 twin scales from each bulb. Treat them with liquid fungicide and store as you would chips. *See* CHIPPING

two-pinnate *See* BIPINNATE

two-ranked *See* DISTICHOUS

umbel This type of flower cluster, or inflorescence, is flat or rounded on top, and all the individual flowers are borne on stalks, or pedicels, that arise from the same point on the stem. The pedicels are more or less equal in length, and umbels are indeterminate, meaning the main stem continues to lengthen after the first flowers open. Although they resemble corymbs in shape, umbels can be distinguished because all the pedicels are attached at the same point on the tip, or apex, of the main stem. There are several types of umbels. A simple umbel has unbranched stems, or pedicles, while a compound umbel bears pedicels topped by separate secondary umbels. Crown vetch (*Cornilla varia*) bears its flowers in simple umbels. Members of the carrot family (Apiaceae, formerly Umbelliferae) bear their flowers in umbels, generally compound ones. These include Queen Anne's lace (*Daucus carota*), dill (*Anethum graveolens*), and fennel (*Foeniculum vulgare*). Ornamental onions (*Allium* spp.) bear their flowers in simple umbels, often nearly round ones. The individual flowers of devil's-walking-stick (*Aralia spinosa*) are borne in umbels, but they are carried in large panicles on racemose branches.

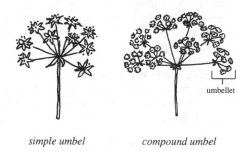

simple umbel   *compound umbel*

umbellate Umbel-like. A flower cluster, or inflorescence, that resembles an umbel but may or may not be a true umbel. Members of the genus *Asclepias* bear their flowers in umbellate cymes.

umbellet The small or secondary umbels in a compound umbel.

umbelliferous Bearing umbels. Members of the carrot family (Apiaceae, formerly Umbelliferae) are all umbelliferous.

umbelliform Umbel-like; a flower cluster, or inflorescence, that resembles an umbel but may or may not be a true umbel.

umbillicus A central depression or navel-like structure. The hilium of a seed is an umbillicus.

umbo A rough, rounded projection or bulge that arises from the center of a structure or organ. Some pine cones have such protuberances on the tips of their scales.

umbonate Bearing umbos.

umbraculate Umbrella- or parasol-shaped.

umbraculiferous Bearing umbrella- or parasol-shaped structures.

unarmed Lacking spines, thorns, prickles, or any sharp points.

unbranched whip *See* WHIP

uncinate Abruptly hooked or barbed at the tip. This term is usually used to describe hairs.

unctuous Appearing greasy or oily.

undercutting Severing the roots of plants grown in the ground in order to encourage the formation of a fibrous root system. This technique primarily is used in nurseries to prepare plants for transplanting.

underlayment A geotextile fabric installed under a flexible water garden liner to protect the liner from being punctured by rocks, roots, or other objects. Commercial underlayment products are available, but old carpet also works. EPDM water garden liners bonded to a geotextile (Geo-Pond and UltiLiner are two brands) do not require an underlayment.

underplant To plant one plant around or under another, usually to achieve a particular look in a design and/or to keep the soil densely covered with plants to prevent weeds. Shrubs can be underplanted with ground covers, for example. Large perennials can be underplanted with smaller ones, and both can be underplanted with bulbs.

undershrub A low shrub or a subshrub.

understock *See* STOCK

undulate Slightly wavy, either up and down or in and out. Many sources use the term undulate to describe the edge of a leaf, leaflet, or other organ that goes up and down, and use the term sinuate to designate an edge that goes in and out.

undulate leaf margin

unequally pinnate *See* ODD PINNATE

unguiculate Having a claw at the base. This term is used to describe petals and sepals that end with a clawlike base.

uni- A prefix meaning one. Unicarpellate means bearing one carpel; uniflorus, one flower; unipetalous, one petal, for example.

unicate Hooked at the tip.

unifoliate A simple leaf. Bearing only a single leaf.

unifoliolate A compound leaf with only a single leaflet remaining.

unilateral One-sided.

unisexual A flower that has either male or female structures (stamens or pistils) but not both (is imperfect). Also used to refer to plants that bear flowers of all one sex, either staminate (male) or pistillate (female). *See* STAMINATE FLOWER, PISTILLATE FLOWER

united Stuck or clinging together, but not actually fused. This term is used to refer to unlike plant parts that normally are separate as well as to similar structures, such as leaves or filaments, that form a unit. *See* ADHERENT, COHERENT

unity A design principle that means all the parts of a garden or flower arrangement are in scale and harmonious, meaning they work together to make a pleasing whole. Unity is subjective, and personal taste and aesthetics figure into whether a composition is considered unified.

unwanted growth A general term sometimes used in pruning references to refer to growth that is crowding the center of a plant, including watersprouts, rubbing and crossing branches, excessive twiggy growth, suckers at the base of the plant, root suckers, and reverted growth. Use thinning cuts to remove all these types of growth. *See* THINNING CUT

urceolate Pitcher- or urn-shaped. This term is used to describe the corolla (petals) of flowers that are rounded or inflated at the bottom and constricted or narrow at the top. Blueberries (*Vaccinium* spp.) and leucothoes (*Leucothoe* spp.) bear urceolate, or urn-shaped, flowers.

urceolate flower

urent Stinging. Bearing stiff, bristlelike hairs that release an irritating fluid upon contact. Nettles (*Urtica* spp.) are armed with stinging hairs, or urents.

USDA United States Department of Agriculture.

utricle An inflated or bladderlike fruit that has a thin wall and doesn't open along definite lines when ripe (meaning it is indehiscent). It bears one or at most two seeds. Job's tears (*Coix lacryma-jobi*) bears utricles.

vaginate Sheathed. Enclosed in or bearing a sheath. The sheathed petioles of grasses are vaginate.

vallecula, *pl*. **valleculae** A furrow, groove, or depression.

vallecular, **valleculate** Bearing or pertaining to valleculae.

valvate Opening by a valve or valves. Many dehiscent fruits have valves that split at maturity to release seeds, including fruits such as capsules, follicles, and legumes.

valve A segment of a dehiscent fruit that opens at maturity.

V-angle *See* CROTCH, CROTCH ANGLE

varicose Enlarged or swollen in spots.

variegate A general term for any plant with variegated foliage.

variegated Striped, edged, or otherwise marked with areas of different colors. Experts use different terms to describe patterns of variegation: *See* BANDED, BLOTCHED, BORDERED, CLOUDED, DISCOIDAL, DOTTED, EDGED, MARBLED, PAINTED, SPOTTED, STRIPED, TESSELLATED, ZONED

variety Botanists and horticulturists use this term in different ways. In botany, the word variety is the taxonomic category between subspecies and forma. It is used to distinguish a group of naturally occurring plants with characteristics that set them apart from other individuals in the species but do not make them distinct enough to be recognized as a separate species in their own right. Botanical varieties are given latinized names, and a variety name is set in italics and preceded by the abbreviation "var." For example:

Salvia sclarea var. *turkestanica*. In horticulture, the terms cultivar and variety can be used interchangeably: The *International Code of Nomenclature for Cultivated Plants* considers the words cultivar and variety as exact equivalents. A horticultural variety (cultivar) is a particular, distinct form of a plant that originated and is maintained in cultivation by either sexual or asexual propagation. A variety also is uniform (the plants have a consistent, predictable appearance) and stable (the plants remain relatively unchanged).

vascular bundle A cluster of vascular tissue in a stem, root, leaf, or other plant part that contains xylem and phloem, which are specialized tissues that move water, minerals, and food through the plant.

vascular cambium *See* CAMBIUM

vascular plant A plant containing vascular tissue or vessels that conduct water, nutrients, sugars, or other substances. Gymnosperms, angiosperms, ferns, and fern allies are all vascular plants. (Ferns and fern allies are sometimes called lower vascular plants.) Algae, seaweed, mosses, and liverworts do not have specialized vascular tissue. *See* VASCULAR TISSUE

vascular tissue Tissue that moves water, minerals, and food molecules through the roots, stems, and leaves of plants. In higher plants, vascular tissue consists of xylem, which moves water, and phloem, which moves minerals and food.

vase life The length of time cut flowers remain fresh and attractive in a vase or other arrangement. To increase vase life, pick flowers at the optimum time and condition them before arranging. (*See* CUT FLOWERS, CONDITIONING FLOWERS) Recut stems under water as you arrange the flowers, use a floral preservative to lengthen life (*See* FLORAL PRESERVATIVE), and make sure containers stay filled with water so the stem tips always are submerged. Replace the water every 2 days or so to discourage bacteria, which will clog stem ends and cause rot. Recut stems that seem to be clogged.

vegetative Leaves, stems, and other non-flowering plant parts. Vegetative growth consists of leaves and stems, but not flowers.

vegetative frond *See* STERILE FROND

vegetative propagation To increase plants without sex. Also called asexual propagation, this is a general term used to refer to all forms of propagation that do not involve seeds. Plants propagated by vegetative means are grown from naturally produced plant parts: *See* BULBIL, CORMEL, OFFSET, PLANTLET, and MOTHER FERN for information on these structures. Various techniques also are used to propagate plants vegetatively (*See* CUTTINGS, DIVISION, BUDDING, LAYERNG, GRAFTING, TISSUE CULTURE). All vegetative propagation techniques yield plants that are genetically identical to their parent plant.

vegetative reproduction Reproducing vegetatively by producing structures such as bulbils, cormils, stolons, or offsetts instead of by producing seeds.

vein A strand of vascular tissue, consisting of xylem and phloem (a vascular bundle), that is visible in a leaf or other plant part.

veinlet A very thin vein.

velutinous Velvety. Covered with short, soft, woolly hairs that are matted down and give the surface a velvetlike look and feel. A velutinous surface has thicker, denser hairs than a tomentose one. Most often used to describe leaf surfaces.

venation pinnate *See* PINNATE VENATION

venation The arrangement of the veins on the surface of a leaf or other organ. Also called nervation.

venation, arcuate *See* ARCUATE

venation, palmate *See* PALMATE VENATION

venation, parallel *See* PARALLEL VENATION

venation, reticulate *See* RETICULATE

venenose Extremely poisonous.

venose Having veins.

ventral The side of a plant part (such as a leaf) that faces toward the main stem, or axis. The top of a leaf is the ventral side. The same as adaxial.

ventricose Having a pronounced swelling or pouch on one side, usually at the bottom. The term gibbous means the same thing, but is used to indicate a less pronounced swelling.

vermiculite A mica-like mineral that is expanded at high temperatures to form lightweight pelletlike granules that retain water but also provide good aeration when added to various potting mixes.

vermiform, vermiculate Worm-shaped. Usually used to describe a pattern of sunken, wavy lines.

vernal Appearing or blooming in spring.

vernalization The process of treating seeds, bulbs, or plants to cause them to break dormancy or flower. This is most often accomplished by storing them in freezing or nearly freezing temperatures. Seeds can be vernalized simply by sowing them outdoors in fall to subject them to winter's cold temperatures; vernalized seeds break dormancy when spring arrives and often grow more rapidly than unvernalized ones. Hardy spring bulbs such as daffodils or tulips that have been potted up for forcing need to be vernalized by holding them in a cold spot for several weeks before they will flower. Biennials such as parsley and most foxgloves (*Digitalis purpurea*) do not flower until they have received a period of cold temperatures.

vernation The manner in which leaves are arranged in a bud.

verrucose Warty. Covered with wartlike lumps. Most often used to describe leaf surfaces.

versatile Attached near the middle rather than at the end and capable of free movement. Some anthers, including those of lilies (*Lilium* spp.), are versatile.

versicolor Variously colored or changeable in color.

vertical line A shape used in flower arranging in which the flowers, leaves, and other plant materials are positioned along a single, main axis or line, vertical to the container or the surface on which it rests. The main line of the arrangement usually is repeated rhythmically on either side with more plant material.

vertical line arrangement

verticil *See* WHORL

verticillaster This type of floral arrangement consists of pairs of cymes attached at the leaf axils. The flowers seem to surround the stem, but since they are not attached individually they form a false whorl rather than a true one. Many members of the mint family (Lamiaceae) produce spikelike flower clusters with individual blooms arranged in this manner, including mints (*Mentha* spp.), bells of Ireland (*Moluccella* spp.), and salvias such as mealy cup sage (*Salvia farinacea*) and scarlet sage (*S. splendens*).

verticillaster

verticillate Forming or appearing to form a whorl. *See* WHORL

verticutter A power tool used in overseeding a lawn that slices through thatch and into soil to prepare the site for sowing. *See* OVERSEEDING

vesiculose Covered with small, bladderlike sacs, called vesicles, that are filled with fluid or air. Most often used to describe leaf surfaces.

vespertine Functioning or opening in the evening.

vessel *See* XYLEM

vestigal *See* RUDIMENTARY

vexillum The large, uppermost petal in a papilionaceous flower such as a sweet pea (*Lathyrus odoratus*). Also called a standard or banner.

viable Capable of living. This term is used to describe seeds that contain a living embryo and are capable of germinating.

villous Covered with long, soft hairs that give the surface a shaggy texture. Most often used to describe leaf surfaces.

vimineous Bearing twigs that are long and flexible. Composed of twigs. Twiglike.

vine A plant that has long, flexible, stems that are unable to support the plant. Vines climb by various means: They can twine around supports such as trellises or other plants, they can stick to objects by holdfasts, or they can climb via tendrils. *See also* CLIMBER

vinegars *See* HERB VINEGARS

virescence, virescent Becoming or turning green or greenish. This term is used to describe plant tissues that become green, but are not normally green.

virgate Long, straight, thin, and erect. Wandlike.

viruses Plant diseases that cause crinkled, deformed leaves that often have yellow-green mottling. Infected plants are stunted or unusually bushy and either do not set fruit or produce deformed fruit that is dry and flavorless. Virus diseases cannot be cured: Pull up and destroy infected plants. Protect crops with floating row covers or use sprays to control the insects that spread the viruses, including aphids, cucumber beetles, leafhoppers, and whiteflies.

viscid Sticky, gluey, or gummy. Covered with a sticky or gummy exudate. Petunias (*Petunia* spp.) have viscid leaves and stems.

viscidulous Slightly sticky or gummy.

viticulture The science and art of growing grapes.

viviparous Sprouting on the parent plant. This term is used to describe seeds or bulbs that sprout and form plantlets while still attached to the parent plant. It is also used to refer to the plants that bear such seeds or plants. Mother fern (*Asplenium bulbiferum*) bears small bulblets on its leaves that sprout into plantlets. In general, plantlets borne in this manner do not get very large or reach maturity unless the leaf is pinned to the ground or to a pot filled with sand or an appropriate rooting medium.

volubile Twining.

volute Rolled up. *See also* INVOLUTE, REVOLUTE

walking ferns *See* MOTHER FERNS

wall nail A specially designed nail that can be pounded into walls and used to attach vines to the wall surface. Wall nails have a strip of soft, bendable lead attached to the head, which can be bent around a vine stem.

warm colors *See* HOT COLORS

warm-moist stratification *See* STRATIFICATION

warm-season grass Grasses that grow best during the summertime, when temperatures are between 80 and 95°F. Warm-season grasses turn brown in fall and remain brown through the winter. Warm-season grasses include zoysiagrass, centipedegrass, bahiagrass, Bermudagrass, St. Augustine grass, and carpetgrass.

warm-weather annuals Also called tender annuals, these are the annuals that thrive in summer heat and fill gardens with color from early summer to fall. Sow seeds for warm-weather annuals outdoors in spring after the last frost date, provided your growing season is long enough. Or start seeds indoors from 6 to as many as 12 weeks before the last spring frost date, depending on the species. Move hardened-off plants to the garden after the last spring frost date. With most warm-weather annuals, it's best to wait to transplant until the soil has warmed up and air temperatures remain above at least 40°F at night; although they may survive cool conditions, plants will be stunted and ones spared exposure to cool temperatures will quickly catch up with and surpass them.

warm-weather crops Vegetable crops that thrive in warm temperatures, including peppers, eggplants, tomatoes, summer squash, lima and snap beans, cucumbers, melons, watermelons, sweet potatoes, and corn. All are grown as warm-weather annuals (*See* WARM-WEATHER ANNUAL).

wart A firm lump or swelling.

water garden liners Various materials are available for lining a water garden. Preformed, rigid units are made of fiberglass or various plastics. Of these, fiberglass units are the best buy because they are rigid, durable, strong, and long-lived. Plastic pond liners are less expensive, but tend to be short-lived. To install a rigid liner, dig a hole to fit its shape, line the hole with sand, carefully level the liner from edge to edge, and then backfill around it to support the sides. Flexible liners can be installed in any shape hole, and are made of PVC and polyethylene as well as rubber (*See* EPDM, BUTYL), which is a much more durable and longer-lived material. Here's how to determine the overall size of the liner required: Maximum width plus twice the depth; maximum length plus twice the depth. Then add 18 inches to both length and width dimensions; this ensures you'll have enough liner to overlap the edges of the hole, plus run down the sides and line the bottom. To install a flexible liner, dig the hole and remove any roots, sharp rocks, or other objects that may damage it. Line the hole with sand, especially if the soil is very rocky. Check to make sure the sides of the hole are level (otherwise the water will look lopsided). Then line the hole with underlayment (*See* UNDERLAYMENT) before spreading the liner. Hold the edges of the liner in place with stones or bricks while filling the hole with water; move the stones as necessary as the liner settles into the hole. Edge water gardens built with either rigid or flexible liners with flagstones or rocks, mortared in place, to hide the liner.

watering from below This technique is valuable when caring for newly sown seeds, seedlings, and cuttings because it prevents them from being washed out of the pots by a flood of water. Watering from below also helps prevent soilborne diseases such as damping off from attacking because it keeps the soil surface slightly dryer than the rest of the medium. To water from below, simply set pots in a flat of water for several minutes until the water is drawn up to the surface via capillary action. Remove the pots to let the water drain away. If containers are sitting in a watertight flat, simply fill it with water and pour off the excess after the soil surface is moist.

water shoots *See* WATERSPROUTS

watersprout A thin, vertical stem arising from a branch that usually is very fast growing and unbranched or nearly so. Also called water shoots, watersprouts seldom flower or bear fruit, and should be removed. They can be removed during the dormant season or in midsummer.

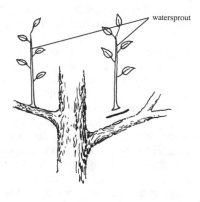

watersprout

water table The top level of the soil that is saturated with water. Damp spots that appear in the lawn during the spring or other times of year, as well as springs, indicate a high water table. Spots on a property that have a high water table are ideal for plantings of marginal- and moisture-loving plants (*See* MARGINAL PLANTS, MOISTURE-LOVING PLANTS). They aren't good places to locate water gardens that are lined with preformed or flexible liners, however. The force of ground water can push a preformed liner right out of the ground, while air in water

causes bubbles that will cause a flexible liner to float up off the bottom of the pool and look decidedly unattractive.

wattle fence A temporary fence constructed by weaving young, straight, pliable stems of shrubs between upright posts.

wavy *See* UNDULATE, SINUATE, REPAND

wax *See* GRAFTING WAX

waxy Plastic- or waxlike in texture and yellowish white in color.

webbed, weblike *See* ARACHNOID

wedge grafting *See* SAW-KERF GRAFTING

wedge-shaped *See* CUNEATE

weed Sometimes defined as "any plant growing where it is not wanted," the term weed is usually used to refer to wild species or non-native plants that pop up in disturbed areas because they self-sow so freely or have invasive, spreading roots. Prevention is very helpful when dealing with weeds. When preparing a new garden bed, remove as many of the weeds as possible—roots and all—before you dig or till. Otherwise you'll chop up and spread roots during the digging process, propagating the weeds in the process. Solarizing soil also helps control weeds. (*See* SOLARIZATION) Repeatedly tilling a site can also work: Remove weeds and prepare the soil, then wait about 2 weeks to let weeds sprout, then till or hoe shallowly to eliminate weeds again. Repeat the process once or twice more before planting. Mulching also is an effective defense against weeds. (*See* MULCH) For best results when weeding, wait until after a rain so it is easier to pull plants out root and all. *See also* FLAMING and HERBICIDES for other weed controls. Other organic control options include pouring boiling water over weeds or pulling off the tops and dousing the roots with a mixture of vinegar and salt. These controls are best in paved areas, where you don't want any plants to grow.

weeders Gardeners have developed various tools for rooting out weeds by hand. Various weeders with heads that resemble those of full-size hoes are available, including Dutch weeders with triangular blades (both left- and right-handed models are available) and collinear weeders, which have a narrow, rectangular blade. A Cape Cod weeder has an L-shaped blade and is handy for working in very tight places—among closely spaced plants, for example. A crack weeder is even narrower and is designed for rooting weeds out of paving cracks and other tight spaces. A farmer's weeder, sometimes called a grub knife, resembles a heavy knife and is useful for removing taprooted perennials and for other tasks such as digging holes or digging up offsets or other small plants. *See also* ASPARAGUS FORK, TROWEL

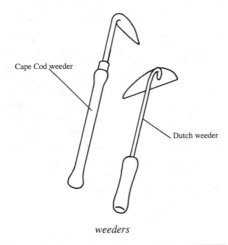

Cape Cod weeder

Dutch weeder

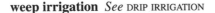

weeders

weep irrigation *See* DRIP IRRIGATION

weevils These are small, hard-shelled beetles with long snouts that usually feed at night and chew notches in leaves, stems, and buds. The larvae are grubs that feed on plant roots. To control them, drench the soil around plants with parasitic nematodes to control larvae. Handpick adults, or treat serious infestations by dusting plants with pyrethrins or rotenone in the evening.

wheel cultivator Also called a wheel hoe, this implement is ideal for anyone with a large garden with straight rows to be weeded or cultivated. It has a single small wheel attached to handles that resemble the handlebars of a bicycle. Most models come with various attachments similar to the many variations of a hoe, including oscillating heads, a head that digs furrows, and a tined cultivator.

wheel hoe *See* WHEEL CULTIVATOR

whip A young, single-stemmed tree, either grown from seeds or grafted, that does not have any side branches. This term also is used to refer to a young, unbranched tree that has been grafted or budded onto a seedling rootstock. Fruit trees, for example, are commonly sold as 1-year-old whips. Also called unbranched whips.

whip graft *See* WHIP-AND-TONGUE GRAFT

whip-and-tongue graft A graft ideal for uniting relatively small stocks and scions (from $^1/_4$ to $^1/_2$ inch in diameter is best) that features interlocking tongues of wood. It can also be used to top-work a small shrub or tree. Stock and scion that are of similar diameters are best, and scions should have two or three buds. To make a whip-and-tongue graft, make a smooth, sloping, 1- to $2^1/_2$-inch-long cut in the top of the stock and the bottom of the scion with a single stroke of a very sharp grafting knife. Starting about one-third down from the tip of each cut surface, make a second cut, about half as long as the first cut. Slice down through the end, parallel to the first on each piece; don't just split the wood along the grain. Then fit stock and scion together with the tongues interlocking and the cambium layers lined up. If stock and scion are not exactly the same diameter, match the cambium layers along one side. The lower tip of the scion should match the lower edge of the cut on the stock; if it sticks out, often a knot of callus will form. Wrap or tie the two pieces together with a rubber budding strip, waxed string, or raffia. Cover the union with grafting wax to prevent dessication, and also dab a bit of wax on the cut end of the scion. Plants grafted in this manner can be planted with the graft union below the soil surface, but once topgrowth has begun, inspect the graft union to make sure it is strong and to remove strips or string before they constrict the stem. *See* GRAFTING

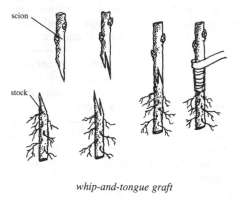

scion

stock

whip-and-tongue graft

whiteflies Tiny flies with white, powdery wings that cluster on the undersides of leaves and fly up in great numbers when disturbed. Both adults and nymphs suck plant juices, making infested plants look yellow, sickly, and stunted. They also exude a sticky honeydew that fosters the growth of black sooty mold as they feed. Whiteflies can be a problem in the garden as well as indoors. Indoors, catch whiteflies on sticky yellow cards or use a hand-held vacuum to suck pests off plants. Spray serious infestations with insecticidal soap, superior oil, pyrethrins, or rotenone.

white-woolly A woolly surface covered with white hairs.

whole-root graft *See* ROOT GRAFTING

whorl Three or more leaves, flowers, petals, or other organs arranged in a circle around a stem at the same node, which is the point on a stem where one or more leaves are attached. Also called a verticil. Bugleweeds (*Ajuga* spp.) bear their flowers in whorls.

whorled leaves

whorled Arranged in a whorl.

wick watering An automatic watering technique that can be used to provide constantly moist soil, which some houseplants require. While commercial systems are available, setting up a plant for wick watering is relatively easy with a thin strip of pantyhose (nylon cord works as well). Gently dump the plant out of its pot and thread the strip of pantyhose up through the drainage hole and along the side of the root ball. Hold it in place as you repot the plant. Cut a small hole in the top of a plastic container and another on one side. Thread the other end of the pantyhose strip into the top of the container, and then keep the container filled with water.

wide rows *See* ROWS

wild-collected Wildflowers that have been dug from natural areas and potted for sale or sold bare-root. Conscientious gardeners avoid wild-collected plants, because the practice depletes native populations of wildflowers. Native orchids, trilliums (*Trillium* spp.), and native lilies (*Lilium* spp.) are frequently wild-collected because they take a lot of time and effort to propagate. When buying wildflowers, ask questions and look for nursery-propagated plants; industry standards allow companies to grow wild-collected plants in the nursery for a year or two and then sell them as "nursery-grown." Extremely inexpensive plants and ones that look like they have been recently potted up (with leaves and stems askew) are two other signs of wild-collected plants.

wildflower garden An informal garden, in sun or shade, that features primarily native plants.

wildlife garden A garden designed to attract all manner of garden visitors from birds, squirrels, and rabbits to toads, frogs, salamanders, butterflies, and insects. The basic requirements of backyard wildlife are food, water, and shelter. Plants provide a basic source of food—berry-bearing shrubs, trees that produce nuts, as well as perennials and annuals that provide seeds, for example.

Other creatures will visit a wildlife garden in search of prey in the form or insects or larger animals. A garden pond or shallow water basins and birdbaths can provide water, while thickets of shrubs and trees—and even brush piles—create shelter that animals require to feel at home. For more information on backyard wildlife, write Backyard Wildlife Habitat Program, National Wildlife Federation, 8925 Leesburg Pike, Vienna, VA 22184. (703) 790-4000 or visit their website at *www.rwf.org/habitats/*.

wilting A plant that has lost turgor in plant cells because it is transpiring more water than it can take up in the roots, thus causing leaves and stem tips to droop.

wilts Both bacteria and fungi cause wilt diseases, and afflicted plants may have yellow or browned leaves that curl upward or drop early. They also commonly wilt and/or are stunted. Symptoms may affect the whole plant or just one side. Prevent wilts by growing resistant cultivars and protecting plants with floating row covers to control cucumber beetles, flea beetles, and other insects that spread the diseases. Remove and destroy infected plants.

windbreak A planting or structure designed to provide protection from prevailing winds. *See* SHELTERBELT

windfall Fruit that has dropped on the ground because of wind or because it is ripe.

wind-pollination Many plants depend on wind to transfer pollen from anther to stigma. Wind-pollinated plants—including oaks (*Quercus* spp.), pines (*Pinus* spp.), and ragweed (*Ambrosia* spp.)—are the bane of allergy sufferers. Corn also is wind-pollinated, and to ensure the production of ears that are well filled with succulent kernels, it needs to be planted in blocks rather than rows. Otherwise, the pollen (produced on the tassels) won't be blown evenly enough to female flowers (the ears).

windrock A condition caused by strong winds that move and damage tree roots and destabilize the tree.

windrow A row of cut hay or grain. A row of leaves blown by the wind. Also, a long, broad compost pile used in commercial composting operations and turned by a front loader or other piece of equipment.

windthrow A tree that blows over because the topgrowth isn't supported by wide-spreading roots. This is usually caused by improper planting. *See* PLANTING

wing A thin, flat extension, which is often membranelike, on an organ such as a stem. Burning bush (*Euonymus alatus*) bears winged stems, for example. *See also* PTEROUS-, -PTEROUS, ALATE Also, a side petal in a paplionaceous flower. *See* PAPILIONACEOUS

winged Bearing wings.

winnow, winnowing Using air to separate seeds or grains from chaff, which are the dry, thin, membranelike scales or bracts that surround them. To winnow, select a spot with a light breeze or sit a few feet away from a fan. Then place seeds in a shallow container and toss them gently in the air, which will carry away the lighter chaff. (If the pods have not released all the seeds, gently crush them before winnowing.) Obviously, too much wind will also blow away the seeds, so experiment to get the right combination before winnowing seeds that are hard to replace.

winter annual An annual that germinates in fall, blooms the following spring, and is dead by summertime, either because it has finished setting seeds or because it has been killed by warm temperatures.

winter bud A dormant vegetative shoot. *See* TURION

winterburn A condition on woody plants such as shrubs and trees caused by winds that dry out bark and leaves. Winterburn kills or damages bark and turns the edges of broad-leaved evergreens brown. *See* EXPOSURE

wintergreen *See* EVERGREEN

winterkill A condition caused by winter temperatures that drop suddenly, killing top growth of trees, shrubs, or other plants that would be hardy under normal conditions. In unusually cold years, winterkill can happen if the ground freezes too deeply.

winter mulch A mulch that is installed in fall to protect plants over the winter. Winter mulches are commonly used in northern gardens or to protect plants that are not quite hardy in the zone they are being grown in. Install them after the ground has frozen completely. Winter mulches should be loose and open and not hold moisture around the crowns: Evergreen boughs, weed-free straw, and saltmarsh hay are all effective. Remove winter mulch in late winter or early spring. *See also* WINTER PROTECTION

winter protection Artificial coverings that protect a plant from inclement winter weather. In the Deep South, a light covering with sheets or blankets for a few nights may be all the winter protection many species require, but farther north, covering the garden with a layer of winter mulch is a common form of winter protection. For best results, use several inches of chopped leaves, saltmarsh hay, or straw, and cover beds only after the ground has frozen. Otherwise, vermin such as voles and mice may move in and feast on the crowns of plants over winter, with the mulch providing a warm protective cover. Remove winter mulch gradually in late winter to early spring as plants begin to grow and temperatures warm up. To protect tender roses and other plants that tend to be winter damaged in a particular zone, surround them with cones or other protective devices stuffed with leaves. Burying plants in shallow trenches is another technique: Figs and climbing roses are often laid on the ground and covered with a mound of loose soil or mulch. Or, mound loose soil or mulch around the crown of the plant. Where wet, rainy winters are the norm, winter mulch may cause more problems than it solves, because it can cause rot. In this case, keep the plants uncovered, and inspect the garden regularly over winter to look for signs of frost heaving. A site with perfect drainage may help plants that resent wet soil in winter.

winter weed A weed that germinates in late summer or fall and blooms and sets seed in early spring.

wiring A technique used by flower arrangers and florists to mount flowers and leaves in corsages, bouquets, or other arrangements. Wiring allows the arranger to use short-stemmed blooms and set them in a particular direction. It is also helpful for reinforcing weak-stemmed plants to achieve a particular effect. In addition, many dried flowers are routinely wired because their stems are so brittle they are essentially worthless in holding the blooms in arrangements. Florist's wire is handiest for wiring, and comes in green, which makes it easy to conceal. Several gauges, or weights, are available: Use heavier gauges for heavier flowers, and lighter ones for more delicate blooms. The exact technique for wiring depends on the bloom. To wire roses or other flowers with a fairly thick base, stick the wire through the base of the flower and twirl the end around the stem bottom to create a new, sturdier stem. Use this procedure for wiring leaves as well. Wire flat-topped flowers such as daisies and strawflowers by sticking the wire up through the center of the bloom, making a hook in the end, and pulling the hook down into the center of the bloom. In this case the end of the wire doesn't need to come all the way through the bloom. If the wires will be visible, cover them with florist's tape. (*See* TAPING) Wiring also is a technique used in bonsai to adjust the position of branches and train growth in a particular direction. Copper or aluminum wire in various sizes, or gauges, is used for this purpose.

wiring

witch's broom A dense cluster of stunted, twiggy growth in a tree or shrub. They can be pruned out if desired. Many dwarf conifers originated as witch's brooms.

wood ashes A valuable source of potassium (from 8 to as much as 15 percent) along with phosphates, iron, magnesium.

wood Dense, hard plant tissue made up of secondary xylem cells. *See* XYLEM

woody Hard and woodlike or nearly so. Ligneous.

woody-based A plant that has succulent, herbaceous stems and woody or somewhat woody growth at the base. This is a general term applied to perennials that usually have longer or larger herbaceous shoots than subshrubs. Many salvias (*Salvia* spp.) are characterized as woody-based perennials. Annuals also can be woody-based; Mexican sunflower (*Tithonia rotundifolia*) and coleus (*Solenostemon scutellarioides*), a tender perennial grown as an annual, develop woody stems as the season progresses. *See also* SUBSHRUB

woolly This is a general term meaning covered with long, soft, usually matted hairs. *See also* LANATE, LANGUINOSE, TOMENTOSE, FLOCCOSE, PANNOSE

wound dressing, wound paint A specialized paint or material used to cover pruning cuts on trees. Using wound dressing generally is no longer recommended.

wounding This technique is invaluable for encouraging root formation in cuttings, especially ones that are slow or difficult to root, because it removes the hardened, lignified layer around the stem base to expose the cambium. To wound a cutting, use a clean knife or razor blade to make a 1-inch-long vertical slice through the bark at the base of the cutting and into the wood. Wound one or both sides of each cutting. Sometimes stripping the leaves off the lower portion of the cutting will suffice if it pulls off enough bark. After wounding, treat the cutting with rooting hormone (make sure to get powder on the whole wounded area) and plant as usual.

wounding

× The character used to designate a plant of hybrid origin. When the × precedes the genus name, it indicates a hybrid between two genera—× *Brassocattleya* is a hybrid between *Brassavola* and *Cattleya*, for example. When the × appears between the genus and the specific epithet, it indicates a cross between two species in the same genus. Goldflame honeysuckle (*Lonicera × heckrottii*) is a cross between *L. × americana* (another hybrid) and *L. sempervirens*.

xeric Characterized by or adapted to dry areas.

xeriscape A garden or landscape designed for a dry region that incorporates various water-saving features to create plantings that are extremely efficient in the use of water. Although xeriscaping was originally developed to help cope with chronic water shortages in the western United States, even gardeners in areas with reliable rainfall benefit from the basic water-saving principles it employs. In a xeriscape, water-saving techniques are incorporated into the design. Principles include: digging the soil deeply and adding plenty of organic matter to encourage deep roots and make plants more drought tolerant; mulching any unplanted soil to conserve moisture; watering efficiently (usually with drip irrigation); using drought-tolerant plants; minimizing lawn areas, which require lots of water to look their best.

xero- A prefix meaning dry.

xeromorphic Having adaptions to dry environments. Cacti and succulents are able to store water to help them withstand dry conditions, for example. Many other desert natives have reduced leaves or leaves that are covered with waxy coatings to lessen water loss.

xerophyte A plant that grows in dry soil or is adapted to dry environments. Cacti and succulents are xerophytes.

xerophytic Able to grow in dry environments.

xylem The main water-conducting tissue of both woody and herbaceous plants, which moves water up out of the soil to leaves and other aboveground plant parts. Xylem consists of living and nonliving cells that have lignified cell walls. In gymnosperms such as conifers, cycads, and ferns, water moves through specialized cells called tracheids, which are nonliving when mature. They lack a nucleus and cytoplasm, and have only a thin membrane at each end as a cell wall. Water moves from cell to cell through tracheids via a series of pits in the cell walls. In angiosperms, or flowering plants, water moves through specialized cells called vessels. Like tracheids, vessels are empty and nonliving when they are mature (they lack a nucleus and cytoplasm). They are lined up end to end, and just as they mature, the cell walls at either end dissolve (or partially dissolve), creating long, continuous columns through which water can pass. Because of their longer length, vessels are less efficient supporting structures than tracheids; in angiosperms, xylem fibers aid in supporting the plant. Primary xylem arises from the apical meristems located in shoot and root tips. Secondary xylem, found in the trunks and branches of perennial woody plants, is created by the vascular cambium, a very thin layer of meristematic cells under the bark. Xylem tissue forms the annual rings of a tree; xylem cells laid down in spring are large and have thin cell walls, making them appear lighter and less dense than those produced in summer, which are smaller and thicker. Secondary xylem is called sapwood when it is still actively conducting water through the plant. As the water-conducting tissues gradually become clogged with substances such as gums and resins, the sapwood turns darker. Eventually, the cells can no longer conduct liquids. The darker wood is called heartwood.

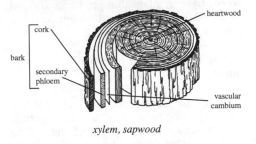

xylem, sapwood

zigzag A shape used in flower arranging in which the main flowers, leaves, and other plant materials are positioned in a restless, Z-shaped pattern.

zigzag arrangement

zoned A variegation pattern in which a curved band or large blotch of one color runs across a different background color. Many bedding, also called zonal, geraniums (*Pelargonium* spp.) have green leaves marked with a darker zone.

zoophilous Pollinated by animals.

zygomorphic This term is used to designate a type of irregular flower that is bilaterally symmetrical, meaning it can only be divided into two mirror-image halves along one plane or line. Snapdragons (*Antirrhinum majus*), gladiolus (*Gladiolus* spp.), and orchids (including *Cattleya* spp. and *Phalaenopsis* spp.) produce zygomorphic flowers. *See also* IRREGULAR

zygomorphic flower

zygote A fertilized egg. The result of the union between a male and female gamete.

BASIC BOTANY

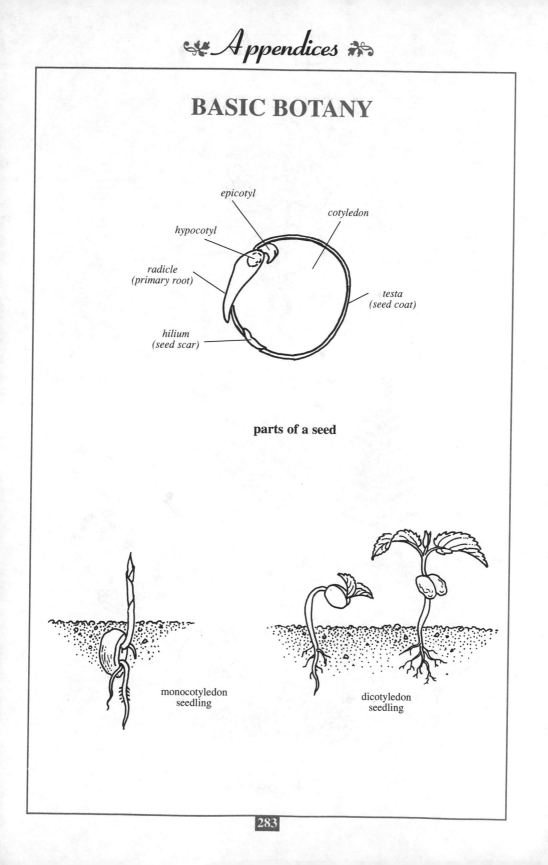

epicotyl

hypocotyl

cotyledon

radicle
(primary root)

testa
(seed coat)

hilium
(seed scar)

parts of a seed

monocotyledon
seedling

dicotyledon
seedling

BASIC BOTANY

Continued

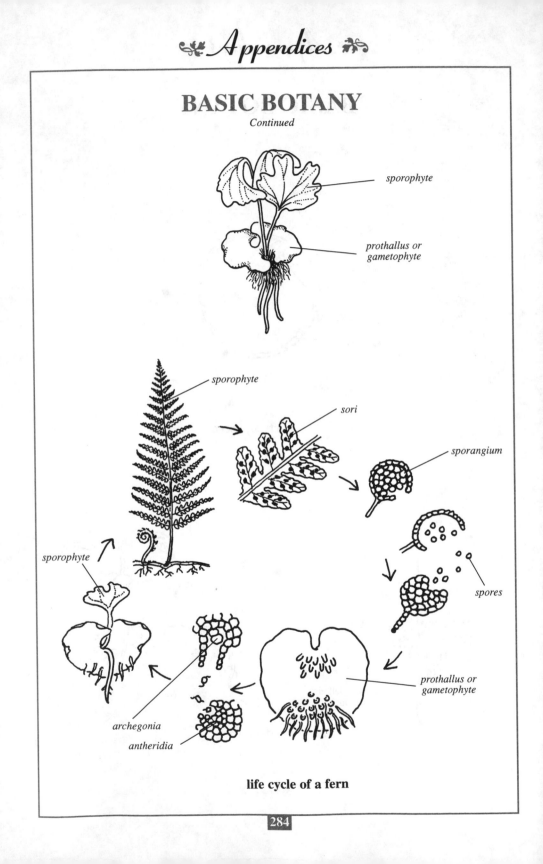

life cycle of a fern

BASIC BOTANY
Continued

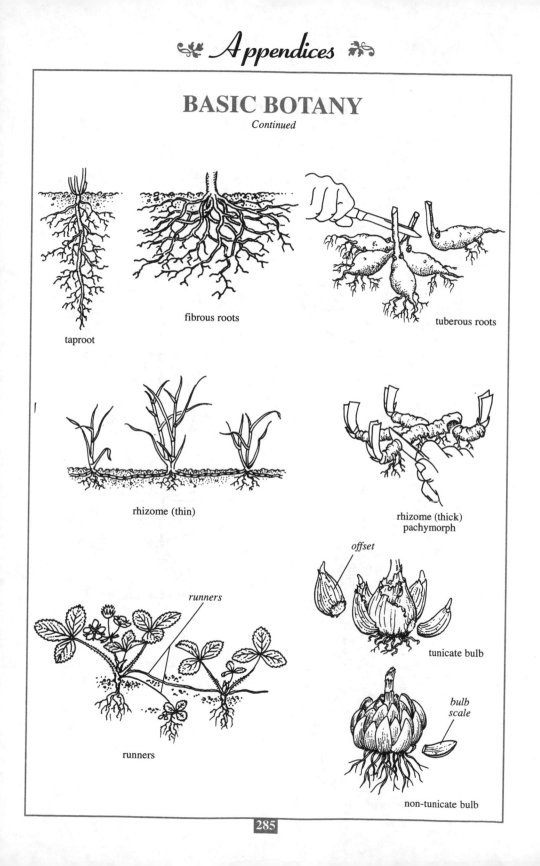

taproot

fibrous roots

tuberous roots

rhizome (thin)

rhizome (thick)
pachymorph

offset

runners

tunicate bulb

bulb scale

runners

non-tunicate bulb

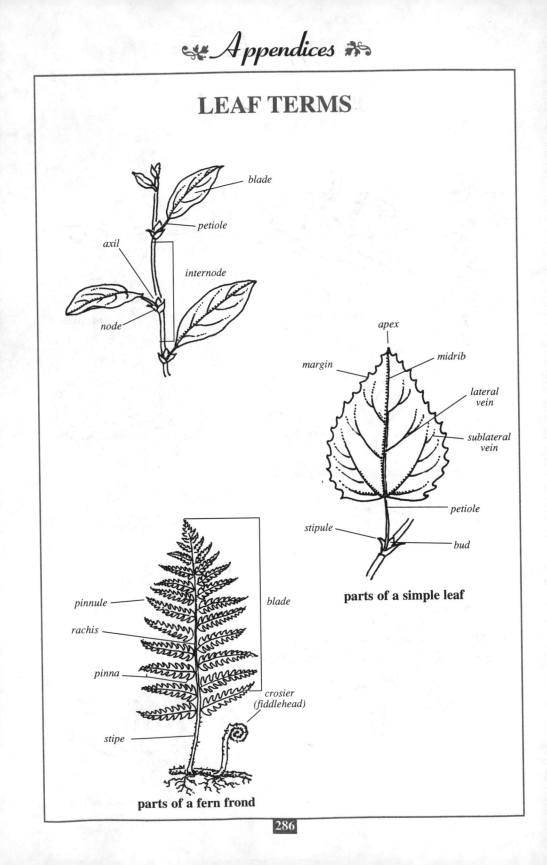

LEAF TERMS

blade

petiole

axil

internode

node

apex

margin

midrib

lateral vein

sublateral vein

petiole

stipule

bud

parts of a simple leaf

pinnule

blade

rachis

pinna

crosier (fiddlehead)

stipe

parts of a fern frond

LEAF TERMS
Continued

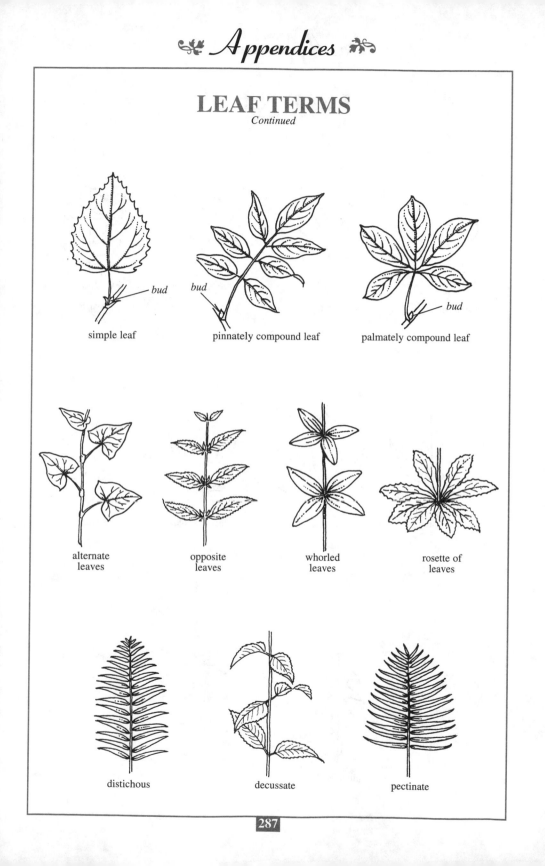

simple leaf

pinnately compound leaf

palmately compound leaf

alternate leaves

opposite leaves

whorled leaves

rosette of leaves

distichous

decussate

pectinate

LEAF TERMS
Continued

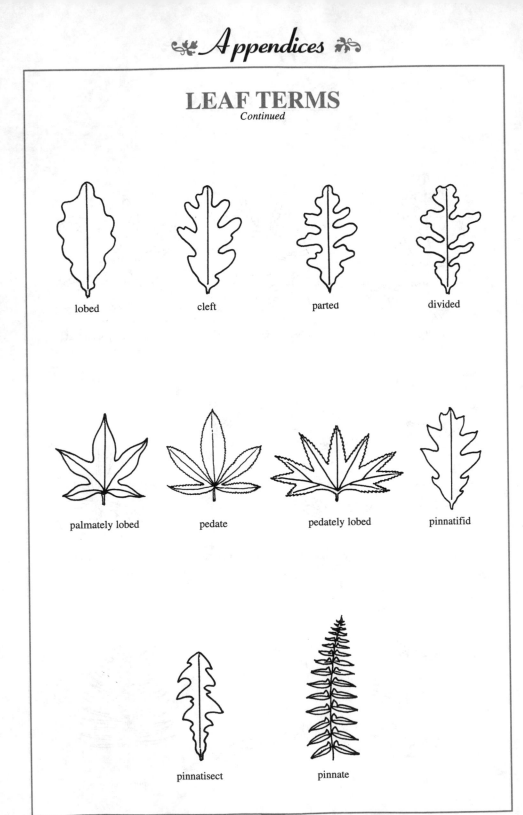

lobed　　　　cleft　　　　parted　　　　divided

palmately lobed　　　pedate　　　pedately lobed　　　pinnatifid

pinnatisect　　　　pinnate

LEAF TERMS
Continued

even pinnate

odd pinnate

pinnate-pinnatifid

bipinnatifid

bipinnate

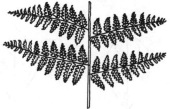

bipinnate-pinnatifid

tripinnate

LEAF SHAPES

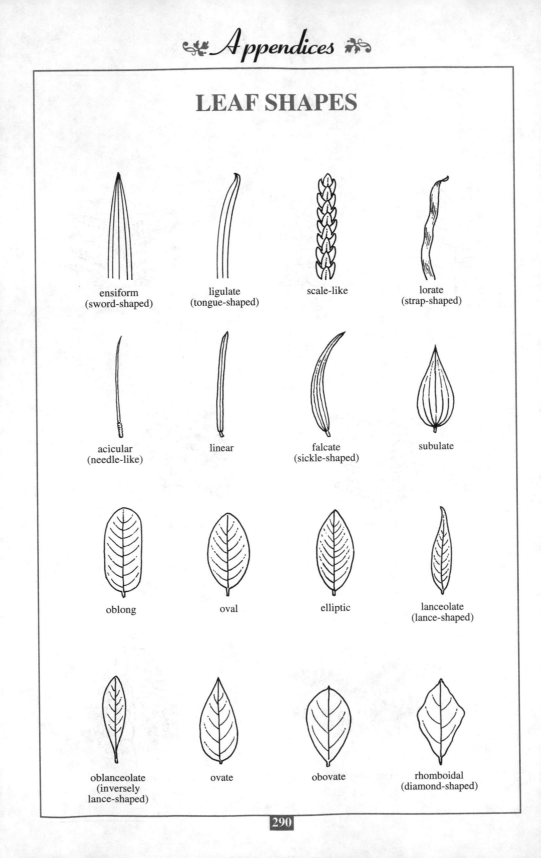

ensiform
(sword-shaped)

ligulate
(tongue-shaped)

scale-like

lorate
(strap-shaped)

acicular
(needle-like)

linear

falcate
(sickle-shaped)

subulate

oblong

oval

elliptic

lanceolate
(lance-shaped)

oblanceolate
(inversely
lance-shaped)

ovate

obovate

rhomboidal
(diamond-shaped)

LEAF SHAPES
Continued

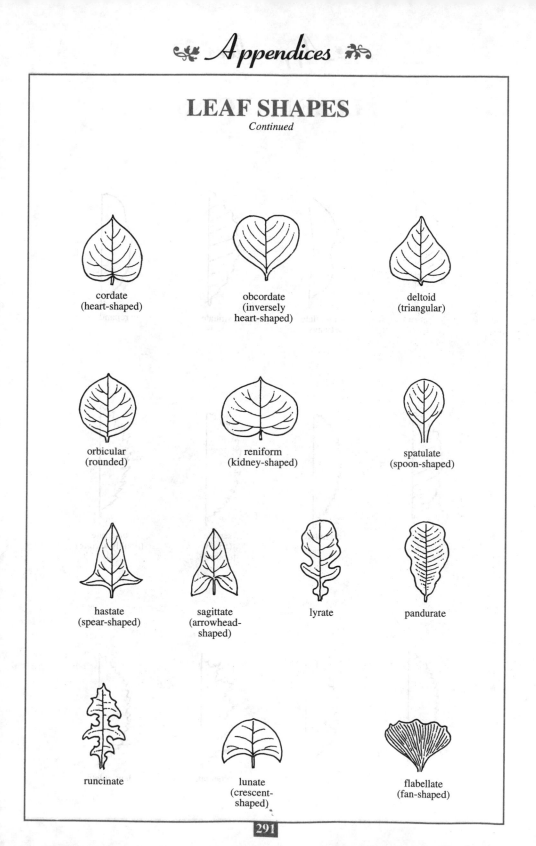

cordate
(heart-shaped)

obcordate
(inversely
heart-shaped)

deltoid
(triangular)

orbicular
(rounded)

reniform
(kidney-shaped)

spatulate
(spoon-shaped)

hastate
(spear-shaped)

sagittate
(arrowhead-
shaped)

lyrate

pandurate

runcinate

lunate
(crescent-
shaped)

flabellate
(fan-shaped)

LEAF MARGINS

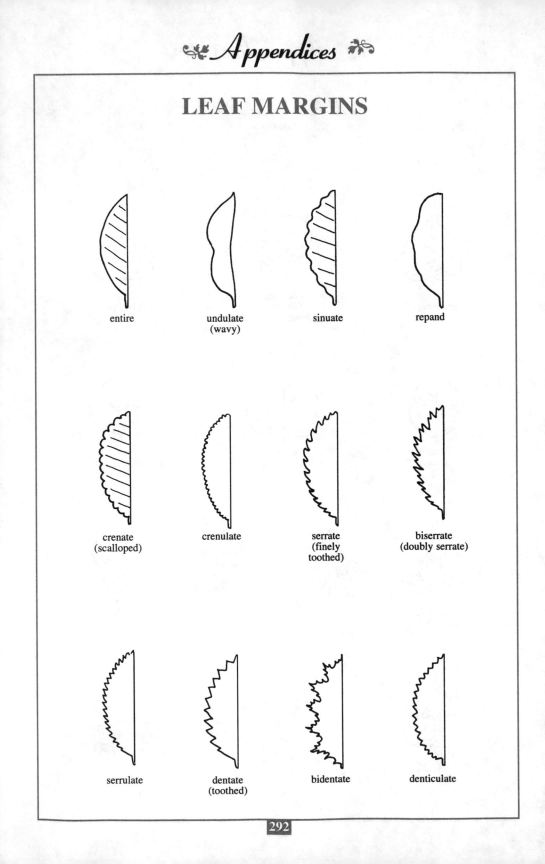

entire

undulate
(wavy)

sinuate

repand

crenate
(scalloped)

crenulate

serrate
(finely
toothed)

biserrate
(doubly serrate)

serrulate

dentate
(toothed)

bidentate

denticulate

LEAF MARGINS
Continued

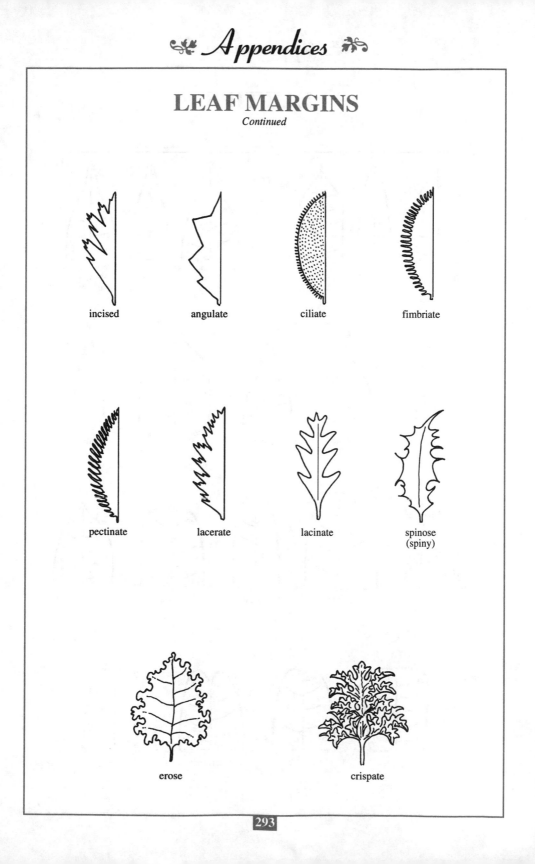

incised

angulate

ciliate

fimbriate

pectinate

lacerate

lacinate

spinose
(spiny)

erose

crispate

LEAF TIPS

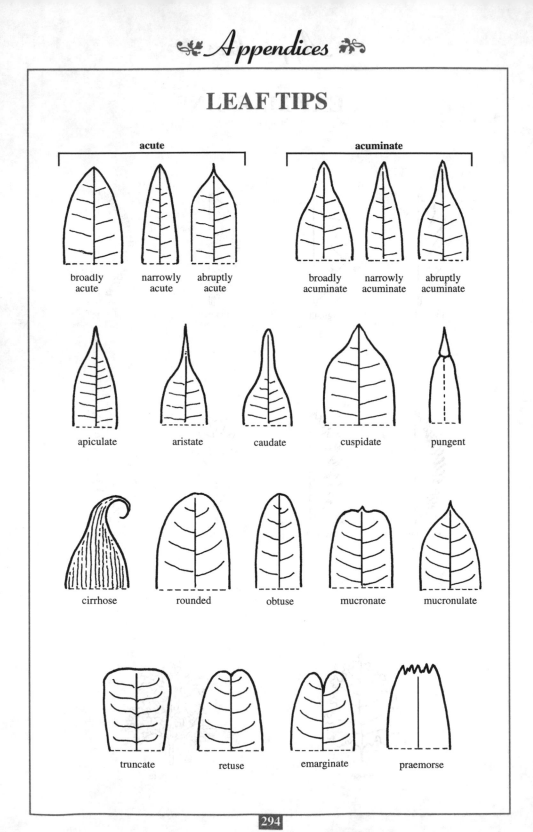

acute

broadly
acute

narrowly
acute

abruptly
acute

acuminate

broadly
acuminate

narrowly
acuminate

abruptly
acuminate

apiculate

aristate

caudate

cuspidate

pungent

cirrhose

rounded

obtuse

mucronate

mucronulate

truncate

retuse

emarginate

praemorse

LEAF BASES

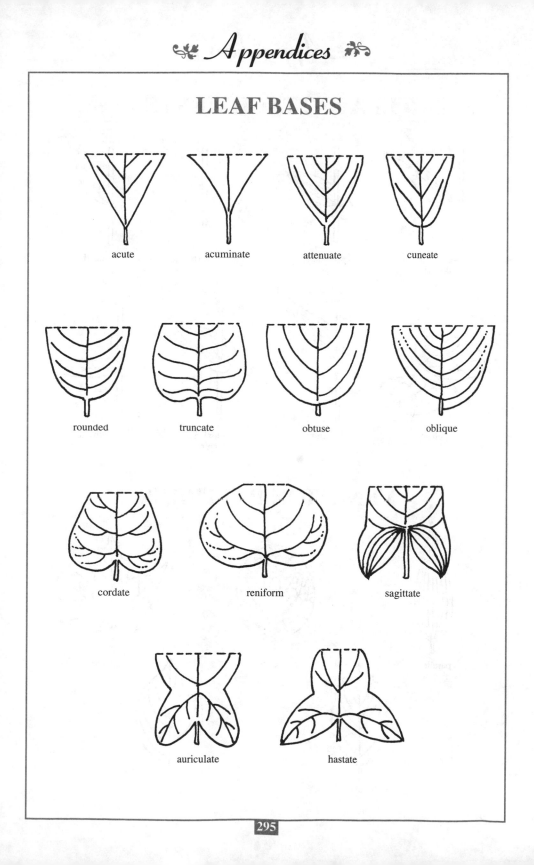

acute   acuminate   attenuate   cuneate

rounded   truncate   obtuse   oblique

cordate   reniform   sagittate

auriculate   hastate

LEAF ATTACHMENTS

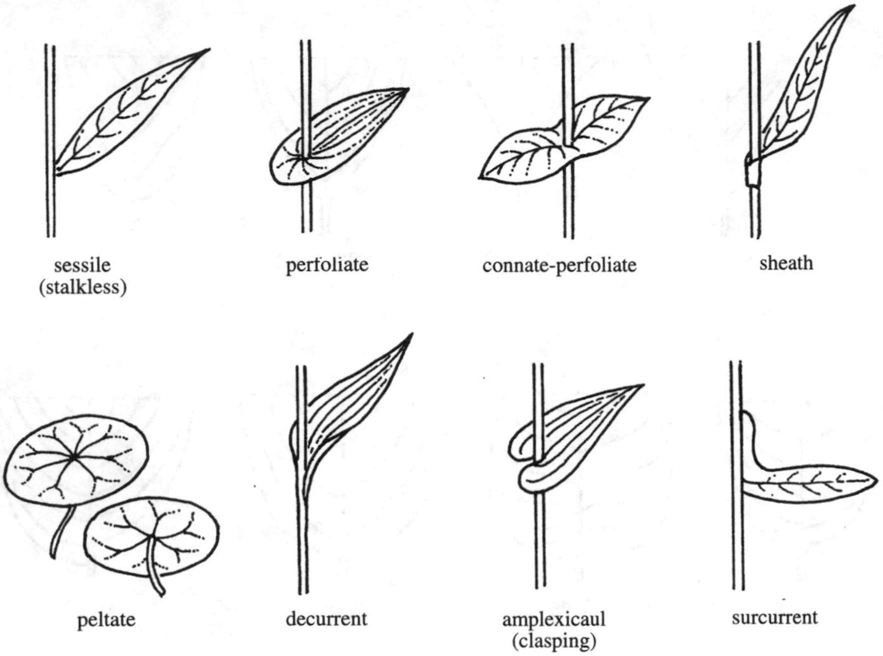

sessile
(stalkless)

perfoliate

connate-perfoliate

sheath

peltate

decurrent

amplexicaul
(clasping)

surcurrent

VENATION PATTERNS

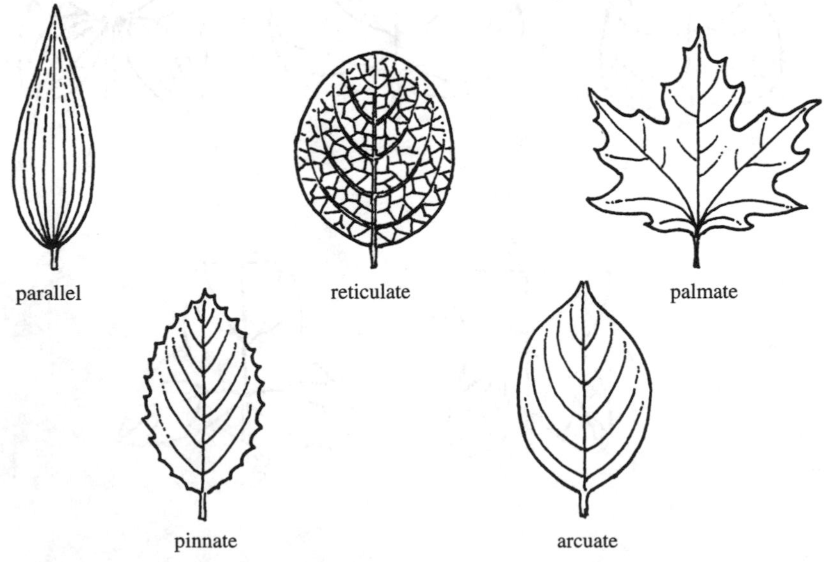

parallel

reticulate

palmate

pinnate

arcuate

FLOWER TERMS

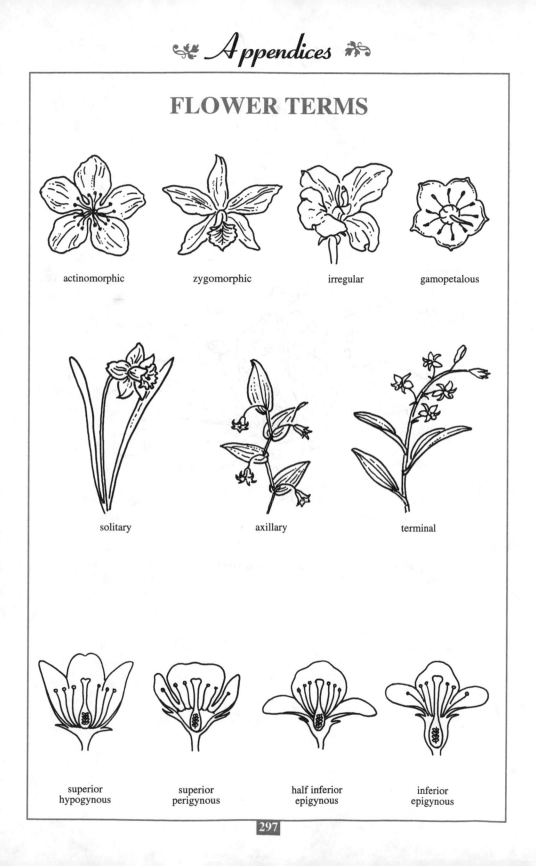

actinomorphic   zygomorphic   irregular   gamopetalous

solitary   axillary   terminal

superior
hypogynous

superior
perigynous

half inferior
epigynous

inferior
epigynous

FLOWER TERMS
Continued

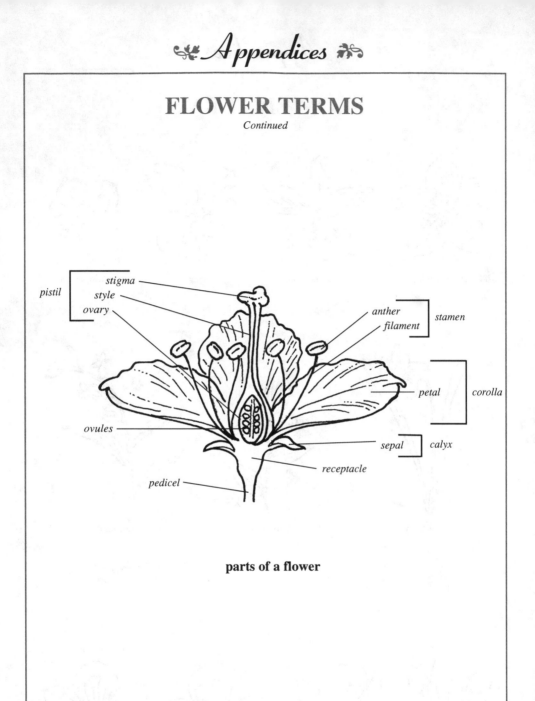

parts of a flower

FLOWER TERMS

Continued

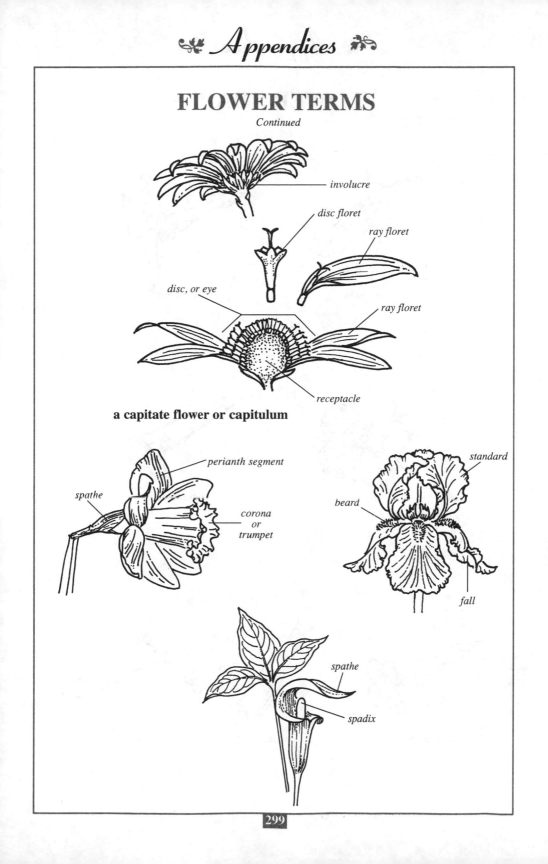

involucre

disc floret

ray floret

disc, or eye

ray floret

receptacle

a capitate flower or capitulum

perianth segment

spathe

corona
or
trumpet

standard

beard

fall

spathe

spadix

FLOWER SHAPES

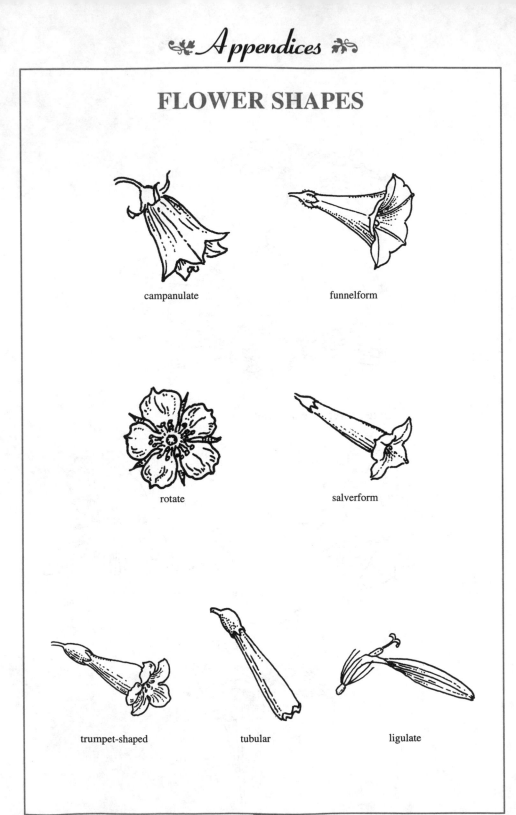

campanulate

funnelform

rotate

salverform

trumpet-shaped

tubular

ligulate

FLOWER SHAPES
Continued

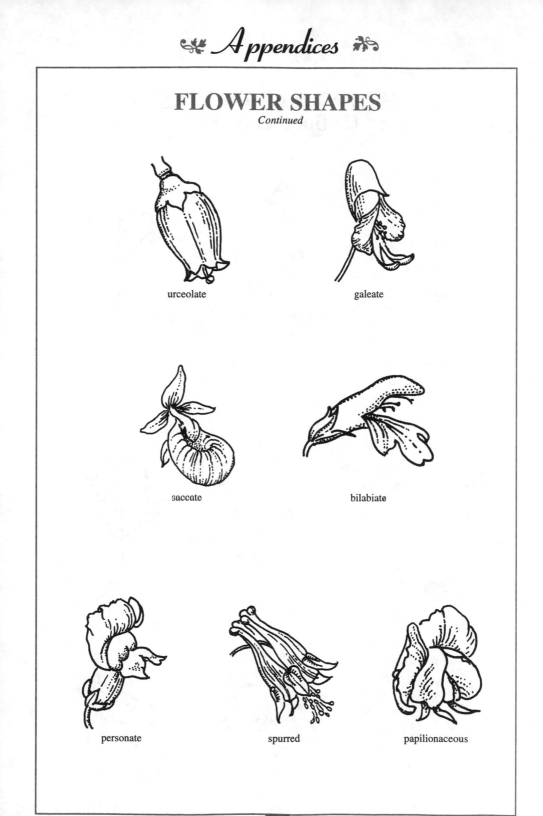

urceolate

galeate

saccate

bilabiate

personate

spurred

papilionaceous

FLOWER CLUSTERS
(Inflorescences)

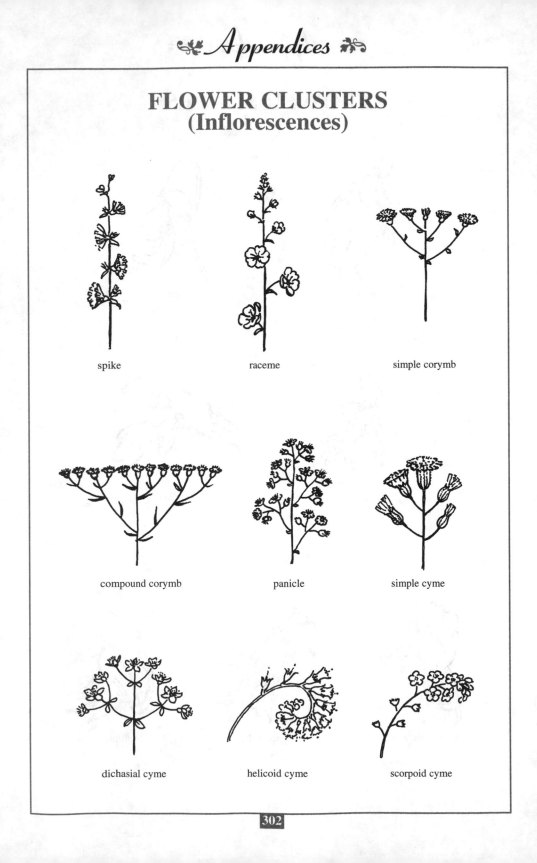

spike

raceme

simple corymb

compound corymb

panicle

simple cyme

dichasial cyme

helicoid cyme

scorpoid cyme

FLOWER CLUSTERS
(Inflorescences)
Continued

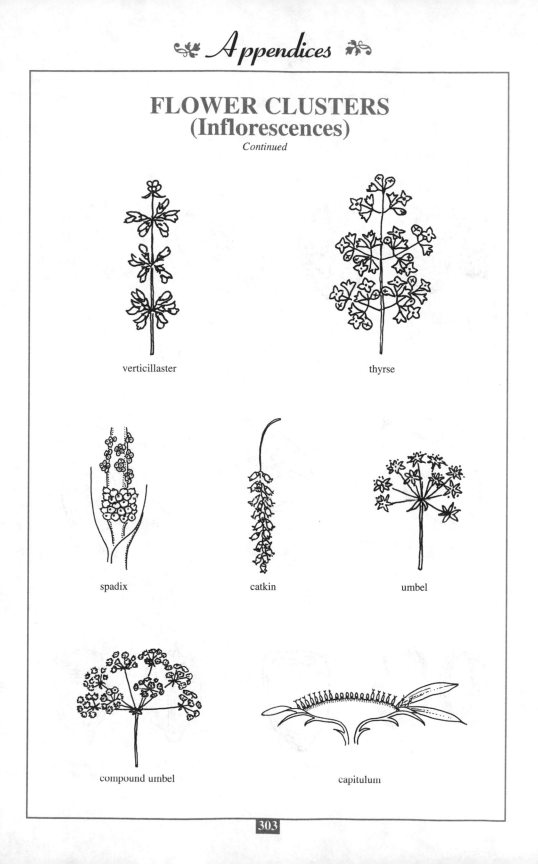

verticillaster

thyrse

spadix

catkin

umbel

compound umbel

capitulum

TYPES OF FRUIT

aggregate

accessory

pome

berry

drupe

hesperidium

pepo

achene

caryopsis

septicidal capsule

poricidal capsule

TYPES OF FRUIT
Continued

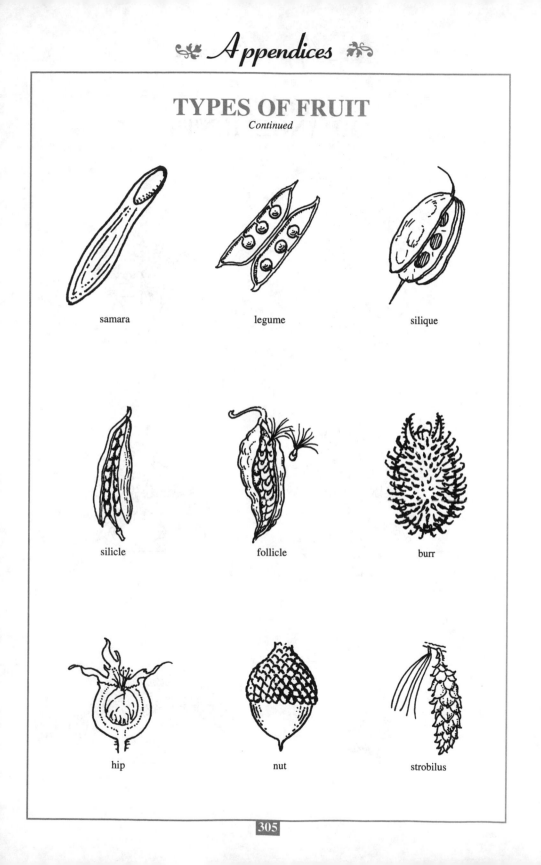

samara

legume

silique

silicle

follicle

burr

hip

nut

strobilus

FLOWER ARRANGEMENTS

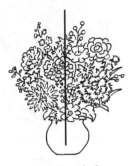

symmetrical
balance

asymmetrical
balance

out of scale

in scale

vertical line

horizontal line

306

FLOWER ARRANGEMENTS

Continued

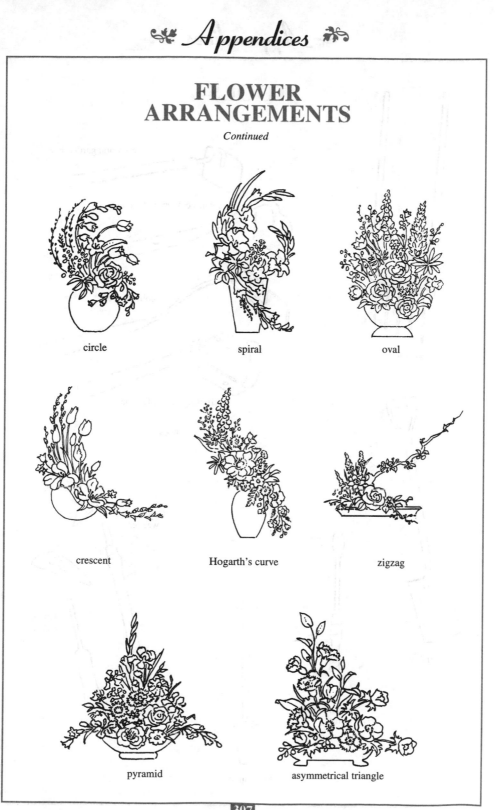

circle

spiral

oval

crescent

Hogarth's curve

zigzag

pyramid

asymmetrical triangle

TOOLS

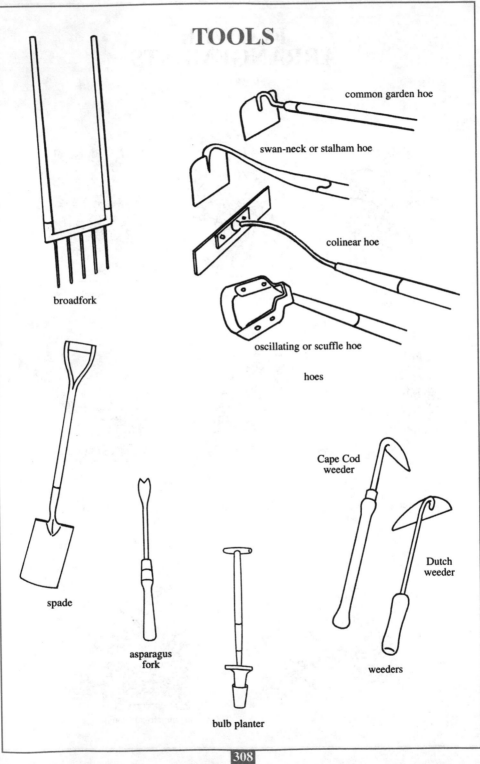

common garden hoe

swan-neck or stalham hoe

colinear hoe

oscillating or scuffle hoe

hoes

broadfork

spade

asparagus fork

bulb planter

Cape Cod weeder

Dutch weeder

weeders

TOOLS
Continued

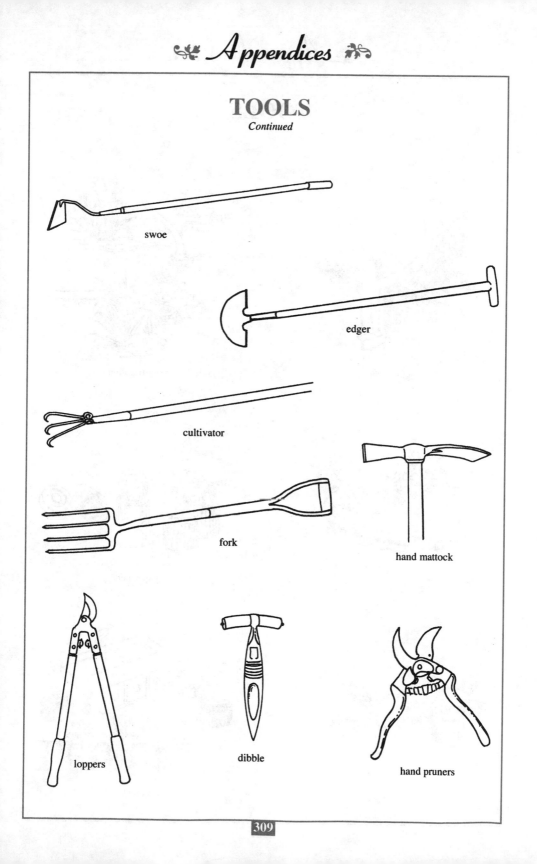

swoe

edger

cultivator

fork

hand mattock

loppers

dibble

hand pruners

TOOLS
Continued

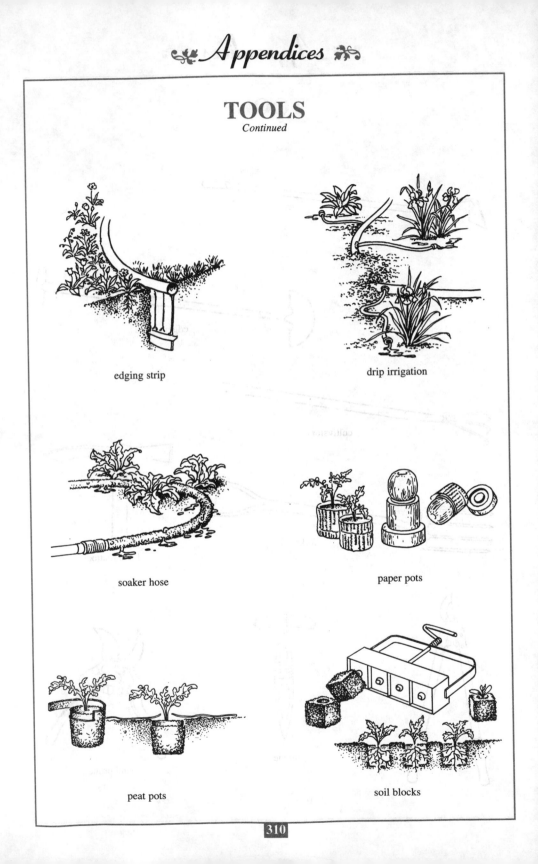

edging strip

drip irrigation

soaker hose

paper pots

peat pots

soil blocks

TYPES OF INSECTS

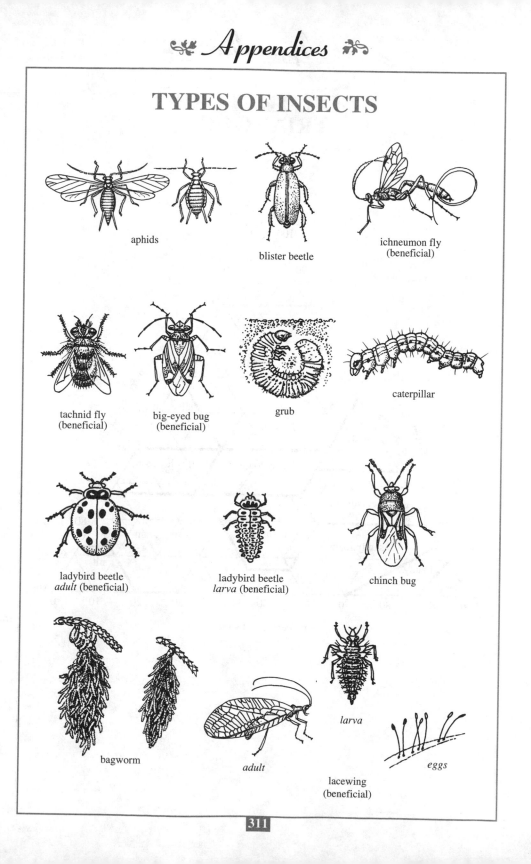

aphids

blister beetle

ichneumon fly
(beneficial)

tachnid fly
(beneficial)

big-eyed bug
(beneficial)

grub

caterpillar

ladybird beetle
adult (beneficial)

ladybird beetle
larva (beneficial)

chinch bug

bagworm

adult

larva

eggs

lacewing
(beneficial)

SOIL TEXTURE TRIANGLE

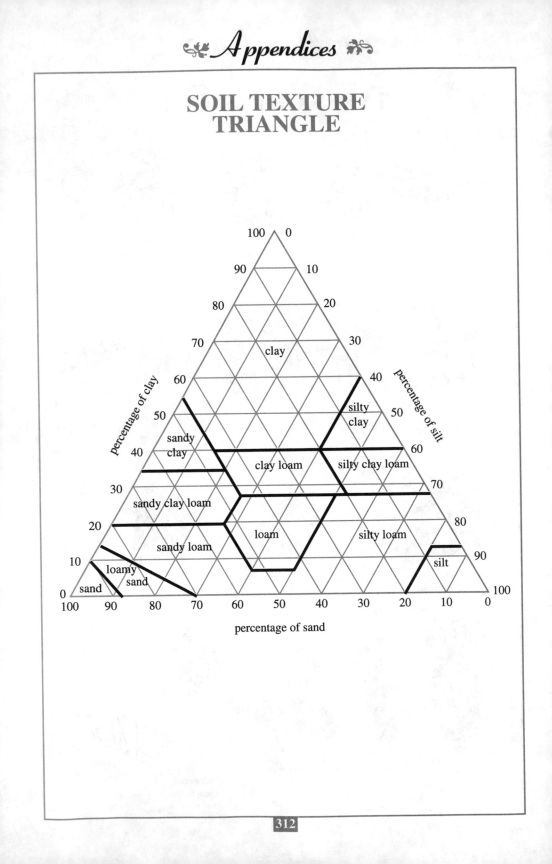

PLANT HARDINESS ZONE MAP

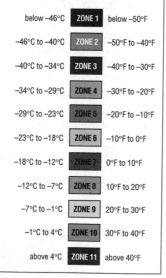

ALASKA

AVERAGE ANNUAL MINIMUM TEMPERATURE

below −46°C	**ZONE 1**	below −50°F
−46°C to −40°C	**ZONE 2**	−50°F to −40°F
−40°C to −34°C	**ZONE 3**	−40°F to −30°F
−34°C to −29°C	**ZONE 4**	−30°F to −20°F
−29°C to −23°C	**ZONE 5**	−20°F to −10°F
−23°C to −18°C	**ZONE 6**	−10°F to 0°F
−18°C to −12°C	**ZONE 7**	0°F to 10°F
−12°C to −7°C	**ZONE 8**	10°F to 20°F
−7°C to −1°C	**ZONE 9**	20°F to 30°F
−1°C to 4°C	**ZONE 10**	30°F to 40°F
above 4°C	**ZONE 11**	above 40°F

To use the map:
- Find the color of your locality and determine its zone number.
- Keep this zone number in mind when selecting perennial plants. Plant and seed catalogs and garden centers will list the hardiness zone of perennial plants. If a plant is listed as hardy in zones 4–9, it will not survive winters in zones 1–3 or summer heat in zones 10–11.

Become a Better Gardener with Barron's

Barron's gardening books feature full-color photographs, beautiful illustrations, handsome line art, easy-to-understand text, instructive diagrams, sidebar features, and detailed indexes.

Cactus

Introduces plant growers to the basics of cactus care and cultivation, then presents an alphabetized directory of roughly 50 varieties—from *Acanthocalycium* to *Uebelmannia pectinifera*.

Paperback, 160 pp., 0-7641-1226-0, $14.95, Can$21.00

Complete Gardener's Dictionary

Over 2,500 definitions for common gardening terms and practices, garden tools and their specific uses, landscape methods, horticulture, soil analysis and care, fertilizing, controlling pests and diseases, and more.

Paperback, approx. 336 pp., 0-7641-0637-6, $13.95, Can$19.50

Family Garden

Looks at yard and patio surfaces, adjoining structures, garden furniture and equipment, garden toys and play spaces, and shows how to make the most out of them as attractive, functional recreation areas.

Paperback, 112 pp., 0-7641-0932-4, $13.95, Can$19.50

500 Popular Annuals and Perennials for American Gardeners

Comprehensive advice on planting, cultivation, and flowering times of plants, with suggestions for attention-catching color combinations in gardens, or in containers for terraces, decks, and patios.

Paperback w/clear vinyl jacket, 288 pp., 0-7641-1177-9 $12.95, NCR

500 Popular Garden Plants for American Gardeners

Features detailed profiles of nearly every desirable garden plant that can grow on the North American continent including trees, annuals, perennials, bulbs, corms, tubers, vegetables, herbs, and many more.

Paperback w/clear vinyl jacket, 288 pp., 0-7641-0850-6 $12.95, NCR

500 Popular Roses for American Gardeners

Contains descriptions for over 500 different rose varieties, categorized by species or wild roses, old garden roses, modern garden roses, and miniature roses.

Paperback w/clear vinyl jacket, 288 pp., 0-7641-0851-4 $12.95, NCR

Gardening for Beginners

Covers garden tools, different types of soil, fertilizers and compost, the details of planting and irrigation, ideas for setting up a beautiful garden and profiles 150 different flowers, shrubs, and grasses.

Hardcover, 194 pp., 0-7641-5164-9 $16.95, Can$22.95

Made for the Shade

Includes detailed descriptions and instructions for nurturing trees, shrubs, ground covers, perennials, bulbs, tubers, and annuals that thrive in shady places.

Paperback, 160 pp., 0-7641-0512-4 $14.95, Can$19.95

Mix & Match Gardening

Includes 60 illustrated plans for garden beds and borders, and advice on best plant locations, soil types, weather, sunlight, shade, and compatible small trees or shrubs that complement flower beds.

Hardcover with concealed spiral binding, 144 pp., 0-7641-5118-5 $24.95, Can$32.50

Barron's Educational Series, Inc.
250 Wireless Blvd.
Hauppauge, NY 11788
In Canada: Georgetown Book Warehouse
34 Armstrong Ave.
Georgetown, Ont. L7G 4R9
Visit our website at: www.barronseduc.com

Stop and Smell the Roses

The Encyclopedia of Roses
Robert Markley

Here is the last word on roses —
a lavish, authoritative, large-
format book that will come as
the answer to any rose lover's
dreams. The book's main
sections deal with:

❀ The history of roses

❀ Detailed botanical
  information

❀ Advice on incorporating
  roses into a garden plan

❀ Information on
  planting and
  nurturing roses

❀ Profiles of all the most
  popular varieties

There is also a wealth of advice on cultivating roses as a
business to produce products for florists as well as health food retailers. This
beautiful, heavily illustrated volume is bound to appeal to the broadest audience.
Dedicated rose growers will be impressed by detailed chapters on rose cultivation,
suggestions for complementary planting, and the many uses of roses down through
the centuries. Beginners will value the book for its clear, easy-to-understand text and
its many instructive diagrams and sidebar features. Unusual in a book for gardeners
is information on the use of roses as herbal medicine, as food, as having symbolic
value for artists and poets, and as ornamental enhancements in the home. This
volume concludes with a detailed glossary and an extensive index. Hundreds of
full-color photos, drawings, and diagrams throughout.

Hardcover w/dust jacket, 240 pp., 9¹/₂" x 11³/₄"
ISBN 0-7641-5193-2 $35.00, Can$46.95

Books may be purchased at your
local bookstore, or by mail from
Barron's. Enclose check or money
order for the total amount plus
sales tax where applicable and
18% for postage and handling
(minimum charge $5.95). Prices
subject to change without notice.

Barron's Educational Series, Inc.
250 Wireless Blvd.
Hauppauge, NY 11788
In Canada: Georgetown Book Warehouse
34 Armstrong Ave.,
Georgetown, Ont. L7G 4R9
Visit our website at: www.barronseduc.com

12/99 (#101)